Automating Science and Engineering Laboratories with Visual Basic®

Automating Science and Engineering Laboratories with Visual Basic®

MARK F. RUSSO

MARTIN M. ECHOLS

JOHN WILEY & SONS, INC.

New York • Chichester • Weinheim • Brisbane • Singapore • Toronto

Library of Congress Cataloging-in-Publication Data

Russo, Mark F.
      Automating science and engineering laboratories with visual basic
   / Mark F. Russo, Martin M. Echols
         p.   cm. — (Wiley-Interscience series on laboratory
   automation)
      Includes index.
      ISBN 0-471-25493-2 (alk. paper)
      1. Laboratories—Data processing.   2. Engineering laboratories—
   Data processing.   3. Laboratories—Automation.   4. Engineering
   laboratories—Automation.   5. Robotics.   6. Robots, Industrial.
   I. Echols, Martin M.   II. Title.   III. Series
   Q183.A1R88   1999   98-30703
   660′.28′002855268—dc21

Printed in the United States of America.
10 9 8 7 6 5 4

To my wife Jean Boyer, for so many things I cannot put into words.
I could not have done it without you.
Mark Russo

To Elaine Echols, for all your patience and support.
Martin Echols

Contents

Introduction

A QUIET REVOLUTION

Microsoft® Visual Basic® is quietly revolutionizing science and engineering laboratories. It used to be rare to find a practicing scientist who could also write a Microsoft Windows® program or build a controller with a graphical user interface. Remaining competent in science or engineering while developing the skills necessary to write Microsoft® Windows® applications was beyond the abilities of most mere mortals.

Things have changed.

It is scarcely possible to go into any modern laboratory these days and not find Microsoft® Visual Basic® hard at work. It is refreshing to discover the number and breadth of applications in laboratories that have been built using Visual Basic®. Often, one finds VB as a custom interface to a barcode reader, balance, analytical instrument, or a large integrated robotic system. Controlling, coordinating, and acquiring data from instrumentation is a common laboratory task, and one in which VB excels. Processing measurements and graphically displaying results are also well within the reach of Visual Basic®.

GENESIS OF THE BOOK

The need for this book grew directly from an observation that many of our colleagues were disappointed with the kind of Visual Basic® training that was available. They complained that popular VB courses presented examples almost exclusively in fields such as finance or human resources, which has little relevance to applications in science and engineering. Our colleagues are using Visual Basic® for data acquisition, instrument control, laboratory user interface development, and other science and engineering laboratory-related tasks. The Visual Basic® tool is the same, whether it is used for human resources applications or for pilot plant control, but the way it is used is very different. This book is aimed directly at the use of Visual Basic® to develop applications that solve problems typically encountered in laboratories of the scientific and engineering community.

A significant portion of the material included in this book comes from a short course that the authors present on a regular basis at a conference called LabAutomation, organized by the Association for Laboratory Automation (ALA). You can learn more about the annual conference and the ALA by visiting the web site http://labautomation.org. The short course began as a single day event, and quickly grew into two full days. Still, there is not enough time in two days to cover all the material that should be included for a solid foundation in the application of Visual Basic® to laboratory computing problems. This book seeks to solve that problem. The topics included in the book cover areas that we have found to be critical for developing Visual Basic® programs in a laboratory environment. Topics covered represent a balance between novel contributions, the desire to provide an all-in-one reference for scientists and engineers, and an attempt to avoid rehashing areas for which there are already several other excellent references.

CONTRIBUTIONS

This book makes contributions in two main areas. First, this book represents the only known volume available that presents techniques for applying Visual Basic® to scientific and engineering laboratory computing problems. The techniques presented represent what we have found to be useful when solving problems that commonly arise in a laboratory using Visual Basic®. Techniques covered include communication through an RS-232 port and TCP/IP network connection, development of robust instrument controllers, and the creation of interactive scientific graphical displays. Examples apply exclusively to problems that typically occur in science and engineering laboratories. Second, the book includes several custom-developed software tools that can be used immediately to build laboratory and other software applications. We developed these tools in the course of solving laboratory computing problems using Visual Basic®. The software tools provided include: a customizable spreadsheet class, a class containing a variety of predefined parsing functions, and a set of new classes that provide for the dynamic graphical display and interactive manipulation of associated data.

PHILOSOPHY

Our approach is to get the reader programming as soon as possible—sometimes even before a topic is explained thoroughly. We have found this to be the most effective way of conveying a programming concept or tool. We feel that a level of comfort with a programming tool before it is understood in detail encourages self-directed exploration, which in turn promotes a deeper level of understanding.

Although this is not an introductory book, it is our desire that the material be accessible to a wide audience. For that reason, several introductory chapters have been provided that review Visual Basic® and other general programming concepts used in the book, but which normally fall outside the scope of knowledge of a typical laboratory professional. This is done in order to assure that as many readers as possible have the opportunity to acquire a good understanding of the material presented.

LEVERAGING SKILLS

This book covers Microsoft® Windows® Visual Basic® 6.0 - For 32-bit Windows Development (VB6). All examples are programmed using the version of the Visual Basic Language included in VB6 and the tools that are distributed with the Professional Edition. Still, it can be very useful for developing programs in other versions of Visual Basic®. All examples will run in version 5.0 of Visual Basic® (VB5), and many of the examples will run directly, or with minimal changes, in version 4.0 of Visual Basic®, or one of the applications that employs Visual Basic for Applications (VBA) as its scripting language. For example, in our own work we have converted many of the examples presented here to Microsoft® Excel 97. This is especially true for examples that involve device communications and control. The code and programming techniques presented in Parts 2 and 3 can be used in Microsoft® Excel 97 to control devices, capture data, and insert it directly into a spreadsheet. For more information on developing scientific and engineering applications in Microsoft® Excel, refer to one of the other John Wiley & Sons excellent books.

WHO IS THIS BOOK FOR?

This book is for the programming and nonprogramming scientific or engineering laboratory professional. It is both tutorial and practical in nature. A healthy introduction is given to many relevant topics, which are then followed by programming examples in Visual Basic®.

It is not assumed that the reader is familiar with concepts such as object-oriented programming, parsing, network communications, and other topics that are important to laboratory computing. Instead, we provide several introductory sections that review the key aspects of each topic. Then we reduce each to practice using examples written in Visual Basic®.

For example, RS-232 and TCP/IP communications are introduced before explaining how to use an RS-232 port or network connection to communicate using Visual Basic®. Topics such as multitasking, parsing, and state diagrams are introduced as a basis for understanding and programming robust instrument controllers. We also provide several ready-to-use code modules that you can plug into your laboratory application right away.

WHAT WILL YOU NEED?

To get the most from this book, you will need the Professional Edition of Microsoft® Windows® Visual Basic® 5.0 or 6.0, and a suitable computer on which to run it. Microsoft lists the following minimum requirements for running VB.

- Microsoft® Windows NT® 4.0 Service Pac 3 or later, or Microsoft® Windows® 95
- An 486/DX microprocessor or higher
- 76 megabytes of available hard disk space for installation
- A CD-ROM drive
- VGA or higher screen supported by Microsoft® Windows®
- 16 megabytes of RAM
- A mouse or other suitable pointing device

You will also need to be familiar with the BASIC programming language. We use no third-party software. Some examples use tools that come only in the Professional Edition of Visual Basic®. If you are doing serious software development, the Professional Edition is necessary anyway. If you are still learning, and not ready to make the investment in the Professional Edition, many of the examples will run in the Learning Edition of Visual Basic® as well.

To run examples that communicate over the RS-232 port, you must have two computers, each with one available RS-232 port, or one computer with two available RS-232 ports, and a suitable serial cable. RS-232 ports are often referred to as "COM1" or "COM2." Be careful. Even though your computer appears to have an RS-232 port, it may not be available for use. Older computers use RS-232 ports for other devices, such as a mouse. It would be tough to run some of the example programs without the benefit of a mouse. Later on we'll describe exact specifications for serial cables.

Ideally, examples that communicate over a network require a computer that is hooked up to a network supporting the TCP/IP communications protocol. In fact, it's not strictly necessary that your computer be connected to a network. Most examples that perform network communications use an address that reflects network data back to the same computer. In this case, it is only necessary that your computer have TCP/IP networking configured properly.

ORGANIZATION

The book is divided into four parts. Part 1 is a review of Visual Basic® 6.0 and the VB Integrated Development Environment. It is not our intention to provide a complete Visual Basic® tutorial or to instruct the reader how to program in the BASIC programming language. Instead, we cover those aspects of Visual Basic® that add to a pre-existing knowledge of BASIC, and are required for a full appreciation of the examples included in the remaining parts of the book.

The ability to perform electronic communications is a fundamental recurring theme in laboratory applications. Part 2 covers several major techniques for communicating: between programs running on the same computer, between programs running on different computers, and between a program and an instrument. Demonstration of the last concept is difficult without having an instrument handy with an appropriate electronic interface; so to solve the problem we developed a program called the Virtual Instrument. This program acts like an instrument that you can communicate with and control using Dynamic Data Exchange, an RS-232 port, and a TCP/IP network connection. Most of the concepts presented in Parts 2 and 3 will be demonstrated using the Virtual Instrument.

Once device communications is mastered, the next step is device control, which is the topic of Part 3. Several techniques for building robust device controllers are investigated and demonstrated using material covered in Part 2 as a basis. After introducing several concepts in the first few chapters of Part 3, we develop a general-purpose framework for device control that can be reused for many different applications. We use this same framework to develop device controllers based on several different communication mechanisms.

Visual Basic® is an excellent environment for developing interactive graphical applications. In Part 4 the fundamentals of graphics programming in Visual Basic® will be reviewed, and a number of techniques for applying graphics to scientific and engineering problems will be demonstrated. Several custom graphical data displays will be constructed that apply specifically to building laboratory interfaces.

CHAPTER DESCRIPTIONS

We begin in Chapter 1 with background information designed to get the reader familiar with Visual Basic® and the range of features that are provided with the Visual Basic Development System. In Chapter 2 we jump right in to the Visual Basic Integrated Development Environment (IDE). Here we will take a tour of all the major IDE components that are used throughout the remainder of the book. The function and features of each component are described with an emphasis on how to use it to get the job done.

While we are not attempting to provide a thorough VB tutorial, we do provide a quick review of the Visual Basic® programming language in Chapter 3. This is especially useful for those who have programmed before, but have not used Visual Basic® to any extent. We anticipate that most readers interested in this book will have had some background in programming. Chapter 3 will help begin to put the Visual Basic® programming language in perspective. This is continued in Chapter 4, where we review the framework provided for creating new applications using VB. We introduce the manner in which applications are organized in VB using modules as well as how they interact.

Visual Basic® offers many sophisticated object-oriented programming features. While it is true that VB does not implement all concepts considered necessary for a complete object-oriented programming language, we can benefit tremendously from what it does include. In Chapter 5 we review the concepts of object-oriented programming and discuss how it is implemented in Visual Basic®. We will make heavy use of these concepts throughout the examples in this book. Mastering the concepts presented in this chapter is necessary for a complete understanding of the material to follow.

Chapter 6 precedes our discussion of device communications by introducing the Virtual Instrument (VI). The VI is a Visual Basic® program that simulates an instrument that accepts commands and generates data. The VI is capable of being controlled remotely. It can be controlled over several different modes of communication. Source code for the VI is included with the software that comes with this book. Appendix C gives detailed instructions on how to build the VI from scratch.

We begin our discussion of device communications in Chapter 7 with a review of Dynamic Data Exchange (DDE). The review presents the necessary concepts in a concise format. This is continued in Chapter 8 with a more detailed presentation of how to establish connections and communicate using DDE. Examples of each style of DDE link are explored by communicating with Microsoft® Excel. The chapter closes with an example of how to establish communications with the Virtual Instrument using DDE.

Chapter 9 is a solid review of RS-232 communications. In order to establish an RS-232 connection and communicate with minimal transmission errors, it is necessary to have a basic understanding of how RS-232 works. The material included in Chapter 9 covers the essential topics. Chapter 10 continues by describing how to perform RS-232 communications using Visual Basic® and the MSComm ActiveX control. An example program is built to send commands to the Virtual Instrument over an RS-232 connection.

Increasingly, laboratory instrumentation is providing the option to communicate over network connections. In Chapter 11 we review Ethernet networks and the commonly used TCP/IP network protocol. Chapter 12 includes a detailed discussion of the Microsoft® Winsock ActiveX control and how it can be used in VB for building a variety of network-enabled programs. Examples of both client and server programs are given. The chapter closes by constructing a program that sends commands to the Virtual Instrument over a TCP/IP network connection.

A strategy for communicating between programs through files is explored in Chapter 13. A class called clsFileComm is constructed, which implements the strategy for file communications. An example uses the class for bidirectional communications.

Chapter 14 describes multithreading and compares it to multitasking. Chapter 15 discusses how the default behavior of Visual Basic® is to run all user code on a single thread. An example demonstrates what happens when one procedure is executed while another is running, and how to use the DoEvents statement to keep your applications responsive.

A description and the basic components of a state diagram are given in Chapter 16, along with an explanation of the importance of tracking state during the development of an instrument controller. Chapter 17 describes one method for implementing state diagrams in Visual Basic®, and demonstrates the concepts with an example that implements the state diagram of the Virtual Instrument.

The fundamentals of parsing are given in Chapter 18. There is much to be gained by using parsing techniques. The most important benefits of parsing are an ability to recognize easily a wide range of valid messages and the generation of truly useful errors when something is unexpected. Well-implemented parsers are one of the primary tools necessary for building robust controllers. The parsing techniques developed are encapsulated in a Parser class that can be used as is, extended, or modified as needed. This is the topic of Chapter 19.

Two models for monitoring a communication channel are presented in Chapter 20. These models are included within a general-purpose framework for building device controllers. Several example programs are developed in Chapter 21 that demonstrate communication channel monitoring techniques and device controller implementation. In particular, a Virtual Instrument controller is developed that interacts with the VI over an RS-232 port. The controller is also modified to operate over a TCP/IP network connection.

One of the most common ways to use a computer in a science or engineering laboratory is to generate plots of experimental data. MSChart is an ActiveX control provided with Visual Basic® that is capable of generating sophisticated plots. In Chapter 22 the MSChart control is described in detail, and several examples are given that demonstrate its capabilities.

Another ActiveX control provided with Visual Basic® for displaying data is MSFlexGrid. The MSFlexGrid control provides an ability to display data as well as graphics in tabular form. It does not include interactive editing capabilities. We will build a spreadsheet class in Chapter 23 that adds interactive editing to MSFlexGrid. Since we provide all the source code for this class, you can easily embed the spreadsheet within your own application and customize editing behavior to suit your needs.

In Chapter 24 we review and demonstrate the fundamentals of generating graphics in Visual Basic®. This is in preparation for Chapter 25, where we use these techniques to build active graphic displays. Two active graphic class examples are created. The StripChart class displays stored data as a scrolling strip chart. As new data are added to a StripChart object, the display automatically updates itself. The GasGauge class displays a data value as a semicircular gauge with a needle and an adjustable background, which divides the gauge into red and green pie slices. The needle changes position automatically when an associated data value changes.

Concepts presented in Chapter 25 are extended in Chapter 26 by adding interactive capabilities. A Knob class is constructed that displays a data value as a rotary-action knob. The Knob display can be clicked and rotated using the mouse to set its value. When a Knob object value changes, it fires an event, which can be used to perform other actions. A Thermometer class is also constructed that indicates Temperature and Threshold values using a traditional glass thermometer graphic with a mercury meniscus. The mercury meniscus can be clicked and dragged with the mouse to set a temperature value interactively. Events are fired when the Temperature property value goes over or under the Threshold. Complete source code is provided for each of these classes. They can be used as is or modified to add new functionality.

ACQUIRING AND INSTALLING THE SAMPLE PROGRAMS

Strictly speaking, you won't need an electronic version of the sample programs that are included with this book. All the code for every example is listed in the pages of the book. From a practical standpoint, you probably don't want to type it all in. But you do have that option.

You can directly download all the completed examples and software tools described in this book from Wiley's ftp site. Use your web browser to visit the URL ftp://ftp.wiley.com/public/sci_tech_med/labvb and download the file labvb6.zip for examples written in version 6.0 of Visual Basic®, or labvb5.zip for examples written in version 5.0 of Visual Basic®. As an alternative, you can run your favorite ftp program, connect to ftp.wiley.com, log in as "anonymous", and get the file /public/sci_tech_med/labvb/labvb6.zip or labvb5.zip in the same directory. To install the software, unzip it with an appropriate utility such as WinZip or PKUnzip. You can buy WinZip or download a trial copy by visiting http://www.winzip.com. The labvb6.zip and labvb5.zip file archives were created with folder information. Make sure you extract an archive with the "User Folder Names" option selected when using WinZip, or the –d option with PKUnzip. This will assure that the necessary folders are recreated from the archive. Neglecting to do this will cause several of the example files to be overwritten.

By making the software available from a Web site, we can continuously improve what you get. We can fix any problems that may occur after the book goes to print and include new software tools as they become available. Keep checking Wiley's web site for new developments.

Automating Science and Engineering Laboratories with Visual Basic®

1

Visual Basic® and the Integrated Development Environment

Visual Basic® is a marvelous Microsoft® Windows® application development tool. As you may already know, it is possible to get your first Windows® program up and running in a matter of minutes. What a feeling of accomplishment! If you're not new to programming, this might raise a red flag. You wouldn't be alone if you thought, "If it's that easy to get started, it must be impossible to develop an application of any significance." Not so! Layer after layer, Visual Basic® lets you get down to any level of complexity that you desire.

On several occasions in this book we will be dealing with aspects of Visual Basic® programming that you may not have come across. To make sure that you have the necessary background, or to refresh your memory, the chapters in Part 1 will review the fundamentals of developing applications in Visual Basic®.

CHAPTER

1

Background

Visual Basic® is an application development tool designed specifically for the Microsoft® Windows® family of operating systems. Visual Basic® provides a powerful and flexible environment, enabling rapid Windows® application development. Applications written using Visual Basic® can cover a broad spectrum of functionality, from a simple special-purpose calculator to a live pilot plant graphical interface, to a complex distributed multitier business system, and more. One of the real strengths of using VB is that it provides you with an ability to write diverse programs for a wide range of applications, with minimal effort.

The Visual Basic® development environment significantly reduces the complexity of writing Windows® applications. The Visual Basic® language is derived from the BASIC programming language syntax, making VB easy to learn and you more productive. Even with its ease of use, VB does not fall flat when it comes time to do more complex development. Visual Basic® supports access to the lowest level of capabilities provided by the operating system.

As we have said, Visual Basic is a development tool that is specific to the Microsoft® Windows® family of operating systems. Programs written in Visual Basic® will not be able to run on other operating systems, such as Mac™OS or any flavor of UNIX. However, within the instrument manufacturing community Microsoft® Windows® is by far the most prevalent operating system in use. With few exceptions, makers of instrumentation either provide Windows®-compatible instrument control software or have publicly committed to making such software available. As a result, for the laboratory professional, this limitation rarely ever causes a problem.

The capabilities of Visual Basic® have expanded dramatically since its first release in early 1991. As the Windows® operating system has evolved, Visual Basic® has followed closely behind with new features that take advantage of operating system advances. Microsoft® has demonstrated its commitment to the language in a number of ways. They have always closely monitored how Visual Basic is being used, and continue to add significant enhancements that reflect the needs of the VB community. For example, beginning with version 5.0, Visual Basic® includes a native code compiler. Prior to version 5.0 all VB programs ran interpreted. Native code compilation was something that VB developers requested that Microsoft® include in the product. With version 6.0, Microsoft® has added a whole range of new tools to support the use of VB in web development, both on the browser and web server sides, and in database development. Microsoft® has also adopted the VB language as the basis for scripting all of their other products, including the entire Microsoft® Office family of products.

OBJECTS AND CONTROLS

To be a successful Visual Basic® programmer you must understand the concept of an object. Objects are everywhere in Visual Basic®. We will discuss VB and object-oriented programming in much more detail later on. But for now, it is sufficient to understand that an object is simply a software component, which encapsulates its properties and related methods into a single reusable unit. It is very much like the code module in traditional approaches to programming, only multiple instances of objects can be created and manipulated in new ways.

Most of what you'll be dealing with in Visual Basic® is packaged as an object of some sort. For example, you will build graphical interfaces on Forms. A Form is a kind of object. It has properties such as Caption, which sets a title that is displayed on the Form, and BackColor, which sets the background color of the Form. Forms also have methods such as Show, which makes the Form visible. The items that you will place onto a Form are also special kinds of objects called ActiveX controls. An example of an ActiveX control is a CommandButton, a standard pushbutton-style graphic interface element that you have probably used over and over again. You can create new instances of ActiveX controls and set their properties to determine how they appear and behave. This is accomplished through the interface or from code. You can also add existing software libraries right into your Visual Basic® development environment simply by making an appropriate reference to the library. By and large libraries offer new functionality through sets of predefined objects, which you can create and manipulate from your Visual Basic® code.

The overall result is to make VB a very easily extensible language. When building an application, much of your development time is spent loading and configuring predefined objects rather than creating them from scratch. Visual Basic® programming has been referred to as a process of stitching together existing objects into a new application (see Figure 1-1).

EVENT-DRIVEN PROGRAMMING

If you've never written a Windows® program before, you may find its structure a bit unusual. Windows® programs do not follow a traditional model of

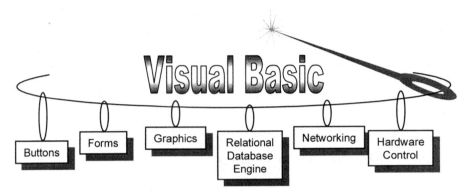

Figure 1-1. Visual Basic® programming.

starting execution at the first line, and continuing sequentially until the last. Instead, the code that makes up your program is divided into procedures, which are executed in response to a stream of events that are received by your program. Events are generated as a result of various kinds of user interaction and other system actions. The order in which your procedures are executed corresponds to the order in which your application receives these events. If no events are received, nothing executes.

The events that occur are each associated with and handled by a particular object. When a VB object receives an event, it executes an associated piece of code called its *event procedure*. For example, a CommandButton object has several associated events, including one called Click. When a user clicks on a CommandButton with the mouse, the object receives the Click event and invokes the Click event procedure. As a VB programmer, you only need to create an instance of the CommandButton object, and optionally add code to the predefined Click event procedure. VB provides all the internal plumbing that connects a CommandButton's graphical interface with its event procedures. Some of the most straightforward VB programs are written simply by creating instances of graphical interface objects and adding code to their event procedures.

Creating a program in Visual Basic® requires you to understand what events will fire in response to other actions, such as a mouse click, a key press, or the arrival of data on a communications port. You must understand how these events will trigger the execution of event procedures, and then add your code so as to cause the desired result. While this does present a unique challenge, it provides a tremendous opportunity for building applications that are flexible and responsive.

With this as a beginning, we are ready to take a look at the application that is used to create, organize, test, and debug new Visual Basic® programs. This application is called the Visual Basic® Integrated Development Environment, or IDE. In the next chapter we will introduce the IDE and its various components. We will also create a simple VB application using the IDE. Our hope is that this will break the ice for those who have never used VB before, or act as a refresher for those who have not used it for some time.

CHAPTER

2

IDE Fundamentals

This chapter is intended for those who have had little or no experience with Visual Basic®. If you are an experienced VB programmer, you can safely skip it. As we discussed in Chapter 1, you can think of Visual Basic® programming as stitching together a set of objects with code. To facilitate the whole process VB comes with an application called the Integrated Development Environment, or IDE. The IDE is really a complete set of integrated tools, designed for creating and managing the various components of a new VB program, for writing code to bind them together, and for testing and debugging the result. The IDE is very easy to use due to its point-and-click graphical interface. In this chapter we will discuss the features of the IDE and how they are used together to create new applications with Visual Basic®.

There are three editions of Visual Basic®. They are the Learning Edition, Professional Edition, and Enterprise Edition. The Learning Edition is meant for those interested only in getting their feet wet. You will be able to complete many of the examples in the book using the Learning Edition, but not all. The Professional Edition includes more functionality than the Learning Edition and several additional tools. All the examples in this book can be completed with the Professional Edition of VB5 or VB6. The Enterprise Edition of VB includes even more tools, primarily for the development of enterprise-wide applications. We will be using the Enterprise Edition of VB6 to introduce VB and demonstrate various IDE features. But have no fear. We used the Enterprise Edition rather than the Professional Edition, since it was the one available to us during the preparation of this book. Furthermore, the VB6 IDE is almost identical to the VB5 IDE. All of what you'll see will apply to each of the different editions in both versions 6.0 as well as 5.0.

When you start up Visual Basic®, a dialog appears asking you to select a project type (see Figure 2-1). By selecting the tabs at the top of the dialog you can select a new, existing, or recent project. For the purposes of this book, we will almost always use a new Standard EXE project type and add additional ActiveX controls as needed. You can also choose to start with a new VB Professional Edition Controls or VB Enterprise Edition Controls project type. The only difference between these types and the Standard EXE project type

6

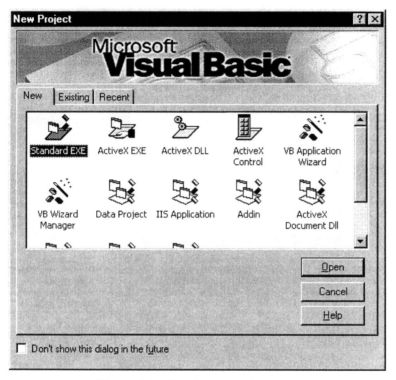

Figure 2-1. Creating a new VB project.

is the default set of ActiveX controls that are included with the project. After selecting a new project type the Visual Basic® Integrated Development Environment will open with one or more default objects. This mode is called *design time*. Design time refers to those activities that you perform while editing the application. Figure 2-2 shows the IDE after opening a new Standard EXE project. The default project name is Project1. The *project* is the entity that binds together all the components that make up a Visual Basic® program. It is within the project that you build your application and manage the associated files and objects. A default Form called Form1 is also created and displayed.

The default Standard EXE is a functional application in the sense that it will run as is, although it won't do very much. If you click the Start button on the IDE toolbar after creating the new project, your blank Form will be created and displayed. Figure 2-3 shows the new blank form running and displayed in front of the IDE. This mode is called *run time*. Run time refers to those activities that you perform while an application is currently running within the IDE. A tooltip popup labeled "Start" is displayed right below the Start button on the toolbar in Figure 2-3.

The Integrated Development Environment is the tool that you will use in order to build and bind together the objects that make up your application.

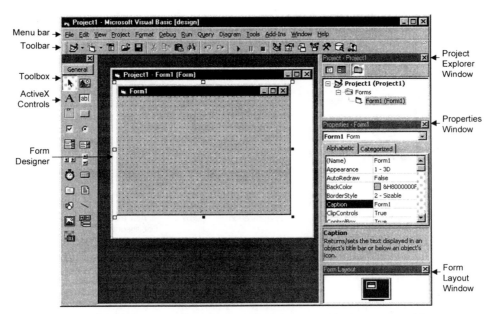

Menu bar →
Toolbar →

Toolbox →

ActiveX
Controls

Form
Designer

Project
Explorer
Window

Properties
Window

Form
Layout
Window

Figure 2-2. The Visual Basic® Integrated Development Environment with a new Standard EXE project.

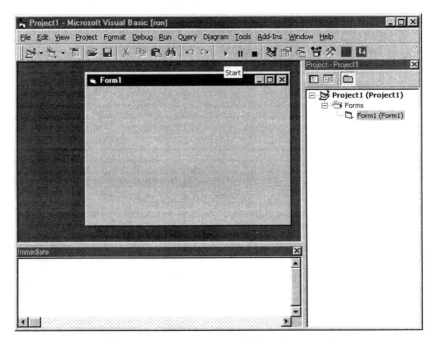

Figure 2-3. A default Standard EXE will run right away.

8

You can add or remove objects, write code, set object properties, design graphical interfaces, test applications by running them in interpreted mode, or compile applications for running stand alone, all from the IDE.

When running a program in interpreted mode from the IDE, your application is partially compiled to a format called *p-code*, which can be efficiently executed by an interpreter. When you compile the application completely down to native code, it can run as a stand alone application outside the IDE. This is a feature that was added in version 5.0 of Visual Basic®. In earlier versions of Visual Basic® an executable file was also created when a VB application was compiled. But running the executable only started the interpreter that executed your VB program by interpreting its p-code, as is the case when running your application from the IDE. The addition of a native-code compiler may, or may not, improve the speed of your application. It all depends on the amount of time your application spends executing VB code. Empirical observations suggest that a "typical" application can only gain a 5% to 10% performance improvement by compiling to native code. This implies that 90% to 95% of the time a typical application is executing precompiled code that makes up one of the various objects included in your application. You'll have to discover for yourself the extent to which native-code compilation will improve the performance of your applications.

A final note before we begin to look at the components of the IDE itself. When running a program within the IDE, it is possible to pause and resume the program. With the application paused, you can do quite a number of things with your program. You can add or delete code, modify the contents of variables, and then resume the application! This can be a very powerful capability, especially when you are not sure how to solve a problem and need to try different approaches. Instead of completely stopping and restarting the application each time a change is made, simply pause the program and edit your code. When resumed, the program will execute the new code. This is a powerful tool for debugging and developing programs in Visual Basic®.

There are many components that make up the Visual Basic® IDE. We will cover the more important IDE components in the following sections.

THE MENU BAR AND STANDARD TOOLBAR

Across the top of the IDE is the Menu bar (see Figure 2-2). The menu bar provides you with access to almost all of the things that you can do in the Visual Basic® IDE. Rather than explore each menu option, we leave it to you to investigate the menu bar on your own. Everything you need is in one of the menus. During your exploration, if you see a useful menu option, it will probably have an associated shortcut key or key combination, which will be displayed to the right of the caption. Try to remember these shortcut key combinations; they will make you more productive as you become a skilled VB programmer. If you ever want help with the menu bar, or any other component in the IDE, select the component and press the F1 key. VB will pop up a help screen to guide you further. Also, don't forget that Windows® makes good use of the right mouse button. Try right-mousing on various IDE components to discover what options appear.

Below the menu bar is a row of graphic buttons called the Standard Toolbar. The buttons on the Standard Toolbar give you access to some of the most frequently used functions in the IDE. To discover the function of a particular button, hover the mouse over the button and wait for a tooltip to pop up. That's how we displayed the Start tooltip in Figure 2-3. There are several additional toolbars available that you can display in the IDE. To see what's available, first select the View menu on the menu bar and choose the Toolbars option from the menu list. Another way that we'll refer to menu options is by concatenating the menu name and menu options together, separated by a vertical bar. So, for example, we also could have referred to this menu option as View | Toolbars. When you select the Toolbars menu option you will get a further submenu that displays all the available toolbars in the IDE. Put a check next to the toolbars that you want to display and uncheck the ones you want to hide.

Before leaving this section, there are a few options in one menu that we want to describe in a bit more detail. The View menu has many helpful functions for quick navigation around your project that too often go unused. Figure 2-4 shows the VB IDE with the View menu open.

The first two options in the View menu are Code and Object. When you are editing an object in VB, such as a Form, you can select the View | Code menu option or press F7 at any time to display the Code window and position the cursor within the code that is associated with the object. Another way to display the Code window is to double-click on the component of interest. To get back to the object, select View | Object or press Shift+F7. This gives you a fast mechanism for jumping between the tools available for editing an object. This is something you will be doing a lot. Figure 2-5 shows the VB IDE after Form1 was selected and the F7 key pressed.

The Definition menu option (Shift+F2) takes you to the definition of the variable or procedure currently under the cursor. The Last Position option (Ctrl+Shift+F2) is very useful in conjunction with the Definition option because it takes you back to where you were when you needed the definition. In fact, VB keeps track of your last eight locations; so you can jump back up to eight times.

THE TOOLBOX AND FORM DESIGNER

Figure 2-6 shows the Toolbox, which contains the ActiveX controls that can be added to an application. ActiveX controls can only be sketched onto the graphical interface of a Form using the Form Designer (Figure 2-2). A control is added to an application by selecting its icon in the toolbox and then

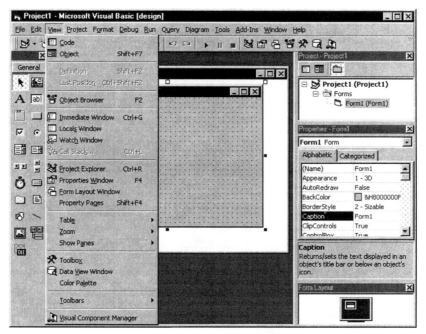

Figure 2-4. The VB IDE View Menu.

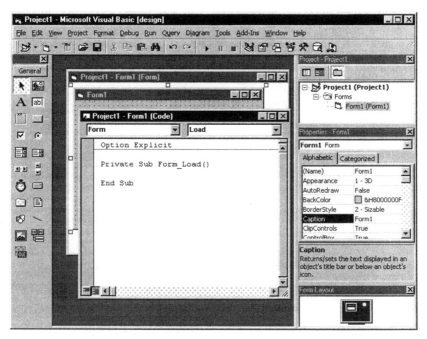

Figure 2-5. The Code Window for Form1.

Figure 2-6. The Toolbox with standard controls.

sketching out a rectangle on the Form where you want the control to be placed. When you release the mouse after sketching the rectangle, the design-time interface of the control will appear. If you are using a sizable control, such as the TextBox or CommandButton control, it will initially be approximately the same size as the sketched rectangle. In other cases the only thing displayed on the Form is an image that is the same as the Toolbox icon. This occurs when there is no run-time graphical interface associated with a control. The MSComm control, which handles RS-232 communications, is an example of such a control. ActiveX controls allow you instantly to add a wide range of functionality to your application. It is no more difficult to add a TextBox to your application for textual input than it is to add a Multimedia MCI control, which allows your application to show digital video clips with full sound.

The Toolbox displayed in Figure 2-6 is configured only with the standard controls. The name and a description appear alongside each control. To learn more about each control, select the control and press F1 for help.

To make other controls available from your Toolbox, choose the Project | Components menu option from the IDE, or type Ctrl+T. You will be presented with the Components dialog (Figure 2-7). Check the ActiveX controls that you want to add to your project and uncheck the ones you want to remove. Generally, you want to include only those components in your Toolbox that you use. Adding controls that you do not use will make the distribution of your final program unnecessarily large, or it will include useless dependencies.

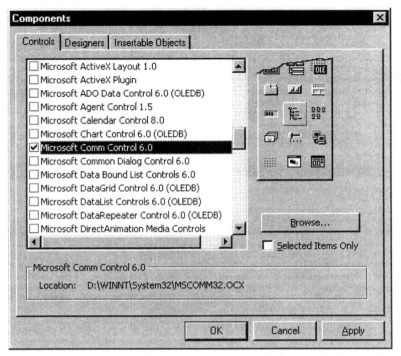

Figure 2-7. Controls can be added to or removed from the Toolbox using the Components dialog.

You are not limited to the ActiveX controls that come with your edition of Visual Basic®. Additional ActiveX controls can be purchased and added to the Toolbox through the Components dialog. There are literally thousands of ActiveX controls commercially available that add a tremendous variety of functionality to your Visual Basic® development environment. The flexibility to add new functionality to your program through the addition of ActiveX controls is another powerful feature of VB. This ability makes Visual Basic® a powerful and extensible development environment. Many instrument manufacturers now ship ActiveX controls with their products. You can even make your own ActiveX controls in VB.

PROJECT EXPLORER

By default, three docked windows are located on the right-hand side of the IDE (see Figure 2-2). The upper window is the Project Explorer. The Project Explorer allows you to navigate between the various components of your project. The Project Explorer organizes and displays components using an expandable tree view, with a top-level category for each type of component included in your project. Component types include Forms, Standard modules,

Class modules, and others. The default Standard EXE project has one default Form module called Form1. You can see it displayed in Figure 2-2.

The names of the objects shown in the Explorer have the form Name(FileName). The name that appears outside the parentheses is the name given to the object in the current application. The name that appears inside the parentheses is the name of the disk file in which the object is stored. The Project Explorer displays the default project as Project1(Project1). The default Form1 appears as Form1(Form1). If you save the project or Form to a file using a new name, the file name will appear within the parentheses in the Project Explorer.

PROPERTIES WINDOW

The window directly below the Project Explorer in Figure 2-2 is the Properties Window. This window gives you direct access to the design-time properties of the currently active object. For example, if Form1 is currently active, then the Properties Window would appear as in Figure 2-2.

Different objects have different properties. Forms have approximately 50 properties that are listed in the Properties Window, while other objects may have only one or two. Some properties are not available at run time, and others are not available at design time. It all depends on the design of the object. Design-time properties can be edited at design time through the Properties Window. You will have to consult the object's documentation or use the Object Browser to learn about run-time object properties.

The one property that all objects have is called Name. It always shows up as the first item in the Properties Window, and is displayed in parentheses. The IDE assigns a default name for each new object. You can change the name of the object by editing the Name property at the top of the Properties Window. Most other properties have default values as well. Often, when a property can be assigned only to a finite list of options, the Properties Window will display a dropdown or popup dialog that lets you conveniently choose a valid value to assign to the property.

RUNNING, MODIFYING, AND DEBUGGING APPLICATIONS

Debugging an application can be a fairly complex problem. Visual Basic® provides a debugging environment that has all the tools you will need to locate and fix programming errors effectively. Another benefit of the debugging environment is that it also allows you to enter and modify code at run time, while the application is paused. This ability can be tremendously helpful in working out programming problems. In this section we will cover the highlights of the debugging environment and point out the features that are the most useful.

As we saw earlier, it is possible to run a Visual Basic® program even if you have not yet added a single line of code. Once you begin writing code, you can run the program at any time to test what you have thus far. Just click the Start button on the Standard Toolbar. When VB runs the application, it translates your code to p-code and executes it using the interpreter. The VB interpreter will report errors as they are encountered.

While the application is running, it is possible automatically to pause it on any executable line of code. To accomplish this, you need to set a breakpoint on the line at which you want execution to be paused. You can set breakpoints on a line by positioning the cursor at any point on the line in the Code window and choosing the Debug | Toggle Breakpoint menu option from the IDE, or pressing the F9 key. Another way to set a breakpoint is to click on the left-hand gray sidebar in a Code window. When a breakpoint is set the executable line of code will turn red, and a red circle will appear next in the sidebar (see Figure 2-8).

When the application hits a breakpoint, it enters break mode. This is indicated in the caption of the IDE in Figure 2-9. At this point the program can be restarted by clicking the Start button on the Standard Toolbar or pressing F5, or it can be stopped altogether by clicking the End button on the Standard Toolbar. The End button has a blue square as its icon.

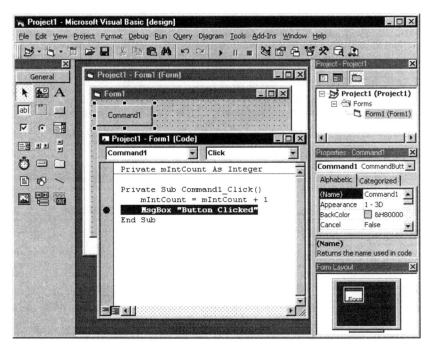

Figure 2-8. Setting a breakpoint.

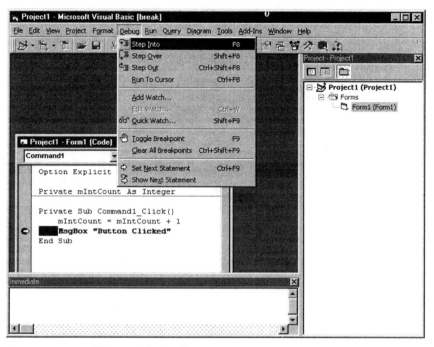

Figure 2-9. A VB application in break mode.

While in break mode the Debug menu offers several powerful functions. You can execute your program one line at a time using the Step Into, Step Over, and Step Out Debug menu options, or you can set the cursor on a line after the current execution point and run the program until it hits that line by selecting the Run To Cursor menu option. The current breakpoints can be modified using the Toggle Breakpoint and Clear All Breakpoints menu options. The value of a variable or expression can be viewed by hovering over it with the mouse. If a value can be determined, it will automatically be displayed in a tooltip style box. Alternatively, select the expression of interest and choose the Quick Watch menu option to display the value once, or add it permanently to the Watches window by choosing the Add Watch menu option. You can also move the current line of execution back or forward by putting the cursor on the new line and choosing the Set Next Statement menu option.

While in break mode you can enter and execute code in the Immediate window, which is generally docked at run time at the bottom of the IDE. In Figure 2-10 the value of the variable mIntCount was displayed by selecting the Immediate window and executing a print statement. The Immediate window can also be used to reassign variable values and run procedures.

VB's debugging environment lets you step through a section of code while watching all the variables and expressions of interest. You can change the code

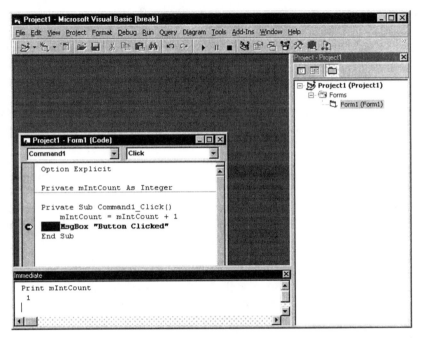

Figure 2-10. Using the Immediate window.

on the fly, reset the line of execution to a point before the new code, and step through it again. If you are trying to interact with an external device but you're not sure exactly how to accomplish it in code, this environment allows you repeatedly to try different approaches until you get the desired behavior, without having to stop the program, make the change, and restart it every time.

A SUMMARY OF THE STEPS FOR CREATING A NEW PROGRAM

The process of building a new Visual Basic® program begins by creating a new Project within the IDE. The project type you choose will depend on the kind of program you want to create. In most cases, we will begin with the Standard EXE project type. The default name for a Standard EXE project is always Project1. You can change the name of the project to something more descriptive by selecting Project1 in the Project Explorer window, and editing the project's Name property in the Properties Window.

Every project must have a startup Form or Standard module. This is the initial module that is executed when the application begins. When a Standard module is used as the startup module, it must have a subroutine named Main, which will be executed when the module loads. Also, programs that utilize a Standard module for startup do not initially (or may never) have a graphical interface. In the default Standard EXE project, Form1 is automatically set as the startup module. This can be changed using the General tab of the Project Properties dialog, which can be displayed by choosing the Project | Properties menu option from the IDE.

Additional Forms and other components can be added to your project by selecting one of the options under the Project menu from the IDE. There are a variety of options depending on the type of program you are writing. We will describe the Form module, Standard module, and Class module in much more detail later on. Consult VB Help for information about the other types of project components that are available.

Use the Toolbox to select and add new ActiveX controls to a Form. Display the Code window for a component by selecting the View | Code menu option, by pressing F7, or by double-clicking on a component. Add code to controls, Forms, and other modules. From the Code window, if not already the case, select the object of interest from the Object box, located in the upper left-hand corner of the window. Then select the object's event to which you want to add code from the list of all available events in the Procedures/ Events box located at the upper right-hand corner of the window. The Code window will display the event procedure. You are ready to enter the code that will execute when the event occurs.

Run your program by pressing the Start button on the Standard Toolbar and test its functionality. Pause the program and debug as necessary. Resume and test again. For more significant changes, end your program and go back to editing.

These simple steps are all that is required to get a simple Windows® application up and running with Visual Basic®. Applications written in VB can be a simple, containing a single Form module with a few controls and a little code, or quite complex, containing hundreds or thousands of procedures, Forms, and other components.

In the next section we'll step through the development of a simple program to demonstrate many of the concepts we have described.

A QUICK START

Let's step through a simple example to demonstrate the process of creating a program in Visual Basic®. We'll avoid the traditional "Hello World" example, and do something that is a little more interesting to science and engineering professionals. The example will simulate the collection of data from a very simple "instrument," filter it, and then display the data.

SELECTING THE PROJECT

If you haven't already done so, start up Visual Basic®. When VB first starts it displays the New Project dialog shown in Figure 2-1. Here we will select the type of project we want to create. For this example select a Standard EXE project type by double-clicking on the Standard EXE icon. The default project will be named Project1 and will have one Form named Form1. If the Form1 Form Designer is not visible, find the Form in the Project Explorer and double-click on it.

SETTING PROJECT AND FORM PROPERTIES

Let's change the names of the Project and Form as well as the Form's Caption. Click on Project1 in the Project Explorer to display the Project properties in the Properties window. Edit the Name property in the Properties Window. In Figure 2-11 we changed the project's name property to "Example."

Now let's change the name of the Form. It is good programming practice to name objects using a prefix that indicates the type of object. This becomes very useful later when working with objects in code. You can identify its type immediately by its name. Click on Form1 in the Project Explorer to display the Form's properties in the Properties window. Edit the Name property. In this example we changed the name of Form1 to "frmMain." The "frm" name prefix indicates that this object is a Form. Table 2-1 also lists some common

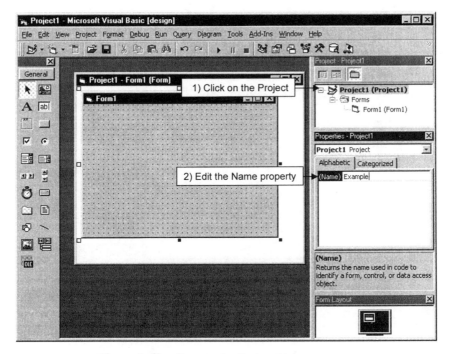

Figure 2-11. Change the Project Name property.

TABLE 2-1. Some ActiveX controls with suggested name prefixes.

ActiveX Control	Prefix	ActiveX Control	Prefix
Label	lbl	TextBox	txt
Frame	fra	CommandButton	btn
CheckBox	chk	OptionButton	opt
ComboBox	cmb	ListBox	lst
HScrollBar	hsb	VScrollBar	vsb
Timer	tmr	DriveListBox	drv
DirListBox	dir	FileListBox	fil
Shape	shp	Line	lin
Image	img	Data	dat
SSTab	sst	CommonDialog	cdl
MSComm	com	MSFlexGrid	grd
PictureBox	pct	MSChart	cht

control name prefixes for your reference. To change the Form's Caption, scroll the Properties window down until you see the Caption property and edit the property value. In Figure 2-12 we have given the frmMain Form the Caption "DataCapture." This is also reflected in the caption of the Form Designer.

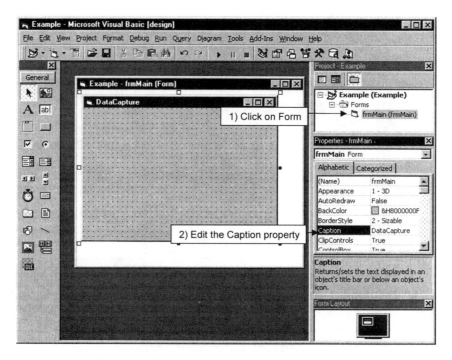

Figure 2-12. Change a Form's Caption property.

ADDING ACTIVEX CONTROLS

The first control we want to add is a Timer. Click on the Timer icon in the Toolbox and sketch a small rectangle to the right side of the frmMain Form. A new Timer control will appear on the Form. Hover the mouse over an icon on the Toolbox to display its name in a tooltip. Repeat the process for two TextBox controls, two Labels, and a CommandButton. Figure 2-13 shows the Form Designer with the newly created controls.

With the new ActiveX controls in place, now is a good time to assign meaningful names and other properties. For this example, we will assign the following property values. Column 1 lists the type of object, column 2 lists the property name, and column 3 lists the property value. Select an object in your project to display its properties in the Properties window. Find a property name and change its value. Repeat the process for all listed object properties. We will use this format throughout the book to list object property values in example projects.

Object Type	Property	Value
Form	Name	frmMain
	Caption	DataCapture
CommandButton	Name	btnStart
	Caption	Start
TextBox	Name	txtDataBuffer
	Text	
TextBox	Name	txtCutOffFilter
	Text	
Timer	Name	tmrDataTimer
	Interval	2000
	Enabled	False
Label	Name	lblDataBuffer
	Caption	Data:
Label	Name	lblCutOffFilter
	Caption	Cut Off Filter:

ADDING CODE TO EVENT PROCEDURES

Now it's time to add the code that you want executed in response to the events that occur in the application. Let's start with the tmrDataTimer Timer control. This control has only one event, the Timer event. When the Timer's Enabled property is set to True, the Timer event fires continuously with an interval determined by the value of the Interval property, which is measured in milliseconds. This will continue until the Timer's Enabled property is set to False. To add code to the Timer event, double-click on the Timer control that is sketched on the Form. The Code window will be displayed and the cursor

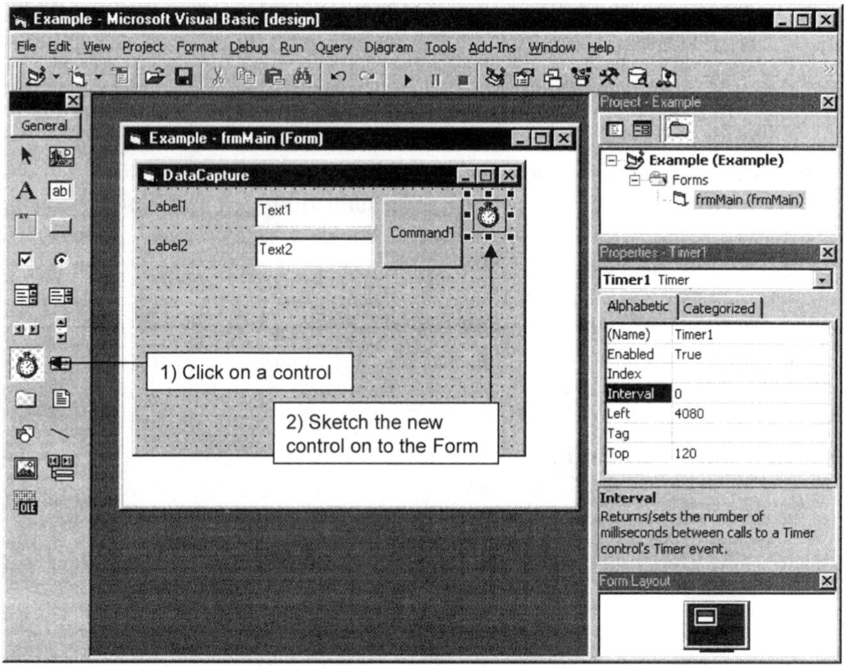

Figure 2-13. Add ActiveX Controls to a Form.

positioned over the Timer event procedure named tmrDataTimer_Timer. Add the following code to the body of the procedure, as shown in Figure 2-14.

```
Private Sub tmrDataTimer_Timer()
   Dim dblDataTmp As Double, dblCutOff As Double

   If IsNumeric(txtCutOffFilter.Text) Then      ' Get the cutoff value
      dblCutOff = CDbl(txtCutOffFilter.Text)
   End If

   dblDataTmp = Rnd                             ' Generate a data point

   If dblDataTmp > dblCutOff Then               ' Filter the data
      txtDataBuffer.Text = dblDataTmp           ' Put the data in the buffer
   End If

End Sub
```

This procedure will produce a random number and save the number in the Text property of the txtDataBuffer Textbox. The first If statement checks to see if a valid number was added to the txtCutOffFilter TextBox. If so, it converts the number to a Double and saves it in the dblCutOff variable. Rnd is a builtin function that generates random numbers in the range 0.0 to 1.0. It is

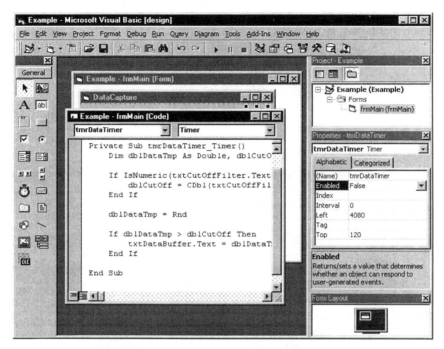

Figure 2-14. Add code to an event procedure.

used here to generate a new number, which is stored in the variable dblDataTmp. After generating the random number, the second If statement tests whether the number is greater than the cutoff value. If it is, the random number is copied to the Text property of the txtDataBuffer Textbox, which displays the number in the TextBox.

Next we'll add code to the btnStart CommandButton to start and stop the Timer. Press Shift-F7 to jump back to the Form Designer. Double-click on the btnStart CommandButton to show the Code window. The default event procedure displayed is for the CommandButton's Click event and is named btnStart_Click. Add the follow code to the btnStart Click event procedure.

```
Private Sub btnStart_Click()
    If tmrDataTimer.Enabled = False Then    ' If the Timer is disabled
        tmrDataTimer.Enabled = True         ' Enable it
        btnStart.Caption = "Stop"           ' Set the caption
    Else
        tmrDataTimer.Enabled = False        ' Otherwise disable it
        btnStart.Caption = "Start"          ' Set the caption
    End If
End Sub
```

This code will cause the CommandButton's function to toggle between enabling and disabling the Timer. Since the Timer starts out with its Enabled property set to False, the first Click event will cause it to be enabled, which initiates data generation. Also, the btnStart CommandButton Caption will be changed to "Stop." The new caption indicates that the next time the btnStart CommandButton is clicked, it will disable the Timer, and data generation will be terminated.

RUNNING A PROGRAM

Now it's time to run and test your program. Click the Start button on the Standard Toolbar of the IDE. The interface of your example program will appear as in Figure 2-15. Click the btnStart CommandButton and watch what happens. The CommandButton Caption changes to "Stop," and a new random number will be generated and displayed in the txtDataBuffer TextBox every two seconds. Enter a cutoff value between 0.0 and 1.0 into the txtCutOffFilter TextBox. Notice how the numbers that are appearing in the txtDataBuffer TextBox are now limited to those that are greater than the cutoff value (see Figure 2-16). Click the btnStart CommandButton one more time. The Caption changes back to "Start," and data generation stops.

As you can see, a significant portion of VB programming involves choosing and configuring the best components for your application. So far we have used TextBox controls for displaying and editing text, Label controls for identifying the purpose of TextBoxes, a CommandButton for initiating and terminating an action, and a Timer to fire periodic events. We added very little code to cause these objects to work together.

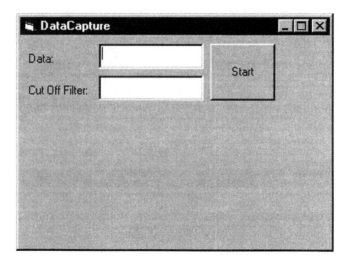

Figure 2-15. The interface right after the example program was started.

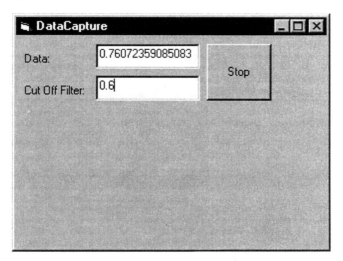

Figure 2-16. The example program in action.

CHARTING THE DATA

Let's modify the example to chart the data we are generating. We will do this by adding a Microsoft® Chart (MSChart) ActiveX control to the application. The MSChart control is a very powerful charting tool that we'll describe in detail in Chapter 22. Here we'll make use of just a few of its features.

Before we can create an MSChart control we need to add it to the Toolbox. Open the Components dialog by selecting the Project | Components menu option from the IDE or pressing Ctrl+T (see Figure 2-7). Scroll down to the option that includes the name "Microsoft Chart Control" and check it. Once you click the OK button on the Components dialog, your Toolbox will be modified to include the MSChart control. Select the MSChart icon on the Toolbox and sketch a new chart onto the frmMain Form. A default MSChart control will appear as in Figure 2-17. Resize the control as needed. You now have powerful charting capability built right into your program.

INTEGRATING THE MSCHART

We will need to set some properties and add a little code to cause the MSChart control to display generated data the way that we want. First, set the following MSChart properties by selecting the MSChart control and editing the property values in the Properties window. These property values will cause 10 data points to be plotted in the default bar chart style.

Object Type	Property	Value
MSChart	Name	chtData
	ColumnCount	1
	RowCount	10
	RowLabel	Data

To cause the generated data to be added to the new chart, we will use the Change event of the txtDataBuffer TextBox. The Change event is fired whenever the Text property of the TextBox changes. Activate the Form Designer and double-click on the txtDataBuffer TextBox. You will be brought to the Code window and positioned over the txtDataBuffer Change event procedure. Add the following code.

```
Private Sub txtDataBuffer_Change()
    Dim dblDataTmp As Double
    Static intNextRow As Integer

    intNextRow = intNextRow + 1          ' Determine the next row
    If intNextRow > chtData.RowCount Then intNextRow = 1
                            ' Get the new data value and add it to the chart
    If IsNumeric(txtDataBuffer.Text) Then dblDataTmp = CDbl(txtData Buffer.Text)
    chtData.DataGrid.SetData intNextRow, 1, dblDataTmp, 0

End Sub
```

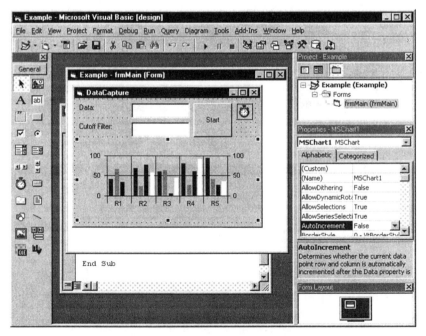

Figure 2-17. Add a new MSChart control.

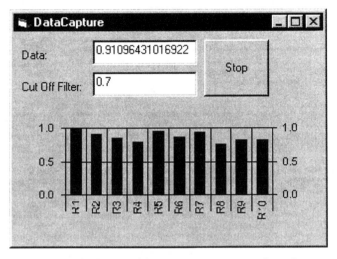

Figure 2-18. The modified example program in action.

When the Text property of the txtDataBuffer TextBox changes, the next row in the chtData MSChart will be determined, and the new data value will be added to the chart.

Run the modified example program by clicking the Start button on the Standard Toolbar of the IDE. Click the Start button on the example and watch what happens. As each point is generated it is also added to the chart. The chart's Y-axis will be scaled automatically to the displayed data. Set a cutoff value in the range 0.0 to 1.0 and notice how only the filtered data is added to chart. Figure 2-18 shows the modified example program in action.

The source code for the complete example is included with the software that is available online. It can be downloaded from Wiley's FTP site, using the instructions detailed earlier. Once you have the software distribution, the source code can be found in the project file named \Part1\Ex1\Ex1.vbp.

IN SUMMARY

This example is intended to simulate a typical laboratory situation and demonstrate how quickly and easily you can create an application to capture data, manipulate it, and display it. We set about 20 property values and wrote only three short procedures. With Visual Basic®, a little effort can go a long way.

3

A Review of the Visual Basic® Language

If you've already programmed with the BASIC language, or another popular computer programming language, you'll find the Visual Basic® language to be very natural. In this chapter we review many of the programming constructs and language elements in order to help you discover how to accomplish common programming tasks in VB. We won't attempt to list all options or cover every syntactical nuance. Refer to help files and other documentation provided with Visual Basic® for these details. If you are already familiar with the Visual Basic® language, you can safely skip this chapter.

DATA TYPES AND ARRAYS

The Visual Basic® language includes many *intrinsic data types* with associated variable types. The keyword Dim is used to declare a new variable. For example, to declare a variable name intCount of type Integer, you would use the following statement.

```
Dim intCount As Integer
```

There are other keywords used to declare new variables with different scope and lifetime, such as Private, Public, and Static. We'll discuss that in the next chapter. Table 3-1 lists the intrinsic data types in VB, including the type name, a brief description, the default value, storage length, and our naming convention prefix. Throughout the examples in this book we will assign names to most variables using the naming convention in Table 3-1. For example, you could tell that the variable named intCount was an Integer by the leading "int" in its name. We won't strictly adhere to the convention, but, when used, it will be accurate.

Visual Basic® is very flexible when it comes to declaring variables. In fact, you can simply refer to a variable in your code without ever declaring it. If

TABLE 3-1. VB variable types with descriptions.

Variable Data Type	Data Type Description	Default Value	Length in Bytes	Variable Name Prefix
Boolean	True or False	False	2	bln
Byte	An integer in the range 0 to 255	0	1	byt
Integer	An integer in the range −32,768 to 32,767	0	2	int
Long	An integer in the range −2,147,483,648 to 2,147,483,647	0	4	lng
Single	A floating point number, roughly in the range −3.402823E38 to 3.402823E38	0.0	4	sng
Double	A floating point number, roughly in the range −1.797693134862232E308 to 1.797693134862232E308	0.0	8	dbl
Decimal	A decimal number, capable of representing up to 28 significant digits. With no decimal places, it can hold numbers in the range +/−79,228,162,514,264,337,593,543,950,335	0	14	dec
String	A sequence of characters	" "	variable	str
Currency	A number with four decimal places, designed for currency calculations. Can hold values in the range −922,337,203,685,477.5808 to 922,337,203,685,477.5807	0	8	crn
Date	A date and time in the range 1 January 100 to 31 December 9999	12:00:00 AM	8	dat
Object	A reference to an object	Nothing	4	obj
Variant	A variable that can hold any intrinsic data type. Data type depends on value.	Empty or 0	variable	vrn

you haven't declared a variable, or provided a type in a variable declaration, it gets the type Variant by default. To force the declaration of all variables in your code, check the Require Variable Declaration option on the Editor tab of the Options dialog under the Tools menu in the VB IDE. We strongly recommend that you always select this option. It is easy for programming errors to go unnoticed when you are not forced to declare all variables. For example, you may declare a variable called intCount as an Integer, and then later on type the variable name intCont in your code, inadvertently leaving out the "u." Without requiring that all variables be declared, VB will happily bring the new variable into existence as a Variant and assign it a default value of 0. The result could be catastrophic.

The Visual Basic® language also allows you to declare arrays of any data type. Arrays can be declared with up to 60 dimensions. Dynamic arrays can be resized at run time and Visual Basic® handles all the memory management for you. For example, the following two statements declare a one-dimensional Integer array and a two-dimensional Double array.

```
Dim arrInts(1 to 10) As Integer
Dim arrMeasure(1 to 8, 1 to 12) As Double
```

As you can see by these examples, the upper and lower bounds of an array can be specified in the declaration. Array bounds can even extend into negative numbers. When arrays are declared, all their elements are initialized to default data type values.

To resize an array it must first be declared to be dynamic. Dynamic arrays are initially declared with no dimensions, and redimensioned at run time using a ReDim statement. For example, in the following statements a dynamic array is declared of type Single, and its size is increased ten times in a loop, while storing the square of the index each time in the new array location. When the Preserve keyword is used in the ReDim statement, the contents of the array are not erased. Leaving Preserve out will cause the contents of the entire array to be erased as well as resized.

```
Dim arrSingle() As Single
Dim I As Integer
For I = 1 To 10
       ReDim Preserve arrSingle(1 To I) As Single
       arrSingle(I) = I * I
Next I
```

Visual Basic® provides a variety of ways to define your own data types. The first is called a *User-Defined Type*, commonly referred to as a UDT. UDTs are similar to C programming language structures. They are made up of a group of variables of any type that are manipulated as a single unit. Following is the definition of a new UDT named Well. The Well type has four data members of types Integer, Double, and Date.

```
Type Well
    intRow As Integer
    intCol As Integer
    dblMeasurement As Double
    datLastModified As Date
End Type
```

Once a UDT is defined, new variables can be declared using the UDT name. In the following series of statements a new variable of type Well is declared with the name MyWell, and its members are assigned values. To access individual member variable values, join the type variable with a member name using a dot.

```
Dim MyWell As Well
MyWell.intRow = 2
MyWell.intCol = 3
MyWell.dblMeasurement = 12.34
MyWell.datLastModified = #1/1/1999#
```

Another way to define a custom type in Visual Basic® is to use something called an *Enumeration* variable. This is similar to an enum in the C programming language. An Enumeration variable is used to conveniently declare a series of named constants. In the lower window of Figure 3-1 a new Enumera-

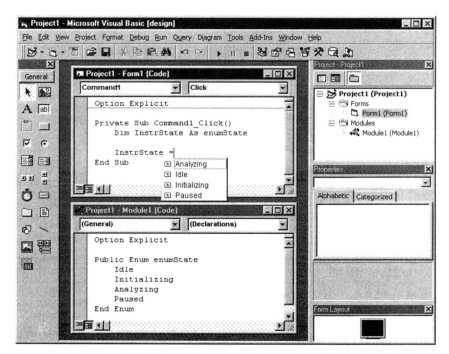

Figure 3-1. The Code Editor's Auto List Members feature with an Enumeration variable.

tion variable called enumState is defined, which includes a series of named constants that identify a set of states. In the upper window a new variable of type enumState named InstrState is declared and is being assigned a value. Since Visual Basic® knows the declared constant names, the Code Editor's Auto List Members feature automatically displays a dropdown list with available options. This feature is handy for remembering predefined constants.

EXECUTION CONTROL

Visual Basic® provides most of the standard execution control programming language constructs. There are primarily two types of looping constructs, For-Next and Do-Loop. An additional While-Wend construct is equivalent to a type of Do-Loop construct. The following statements implement a loop that increments a variable named I from a value of 1 to 10 with an increment of 2.

```
For I = 1 To 10 Step 2
      MsgBox I
Next I
```

A Do Loop repeatedly executes a group of statements based on the result of a condition. The condition can be checked each time before the group of statements is entered, or after the group of statements has completed execution. The loop continues while a condition is true or until a condition becomes true. For example, the following Do Loop repeats while the value of I is less than 10. The loop will never be entered if I is initially equal to or greater than 10.

```
Do While I < 10
      I = I + 1
Loop
```

The next example will continue to loop until the value of I is greater than 10. The body of the loop will always execute at least once, regardless of the initial value of I. Either of the While or Until conditions can be used before the loop or after the loop.

```
Do
      I = I + 1
Loop Until I > 10
```

The Visual Basic® language includes If-Then-Else and Select-Case conditional constructs. An If-Then-Else construct may include an arbitrary number of conditions by adding ElseIf statements. For example, the following If-Then-Else construct will pop up a different error message depending on the value of the variable name intErrCode.

```
If intErrCode = 3 Then
        MsgBox "Error. Return without GoSub"
ElseIf intErrCode = 5 Then
        MsgBox "Error. Invalid procedure call"
ElseIf intErrCode = 6 Then
        MsgBox "Error. Overflow"
Else
        MsgBox "Unknown Error"
End If
```

This can also be written using a Select-Case conditional construct, as in the following:

```
Select Case intErrCode
Case 3
        MsgBox "Error. Return without GoSub"
Case 5
        MsgBox "Error. Invalid procedure call"
Case 6
        MsgBox "Error. Overflow"
Case Else
        MsgBox "Unknown Error"
End Select
```

PROCEDURES

Visual Basic® offers a handful of ways to define procedures. If you have never programmed in Visual Basic® before, some will be familiar and others may be brand new. We'll introduce *subroutines*, *functions*, and *event procedures*. Two additional types of procedures, called *object methods* and *property procedures*, will be introduced in Chapter 5 when we cover object-oriented programming in Visual Basic®.

A subroutine is a procedure that accepts a series of arguments and has no return value. As an example, let's take the previous Select-Case statement and add it to a subroutine called HandleError. In Figure 3-2 the upper portion of the displayed window shows the defined subroutine. Below that, we are in the middle of entering a statement that calls the HandleError subroutine. You can see that the Code Editor's Auto Quick Info feature has listed the subroutine declared argument and data type. This is a great reason to give your arguments meaningful names.

A function is similar to a subroutine, only it returns a value. The type of value returned is indicated by the type that appears at the end of the first line in a function declaration. In Figure 3-3 we have converted the HandleError subroutine into a function that returns a Boolean value. The function indicates whether or not the error code was recognized.

We've already seen examples of event procedures, which are just subroutines that are automatically executed in response to a particular Windows® event. For example, the Command1_Click subroutine in Figures 3-2 and 3-3

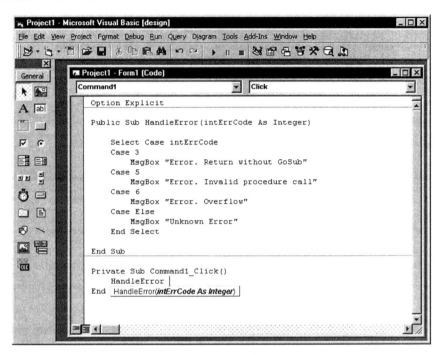

Figure 3-2. The Code Editor's Auto Quick Info feature shows procedure arguments while entering a subroutine call.

is invoked when a CommandButton named Command1 is clicked. You can also call event procedures from code as if they were normal subroutines.

ARGUMENT PASSING

There are essentially two ways that a value can be passed to a procedure as one of its arguments. These are called *pass by value* and *pass by reference*. When a variable is passed to a procedure by value, only a copy of the value stored by the variable is actually passed to the procedure. A change made to the argument's value within the procedure will have no effect on the value of the original variable outside the procedure, since the passed value is only a copy. When an argument is passed by reference, the argument variable within the procedure will refer to the exact same value as the argument variable originally passed to the procedure. Changes to the value of the argument variable within a procedure will be reflected in the value of the passed variable when the procedure exits, since the two variables refer to the same value.

You can determine how an argument is passed to a procedure in two ways. If you precede an argument declaration in a procedure definition with the keyword ByVal or ByRef, when the procedure is called, the argument vari-

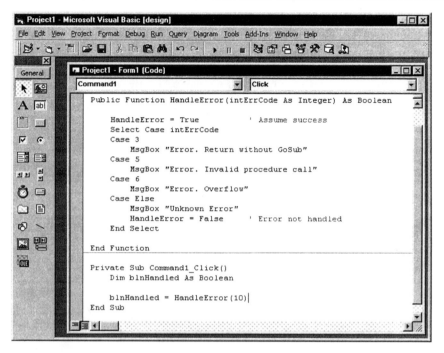

Figure 3-3. HandleError is converted to a function that returns a Boolean value.

able will be passed to the procedure by value or by reference, depending on the keyword used. For example, consider the following subroutine called DoubleIt and the Command1_Click event procedure. DoubleIt multiplies an Integer argument by 2 and reassigns the result to the variable. Command1_Click assigns the variable I a value of 1, passes I to DoubleIt, and displays the value of I after DoubleIt exits.

```
Private Sub Command1_Click()
    Dim I As Integer

    I = 1
    DoubleIt I
    MsgBox I
End Sub

Sub DoubleIt(ByRef intVal As Integer)
    intVal = intVal * 2
End Sub
```

The argument intVal in the DoubleIt subroutine definition is declared using the ByRef keyword. When the subroutine is called, the argument will be passed by reference. When intVal modifies its value, the change will also be reflected in the variable I, since intVal and I refer to the exact same value. When the Command1 CommandButton is clicked, a MessageBox will appear displaying a "2." If DoubleIt is redefined using the ByVal keyword in place of ByRef, a copy of the variable I will be passed to the subroutine instead and stored in intVal. The copy will be modified when intVal is reassigned. When DoubleIt exits, the original value of I remains unchanged. This will be indicated by the MessageBox, which will display a "1." By default, arguments are passed to procedures by reference.

The second way to determine how variables are passed to procedures is with the syntax used to call the procedure. Let's consider another subroutine called SquareIt, defined as follows:

```
Sub SquareIt(intVal As Integer)
    intVal = intVal * intVal
End Sub
```

When the subroutine is called with no parentheses surrounding its arguments, all arguments are passed by reference. For example, the following Command1_Click event procedure will result in a MessageBox that displays a "4":

```
Private Sub Command1_Click()
    Dim I As Integer

    I = 2
    SquareIt I
    MsgBox I
End Sub
```

If the subroutine call is modified to include parentheses, the variable is automatically passed by value. For example, if the subroutine call is modified to the following statement, the resulting MessageBox will display a "2."

```
SquareIt (I)
```

A similar rule applies to function calls. Functions always have parentheses surrounding their arguments. The syntactic difference that results in a change in the way variables are passed is whether or not the return value from the function is retrieved. As an example, consider the following function called CubeIt, which returns the cube of the passed integer. The function reassigns the passed argument in the process of computing the cube.

```
Function CubeIt(intVal As Integer) As Integer
    intVal = intVal ^ 3
    CubeIt = intVal
End Function
```

When the return value of the function is retrieved, for example, by assigning it to another variable, the argument I is passed by reference, and the MessageBox will display an "8."

```
Private Sub Command1_Click()
    Dim I As Integer, I2 As Integer

    I = 2
    I2 = CubeIt(I)
    MsgBox I
End Sub
```

If the function call is modified to exclude the retrieval of its return value, as
in the following example, the argument I is automatically passed by value,
and the MessageBox will display "2," indicating that I remains unchanged.

```
Private Sub Command1_Click()
    Dim I As Integer, I2 As Integer

    I = 2
    CubeIt (I)
    MsgBox I
End Sub
```

Experiment with your own examples until you understand the difference
between call by value and call by reference. Make sure that you appreciate
how the ByVal and ByRef keywords as well as how the calling syntax of a subroutine and function affect the way arguments are passed. A solid comprehen-
sion of these subtleties will save hours of debugging later on.

4

The Structure of a Visual Basic® Application

As we've already mentioned, the project is the entity that binds together all the components that make up a Visual Basic® program. You can see all project components using the Project Explorer window (see Figure 4-1). The information describing the components of a project is stored in a project file, which uses the ".vbp" extension. Project files are formatted as plain text; you can edit them with a simple text editor. If you do, be very careful not to make any modifications or save the project file in a format other than plain text. You could easily corrupt the file, making it unreadable by Visual Basic®. Having said that, it is worth looking at the contents of a project file. You may be surprised at what you find.

MODULES

All the Visual Basic® code that you'll write is stored in modules, which are added to a project. There are three main types of modules in VB. They are the *Standard module*, *Form module*, and *Class module*. Each module is saved as plain text in a separate file with a unique extension.

The Standard module is very much like the traditional code module found in several programming languages. If you've ever programmed in a language that permits the creation of code modules, you'll probably find the Standard module to be very similar. Standard modules are plain text files that consist of a brief header followed by declarations and finally procedure definitions. Standard module file names use a ".bas" extension. Any code that exists within a procedure is said to be at the *procedure level*. Any other code in a module is said to be at the *module level*. All module-level declarations must come before procedure definitions in Standard and other VB modules.

Only one instance of a given Standard module will exist in your program at any time, and it will exist for the lifetime of your program. If you've never

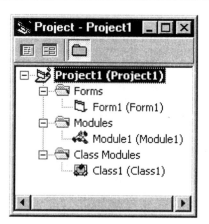

Figure 4-1. Project Explorer window showing the components of a project named Project1.

worked with VB, or another modern programming language, you might find this to be an obvious statement. As it turns out, in VB it's the exception. You can create multiple instances of both Form and Class modules at run time.

To add a new Standard module to your VB project, select the Project | Add Module menu option from the VB IDE menu bar. After choosing to create a new module, VB presents you with the Code window for the Standard module. The Code window at the bottom of Figure 3-1 is for a Standard module. You can have as many Code windows as you have modules in your project. You can enter declarations and procedure definitions into a Code window at any point while the project is not running. At the top of a Code window are two dropdown boxes. The one on the right will always display the current section of the module occupied by your cursor. When your cursor is in a procedure, the procedure name will appear in the dropdown. The area that precedes any procedure definition is called the *Declarations section*. When your cursor is in that section of a module, the upper right dropdown will display "(Declarations)."

A Form module has a Code window that appears similar to the Standard module; declarations are entered at the top followed by procedure definitions. Beyond code structure, similarity between the two modules rapidly diminishes.

Of the three types of modules, the Form module is the only type that has an associated graphical interface. You've already seen how Forms can be created and controls sketched onto a Form. Double-clicking on a control or the Form itself will bring up the Form's Code window. Module-level declarations and procedure definitions that relate to the Form or one of its components are entered into the Code window. There is only one Code window for each Form module. In addition to your own subroutine and function procedures, a Form's Code window is where all event procedures are added to handle the events of any control sketched onto a form, or any other object that is created within the form. There are two dropdowns at the top of a Form's Code window, identical to a Standard module Code window. The dropdown in the upper left of the Form's Code window is called the *Object Box*. It displays all objects with procedures that you can define in the module. The upper right dropdown, called the *Procedures/Events Box*, displays all procedures associated with the object displayed in the Object Box.

To add a new Form module to your project, select the Project | Add Form menu option from the VB IDE menu bar. You are presented with the Add Form dialog, which provides a healthy list of predefined Form templates from which you can choose. VB provides Form templates for a variety of purposes, including a Log In Dialog, Splash Screen, and Web Browser. When choosing a template other than the basic Form template, your new Form will be initialized with a set of controls as well as variable declarations and procedure definitions that work together for a common purpose. For example, if you create a new Form using the Browser template, you will get a new Form with a WebBrowser control, and a toolbar and URL dropdown that implements the functionality of a basic web browser. Figure 4-2 shows a VB project with a Form window and Code window for a new Form module.

All information about a Form is saved in a single file with a ".frm" extension. This file is also a formatted plain text file. At the top of a form file is

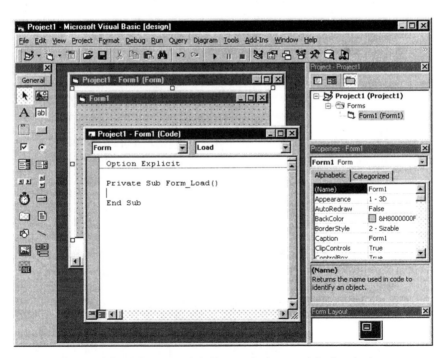

Figure 4-2. A Form module Form window and Code window.

the definition of the Form and all components associated with the Form. Declarations and procedure definitions follow.

The third type of module is a Class module. Class modules are used to define new object types in VB. Classes are very similar to Forms, only they have no graphical interface. We'll defer the details of Class modules until Chapter 5, when we discuss object-oriented programming in Visual Basic®.

SCOPE AND LIFETIME

Anything that can be declared or defined in a Visual Basic® project has *scope* and *lifetime*. Scope determines the program locations from which an entity can be accessed. Lifetime refers to the period of time during which an entity is loaded in memory and accessible from some location in a program. Where and how you make your declarations and define your procedures will determine how they can be used. The main statements that are used for making declarations are *Public*, *Private*, *Static*, and *Dim*.

As we've seen, variables can be declared within a procedure or outside a procedure in a module's declarations section. No matter how you declare a variable, if it is declared from within a procedure, the variable will only be available to program statements that are also within the procedure. Variables declared within a procedure are referred to as *procedure-level variables*. In most of the example code that we present, the Dim statement is used to declare procedure-level variables.

When a variable is declared in the declarations section, it is referred to as a *module-level variable*. The keyword used to declare the variable will determine program locations from which it can be accessed. Variables declared as Private will only be available to program statements that are included in that module. Variables declared as Public will be available to program statements outside the module as well. For example, consider the following two declarations made in the declarations section of a module called MyModule.

```
Public mIntPublicData As Integer
Private mIntPrivateData As Integer
```

From anywhere in MyModule, a statement that refers to either variable will work fine. Outside a module public variables can be properly scoped using the module name and a dot. The statement MyModule.mIntPublicData will successfully access the public variable, but MyModule.mIntPrivateData will generate an error. A module-level variable declared using Dim will behave the same as if it were declared using Private.

The same scoping rules apply for procedures. Procedures declared using Private will be available only to program statements within the module. Public module procedures will be available throughout your program. Access pub-

TABLE 4-1. Summary of declaration statements, scope, and lifetime.

Declaration	Statement	Scope	Lifetime
Procedure-level	Dim	Procedure	While procedure is active.
Procedure-level	Private	Procedure	While procedure is active.
Procedure-level	Static	Procedure	For entire life of module.
Module-level	Dim	Module	For entire life of module.
Module-level	Private	Module	For entire life of module.
Module-level	Public	Application	For entire life of module.

lic module procedures by scoping a procedure call with the name of the module in a manner similar to the way public module variables are accessed.

Variables declared within a procedure using the Private or Dim statements come in to existence after the procedure is invoked, and go out of existence when the procedure exits. Public variable declarations are not permitted within a procedure. The lifetime of procedure-level variables declared using Private or Dim is the same as the lifetime of the procedure. Procedure-level variables declared using the Static statement are different. Static variables exist for the lifetime of a module. Nevertheless, they are not accessible from outside the procedure. Static procedure variables are useful for applications that need to track the number of times a procedure is called since they retain their data between procedure calls.

Table 4-1 summarizes the various declaration types, scope, and the lifetime of the declared language element.

CHAPTER

5

Object-Oriented Programming in Visual Basic®

Object-oriented programming (OOP) has had a dramatic impact on the creation of software. OOP provides a programming framework that results in code that is better structured, more robust, and more easily reused. We will use concepts from object-oriented programming in many of our examples. To get a full appreciation for how these examples operate, how they are designed, and how best to make use of them, it is important to be familiar with object-oriented programming. This chapter is a crash course in the essential characteristics of OOP and to what extent it is implemented in the Visual Basic® language.

OBJECT-ORIENTED PROGRAMMING

The object-oriented programming paradigm is a way of thinking about the development of software. It provides a structured framework in which it is natural to follow good programming practices. One way to think of OOP is as a superstructure for the traditional procedural approach to programming, which is used with the BASIC or C programming languages.

A purely object-oriented program is composed of a collection of software entities called *objects*. An object is essentially a computer model that *encapsulates* the state (*properties*) and behavior (*methods*) of the modeled entity. Encapsulation of state and behavior is one of the central tenets of object-oriented programming, and it is one of the primary reasons for many of the benefits of OOP.

Objects in object-oriented programs interact by passing *messages*, which are requests that an object manipulate its own properties by executing one of its methods. Message passing is analogous to procedure calling. In "pure" object-oriented programming, the only way that an object's properties can be manipulated is through its methods. Direct access to an object's properties is strictly forbidden. An object has the sole responsibility for maintaining the integrity of its properties. If direct access to an object's properties is allowed, the object cannot guarantee integrity. In practice, this constraint is often relaxed.

Encapsulation and message passing result in many benefits. Using encapsulation, the implementation details of complex methods can be hidden. It is not necessary that a user of an object understand how its methods work. It is only necessary to understand how to use the object's *interface*, that is, how to request that an object execute its methods. Complex problems can be dealt with at higher levels of abstraction since objects encapsulate implementation details within their methods. As a result, objects become reusable software components by minimizing their interdependencies. This, in turn, has the potential to increase software development productivity substantially.

A *class* is an object template used to create new object *instances*. A class defines the type of properties that will be contained in an object and how its methods are implemented. An instance is a particular occurrence of an object that actually holds property values and has access to a common set of methods. The generic term *object* can be used to refer to a class or an instance. It is often used when the distinction is obvious by the context, or not important.

In many object-oriented programming languages classes can be organized in an *inheritance* hierarchy, which can be drawn as an inverted tree, similar to the way a family tree is drawn. When a *subclass* (lower in the hierarchy) inherits a *superclass* (higher in the hierarchy), it implies that there exists an "is-a" relationship between the classes. The subclass is a type of superclass. It follows that an instance of a subclass should have its own copy of the properties defined in the inherited superclass, as well as access to superclass methods. After all, if a subclass is actually a type of superclass, it ought to have the same properties and methods. Gaining real benefits from inheritance can be tricky. We won't discuss class inheritance further, since VB doesn't offer it directly.

The last characteristic of object-oriented programming that we'll discuss is a concept called *polymorphism*. The term *polymorphic* is used to describe something that can exist in many forms. The most common types of polymorphism in OOP involve objects and methods. As we've mentioned, in an inheritance hierarchy a subclass is a type of its superclass. Therefore, multiple subclasses represent many different forms of their common superclass. Subclasses are an embodiment of *object polymorphism*. Visual Basic® provides this kind of polymorphism using a different language mechanism called an *Interface*. Refer to VB help files and documentation to learn more about Interfaces.

Methods yield another style of polymorphism in OOP. To demonstrate the concept of *method polymorphism*, consider two shape objects, a Rectangle and a Circle. Each object implements a method called Area that calculates and returns the area of the shape object. The two Area methods use different functions to accomplish the calculation. The function used depends on the object that implements the method. If we consider the calculation of a shape's area to be a single operation, then it is polymorphic since it has two forms, or implementations.

Polymorphic methods can be taken a step further. It is usually possible to define more than one method in the same class with the same method name. The method name is said to be *overloaded*, since it is used more than once. The implementation of each method is typically different. The number and type of arguments determine which implementation is executed when the overloaded method is called. Visual Basic® implements a limited form of single-class polymorphic methods called *Property Procedures*.

Applying object-oriented programming techniques comes with many additional rewards. The code that results can often be reused. You can leverage your programming efforts in future projects, thereby maximizing your own productivity. It is also easier to produce more robust software by using OOP techniques. Encapsulation promotes the organization of your code into distinct functional units, which avoids the "spaghetti code" syndrome. Encapsulation also provides for better debugging capabilities. When something goes wrong, it is usually easy to localize the problem quickly, fix it in one place, and have the fix automatically take effect everywhere the object is used.

Object-oriented programming techniques enhance the production of quality software by providing every opportunity to write well-structured code. Of course, OOP is not required to produce quality software. For years, skilled programmers have achieved the same results with sound software engineering practices. OOP techniques simplify the process, while providing a greater chance for a successful outcome.

Microsoft® Visual Basic® is not considered to be a complete object-oriented programming language since it does not provide true inheritance. For that reason, VB is sometimes referred to as object-based, as opposed to object-oriented. Whatever term you prefer, the VB language does include some powerful programming tools for creating and manipulating objects. Let's explore the object-oriented features of the Visual Basic® language.

DEFINING NEW CLASSES IN VISUAL BASIC®

To create a new class in a VB project, select the Project | Add Class Module menu option from the IDE menu bar. A new Class module is added to your project. It appears very similar to a standard module, but can behave very differently (see Figure 5-1). Similar to Standard modules, Class modules are stored in a separate plain text file, but are distinguished by using the ".cls" file extension. The complete class definition is stored in the file. To reuse a class that has already been defined elsewhere, simply include the class mod-

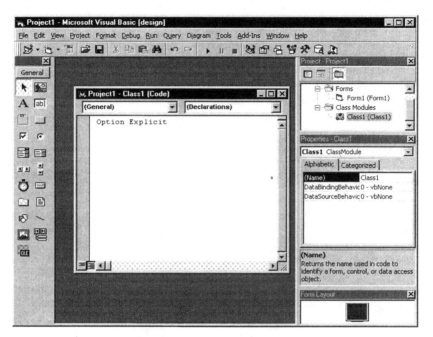

Figure 5-1. A new VB Class module.

ule file into your project by choosing the Project | Add File menu option from the IDE menu bar and selecting the file.

Each class has a Name property, which will be used to create a new instance of the class. Additionally, when you originally create your project, if you choose a project type of ActiveX EXE or ActiveX DLL you have the option to allow other programs to create and use instances of your class. Classes in ActiveX EXE and ActiveX DLL projects have an additional property called *Instancing*, which determines how you wish to share your new class with other programs. Since we won't be using this feature, we'll leave it to others to describe. A good place to start is the documentation that comes with Visual Basic®.

All the code that defines a class is placed in the Class module (see Figure 5-2). The contents of a Class module are similar to a Standard or Form module. Procedure definitions and module-level variables can be private or public. Public variables and procedures are accessible from outside the Class module, and private variables and procedures are restricted to access from within the module only. An object's public variables are exposed as properties, and its public procedures are exposed as methods.

Unlike a Standard module, but similar to a Form module, more than one instance of a Class module can be created. Actually, a class module is very much like a Form module, only without the graphical interface. When a new

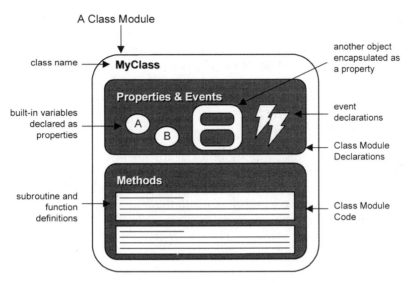

Figure 5-2. *Schematic of a VB Class module.*

class module is defined, it can be referred to by name as if it were a new data type, although there are some important differences between object variables and the intrinsic VB data types such Integer or String.

When an Integer variable is declared using the Dim statement, the integer exists and is initialized to a value of zero. When an object variable is declared, the object does not yet exist. An object variable only holds a *reference* to an object, not the object itself. To bring an object into existence, a second step must be performed.

Let's assume that we've created a new Class module and named it clsExperiment. To create a new instance of the clsExperiment class, we must first create an object variable to hold a reference to the object instance. This is accomplished with the following statement:

```
Dim mExperiment As clsExperiment
```

Once the object variable is declared, we can create a new clsExperiment object and store a reference to the new object in the object variable. To do this, use the Set and New keywords:

```
Set mExperiment = New clsExperiment
```

You can create a new object at the same time you declare an object variable using the following modified declaration, which adds the New keyword.

```
Dim mExperiment As New clsExperiment
```

Object variables are scoped like any other variable in VB. They can be public or private, declared within procedures, or at the module level.

We've already mentioned that public module-level variables are accessible from outside a class module as the object's properties. We can add a property to the clsExperiment class called NumPoints by adding the following module-level declaration to the clsExperiment class module:

```
Public NumPoints As Integer
```

We can then access this property of a clsExperiment object using dot notation in a manner that is similar to the way we accessed the members of a User-Defined Type. For example, if we wanted to set the number of points in a clsExperiment object, we could do so with the following statement after creating the mExperiment object.

```
mExperiment.NumPoints = 25
```

Likewise, public procedures declared within a Class module are also accessible using dot notation as class methods. For example, if we defined a procedure in the clsExperiment class called StandardDev, which computed and returned the standard deviation of all data stored in the clsExperiment object, we can call it using a statement such as:

```
sngStDev = mExperiment.StandardDev()
```

Another kind of procedure, unique to object modules, is something called a *property procedure*. Property procedures provide object modules with a limited form of single-class polymorphic methods, since they allow more than one procedure within an object module to be defined using the same procedure name. The syntax for calling a property procedure is the same as that used to access an object property, hence its name. The particular property procedure that is executed is determined by the way it is called.

There are three kinds of property procedures. They are called *Property Get*, *Property Let*, and *Property Set*. Let's return to the NumPoints property of the clsExperiment object. Instead of declaring a public NumPoints variable within the clsExperiment class, we can do something more powerful. Let's declare a private array of single precision numbers within the class module, along with a Property Let procedure and a Property Get procedure:

```
Private mSngPoints() As Single

Public Property Let NumPoints(intPts As Integer)
    ReDim Preserve mSngPoints(1 To intPts) As Single
End Property

Public Property Get NumPoints() As Integer
    NumPoints = UBound(mSngPoints)
End Property
```

The NumPoints Property Let procedure is invoked with a statement like the previous assignment.

```
mExperiment.NumPoints = 25
```

But instead of merely saving the value passed to NumPoints, the NumPoints Property Let procedure uses the given integer to redimension the private mSngPoints dynamic array to hold the specified number of experimental data points. The NumPoints Property Get procedure is invoked when the NumPoints object property is retrieved, as in the following statement.

```
intNumPoints = mExperiment.NumPoints
```

The Property Get returns the upper dimension of the private array using the builtin UBound function. In this example, the mSngPoints array must be dimensioned before calling the NumPoints Property Get in order to prevent a run-time error.

A Property Set procedure is defined when assigning a property that is a reference to an object. Property Set procedures are invoked when the Set keyword is used.

Property procedures provide much more control over access to object properties. For example, it is possible to cause a property to be read-only by only defining a Property Get procedure. Without a corresponding Property Let procedure, there is no means to assign the object property. It is also possible to make a property write-once by defining a Property Let procedure such as the following, which uses a Static variable:

```
Public Property Let NumPoints(intPts As Integer)
    Static blnAlreadyDimensioned As Boolean

    If blnAlreadyDimensioned = True Then
        MsgBox "Sorry.  The number of data points has already been set."
        Exit Property
    Else
        ReDim Preserve mSngPoints(1 To intPts) As Single
        blnAlreadyDimensioned = True
    End If
End Property
```

Custom events can be declared in VB classes, and raised from within class procedures at appropriate times. The result is to invoke the associated event procedure, which is defined by the user of the object. Let's add a new event to the clsExperiment class called ArrayFilled, which fires when the mSngPoints array is full. The event passes the total number of points that has been added to the mSngPoints array. The ArrayFilled event is raised from a new method called AddPoint, which adds a given value to the next available position in the mSngPoints array and increments a module-level counter variable called mIntNextPoint. When the counter equals the upper bound of the array, the event is fired. The following lines of code, added to the clsExperiment class module, provide this functionality

```
Public Event ArrayFilled(intPts As Integer)

Private mIntNextPoint As Integer

Public Sub AddPoint(sngPt As Single)
    mIntNextPoint = mIntNextPoint + 1
    mSngPoints(mIntNextPoint) = sngPt

    If mIntNextPoint = UBound(mSngPoints) Then RaiseEvent ArrayFilled(mIntNextPoint)
End Sub
```

In order to get access to the ArrayFilled event procedure, the mExperiment object variable must be declared using the *WithEvents* keyword. For example, if we declare the mExperiment variable in the declarations section of a Form module using WithEvents, we will have access to the ArrayFilled event procedure of mExperiment through the Form's code window. Figure 5-3 demonstrates that the code window knows about the mExperiment object and its ArrayFilled event procedure.

SOME USEFUL OBJECTS IN VB

A wide range of objects is included in the libraries that ship with Visual Basic®. It has been said that the hardest part about learning Visual Basic® is not the

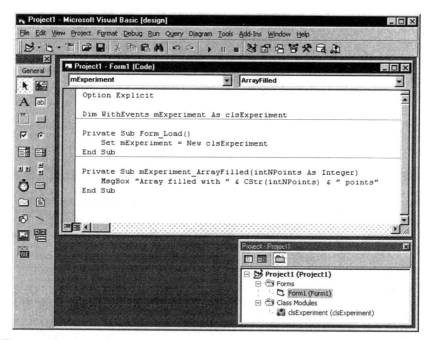

Figure 5-3. Accessing the ArrayFilled event procedure of a clsExperiment object.

language, but how to make optimal use of its objects. Throughout this book we will come across a number of objects that are provided by Visual Basic®, which we will use in a variety of ways to develop programs to automate science and engineering laboratories. We'll get started in this section by introducing a few of the objects that are used repeatedly throughout our examples.

There are sophisticated debugging tools built right into Visual Basic®, but sometimes you just want a simple print statement to follow the progress of your program. VB provides that through the *Debug object*. The Debug object has two methods and no properties or events. Debug's two methods are Print and Assert. Print takes a comma- or semicolon-separated list of arguments and prints them to the Immediate Window (see Figure 5-4). Assert takes a single boolean argument. It will suspend execution if the program is running in the IDE and its argument has a value of False.

Screen is another handy object built into Visual Basic®. The Screen object represents the entire Windows® desktop as an object. It has a number of handy properties that can be used to manipulate your interface. We frequently use the MousePointer property of the Screen object when we need to change the mouse cursor to indicate that a long process is occurring. Setting the MousePointer property to one of several predefined constants will automatically change the cursor. Search VB Help for "MousePointer Constants" to see a list of all predefined constants.

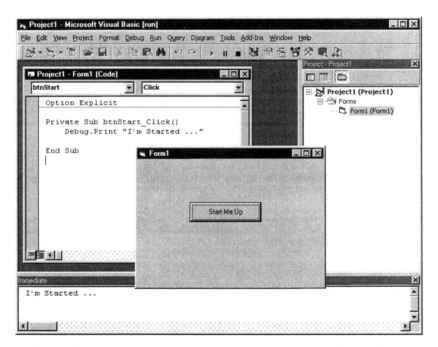

Figure 5-4. Printing to the Immediate Window with the Debug Object.

HANDLING RUN-TIME ERRORS WITH ON ERROR AND THE ERR OBJECT

Another very useful object provided with VB is called *Err*. The Err object contains information about run-time errors. The Err object Number property contains the number identifying the last run-time error, and the Description property contains a description of the error. To raise an error yourself, call the Err object Raise method. To clear the Err object property values, call the Clear method.

The Err object is most effectively used with the On Error statement to handle run-time errors. An On Error statement is used to indicate what VB should do when a run-time error occurs. When you invoke an On Error Goto statement, a run-time error will cause VB to jump to the line with the indicated label. For example, consider the following Click event procedure of a CommandButton named btnTrouble. An On Error Goto statement indicates that when a run-time error occurs, the program should jump to the line labeled "ErrorHandler." Following execution from this line, you will see how Err object properties are used to display a message box indicating the error that occurred (see Figure 5-5).

```
Private Sub btnTrouble_Click()
    On Error GoTo ErrorHandler
    Dim sngX As Single

    sngX = 1# / 0#

    Exit Sub
'_____
ErrorHandler:
    MsgBox "Error " & CStr(Err.Number) & ": " & Err.Description

End Sub
```

To cancel an error handler, use the On Error Goto statement with a line number of 0, as in the following statement:

```
On Error Goto 0
```

If you don't use an On Error statement at all, run-time errors are fatal. See VB Help for more about error handling and the Err object.

UNDERSTANDING COLLECTIONS

A very special object included with Visual Basic® is the *Collection*. A Collection is a general-purpose container for holding ordered collections of other objects and other items. The items contained in a Collection do not have to be of the same type. Understanding how the Collection object works is important, since Visual Basic® uses Collections throughout its libraries.

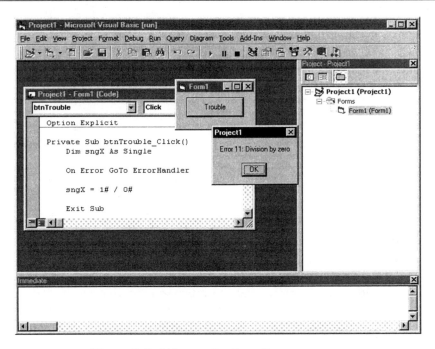

Figure 5-5. Using an On Error Goto statement.

Collection objects can be created like any other object. For example, the following statement creates a new Collection object called colExperiments:

```
Dim colExperiments As New Collection
```

The Count property of the Collection object returns the number of items currently stored in a Collection. The Add method adds a new item to a Collection with an optional string that is used as a key for easy access later on. The Item method takes an index and returns a reference to the item that is identified by the index in the Collection. The index argument can be either a number indicating the position of the item in the Collection or the key provided when the item was added to the Collection. The Remove method takes a similar index argument as Item, only the identified item is removed from Collection. More information about the syntax of Collection properties and methods is available from VB Help.

There are a few concepts that should be thoroughly understood in order to make the most effective use of Collections. In Visual Basic®, an object is not actually removed from memory until there are no more references to it. Every object tracks the number of times it is referenced. When a reference to an object is assigned to a new variable, the object increments its reference count. When the variable is deleted, or set to Nothing, the object reference count is decremented.

An object is not actually stored by a Collection when it is added using the Collection's Add method. Instead, a new object reference is stored in the Collection. Adding an object to a collection causes its reference count to increment. For example, consider the following lines of code:

```
' Create a new Experiment and Collection
Dim mExperiment As New clsExperiment
Dim colExperiments As New Collection

' Add the Experiment object to the Collection
colExperiments.Add mExperiment

' Clear the mExperiment object variable reference
Set mExperiment = Nothing

' Clear the Collection reference
colExperiments.Remove 1
```

A new clsExperiment object is created, and a reference to the object is stored in the mExperiment variable. A new Collection object is also created called colExperiments. Immediately after the mExperiment object is added to the colExperiments Collection, there are two references to the clsExperiment object. The first reference is stored by the mExperiment variable, and the second by the colExperiments Collection. At this point there exists one clsExperiment object and two references to it. A change made to the object referred to by the mExperiment variable would also be reflected in the object referred to by the Collection. The reason is obvious: They are the same object. When the mExperiment variable is set to Nothing, the clsExperiment object reference count is decremented to a value of one. The object still exists because the Collection still refers to it. When the object is removed from the colExperiments Collection, its reference count is decremented to zero, and the object is finally removed from memory.

You will come across Collections throughout Visual Basic®'s libraries. Two useful Collections are the *Forms* Collection and the *Controls* Collection. The Forms Collection holds references to all the Forms that are currently loaded in a Visual Basic® program. Each Form has a Controls Collection that holds references to all controls on the Form. You can loop over the Forms and Controls Collections using the Count property and Item method or a For Each statement to access all the Forms in your program and the Controls on each Form.

THE OBJECT BROWSER

The *Object Browser* is the definitive method for finding out about the objects and other items to which you have access. To display the Object Browser, select the View | Object Browser option from the IDE menu (see Figure 5-6). The dropdown box in the upper left-hand portion of the Object Browser win-

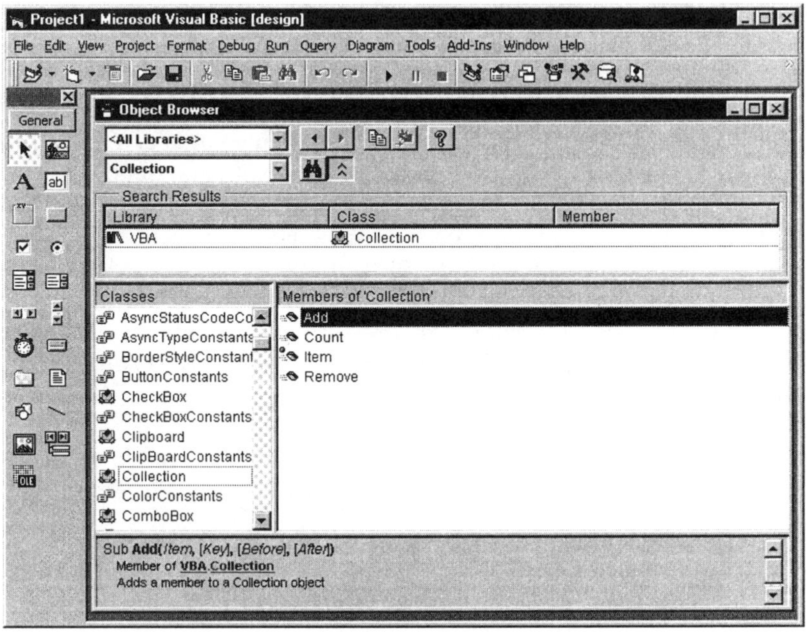

Figure 5-6. The Visual Basic® Object Browser.

dow lists all the libraries that are currently loaded in VB. You can add or remove libraries through the References Dialog, which is available through the Project | References IDE menu option, or the Components Dialog, which is available through the Project | Components IDE menu option. You can browse all libraries at once or one at a time by selecting the library of interest. The Object Browser lists all object classes, Enums, modules, Type declarations, and globals that are currently available in the pane on the left portion of the window.

If you select a class from the list on the left, all class members will be listed in the pane on the right. Class members include properties, methods, and events. Click on a class property in the right pane of the Object Browser to see its data type and membership. Click on class procedures and events to see their arguments and membership. Follow links for more detail.

Select "<globals>" from the top of the list in left pane to see all globally defined procedures, constants, and properties. Click on an item in the right pane to get more information and pertinent links. Similarly, select an Enum or Type from the left pane of the Object Browser to list members in the right pane. Click on an item in right pane to see predefined value, data type, or membership. Follow the links for more detail.

The Object Browser is a valuable resource. It gives you direct access to the objects and other items that are included in a library. On infrequent occasions, we have found the VB documentation to be wrong or incomplete. In these cases the Object Browser was always able to fill in the missing information.

WRAPPING UP

We have introduced the Visual Basic® Integrated Development Environment, the VB language, the structure of a Visual Basic® program, and the object-oriented features of VB, but we have only scratched the surface. You will have to study other resources to appreciate fully the breadth and depth of features that are available to a programmer using Visual Basic®. A newcomer to VB may find this to be a daunting prospect. Actually, it is good news. It's good because it is easy to get started with VB, and add to your knowledge as you go along. Knowing that there is a wide variety of tools that you can bring to bear on any given problem should make you feel comfortable. Chances are good that you will be able to use your knowledge of VB to solve the great majority, if not all, of your laboratory computing needs, and it will be a long time before you run into any limitations.

Let's move to the core of the book and discuss how to use VB to automate tasks commonly encountered in science and engineering laboratories.

2

Device Communications

Communication is at the heart of most science and engineering laboratory applications. Whether it involves reading a measurement from a sensor, collecting data from a data acquisition board, transmitting data to a remote computer, or sending commands to a remotely controlled device, communications is one of the critical functions performed by computers in a laboratory.

Visual Basic® provides a variety of ways to communicate to external hardware devices and separate software programs that are running on the same machine, connected through a cable, or at the other end of a network. In the chapters of Part 2 we will explore many of the ways to communicate using Visual Basic®.

CHAPTER

6

Introducing the Virtual Instrument

Before we begin, we need someone or something with which to communicate. Of course, that will likely be unique for each application. So, how do we proceed? We would have liked to include a laboratory instrument with this book, but that presents certain logistical problems and likely would have had an undesired impact on the price. Instead, we designed the software equivalent—the *Virtual Instrument.*

The Virtual Instrument (VI) is a program designed for the purpose of demonstrating techniques of communication and device control in Visual Basic®. The Virtual Instrument was itself written in Visual Basic® using many of the concepts presented in this book. Source code for the Virtual Instrument is provided with the code available online in the folder \Vi. Instructions for building the VI from scratch are given in Appendix C. To run the Virtual Instrument, double-click on the executable (Vi.exe) in the \Vi folder, or load and run the project, \Vi\Vi.vbp. Figure 6-1 displays the Virtual Instrument main interface.

The Virtual Instrument simulates a real instrument that measures a series of data points. The VI can be controlled remotely through Dynamic Data Exchange (DDE), over an RS-232 port, or over a TCP/IP network connection. The data it generates can also be collected remotely from an RS-232 port or TCP/IP network connection. We will discuss DDE, RS-232, and TCP/IP networking extensively in the chapters that follow.

Let's take a quick look at the user interface of the VI. Like any real instrument, before it is possible to interact with the front panel, the Virtual Instrument must be turned on. This is done by clicking on the On/Off toggle button in the lower right-hand corner of the interface. When the VI comes on, the red "light" turns green and the command button caption changes from "On" to "Off". This indicates that the VI is on, and that the next time the On/Off button is clicked the VI will turn off.

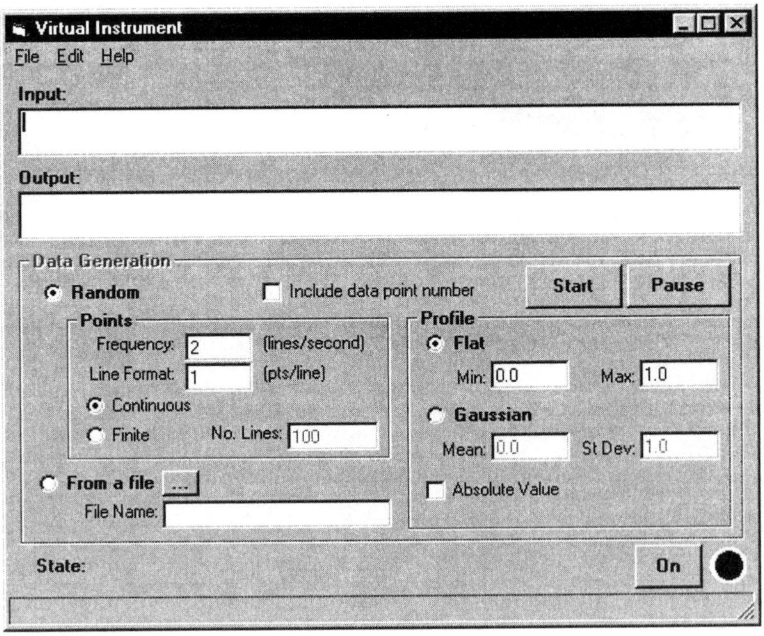

Figure 6-1. The Virtual Instrument main interface.

When the VI is first turned on, by default communication with the RS-232 port called "COM1" is enabled, and network communication is disabled. To modify RS-232 port communication parameters, select the RS232 Port Settings menu option under the Edit menu, as in Figure 6-2. You will see the Communications Settings dialog box with all available options. Also under the Edit menu are options that allow you to modify the network communication parameters as well as transmission formats (Figure 6-3). By default, network communication is disabled, and data transmissions will be comma separated and terminated with a carriage-return character.

Text boxes labeled "Input" and "Output" in the upper portion of the interface always indicate what the instrument is receiving (Input) and what it is sending (Output). You can use what is being displayed in these two boxes to monitor the activity of the Virtual Instrument.

The frame labeled "Data Generation" below the Output box includes options to modify the characteristics of data that will be generated. The frame and its contents are disabled until the VI is turned on. It is possible to generate random data by choosing the "Random" option, or data can be read and transmitted from a file by choosing the option "From a file" and specifying a file name. A sample data file is provided in the folder \Vi called "data.txt."

When the "From a file" option is chosen, the VI reads one line at a time from the specified file and displays it in the Output box. If RS-232 communi-

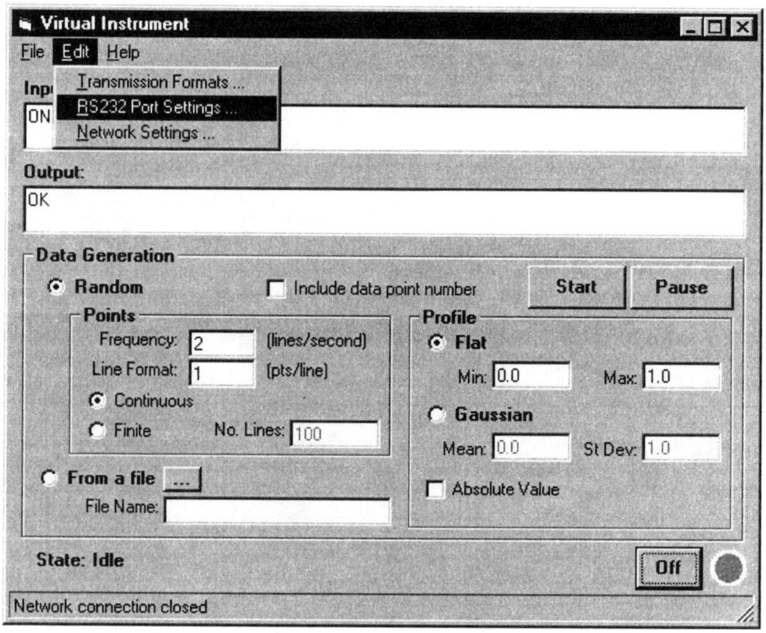

Figure 6-2. Initiating Virtual Instrument RS-232 Communications.

cations or network communications is enabled, each line will also be sent to the RS-232 port or network, respectively. Entering a value into the text box labeled "Frequency" in the Data Generation frame sets the rate at which data are read and transmitted.

The "Random" data generation option offers a variety of ways to tailor randomly generated data. From the Points frame you can set the number of random data points per line that will be generated by entering the number into the "Line Format" text box. The VI can be instructed to generate a finite number of random lines of data, or the data can be generated on a continuous basis. This is determined by choosing the "Continuous" or "Finite" option buttons. To generate a finite number of lines of data, that number is entered into the "No. Lines" text box. A sequential number can be added to the beginning of each line by selecting the "Include data point number" check box. In the Profile frame you can choose the distribution from which to sample random data and the characteristics of the distribution. A flat profile samples evenly over the specified range, and a Gaussian profile produces random numbers that will generate a bell-shaped curve with the specified mean and standard deviation. When the "Absolute Value" check box is selected, the absolute value of all random numbers generated will be returned. When choosing a Gaussian distribution with a zero mean, selecting the "Absolute Value" check box is equivalent to sampling randomly from only the positive half of the distribution. This can help generated data to appear more realistic.

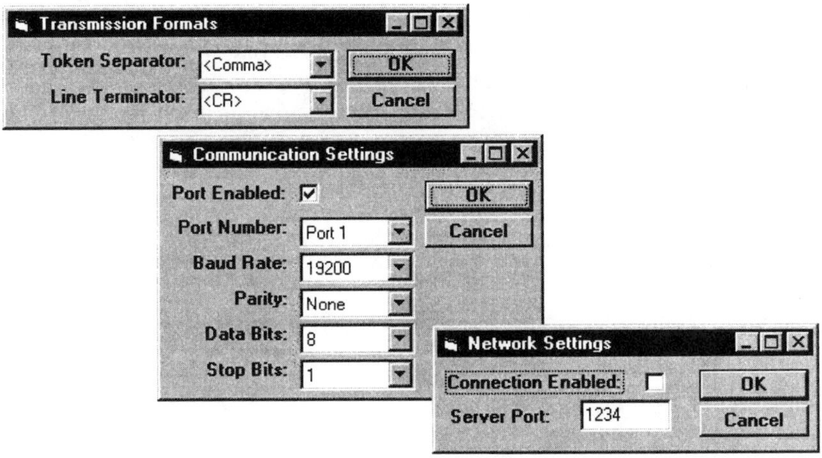

Figure 6-3. RS-232 Communication Settings, Network Settings, and Transmission Formats dialog boxes.

Data generation is initiated or terminated by clicking the Start/Abort toggle button. The current button label indicates the available option. In a similar manner, data generation can be paused or resumed using the Pause/Resume toggle button.

The VI responds to six commands through a remote connection. Command names and a description of each are listed in Table 6-1.

The "Analyze" command takes an optional integer argument that indicates the number of points to generate. If no argument is provided, data are generated continuously. The six commands correspond to the three toggle buttons, On/Off, Analyze/Abort, and Pause/Resume. These commands will be used later when we begin to communicate with and control the Virtual Instrument.

Run the program Vi.exe or load and run the project file \Vi\Vi.vbp in Visual Basic®. Test the functions of the VI in order to get comfortable with its operation. Notice how each command shows up in the Input box when a toggle

TABLE 6-1. Virtual Instrument Commands

Command	Explanation
ON	Turns the Virtual Instrument on.
ANALYZE [*num points*]	Begins the generation of data. Takes an optional argument indicating the number of points to generate.
PAUSE	Pauses data generation.
RESUME	Resumes data generation.
ABORT	Terminates the generation of data.
OFF	Shuts the Virtual Instrument off.

button is clicked. The purpose of the interface is really only to provide a way to pass commands to the VI interactively. Also notice that there is always a well-defined response to a command in the Output box. We will use these responses in Part 3 to build a controller for the Virtual Instrument.

CHAPTER

7

Dynamic Data Exchange

As its name implies, Dynamic Data Exchange (DDE) is a Microsoft® Windows® operating system technology developed to provide a channel through which data can be exchanged from one Windows® application to another. This channel is called a *conversation*. As it turns out, DDE is much more than a way to copy data between applications. In a very real sense Dynamic Data Exchange is a form of communication, and when the applications that need to communicate both support DDE, it can be used very effectively for this purpose.

DDE can be used to perform a variety of tasks in a laboratory. Perhaps the most common use of DDE in a laboratory setting is to copy data automatically between an instrument control program or data acquisition program, and a spreadsheet such as Microsoft® Excel. The spreadsheet can be used to provide calculated numbers as parameters for another program, or further to process or display measured or calculated data originating elsewhere.

A DDE conversation is designed to be unidirectional; a data item is copied from the application that generated or acquired the data to the receiving application. But as you'll see, DDE provides a means by which communication in the opposite direction is also possible. A distinct DDE conversation is always based on a single data item in each of the communicating applications.

THE DDE MODEL

The model by which a DDE conversation is established is not symmetric. This often causes confusion. The two applications engaged in a DDE conversation play different roles and have different functions available to them. Figure 7-1 illustrates the concept.

The application that provides the data for the conversation is called the *Source*. The *Destination* assigns the value of its local data item to the value of the linked data item in the Source. Table 7-1 describes the roles of the two applications engaged in a DDE conversation in a bit more detail.

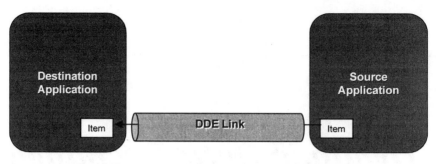

Figure 7-1. Schematic representation of a DDE link.

TABLE 7-1. Roles of a DDE Destination and Source application.

DDE Destination	DDE Source
Initiates the DDE link	Responds to the request for a DDE link
Owns the data item that is updated by the Source	Provides the data item that is the source of data for the DDE link
Can request that the Source execute a command	Can receive a command from the Destination and react in a predefined manner
Can update a Source's data value by "poking"	Can have its data value modified by a poke command issued by the Destination

ESTABLISHING A DDE CONVERSATION

Three pieces of information must be known before a Destination application can establish a DDE conversation with a Source Application. These are:

1. The Source *Application Name*,
2. The *Topic* of conversation, and
3. The data *Item* about which the conversation will take place.

The Application Name is usually the name of the executable file, leaving off the extension. For Microsoft® Excel, the Application Name used to establish a DDE conversation would be "Excel."

The Topic and Item available for a DDE conversation in a Source application must be provided by the creator of the software, and can usually be found in the software documentation. In the case of Excel, a Topic is the name of a file containing a Workbook, with the file name in square brackets, followed by the name of a particular Worksheet in the Workbook. An Item in Excel can be the name of a cell, in "R1C1" notation, or other object such as an Excel Chart. The exact format depends on what has been defined by the Source application.

CHAPTER

Using Dynamic Data Exchange in Visual Basic®

As an example, say we want to use a number calculated in Excel as a parameter that tells a data acquisition program how many measurements to take. The calculated number of points is placed in the cell in the first row and first column of worksheet called Sheet1. The following DDE parameters would be required to establish a conversation with an Excel 97 workbook saved in the file \Part2\Ex1\Crnchdat.xls.

Application Name:	"Excel"
Topic of Conversation:	"C:\Part2\Ex1\[Crnchdat.xls]Sheet1"
Data Item:	"R1C1"

INITIATING AN AUTOMATIC LINK MODE DDE CONVERSATION WITH EXCEL

The first step is to locate and open an existing Excel Workbook, or create a new one. If a new workbook is created, it is important to save it at least once before trying to initiate a DDE conversation. This is required by the DDE conversation creation mechanism. The previously mentioned file named \Part2\Ex1\Crnchdat.xls is included with the downloadable software. Open the file with Microsoft® Excel 97, or go ahead and create a new workbook with the same name. You can use previous versions of Microsoft® Excel as well. Don't forget to save the new Workbook first!

In a new VB project add to Form1 a new TextBox called txtConnect and a CommandButton called btnConnect. Properties for these objects are as follows.

Object Type	Property	Value
TextBox	Name	txtConnect
	Text	
CommandButton	Name	btnConnect
	Caption	Connect

Also add the following code to the btnConnect CommandButton Click event procedure. Make sure that the LinkTopic argument reflects the actual path to your saved Excel file.

```
Private Sub btnConnect_Click()
    ' Establish an Automatic Link Mode DDE conversation between txtConnect and Excel
    With txtConnect
        .LinkMode = vbLinkNone
        .LinkTopic = "Excel|C:\Part2\Ex1\[Crnchdat.xls]Sheet1"
        .LinkItem = "R1C1"
        .LinkMode = vbLinkAutomatic
    End With
End Sub
```

While Excel is still running with the workbook open, run your new Visual Basic® program. When you click on "Connect" a conversation will be established between Excel and the txtConnect TextBox control (see Figure 8-1). When you enter something into the cell in row 1, column 1 of Sheet1 in the Workbook and hit enter, it will immediately be copied to the TextBox in your VB application over the DDE conversation. By the way, the two funny vertical bars that show up in the txtConnect TextBox of Figure 8-1 are the car-

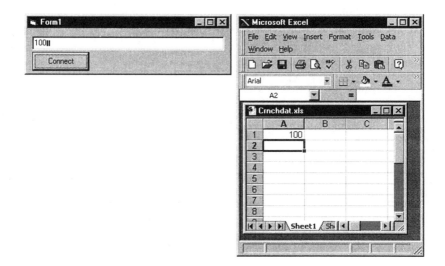

Figure 8-1. DDE in Action.

TABLE 8-1. DDE conversation Link Modes.

Link Mode	Description
Automatic	Destination data is automatically updated when Source data changes.
Manual	Destination data is updated only when the Destination application requests it.
Notify	The Destination application is notified when Source data changes. It is up to the Destination application to request that its data be updated.

riage return and linefeed characters that terminate the contents of the Excel cell. VB prints a vertical bar when it doesn't know how to print a character.

Now that you've actually done it once, let's go back and take a closer look at what happened.

DDE LINKS—TYPES OF DDE CONVERSATIONS

There are three modes in which a DDE conversation can occur. They are *Automatic Link* mode, *Manual Link* mode, and *Notify Link* mode. In the previous example the mode in which the DDE conversation was established with Excel was the Automatic Link mode. This was determined when the LinkMode property of the txtConnect TextBox was set to the predefined constant *vbLinkAutomatic*. Table 8-1 lists the three styles of DDE conversations and describes how each operates.

To set the mode in which an appropriate VB control initiates a DDE conversation, set the control's LinkMode property to one of the predefined VB constants in Table 8-2.

Only three controls provided with Visual Basic® can act as a Destination in a DDE conversation: a TextBox, a Label, and a PictureBox. You'll find the LinkMode and other DDE-related properties in the Properties Window while editing an instance of one of the controls.

We've seen the Automatic Link mode in action. Let's look at the Manual and Notify Link modes and see what they do.

TABLE 8-2. Predefined DDE conversation Link mode constants.

Link Mode	Predefined VB Constant
Automatic	vbLinkAutomatic
Manual	vbLinkManual
Notify	vbLinkNotify

A MANUAL LINK MODE DDE CONVERSATION WITH EXCEL

To change the link mode of the previous example, simply change the LinkMode property of the TextBox to the constant vbLinkManual. The btnConnect CommandButton Click event procedure will look as follows:

```
Private Sub btnConnect_Click()
    ' Establish a Manual Link Mode DDE conversation between txtConnect and Excel
    With txtConnect
        .LinkMode = vbLinkNone
        .LinkTopic = "Excel|C:\Part2\Ex1\[Crnchdat.xls]Sheet1"
        .LinkItem = "R1C1"
        .LinkMode = vbLinkManual
    End With
End Sub
```

When data change in Excel, the contents of the txtConnect TextBox will no longer be updated automatically. We need to do something else in order to cause the update to occur. We need to call the LinkRequest method of the TextBox. A second button called btnUpdate is added to the first example and given the caption "Update." Following is the Click event procedure of btnUpdate in which the LinkRequest method is called.

```
Private Sub btnUpdate_Click()
    ' Request that Excel update the linked data item.
    txtConnect.LinkRequest
End Sub
```

If Excel is not already running, start up Excel and open the file \Part2\Ex1\Crnchdat.xls. Make sure your project is modified as outlined above and run it. When "Connect" is clicked the contents of the TextBox does not change. Only after "Update" is clicked, do the data in Excel actually get copied over (see Figure 8-2). Change the data in Excel again and notice that the contents of the TextBox do not change until "Update" is clicked again.

A NOTIFY LINK MODE DDE CONVERSATION WITH EXCEL

The last mode of DDE conversation that is possible is Notify Link. To establish a Notify Link DDE conversation, the LinkMode property of the TextBox is set to vbLinkNotify, as follows:

```
Private Sub btnConnect_Click()
    ' Establish a Notify Link Mode DDE conversation between txtConnect and Excel
    With txtConnect
        .LinkMode = vbLinkNone
        .LinkTopic = "Excel|C:\Part2\Ex1\[Crnchdat.xls]Sheet1"
        .LinkItem = "R1C1"
        .LinkMode = vbLinkNotify
    End With
End Sub
```

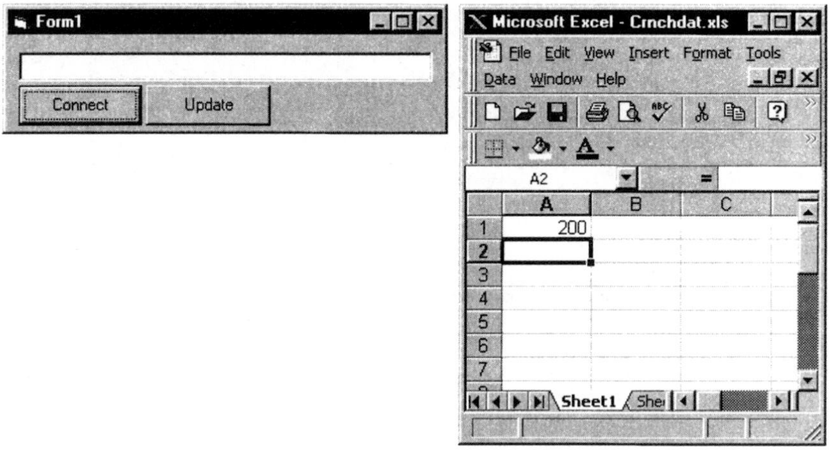

Figure 8-2. A Manual Link DDE Conversation. Data are not updated in a Manual Link until requested.

When data in Excel change the VB program will automatically be informed that a change has occurred by remotely firing the LinkNotify event procedure of the Destination TextBox (Figure 8-3). Appropriate VB code should be added to this event procedure to react to the change notification. If we want to update the contents of the TextBox automatically whenever data change, we could call the LinkRequest method from the LinkNotify event procedure. This is demonstrated in the following LinkNotify event procedure.

```
Private Sub txtConnect_LinkNotify()
    ' Automatically request that the linked data be updated whenever a change occurs.
    txtConnect.LinkRequest
End Sub
```

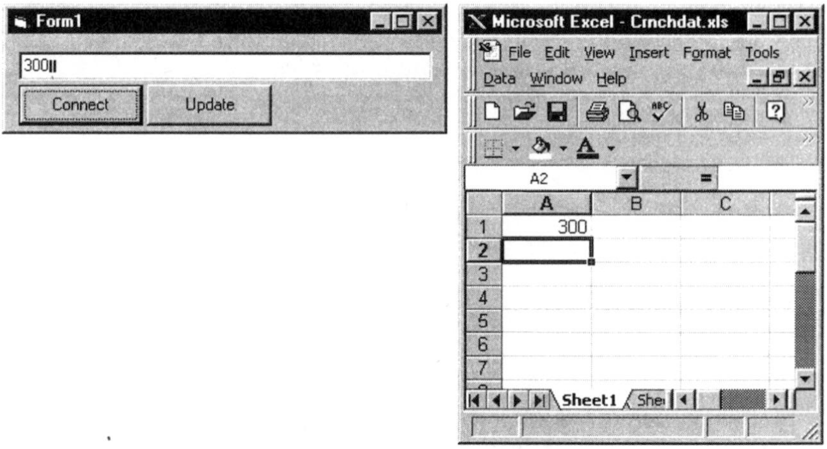

Figure 8-3. A Notify Link DDE Conversation updates data when changed.

The result is very similar to an Automatic Link mode DDE conversation. The difference is that now we have the option to add additional code to the LinkNotify event procedure to perform other functions. For example, we may want to compare the new value each time it changes to an upper threshold and sound an alarm when the threshold is exceeded.

A sample application that illustrates these concepts, as well as a few more, is included with the code available online in the folder \Part2\Ex1.

CREATING A DDE SOURCE APPLICATION

Visual Basic® can also be used to develop applications that act as a Source in a DDE conversation. Only a Form object can be configured to act as a DDE Source. Once a Form is established as a Source, the default property of any control on the Form can act as the data item in the conversation.

To permit a Form to accept connection requests from a DDE Destination, you only need to set two properties in the Properties Window of the Form. This must be done at design time. They are as follows.

Form Property	Description
LinkMode	Must be set to "1 – Source" to tell VB that the Form will accept DDE conversation requests.
LinkTopic	A string naming the Topic that must be used by the DDE destination application when requesting a conversation.

The two projects located in \Part2\Ex2 of the downloadable software distribution called Destntn.vbp and Source.vbp implement simple DDE Destination (Destntn.vbp) and DDE Source (Source.vbp) applications in Visual Basic®.

To build a simple DDE Source application, create a new project and sketch a single TextBox onto the Form. Set the properties as follows.

Object Type	Property	Value
Form	Name	frmSource
	LinkMode	1 – Source
	LinkTopic	DDESource
	Caption	DDE Source
TextBox	Name	txtData
	Text	

No code is necessary in this application in order for it to act as a Source in a DDE conversation. The only critical properties are LinkMode and LinkTopic, which belong to the main form called frmSource. It is important to compile your DDE Source application to an executable file. In this example, give your executable the name "Source.exe."

To create the DDE Destination application, create another new project and add a TextBox and two CommandButtons with the following properties:

Object Type	Property	Value
Form	Name	frmDestination
	Caption	DDE Destination
CommandButton	Name	btnConnect
	Caption	Connect
CommandButton	Name	btnUpdate
	Caption	Update
TextBox	Name	txtConnect
	Text	

As in the previous example, it is necessary for the DDE Destination application to contain code that establishes a link with the DDE Source. This is accomplished with the following Click event procedure for the btnConnect CommandButton. Notice the value of the LinkTopic property in the btnConnect Click event procedure.

```
Private Sub btnConnect_Click()
    With txtConnect     ' Establish a DDE connection
        .LinkMode = vbLinkNone
        .LinkTopic = "Source|DDESource"
        .LinkItem = "txtData"
        .LinkMode = vbLinkAutomatic
    End With
End Sub
```

The format for identifying a DDE Source application created in VB is the name of the executable (no extension) followed by a vertical bar (a pipe) and the value of the LinkTopic property of the Source Form. We gave the LinkTopic property of the frmSource Form in the Source application the name "DDESource." Therefore, the LinkTopic property of the txtConnect TextBox is set to "Source|DDESource." The LinkItem property can be set to the name of any control on the Source form. In this example there is only one control, the TextBox named txtData. Accordingly, the LinkItem property of the txtConnect control is set to "txtData." The mode for the DDE connection is an Automatic Link type; so the LinkMode property is set to the constant vbLinkAutomatic.

To make things more interesting, some code was added to the Change event procedure of the txtConnect TextBox. When the value of the Text property of the TextBox changes, if the value is numeric, it is compared to a threshold value of 100. If that threshold is exceeded, the background color of the Destination form is changed to red. A visual signal such as this is more effective at grabbing the attention of an operator.

```
Private Sub txtConnect_Change()
    ' If linked value exceeds threshold then change form color
    Dim sngValue As Single
    If IsNumeric(txtConnect.Text) Then
        sngValue = CSng(txtConnect.Text)
        If sngValue > 100# Then
            frmDestination.BackColor = &HFF&          ' Red
        Else
            frmDestination.BackColor = &H8000000F     ' Gray
        End If
    End If
End Sub
```

Compile and run the Source.exe executable and the Destntn.exe program from the same folder. This can be done by double-clicking on the executable names while in the Windows® Explorer. If you are running the Destination program from within VB, make sure you start VB and load the project by double-clicking on the Destntn.vbp file. This is important since we did not specify the complete path of the Source program in the LinkTopic property of the txtConnect TextBox in the Destination. With no path, the Destination application will first look in its own home folder for the Source application with which to establish the DDE link. A trappable error will occur if the Source application cannot be found.

When both applications are running, click the Connect button on the Destination application to establish the automatic DDE conversation. Type a number into the TextBox of the Source application. Since an Automatic Link has been established, the number will immediately show up in the TextBox of the Destination application. When the number exceeds the threshold value, the form background color will change to red. Figure 8-4 shows the two applications in action. The Destination application's Form color is red, indicating that the threshold has been exceeded. Since Figure 8-4 is not printed in color, the Form actually appears as more of a dark gray.

REMOTELY EXECUTING COMMANDS IN A DDE SOURCE APPLICATION

DDE Source applications can do more than just provide data to Destination applications. Source applications can also respond to a command issued by the Destination. To make that possible the Source must first create a command processor, which should be invoked by the LinkExecute event procedure of the Source Form.

Figure 8-4. A DDE Source and Destination Application in VB.

Let's say we want our Source application to be able to respond to a Reset command that sets its data value to zero. We can do this by adding the following code to the LinkExecute event procedure of the frmSource Form in the previous example.

```
Private Sub Form_LinkExecute(CmdStr As String, Cancel As Integer)
    ' Respond to DDE commands
    Dim strCommand As String

    ' Format command
    strCommand = Trim$(Ucase$(CmdStr))

    ' Process command
    Select Case strCommand
    Case "RESET"          ' Set data value to 0
        txtData.Text = 0
    End Select

    ' When successful, set Cancel to False.
    Cancel = False
End Sub
```

The LinkExecute event procedure has two arguments. The first argument, represented by the string variable CmdStr, is the command that is passed by the Destination application. The second argument, represented by the integer variable Cancel, indicates whether the command string was accepted or refused by the Source application. Setting Cancel to anything other than 0 (the predefined value of False) is a way to notify the Destination application that the command was rejected.

The body of the LinkExecute method in the above example checks for the command string "RESET." If found, it sets the text in the txtData TextBox to a value of zero. With an automatic DDE link established, the "0" will be copied back to the destination and cause the form background color to revert to gray.

To send a command to the Source, call the LinkExecute method of the control in the Destination with which the DDE conversation is established. Add a new CommandButton to the previous DDE Destination example project with the following properties:

Object Type	Property	Value
CommandButton	Name	btnReset
	Caption	Reset

Add the following Click event procedure to the btnReset CommandButton:

```
Private Sub btnReset_Click()
    ' Execute the DDE Source RESET command
    txtConnect.LinkExecute "RESET"
End Sub
```

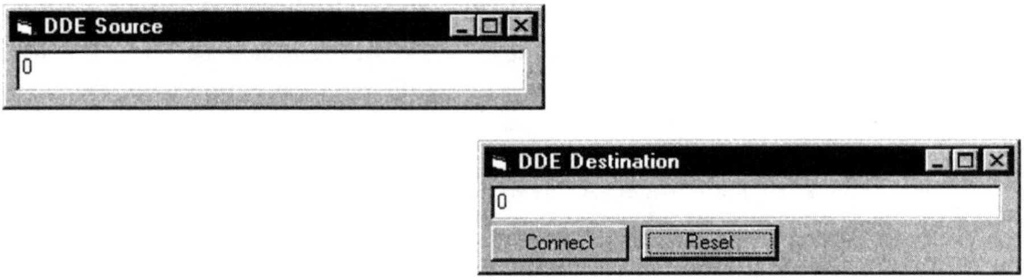

Figure 8-5. The Reset button executes a Source LinkExecute command.

Proceeding as before, compile the new Source and Destination applications to executables and run them from the same folder (See Figure 8-5).

After both applications are running, click "Connect" to establish the DDE conversation and begin entering numbers into the Source TextBox to simulate Source data generation. To reset the value in the Source, click "Reset" on the Destination.

Using the LinkExecute method and event procedure it is possible to make very sophisticated DDE Source applications that can be controlled remotely by DDE Destination applications. A command language can be devised with an interpreter embedded in the Source application, which in turn can control a laboratory instrument or other device. Complete control can be accomplished through a DDE link.

If we only want to change the value of an ActiveX control in a Source, as we did in the previous example, there is a simpler mechanism for getting the job done. We can use the LinkPoke method of the Destination Link control. The LinkPoke method copies data in a Destination control to the linked Source control. It is essentially the reverse of the standard DDE link from Source to Destination.

To demonstrate, add a third button to the Destination application with the following properties.

Object Type	Property	Value
CommandButton	Name	btnPoke
	Caption	Poke

Execute the LinkPoke method of the txtConnect TextBox from the btnPoke CommandButton Click event procedure.

```
Private Sub btnPoke_Click()
    ' Copy data in the txtConnect TextBox back to the Source.
    txtConnect.LinkPoke
End Sub
```

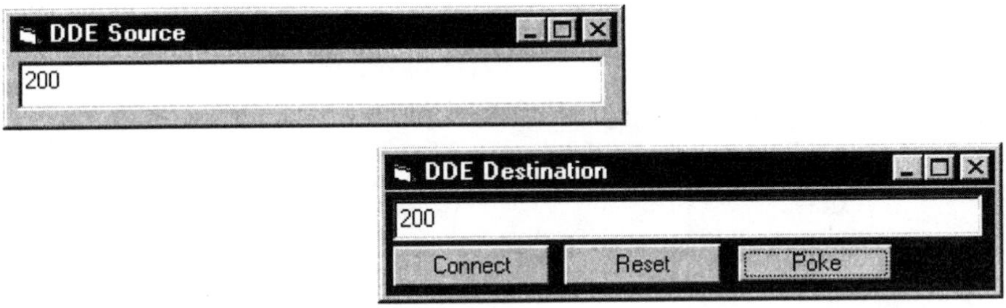

Figure 8-6. Data from the Destination are "Poked" into the Source.

Now if we run the Source and Destination applications and establish the DDE connection, we can enter a value into the Destination txtConnect TextBox and click "Poke." The value in the TextBox will be copied over the DDE link and placed in the txtData TextBox of the Source application. Again, since we have an Automatic Link established, the data will also be copied back to the Destination through the forward DDE link, but the change won't be noticed since the data are identical (see Figure 8-6).

Code for both the DDE source and destination projects can be found with the code available online in the folder \Part2\Ex2.

HANDLING DDE ERRORS

A DDE error, improperly trapped, can cause your program to stop running. That's why it is necessary to trap and handle DDE errors at run time.

There are two types of DDE errors. The first type occurs when an application attempts to perform an illegal DDE operation. This type of error can be trapped within the code that made the illegal call. The second type occurs when a DDE error is not related to any particular Visual Basic® procedure.

In previous examples, if the Source application was not started before an attempt to establish a DDE conversation, an error occurred and the Destination application ended. The error was something like "Run-time error 282. No foreign application responded to a DDE initiate." This will not do in any real-world situation. How can we address this problem? Like any other run-time error, we can trap it and attempt to respond gracefully.

When Error 282 occurs, the Source application is not running. We can respond to the error by attempting to start the Source application from the Destination. To demonstrate this, let's expand the Click event procedure of the btnConnect CommandButton in the previous example. We can trap Error 282 and attempt to start the Source application using the VB Shell command. If successful, the error handler routine will execute a Resume command, which attempts to establish the connection. This is implemented in the following expanded version of the Click event procedure.

```
Private Sub btnConnect_Click()
    ' Establish a DDE conversation between txtConnect and Excel
    Dim dblTaskID As Double

    On Error GoTo ConnectErrorHandler

    With txtConnect
        .LinkMode = vbLinkNone
        .LinkTopic = "Source|DDESource"
        .LinkItem = "txtData"
        .LinkMode = vbLinkAutomatic
    End With

    Exit Sub

ConnectErrorHandler:
    Select Case Err.Number
    Case 282    ' No foreign application responded to a DDE initiate
        dblTaskID = Shell("Source.exe", vbNormalFocus)
        If dblTaskID > 0& Then
            Resume    ' Try again
        Else
            MsgBox "Error.  Could not start Source application"
        End If
    Case Else
        MsgBox "Error " & CStr(Err.Number) & " on Connect.  " & Err.Description
    End Select
End Sub
```

Table 8-3 summarizes several of the DDE errors that relate to specific VB procedures. These can be trapped at run-time.

The second type of DDE error is not related to any particular VB procedure. When one occurs, VB informs you of the error by raising the LinkError event. Both DDE sources and DDE destinations have LinkError event procedures. When raised, VB passes an integer to the LinkError event procedure that identifies the error that occurred. Table 8-4 lists predefined DDE LinkError constants with brief descriptions.

DDE-RELATED METHODS AND EVENT PROCEDURES

There are several DDE-related procedures that can be fired automatically. Adding appropriate code to event procedures can substantially increase the robustness of an application. Table 8-5 summarizes DDE-related methods and event procedures. In the table each procedure is named, the form in which it is available on the Destination and/or Source sides of a DDE conversation is identified, and a brief description is given.

COMMUNICATING WITH THE VIRTUAL INSTRUMENT USING DDE

The Virtual Instrument described in Chapter 6 was designed to accept DDE conversations and respond to commands issued using the LinkExecute

TABLE 8-3. Some trappable DDE errors.

Error Code	DDE Error Message	Description
282	No foreign application responded to a DDE initiate	VB could not find an application whose name and topic matched the LinkTopic property value
285	Foreign application won't perform DDE method or operation	For some reason, the DDE method or operation that was requested failed to execute
286	Timeout while waiting for DDE method or operation	This error occurs when a DDE method did not execute within a predetermined time. Try increasing the LinkTimeout property
287	User pressed Escape key during DDE operation	The Escape key cancels a pending DDE method or operation
288	Destination is busy	The other application is too busy handling other tasks to respond to the DDE request
290	Data in wrong format	The data exchanged over a DDE link were in a format that was not expected. Check that the link is established with the right control
293	DDE method invoked with no channel open	The link was terminated or modified.
295	Message queue filled; DDE message lost	The DDE link can't keep up with the number of operations requested
297	Can't set LinkMode; invalid LinkTopic	An attempt at setting the LinkMode property failed

TABLE 8-4. LinkError event procedure error constants.

LinkError Constant	Description
vbWrongFormat	Another application requested data in the wrong format
vbDDESourceClosed	The Destination application attempted to continue after the Source was closed
vbTooManyLinks	All source links are in use
vbDataTransferFailed	Data in Destination failed to update

method. The parameters required to establish a link with the Virtual Instrument are as follows:

Application Name	"VI"
LinkTopic	"VI | VI"
LinkItem	"txtOutput"

Commands available through a DDE conversation with the Virtual Instrument are the same as listed in Table 6-1. This is sufficient information to build a program that establishes a DDE conversation with the Virtual Instrument and sends commands to it over the DDE link.

Take a look at the VI source code to see how the VI was configured to be a DDE Source application. The source code can be found in the folder \Vi included with the downloadable software. Only the LinkExecute, LinkClose, and LinkOpen event procedures of the frmMain Form include code. The LinkMode and LinkTopic properties of frmMain are also set appropriately.

Create a new project with one Form, two CommandButtons, a TextBox, and a ComboBox as follows (see Figure 8.7). You can find the completed DDE Commander project in the folder \Part2\DDECmdr of the code available online.

Object Type	Property	Value
Form	Name	frmDDECommander
	Caption	DDE Commander
CommandButton	Name	btnConnect
	Caption	Connect
CommandButton	Name	btnExecute
	Caption	Execute
TextBox	Name	txtOutput
	Text	
ComboBox	Name	cmbCommand
	Text	

When the Form is loaded, the cmbCommand ComboBox is filled with valid VI commands.

TABLE 8-5. DDE-Related Methods and Event Procedures.

Procedure	Source	Destination	Description
LinkOpen	Event	Event	Occurs on both sides of a conversation when it is initiated
LinkClose	Event	Event	Occurs on both sides of a conversation when it is ended
LinkError	Event	Event	Occurs on either side when a DDE-related error occurs
LinkSend	Method	-	Transfers data in a PictureBox to the Destination
LinkNotify	-	Event	Occurs in Destination with a Notify Link conversation when Source data changes
LinkExecute	Event	Method	Executed by Destination and raised in Source with a command string as the argument
LinkPoke	-	Method	Executed by Destination to update Source control data
LinkRequest	-	Method	Executed by Destination to request that Source update link data

```
Private Sub Form_Load()
    ' Fill the ComboBox with VI commands for convenience.
    With cmbCommand
        .AddItem "Analyze"
        .AddItem "Abort"
        .AddItem "Pause"
        .AddItem "Resume"
        .AddItem "Off"
    End With
End Sub
```

The btnConnect and btnExecute CommandButton Click events contain the following code:

```
Private Sub btnConnect_Click()
    ' Establish a connection with the VI
    Dim dblTaskID As Double

    On Error GoTo btnConnect_ClickErrorHandler

    With txtOutput
        .LinkMode = vbLinkNone
        .LinkTopic = "VI|VI"
        .LinkItem = "txtOutput"
        .LinkMode = vbLinkAutomatic
    End With

    Exit Sub
'_____
btnConnect_ClickErrorHandler:
    ' Handle run-time DDE errors
    Select Case Err.Number
    Case 282    ' No foreign application responded to a DDE initiate
        dblTaskID = Shell("Vi.exe", vbNormalFocus)
        If dblTaskID > 0& Then
            Resume      ' Try again
        Else
            MsgBox "Error.  Could not start the VI"
        End If
    Case 293    ' DDE method invoked with no channel open
        MsgBox "Error.  Please turn the VI On before establishing a DDE connection."
    Case Else
        MsgBox "Error " & CStr(Err.Number) & " on Connect.  " & Err.Description
    End Select
End Sub

Private Sub btnExecute_Click()
    ' Send a command to the VI
    On Error GoTo btnExecuteErrorHandler

    txtOutput.LinkExecute cmbCommand.Text

    Exit Sub
'_____
btnExecuteErrorHandler:

    Select Case Err.Number
    Case 293    ' DDE method invoked with no channel open.
        MsgBox "Error.  Is the VI running?  The DDE channel is closed."
    Case Else
        MsgBox "Error " & CStr(Err.Number) & ": " & Err.Description
    End Select
End Sub
```

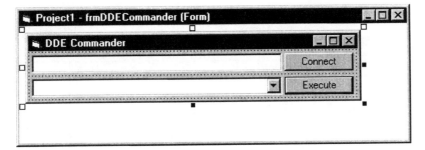

Figure 8-7. The DDE Commander Form in Design Mode.

Finally, trap errors in the txtOutput TextBox LinkError event procedure.

```
Private Sub txtOutput_LinkError(LinkErr As Integer)
    ' Notify user of any DDE-related errors
    Dim strMsg As String

    Select Case LinkErr
    Case vbDDESourceClosed
        strMsg = "Error. The DDE Commander attempted to continue after the VI closed."
    Case vbTooManyLinks
        strMsg = "Error. All VI DDE links are in use."
    End Select

    MsgBox strMsg
End Sub
```

In the Click event procedure of the btnConnect CommandButton, an Automatic Link DDE conversation is established between the txtConnect TextBox of the DDE Commander application and the txtOutput TextBox on the Main form of the Virtual Instrument. Two errors are trapped. If the VI is not running (Error 282), an attempt is made to start it. This attempt is really only for demonstration purposes. In this case it actually doesn't do us any good to start up the VI, because it won't respond until it is turned on. The DDE link will be refused (Error 293) while the VI is off.

Clicking "Execute" on the DDE Commander sends the string currently in the cmbCommand ComboBox to the Virtual Instrument to be executed as a command. If the VI is turned off or closed, the DDE conversation is terminated. Attempting to execute a command at that point will cause an error (Error 293) that is trapped in the btnExecute Click event procedure.

To run the example, do the following:

1. Run the Virtual instrument by executing Vi.exe.
2. Turn the VI on by clicking "On"
3. Compile and run the DDE Commander application.
4. Click "Connect" on the DDE Commander application to establish a DDE conversation.

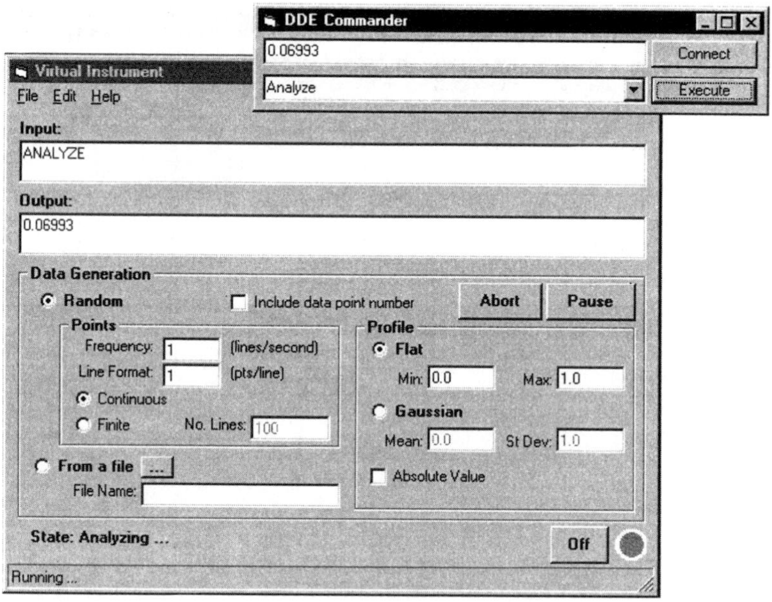

Figure 8-8. The Virtual Instrument under command of a DDE Commander.

5. Select a command in the cmbCommand ComboBox.
6. Click "Execute" to send the command to Virtual Instrument over the DDE Link.

As soon as a DDE conversation is established, you'll see the message "DDE Link Initiated" in the status bar of the VI. After the conversation is established, select the command string "Analyze" in the cmbCommand ComboBox and click "Execute." You will see the VI begin to generate data. Since the DDE conversation is with the txtOutput TextBox of the VI, all output of the VI will be copied over the Automatic Link DDE conversation to the txtConnect TextBox of the DDE Commander application. Figure 8-8 illustrates the process. Select another VI command and click "Execute" again.

9

RS-232 Communications

The RS-232 communications protocol is one of the more popular protocols in use for communicating with laboratory instrumentation. All Intel processor-based personal computers come with one or two ready-to-use RS-232 ports on the back of the box. In addition, the Visual Basic® development environment includes an ActiveX control that makes communications over an RS-232 connection simple. You already have everything you need for RS-232 communications.

The name RS-232 refers to Recommended Standard number 232, which was proposed by the Electronic Industries Association (EIA). It has since been accepted as a standard by the International Standards Organization (ISO), and is described in ISO document 2110. The standard is not rigidly defined, which often causes variations in implementation and increased installation complexity.

RS-232 is a *serial* protocol, which means that one bit is sent over the cable at a time. The standard can be implemented in as little as two wires, a signal and a ground. More often there are at least three wires involved. Cabling for RS-232 connections is relatively inexpensive and can take advantage of existing unused networks. The standard specifies that reliable communication must be possible over connection lengths up to 15 meters at 19.2 kHz. In practice much longer lengths of cable are used at higher data communication rates.

CONFIGURATIONS

The RS-232 protocol was originally designed for communications between a terminal or a computer and a modem (Figure 9-1). In practice, RS-232 has been used for a wide variety of additional purposes, including communications between two computers, a computer and a printer, and a computer and a laboratory instrument (Figure 9-2). In these situations no modem is used; data are transmitted directly from one device to another.

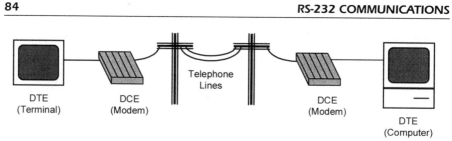

Figure 9-1. Intended configurations for using the RS-232 protocol.

The creators of the original RS-232 specification had two kinds of devices in mind, a *terminal device* that is the ultimate generator and receiver of data, and a *communications device* that converts data to be transmitted into a form that is suitable for sending over a telephone line. For this reason the RS-232 specification is not symmetric. At one end of a standard RS-232 cable is the *Data Terminal Equipment* (DTE) device, and at the other end is the *Data Communications Equipment* (DCE) device. In practice, the difference amounts to the way the wires in the cable are connected. We'll talk more about this in the upcoming section that covers the physical connection.

TRANSMISSION STYLES

Communications over an RS-232 connection can be *uni-* or *bidirectional*. In the case of a unidirectional conversation, one device at the end of the RS-232 cable is designated the *speaker* or transmitter, and the other the *listener* or receiver. This style of communication is referred to as *simplex*.

It is possible to extend the simplex style of communications to a model that is similar to a pair of hand-held "walkie-talkie" radios. Only one of the two involved in the communication can speak at a time while the other listens.

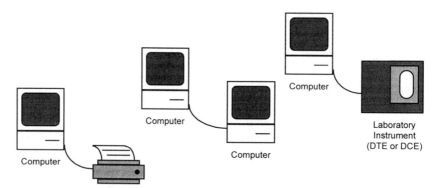

Figure 9-2. Additional configurations for using the RS-232 protocol.

But the roles can switch, ultimately producing a pseudobidirectional communication. When RS-232 communications use this model, it is called *half-duplex*.

The most popular style of RS-232 communications is *full duplex*; both parties can simultaneously transmit and receive. To implement full duplex RS-232 communications, a minimum of three wires are necessary, two signal wires and a ground.

SYNCHRONIZING COMMUNICATIONS

The two communicating devices must also remain in sync to communicate effectively. There are two ways to accomplish this. One is to send timing data continuously over a serial connection so that the two communicating devices are always coupled. These data can be thought of as a "heartbeat" shared by the two devices. Whenever data are to be transmitted on a *synchronous* connection, it can be done very efficiently within this framework since it is not necessary for the two communication devices to synchronize. Synchronization is maintained continuously.

In practice, *asynchronous* RS-232 communications is the preferred option for laboratory-scale serial communications. In asynchronous RS-232 communications, data are sent only when they are ready. There is no continuous form of communication between the communicating devices as is the case with a synchronous RS-232 link. Still, some form of synchronization must occur. This is accomplished with what is known as *start* and *stop bits*.

A start bit is exactly that, a bit sent to signal the beginning of a number of data bits to follow. The purpose of the start bit is to indicate to the device at the other end of the connection that data are about to be transmitted. It gives the receiving device an opportunity to sync its clock to the incoming signal. Similarly, one or more stop bits can be sent at the end of a series of data bits that signals to the receiving device that the particular data transmission is complete. The number of start and stop bits to be used over an RS-232 communication link is an option that must be set before communication is initiated.

DATA BITS

The number of bits of data that are sent between start and stop bits is another parameter that must be set before initiating communication. Typical values are 7 and 8 data bits. Settings of 5 and 6 data bits can be used effectively when the data to be transmitted can be encoded in a limited character set. Limitation of the character set can be traded off for increased data transmission rates. When sending exclusively printable text over an RS-232 communications link,

7 data bits are sufficient since seven bits are all that are necessary to represent all the printable characters. When binary data are being transmitted, a setting of 8 data bits is required, one for each bit in a byte.

ERROR CHECKING

A limited form of error checking can be included right in the RS-232 data stream. A *parity bit* can be added between the last data bit and the first stop bit. The parity bit can be used in one of four ways, or not at all.

When used, the value of the parity bit can indicate whether the sum of data bits in the current set is even or odd. In the case of *odd parity*, the value of the parity bit is set in order to make the sum of data and parity bits turn out to be an odd number. When using *even parity*, the parity bit value is set so that the sum is an even number. If the sum does not match the specified parity, a *parity error* occurs.

Two less commonly used forms of parity are *mark parity* and *space parity*. With mark parity, the parity bit is always set to 1. During transmission, if mark parity is on and the parity bit is 0, a parity error occurs. Even parity is similar, always requiring a 0 parity bit. The mark and space parity options are used infrequently.

To illustrate several of these concepts, imagine that we want to transmit the string "123" over an RS-232 connection. Let's say we are using 7 data bits, odd parity and one stop bit. The series of data bits that would appear on the serial port is given in Figure 9-3.

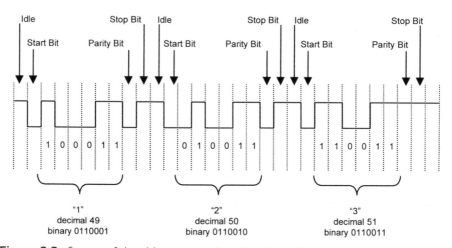

Figure 9-3. Stream of data bits representing the string "123" using RS-232 communication parameters: 7 data bits, odd parity, 1 stop bit.

The characters "1," "2," "3" are represented by the ASCII codes 49, 50, and 51, respectively. Their binary representation is also given in Figure 9-3. The order of transmission is from left to right. Notice that the order of the data bits is sent in reverse.

TRANSMISSION RATE—BAUD

The rate at which data are transmitted over an RS-232 cable is measured in hertz (Hz, cycles per second) and is most often referred to as *baud rate*. Common baud rates are 2400 Hz, 9600 Hz, 19.2 kHz, and 28.8 kHz. The relationship between baud rate and data transmission rate depends on the data transmission options chosen. For example, if the RS-232 communication link will use one start bit, one stop bit, no parity bits, and 8 data bits, a total of ten bits must be transmitted for each byte of data. In this case the data transmission rate will exactly be equal to the baud rate divided by ten. Different options may require that more or fewer bits be transmitted for each byte of data. Dividing baud rate by ten is usually a good estimate of bytes per second transmitted.

RS-232 PIN ASSIGNMENTS

The RS-232 standard defines and assigns pin numbers to 25 lines that can be used in an RS-232 cable. In practice, only 11 are used to any great extent. These are defined for a DTE device in Table 9-1.

Of these 11 lines, only 2, 3, and 7 are used to transmit the actual data. At a minimum, these are the three lines that must be connected to establish a full duplex connection. Other lines are used primarily for signaling and flow control.

FLOW CONTROL

Data received on a computer's RS-232 port are stored in a receive buffer from which data can be removed and processed by an application running on the computer. This buffer is of finite size and can fill quickly. To prevent lost data from a buffer overflow there must be a mechanism for informing the sending device to stop transmitting until data in the receive buffer can be processed. Methods for starting and stopping data transmission are referred to as *flow control.*

When used, flow control can come in two forms, hardware and software.

As discussed previously, when an RS-232 communications channel is half-duplex only one device can be transmitting and the other receiving at any time. When one of the two devices wants to send data, it asserts the predefined

TABLE 9-1. Most commonly used lines in an RS-232 connection with DTE device pin assignments.

Pin Number	Function	Abbreviation	Description
1	Protective Ground		Ground for safety
2	Transmit Data	TD	Used to transmit data
3	Receive Data	RD	Used to receive data
4	Request to Send	RTS	Indicates that data are ready to be sent
5	Clear to Send	CTS	Indicated that data are ready to be received
6	Data Set Ready	DSR	Indicates that the DCE device is ready
7	Signal Common		Common for signal lines
8	Data Carrier Detect	DCD	Indicates that the phone line is active
20	Data Terminal Ready	DTR	Indicates that the DTE device is ready
22	Ring Indicator	RI	Indicates the presence of an incoming call

RS-232 line called *Request To Send* (RTS), indicating to a modem that it has data to be sent over a telephone line. When the receiving device is ready to receive the data, it responds by asserting the *Clear To Send* (CTS) line. When the modems are ready, transmission begins. This exchange is called hardware flow control or *hardware handshaking*.

This same exchange can be used even when a modem is not involved. Two communicating devices can indicate that data can or cannot be transmitted using the RTS and CTS lines. For example, when a computer would like to send data to a printer, it can assert the RTS line. The printer can stop the flow of data to prevent overflow of its print buffer by asserting the CTS line. Other laboratory devices can use this same flow control mechanism for a similar purpose.

A software approach is also available for controlling the flow of data over an RS-232 communications channel. This involves the use of two special characters called XON and XOFF. When operating under software flow control, if a device encounters an XOFF character on its input stream, it is a signal from the other device that any further transmissions should be suspended. An XON character on the input stream indicates that transmission can resume.

The DC1 (ASCII character code 17) and DC3 (ASCII character code 19) characters are usually used for the XON and XOFF characters, respectively. Refer to the ASCII character code table in Appendix A.

THE PHYSICAL CONNECTION

There are two cable connector styles for RS-232 cables that are in common use. They are the DB25 connector and the DB9 connector. Figure 9-4 illustrates these two connector styles. Corner pins are labeled in the diagrams; intervening pins are numbered sequentially. Number assignments in the diagrams are made as if the connectors were being viewed on the back of a computer. When looking at a connector on a cable, pin assignments can be determined by using the mirror image of these diagrams obtained by rotating along the center vertical axis.

The "DB" in DB9 and DB25 refer to D-shell style connectors. They can be male or female. By convention, male connectors are used on the back of a computer for the RS-232 port. You may also find a female DB25 connector on the back of a PC. This is the parallel port.

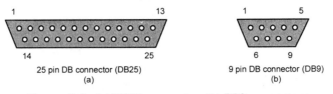

Figure 9-4. (a) DB25 connector, (b) DB9 connector.

In the case of the DB25 connector, pin functions are identical to assignments made in Table 9-1. The DB9 pin function assignments are somewhat different. They are given for a DTE device in Table 9-2.

Finding the right cable to make a connection between two RS-232 devices can be a frustrating endeavor. How the cable is wired depends on the type of devices on either end of the connection as well as options used during communications. With a good understanding of the purpose of each line and the common pin function assignments, it is possible to determine the right RS-232 cable for any situation.

There are a few common cable configurations that satisfy the vast majority of cases. Wiring for these configurations are given in Figure 9-5. Diagram (a) shows a simple straight-through cable where all major pins are connected to each other. Diagram (b) includes only the pins necessary for data transfer, that is, TD, RD, and Signal Common.

Diagram (c) illustrates a minimal *null-modem* configuration. As the name suggests, a null-modem cable is used without a modem directly to connect two devices of the same type. In other words, to connect a DTE device to another DTE device, or a DCE device to another DCE device, a null-modem cable is required. The reason is evident by observing the cable configuration. The DTE device defines pin 2 as TD (Transmit Data) and pin 3 as RD (Receive Data). Two like devices can be connected together successfully by swapping these two pins on one side of the connection. In a null-modem cable, TD is properly connected with RD, and RD with TD.

Diagram (d) illustrates connections for a null-modem cable where handshaking and other signal lines are properly connected as well. RTS (Request To Send) and CTS (Clear To Send) are cross-connected in order to satisfy hard-

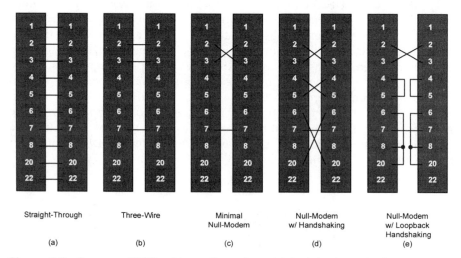

Straight-Through   Three-Wire   Minimal   Null-Modem   Null-Modem
                                          Null-Modem   w/ Handshaking   w/ Loopback
                                                                                Handshaking
      (a)   (b)   (c)   (d)   (e)

Figure 9-5. Common DB25 cable configurations: (a) Straight-through, (b) three-wire, (c) minimal null-modem, (d) null-modem with handshaking, (e) null-modem with loopback handshaking.

TABLE 9-2. DB9 connector pin functions for a DTE device.

Pin #	Function	Abbrev.	Description
1	Data Carrier Detect	DCD	Indicates that the phone line is active
2	Received Data	RD	Used to receive data
3	Transmitted Data	TD	Used to transmit data
4	Data Terminal Ready	DTR	Indicates that the DTE device is ready
5	Signal Common		Common for signal lines
6	Data Set Ready	DSR	Indicates that the DCE device is ready
7	Request to Send	RTS	Indicates that data are ready to be sent
8	Clear to Send	CTS	Indicated that data are ready to be received
9	Ring Indicator	RI	Indicates the presence of an incoming call

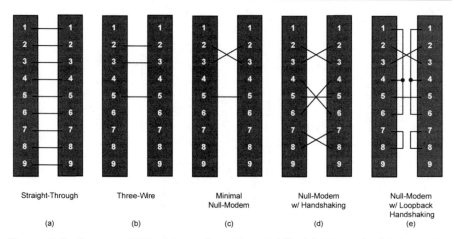

Straight-Through	Three-Wire	Minimal Null-Modem	Null-Modem w/ Handshaking	Null-Modem w/ Loopback Handshaking
(a)	(b)	(c)	(d)	(e)

Figure 9-6. Common DB9 cable configurations: (a) Straight-through, (b) three-wire, (c) minimal null-modem, (d) null-modem with handshaking, (e) null-modem with loopback handshaking.

ware handshaking requirements. DSR (Data Set Ready) and DCD (Data Carrier Detect) on each side are connected with DTR (Data Terminal Ready) on the alternate side in order to satisfy the requirement that the two devices be ready and the phone line appear active.

Diagram (e) also illustrates a null-model cable with handshaking and other signal lines. This time, though, the handshaking and other signals are looped back to the same connector. This tricks the communicating device into thinking that it is successfully handshaking and signaling with another device, when in fact the signals are remaining local.

Figure 9-6 illustrates DB9 connector wiring for the five common RS-232 cable configurations.

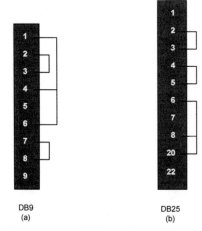

DB9
(a)

DB25
(b)

Figure 9-7. Wiring for (a) DB9 and (b) DB25 loopback plugs.

TABLE 9-3. Summary of RS-232 parameters and common options.

RS-232 Parameter	Options
Transmission Rate	2400 Hz, **9600 Hz**, 19.2 kHz, 28.8 kHz
Number of Data Bits	5, 6, 7, **8**
Number of Stop Bits	**1**, 2
Parity Bit	**None**, Even, Odd, Mark, Space
Handshaking	**None**, Hardware, XON/XOFF
Cabling	Straight-through, three-wire, null-modem, null-modem with handshaking, Null-modem with loopback handshaking

It is possible to test the RS-232 ports on a single computer by plugging one end of a null-modem cable into one port and the other end into a second port. Programs that perform RS-232 communications can be run simultaneously on the same computer if configured to use different ports.

Since an RS-232 port is bidirectional, testing can even occur when only a single port is available. In this case a *loopback plug* must be used. A loopback plug is configured to loop outbound data and signal pins back to the input pins. A single program could open the port, send data out the port, and read it back in from the same port. Figure 9-7 illustrates loopback plug wiring for DB9 and DB25 connectors.

CABLE LENGTHS

The original intention of RS-232 was to establish connections of a local nature, for example, between a terminal and a modem. The specification requires that a connection at 19.2 kHz be able to transmit data reliably over a length of 15 meters. In practice, RS-232 connections can be run successfully at 30 or more meters. This is especially true when lower transmission rates can be tolerated. In general, the lower the transmission rate, the longer the cable can be.

RS-232 COMMUNICATION OPTIONS SUMMARY

More often than not, establishing a successful RS-232 connection boils down to two primary concerns. First, the type of each device must be determined in order to choose the correct cable. That is, do you have two DTE devices, two DCE devices, or one of each? Consult instrument manuals for this information. Second, the parameter settings for RS-232 communications must be determined and configured to be identical on both sides.

To make this process a bit less painful, Table 9-3 lists the RS-232 choices to be made prior to establishing a connection. The most common set of options, determined through experience, is given in bold in the second column.

10

RS-232 Communications in Visual Basic®

THE MSCOMM ACTIVEX CONTROL

Most mature programming languages provide a way to communicate over an RS-232 port, and Visual Basic® is no exception. As with most capabilities in Visual Basic®, RS-232 communications comes by way of an ActiveX control. The MSComm control encapsulates the low-level function calls for performing RS-232 port communications and exposes the capability through the control's properties and events. It is interesting to note that the MSComm control has no methods.

MSCOMM PROPERTIES

Interaction with the RS-232 port using VB involves setting and reading properties of the MSComm control. There are several properties, but only a few are generally necessary to establish a connection and communicate. These are listed and described briefly in Table 10-1.

A QUICK START

Let's get started right away with a simple example that demonstrates the MSComm control and RS-232 serial port in action. This example illustrates the basics of using the MSComm control. It requires a loopback plug, and can be executed on a computer with only one RS-232 port. If you only have an RS-232 cable and no loopback plug, plug one end of the cable into the RS-232 port and connect lines 2 and 3 on the other end. With a female plug, the small loop of a standard-sized metal paperclip will suffice as a jumper to connect the lines.

TABLE 10-1. Frequently used MSComm control properties.

MSComm Control Property	Description
CommPort	Sets or gets the number of the RS-232 port
Settings	Sets or gets the baud rate, parity, data bits and stop bits as a comma-separated string
InputMode	Determines whether data will be read as a string or in binary form
Handshaking	Sets or gets the handshaking protocol to use
PortOpen	Opens or closes the RS-232 port
Input	Fetches and removes data from the receive buffer
Output	Puts data into the transmit buffer
InBufferCount	Gets the number of characters in the receive buffer
RThreshold	Sets or gets the number of characters received before firing the OnComm indicating that event
SThreshold	Sets or gets the number of characters in the transmit buffer, be low which the OnComm event will be fired indicating the event
CommEvent	Holds a constant defining the most recent communications event

Open a new project and add two CommandButtons, two TextBoxes, and an MSComm control to Form1. If the MSComm control does not show up in your toolbox, choose the Components option from the Project menu on the main VB toolbar, or type Ctrl+T. Make sure that the "Microsoft Comm Control" option is checked (see Figure 10-1). The code for this example can be found in the folder \Part2\Ex3 of the code available online.

Assign the following property values to your new controls:

Object Type	Property	Value
TextBox	Name	txtSend
	Text	
TextBox	Name	txtReceive
	Text	
CommandButton	Name	btnSend
	Caption	Send
CommandButton	Name	btnReceive
	Caption	Receive

To demonstrate the basics of using the MSComm control, the btnSend CommandButton will take the contents of the txtSend TextBox and send it out the RS-232 port. The btnReceive CommandButton will copy whatever is in the RS-232 port receive buffer to the txtReceive TextBox.

As soon as Form1 is loaded, we would like to configure and open the RS-232 port. To accomplish this we use the CommPort, Settings, and PortOpen properties. Add the following code to the Load event procedure of Form1:

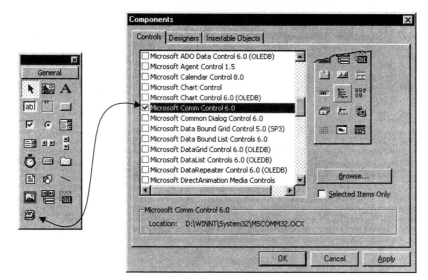

Figure 10-1. Select the Microsoft Comm Control option in the Components dialog to cause the Comm Control to appear in your toolbox.

```
Private Sub Form_Load()
    ' Configure and open the comm port
    With MSComm1
        .CommPort = 1
        .Settings = "9600,N,8,1"
        .PortOpen = True
    End With
End Sub
```

We chose to use port 1 in the example. Make sure that your computer has a COM1 (the name of the port), and that it is available for use. Communications settings are 9600 Baud, no parity, 8 data bits, and 1 stop bit. Since the port is communicating with itself through a loopback plug, practically any valid settings will suffice. Setting the PortOpen property to True causes the RS-232 port to be opened and made ready for communication.

To send data out the RS-232 port and read data in from the RS-232 port, use the Output and Input properties. Add the following code to the btnSend and btnReceive Click event procedures:

```
Private Sub btnSend_Click()
    ' Send data out the comm port
    MSComm1.Output = txtSend.Text
End Sub

Private Sub btnReceive_Click()
    ' Receive data from the input buffer
    txtReceive.Text = MSComm1.Input
End Sub
```

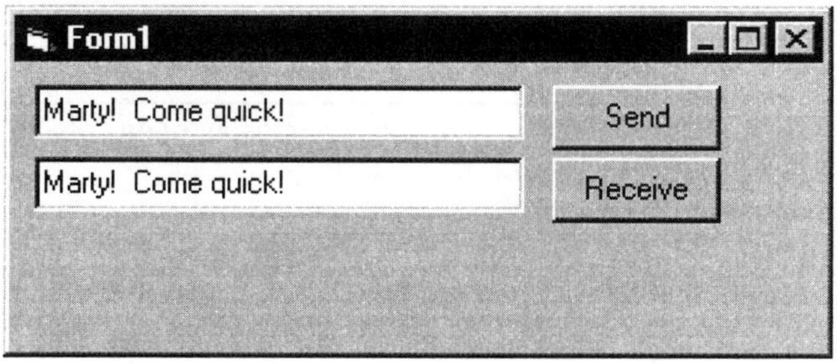

Figure 10-2. Testing RS-232 port communications with a loopback plug.

To see the example in action (Figure 10-2), do the following:

1. Double-check that the loopback plug is firmly placed in an available RS-232 port.
2. Run the project.
3. Enter some text into the txtSend TextBox and click "Send" to transfer the text to the RS-232 port.
4. Click "Receive" to copy the text from the port's receive buffer into the txtReceive TextBox.

MSCOMM PROPERTIES IN MORE DETAIL

We've seen the basics of RS-232 communication using the MSComm ActiveX control. Now let's look into the functionality of the control in more detail. It is useful to remember that the MSComm control has no methods. All your interactions with the control will be accomplished by setting and reading its properties.

The MSComm control's CommPort property is used primarily to set the number of the RS-232 port to use for communications. The property should be assigned an integer value, which is most often 1 or 2. It can also be read to determine the port number that is in use. An error will occur when this property is not set correctly. Make sure you know how many ports are available on your computer and their numbers.

The Settings property takes a string that defines the parameters for communications. The string contains four data items separated by commas. These items are the Baud rate, the parity, the number of data bits, and the number of stop bits. Table 10-2 summarizes the possible values for these four settings. Defaults are shown in bold. For parity, "E" stands for even parity, "M" for mark parity, "N" for no parity, "O" for odd parity, and "S" for space parity.

As described in Chapter 9, handshaking is a technique for metering the flow of information over an RS-232 connection. The MSComm ActiveX control sup-

TABLE 10-2. MSComm Settings property value options.

MSComm *Settings* Parameter	Possible Values
Baud Rate (Parameter 1)	110, 300, 600, 1200, 2400, **9600**, 14400, 19200, 28800
Parity (Parameter 2)	E, M, **N**, O, S
Data bits (Parameter 3)	3, 4, 5, 6, 7, **8**
Stop bits (Parameter 4)	**1**, 1.5, 2

ports hardware and software forms of handshaking, or no handshaking at all. To choose the form of handshaking to be used, set the MSComm control's Handshaking property to one of the predefined VB constants listed in Table 10-3.

The PortOpen property is used to open and close the port. Set PortOpen to True in order to open the port and False to close the port. If you are going to set the CommPort, Settings, or Handshaking properties, it is important that you do so before the port is opened.

To send data out the RS-232 port, set the Output property of the MSComm control to the data to be sent. Both string and binary data can be transmitted using the MSComm control. To send string data, simply set Output to the string to be sent. When sending binary data, fill a byte array with the appropriate data and assign it to a variable of type Variant. Assign Output to the Variant containing the byte array.

Both binary and string data can be received over the RS-232 port. The format in which data are received is determined by setting the InputMode property to one of the predefined constants listed in Table 10-4.

To receive data from the RS-232 port, assign a variable to the Input property of the MSComm control. If receiving binary data, use a variable of type Variant and then reassign the Variant variable to a byte array variable. If receiving string data, a string variable can be used. After the value of Input is assigned to a variable, Input is automatically cleared. When there is nothing available to be read off the RS-232 port, Input will return an empty string.

Often it is useful to be able to determine how many data characters are waiting to be read without actually pulling them out of the receive buffer. The InBufferCount property of the MSComm control returns the number of characters waiting in the receive buffer. After reading data in the receive buffer

TABLE 10-3. MSComm Handshaking property constants.

Handshaking Constant	Description
comNone	No handshaking. This is the default.
comXOnXOff	XON/XOFF (hardware) handshaking.
comRTS	RTS/CTS (software) handshaking.
comRTSXOnXOff	Both hardware and software handshaking.

TABLE 10-4. MSComm InputMode property constants.

InputMode Constant	Description
comInputModeText	Data are received as a String. This is the default.
comInputModeBinary	Data are received in binary form.

by assigning an appropriate variable to the Input property, the receive buffer is cleared and the InBufferCount property goes to zero.

Whenever a significant communications event or error occurs, the CommEvent property of the MSComm control changes its value to a constant that indicates the event or error. An example of a significant communications event is when data arrive in the receive buffer. When this happens, the CommEvent property will change to a value that indicates that new data have arrived. Table 10-5 lists several of the predefined constants, which can be used to compare with the current value of CommEvent. See the CommEvent property in VB Help for a complete listing of CommEvent constants.

The MSComm control can be configured to wait to change its CommEvent property until after a certain number of characters have been received. The RThreshold property determines the number of characters received before CommEvent changes to a value indicating that data have been received. For example, if you only wanted to know when there were ten or more characters on the receive buffer, set RThreshold to a value of 10.

The value of the SThreshold property determines when you will receive notification that all but a certain number of characters have been sent from the transmit buffer. For example, if SThreshold is set to 10, the CommEvent property will change to indicate that data in the transmit buffer have been sent when the number of characters in the transmit buffer goes from 10, or higher, to 9, or lower.

When the CommEvent property changes its value, the MSComm OnComm event fires. This feature makes it possible to build powerful event-driven

TABLE 10-5. Common CommEvent property constants.

CommEvent Constant	Description
comEvSend	There are fewer than Sthreshold number of characters in the transmit buffer
comEvReceive	There are Rthreshold number of characters in the receive buffer
comEvEOF	An End-Of-File (EOF) character was received (EOF = ASCII 26)
comEventRxOver	Receive Buffer Overflow; the receive buffer is full
comEventRxParity	Parity Error; a parity error was detected
comEventTxFull	Transmit Buffer Full; there is no room left in the transmit buffer to add more data

RS-232 communications programs in VB. This is covered in detail in Part 3 when event-driven device control is discussed.

BUILDING AN RS-232 COMMANDER FOR THE VIRTUAL INSTRUMENT

Let's take what we've learned about the MSComm control and build a program to send commands to the Virtual Instrument over an RS-232 connection. For this example you'll need to connect two available RS-232 ports with a null-modem cable. The two ports can be on the same computer, or on different computers (See Figure 10-3). You will find the source code for this example in the folder \Part2\RS232Cmdr of the code available online.

Create a new project and add one TextBox, one CommandButton, and one MSComm control to Form1 (see Figure 10-4). If the MSComm control does not appear in your toolbox, make sure that the "Microsoft Comm Control" option in the Components dialog is selected as in Figure 10-1.

Assign the following properties to the new controls:

Object Type	Property	Value
Form	Name	frmRS232Commander
	Caption	RS-232 Commander
TextBox	Name	txtSend
	Text	
CommandButton	Name	btnSend
	Caption	Send
MSComm	Name	MSComm1

When the form loads, we want to configure and open the RS-232 port. Add the following code to the Load event procedure of your frmRS232Commander main Form.

```
Private Sub Form_Load()
    With MSComm1        ' Set up the comm control
        .CommPort = 2
        .Settings = "19200,N,8,1"
        .PortOpen = True
    End With
End Sub
```

In this example we've chosen to use a Baud rate of 19.2 kHz, no parity, eight data bits, and one stop bit. These are the default RS-232 communication parameters of the Virtual Instrument. Also by default, the VI listens to port 1. Therefore, in the example we have chosen to use port 2. This setup will work on a computer with two available RS-232 ports connected together with a null-modem cable. If you are going to run the VI on one computer and

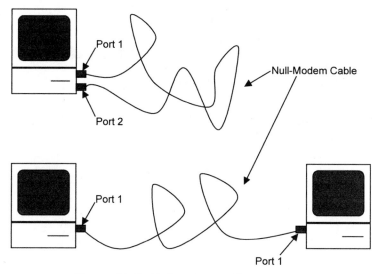

Figure 10-3. Null-modem cable connections.

control it from another computer, make sure you set the port number on the controlling computer to an available port and plug the null-modem cable into that port as well.

Add the following code to the btnSend CommandButton click event procedure.

```
Private Sub btnSend_Click()
    ' Send contents of the text box out the RS-232 port
    MSComm1.Output = txtSend.Text & vbCr
End Sub
```

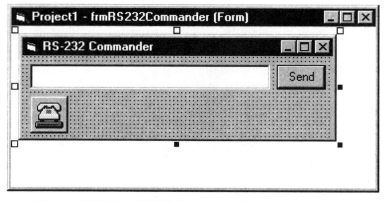

Figure 10-4. The RS-232 Commander form in design mode.

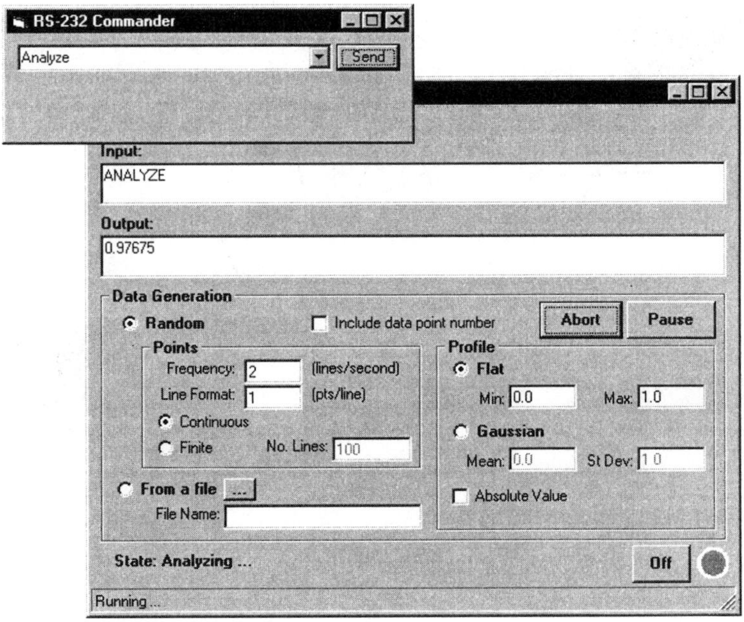

Figure 10-5. The RS-232 Commander communicating with the VI.

The btnSend click event procedure takes the text from the txtSend TextBox and sends it out the RS-232 port. Before it sends the text it adds a carriage return onto the end. The carriage return is obtained using the builtin VB constant called vbCr. The VI is expecting a carriage return at the end of each message that it receives. Without the carriage return, the VI believes that the communicating program is still transmitting the message and will wait.

Once your program is finished and your cables are connected, you can give it a try.

1. Run the VI, making sure that the communication parameters and port number are set correctly by looking at the "RS-232 Port Settings . . ." option in the "Edit" menu.
2. Turn the VI on by clicking "On".
3. Run the RS-232 Commander example program.
4. Select "Analyze" from the ComboBox and click "Send".

Unlike the DDE Commander example, it was not necessary to establish a connection with the VI. Opening the RS-232 port is all we can do. It is not known if there is something listening at the other end of the port until it responds. Figure 10-5 shows the RS-232 Commander in action.

11

TCP/IP Networking

The popularity of the Internet has increased interest in using a network as a means for communication. This is true not only for communications between computers, but also between computers and laboratory instruments. Just as printers now support network connections, as opposed to the more common serial or parallel port connections, a variety of instruments have begun to follow suit. Devices are available that act as an "adapter" for bridging an RS-232 port and a network. This allows you easily to put an RS-232 instrument onto a network.

Third-party networking controls have been available for Visual Basic® for some time. Networking controls now come with the Professional and Enterprise editions of Visual Basic®. In this chapter we will discuss TCP/IP networking. In the next chapter we will show how to use the ActiveX networking controls provided with Visual Basic® to communicate with laboratory instruments over a TCP/IP network.

NETWORKING PROTOCOLS

Before two devices on a network can communicate, they must both speak a common language. Network languages are called *protocols*. Protocols are a set of predefined data formats and rules for how two network devices are to engage in an orderly conversation. For example, the rules of a network protocol might go something like this:

1. The Client computer will request a connection with the Server computer over the network.
2. The Server will accept or ignore the connection request.
3. When the connection is accepted, the Server will immediately identify itself in a predefined format.
4. The Client will then introduce itself in a predefined format.

5. The Client will then inform the Server of the kind of information it is about to transmit.

6. The Server will respond with a code indicating if it can accept the information.

. . . and so on. Networks work because of well-defined network protocols.

The network protocol used and made popular by the Internet is called *TCP/IP*. To communicate over the Internet a device must speak TCP/IP, although a connection to the Internet is not required in order to use TCP/IP. It only takes two computers that speak TCP/IP and a connection to create a TCP/IP network. TCP/IP is actually a suite of higher-level protocols based on a lower-level protocol called the *Internet Protocol*, or IP.

INTERNET PROTOCOL

Internet Protocol (IP) is the basis upon which all TCP/IP protocols are built. With IP, a message is broken up and exchanged over a network in discrete chunks called *packets* or *datagrams*. In addition to a portion of a message itself, each packet contains other information, including the address of the computer to which the message is sent. With the destination address as part of the message, the network can route the packet as needed over the network in order to get it where it is going. It's possible for the packets that make up a message to take different routes to get to its destination. With IP, the order in which packets arrive at a destination is not guaranteed.

In the current version of IP (called IPv4) addresses of network devices are made up of four 8-bit bytes. Each byte is typically written in decimal notation and separated with a dot. For example, the address of the computer at John Wiley and Sons, Inc., from which the software for this book can be downloaded is currently 199.171.201.10. The 32 bits that makes up IPv4 addresses provides up to 2^{32}, or about 4 billion, possible addresses. This may seem like a lot, but with the way that IP addressing works, there is a concern that usable addresses will soon run out. The next version of IP is called IPv6. It provides for 2^{128} possible addresses. This is substantially larger and should provide us with available IP addresses for some time to come. IPv6 can also automatically configure computers and other TCP/IP devices. This is compared to the current version, where IP addresses often must be set manually.

The special IP address 127.0.0.1 is reserved for the *localhost*. The localhost is the same network device that sends a message. In other words, the address 127.0.0.1 provides a loopback mechanism that acts in a very similar manner to the RS-232 loopback plug described in Chapter 9. This address can be useful for testing purposes, as was the case with the RS-232 loopback plug.

One troublesome aspect of computer addresses is that they may have to change, and can do so without notice. Programs that depend on the address of a remote computer to establish a connection will fail if the remote address is changed. To solve this problem a database has been established that maps IP addresses to computer names. A typical name for a computer on the Internet would look something like *ftp.wiley.com*. When an attempt is made to establish a connection with a computer by its name, the name is first used to look up the computer's address, which in turn is used to establish the connection. This way, if the address of a computer changes, or if the name of a computer must be reassigned to another computer with a different address, only the database entry needs to be modified to reflect the change. All programs that use the name remain functional. This database of information is available from a computer on an IP network that runs a program called a *Domain Name Server* (DNS). Copies of the Domain Name Server database for the Internet exist on networked computers throughout the world. When a change is made to one DNS database, the DNS communicates that change to its neighboring DNS databases, which store the change and relay the information on. The change propagates through the world until all DNS databases have made the change. The address of a DNS still must be known. This address is one of the parameters that you'll have to set when your computer is configured for TCP/IP networking.

Protocols that are implemented on top of IP are classified as being either *connection oriented* or *connectionless*. With a connection-oriented protocol, two communicating devices must be activated and agree to take part in the communication before data can be exchanged. Establishing a connection-oriented protocol is like making a phone call; the connection request is sent by dialing the phone and accepted by answering on the other end before a conversation can begin. A connectionless protocol is more like sending a message by carrier pigeon. The message is created and sent on its way, possibly using multiple pigeons. There is no guarantee that the message will arrive at its destination.

TRANSMISSION CONTROL PROTOCOL

The most important networking protocol implemented on top of IP is called Transmission Control Protocol (TCP). TCP is connection oriented; it offers guaranteed delivery of a message while preserving the order in which the packets were originally sent. A TCP connection creates a reliable, full-duplex byte stream between two communicating network devices. A TCP connection follows the Client-Server model for communications, that is one device involved in the network connection requests the connection (the Client), and the other accepts the connection (the Server). Once the connection is established, the two devices can simultaneously and reliably exchange information.

Internet services that are most familiar, such as e-mail and file transfer, are themselves based on TCP.

USER DATAGRAM PROTOCOL

User Datagram Protocol (UDP) is also implemented on top of IP. UDP is connectionless; delivery is not guaranteed. By not requiring an active connection, UDP uses less overhead and is typically much faster than TCP. An example of a higher-level protocol that is based on UDP is DNS, the method by which one network device can look up another network device address using its name.

PORTS

Once a computer or instrument is connected to a network, it can engage in several conversations simultaneously, even though there is only a single physical connection. Compare this to RS-232, where additional ports and cables are required in order to establish additional connections. So, how can a network device keep track of several logical connections over a single physical connection? The answer is through the use of *ports*.

A port is a *logical* conduit through which a process on a network device connects to a network. Both processes engaged in a network connection pass information back and forth through ports to the network. A number identifies a particular port, and may or may not be the same on each side of a network connection. Only one process can be attached through a port to the network at any time. The most important thing to remember is that both an IP address and a port number are required to establish a connection over a TCP/IP network.

Figure 11-1 represents the use of ports in a TCP/IP network connection. The gray area between the two connected devices represents the network. Each device is connected to the network through one or more ports, which

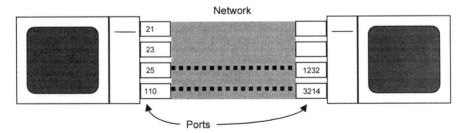

Figure 11-1. Two devices connected over a TCP/IP network through ports.

are labeled with numbers. Dotted lines connecting ports through the network represent logical network connections established between devices through their ports.

WELL-KNOWN SERVICE PORTS

Most well-established TCP/IP network services are associated with a particular port number. For example, when you want to view a web page from Microsoft®'s web server, your web browser requests a connection with the computer(s) called www.microsoft.com on port number 80. Common practice is for web servers to *listen* to port 80 for incoming connection requests. These predefined port number assignments are called *Well-Known Service Ports*. Table 11-1 lists a few of these Well-Known Service Port assignments.

SOCKETS

The last item that we need to know about in order to complete our understanding of TCP/IP network connections is called a *socket*. A socket is the software entity used by a process that actually establishes the network connection. TCP/IP network connections are established through ports and over wires, but the ultimate end-point in an application program is the socket. Sockets include functionality for connecting to ports, requesting connections, listening for connection requests, and accepting connection requests. From a programmer's perspective a socket is the thing with which you interact.

Figure 11-2 illustrates two computers that are engaged in network communications. The computer represented by the box on the left is the Server; it provides various network services. The box on the right represents a typical networked Client computer. The client computer is running two programs, a web browser and mail reader. The server is running a mail server and a web server. Circles with an arrow within each box represent these programs (pro-

TABLE 11-1. Some Well-Known Service Port assignments.

Network Service/Protocol	Description	Port Number
Echo	Returns what is sent	7
File Transfer Protocol (FTP)	Transfers files over a network	21
Telnet	A remote terminal emulator	23
Simple Mail Transfer Protocol (SMTP)	Transfers e-mail over a network	25
Hypertext Transfer Protocol (HTTP)	Transfers web pages and other documents over a network	80

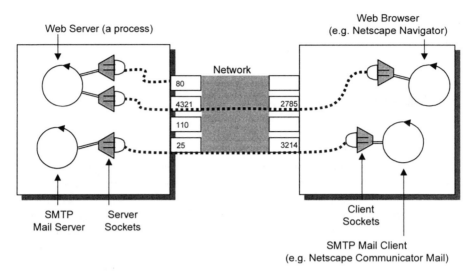

Figure 11-2. Sockets are network connection endpoints.

cesses). Each of these processes is engaged in one or more network connections. This is accomplished through sockets.

It is important to note that when a listening server socket receives a connection request, it need not be the same socket to accept the connection. When a client socket requests a connection with a listening server socket, it is standard practice for a server program to create a new socket and direct it to accept the connection on a random available port. This way the original server socket can continue to listen on the well-known port for new connection requests. The web server in Figure 11-2 is engaged in one network connection with a web browser and is simultaneously listening on port 80 for new connection requests.

THE CLIENT–SERVER MODEL

The terms *Client* and *Server* can have different meanings depending on how they are used. For the purposes of this section, the Client program is the one that requests a network connection, and the Server program is the one that is listening for a connection request, and potentially responds to the request.

Figure 11-3 illustrates a typical series of events that occur during the lifetime of a Client and Server program. The left column of events refers to the Server, and the right column to the Client. Time proceeds from the top of the diagram to the bottom. The diagram assumes that the Server accepts the Client's connection request. As we've mentioned, in addition to accepting the

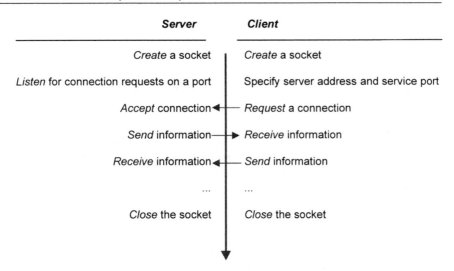

Figure 11-3. The Client–Server Model.

connection itself, the Server can direct another socket to accept the connection, or even ignore the connection request all together.

WINDOWS SOCKETS (WINSOCK)

TCP/IP and sockets were originally born out of the UNIX world, and only later added to Microsoft® Windows® as popularity grew. The implementation of sockets for Windows® is called *Windows Sockets*, or *Winsock.*

Early on, implementations of sockets for Windows® were created by different software vendors and naturally had different application program interfaces (API). It was not uncommon to hear about software that required a certain implementation and revision of Winsock before it would operate correctly. To address the problem, a group of companies got together and agreed on a standard Winsock API. This made the use of network software in Windows® much less painful. Now, TCP/IP-based applications in Windows® can run using any implementation of Winsock provided the application and the implementation of Winsock both strictly adhere to the standard Winsock API.

The Winsock API is a set of standard function definitions contained in a library that implement sockets in Windows®. The functions included in the Winsock library perform a variety of tasks, including the following:

- Create and destroy sockets
- Listen to a port, request and accept connections, close connections

- Send and receive data over a network connection
- Convert between host name and IP addresses

ETHERNET NETWORKS

Ethernet is the network over which TCP/IP is typically spoken, although Ethernet networks also carry other protocols such as Novell and AppleTalk (a.k.a. EtherTalk). Ethernet consists of the *medium* (cable, connectors, etc.) over which signals are transmitted, the *frame* (the data that move over the network as a discrete package), and a set of rules for how to transmit frames. Data that make up higher-level protocols, like those included in TCP/IP, are embedded within frames handled by an Ethernet network.

Media systems and data transmission rates are used to characterize Ethernet networks. The cable originally used for Ethernet networks was a thick coaxial style. Thinner coaxial and "twisted-pair" cable styles are more popular. Fiber optic cable is also becoming more popular. Currently, the most common desktop computer data transmission rate for Ethernet networks is 10 million bits per second (10 Mbps). This is being steadily replaced with the most recent standard, which calls for transmission rates of 100 Mbps.

Shorthand names for Ethernet media systems indicate media type, signaling, and data transmission rates (see Table 11-2). The first number in the shorthand refers to data transmission rate, "10" for 10 Mbps and "100" for 100 Mbps. The "BASE" in the shorthand refers to *baseband*, which is a type of signaling in which Ethernet signals are the only signals carried over the media. The final characters in the shorthand refer to the media type. Table 11-2 summarizes several Ethernet media system shorthand names and their characteristics.

The 10BASE-T (a.k.a. twisted-pair) Ethernet media is by far the most popular. It employs two pair of wires in the cable; one pair is for receiving data signals, and the other is for transmitting data signals. Eight-pin, RJ-45 style connectors terminate 10BASE-T cables. RJ-45 connectors are very similar to the 4-wire RJ-11-style connectors now commonly used in residential modu-

TABLE 11-2. Ethernet media system shorthand names and descriptions.

Shorthand	Media Type	Cable Length	Transmission Rate
10BASE5	Thick coax	500 meters	10 Mbps
10BASE2	Thin coax	185 meters	10 Mbps
10BASE-T	Two twisted-pairs	100 meters	10 Mbps
10BASE-F	Fiber optic	1000 meters	10 Mbps
100BASE-TX	Two twisted-pairs	100 meters	100 Mbps
100BASE-T4	Four twisted-pairs	100 meters	100 Mbps
100BASE-FX	Fiber optic	412 meters	100 Mbps

**TABLE 11-3. Pin assignments for RJ-45-style
10BASE-T Ethernet connectors.**

Pin #	Signal	Description
1	TD+	Positive Transmit line
2	TD–	Negative Transmit line
3	RD+	Positive Receive Line
4	Unused	
5	Unused	
6	RD–	Negative Receive Line
7	Unused	
8	Unused	

lar phone systems. Of the eight pins in a 10BASE-T connector, only four are used. Table 11-3 illustrates pin assignments for the connector.

The signals in each pair of wires in a 10BASE-T cable are polarized with opposite polarity, as indicated in Table 11-3 by (+) and (–) in the signal designation. Pins 1 and 2 connect to the data transmission twisted pair, and pins 3 and 4 connect to the data receive twisted pair.

10BASE-T media systems make use of *repeater hubs* to join cable segments and attach a small group of networked devices to a larger network. A repeater hub is a device that repeats signals coming in on each port to all other ports in the hub. A hub can be used to create a small Ethernet network simply by

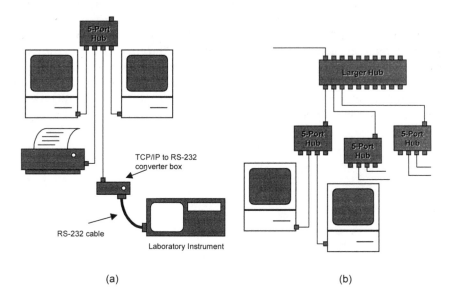

(a)   (b)

Figure 11-4. (a) An isolated Ethernet network; (b) a subnet connected to a larger Ethernet network.

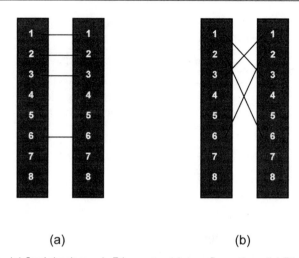

(a)   (b)

Figure 11-5. (a) Straight-through Ethernet cable configuration; (b) Ethernet crossover cable configuration.

plugging all appropriately equipped devices into the hub. All devices on this smaller network can be included in a larger network by running a cable from one of the free ports in a hub to the hub of a larger network (see Figure 11-4). 5-port 10BASE-T hubs are very common and have become a standard item in most computer retail stores and mail-order computer supply establishments.

If only two network devices are to be connected to create a (very small) two-node Ethernet network, a single *crossover cable* can be used instead of a hub. Most 10BASE-T cables are *straight-through*, meaning that the corresponding pins on each connector are connected through the cable. Crossover cables, like RS-232 null-modem cables, connect inputs on one end of the cable to outputs on the other end (see Figure 11-5). In other words, Ethernet crossover cables have transmit data pins on one connector wired to receive data pins on the other connector, and vice versa.

12

TCP/IP Networking in Visual Basic®

Like everything else in Visual Basic®, networking is easy. Two ActiveX controls included with the Professional and Enterprise Editions of Visual Basic® provide the basic functionality for performing a wide variety of TCP/IP network communications. We'll describe one of these ActiveX controls in this chapter and present several examples of using it for laboratory applications.

THE WINSOCK ACTIVEX CONTROL

One of the two new controls for TCP/IP networking provided in the Professional and Enterprise editions of Visual Basic® is appropriately called the Winsock control. The Winsock control encapsulates the Winsock library as an ActiveX control. Using the control, it is possible to create sockets and perform TCP- and UDP-style communications over a TCP/IP network. Moving TCP/IP communications into an event-based framework is powerful. All important communications events are linked to event procedures of the control. The Winsock control makes TCP/IP network programming easy!

WINSOCK CONTROL PROPERTIES

You'll find that the properties of the Winsock control include exactly what is needed to perform TCP or UDP network communications. Table 12-1 describes several of the important Winsock control properties. You can set the communications protocol, the name or IP address of the remote machine, and the remote and local port to use when establishing the communication link.

Another important property of the Winsock control is called State. This property is read-only and available only at run time. It can be used to find out what the control is currently doing. Table 12-2 lists the predefined con-

TABLE 12-1. Important Winsock control properties.

Winsock Property	Description
RemoteHost	Sets/gets name or IP address of remote host machine
RemotePort	Sets/gets the port number on the remote host to which the connection should be made
LocalPort	The local port to be used by client or server for socket connection
Protocol	The IP protocol to use (TCP or UDP)
State	The current state of the control; identifies whether the control is closed, open, listening, connected, error, etc.

stants that can be used to decipher the State property value with a description of each. We'll use State in several examples to determine what to do next.

WINSOCK CONTROL METHODS

Table 12-3 describes several of the important methods of the Winsock control. The order that they appear in the table is typically the order in which they are used. All methods need not be used during network communications. It all depends on the function of the communicating program.

Winsock methods include the ability to listen for an incoming connection request and accept a request. The Listen and Accept methods are used for these purposes. The Connect method is the way to initiate a connection request. Exchanging data over a connection is accomplished with the SendData and GetData methods. The Close method closes a connection. We'll describe the use of these methods in more detail in coming sections.

TABLE 12-2. Winsock State property constants and descriptions.

Winsock State Property Constant	Value	Description
sckClosed	0	The socket is closed (default)
sckOpen	1	The socket is open
sckListening	2	The socket is listening
sckConnectionPending	3	A connection is pending
sckResolvingHost	4	A host is being resolved
sckHostResolved	5	Host is resolved
sckConnecting	6	A connection is being established
sckConnected	7	A connection has been established
sckClosing	8	The peer is closing the connection
sckError	9	An error has occurred

TABLE 12-3. Important Winsock control methods.

Winsock Method	Description
Connect	Executed by client to request a connection with server
Listen	Creates a socket and listens for client connection requests
Accept	Accepts a client connection request
SendData	Sends data to remote computer over network
GetData	Retrieves data sent by remote computer over network
Close	Closes an open socket

WINSOCK CONTROL EVENTS

As mentioned previously, the real power of the Winsock control comes when programming its events. As you can see from Table 12-4, it is possible to attach code to a request for a connection, the actual establishment of a connection, arrival of data, the closing of a connection, a communications error, and more.

In the next section we'll show how to use these events as well as the properties and methods of the Winsock control to establish and communicate over TCP/IP network connections using VB.

ELEMENTS OF VB TCP/IP CLIENTS AND SERVERS

In order to demonstrate how to use the Winsock control, let's create a simple TCP/IP client program and a simple server program. We'll do only what is necessary to create a network connection and transmit data over the connection in order to demonstrate the concepts.

Create a new project and add two TextBoxes, two CommandButtons, and a Winsock control to Form1 as in Figure 12-1.

TABLE 12-4. Important Winsock control events.

Winsock Event	Description
ConnectionRequest	Fired when a client requests a connection
Connect	Fired when a client connection has been established
DataArrival	Fired when data arrive on an open socket
Close	Fired when a connection is closed by the remote computer
Error	Fired when a communication error occurs

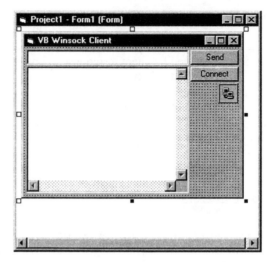

Figure 12-1. Sample TCP/IP client program form design.

Assign the following property values to your client program controls:

Object Type	Property	Value
Form	Name	frmClient
	Caption	VB Winsock Client
TextBox	Name	txtCommand
	Text	
TextBox	Name	txtResponse
	Text	
	MultiLine	True
	ScrollBars	3 - Both
CommandButton	Name	btnSend
	Caption	Send
CommandButton	Name	btnConnect
	Caption	Connect
Winsock	Name	sckClient

The first thing we need to do programmatically is to connect to a server. The code in the following click event procedure of the btnConnect CommandButton does just that.

```
Private Sub btnConnect_Click()
    ' Attempt to connect to a server
    ' TCP is the default protocol
    With sckClient
        If .State <> sckClosed Then .Close
        .RemoteHost = "127.0.0.1"
        .RemotePort = 1234
        .Connect
    End With
End Sub
```

First the state of the Winsock control is checked. If not already closed, the Close method is called, which assures that the socket is closed.

The RemoteHost and RemotePort properties are set. These properties can be assigned values at any point prior to a connection request. They can be initialized when the form is loaded, or at another time. But they must be assigned values before a connection is requested. The RemoteHost property can be assigned to either the remote computer host name or its IP address. For example, let's say that in company XYZ there is a computer named ABC. The host name of that computer is "abc.xyz.com." The RemoteHost property can be set to either "abc.xyz.com" or the IP address of the computer. In this example we are using the localhost IP address 127.0.0.1. By using this address we can run both the example client and server programs on the same machine, and we don't actually have to be connected to a network. If you have two networked Windows® computers, you can replace this address with the host name or IP address of the computer that will run the server program.

The port on which the server program will be listening is also set. The connection request will be made on that port. If the server is listening on a different port, the connection attempt will fail. For this example we arbitrarily chose the port number 1234. It is always safer to pick a server port number above 1023 since port numbers in the range 0 to 1023, are reserved for other purposes.

Once a connection is established, we can send data to the program at the other end of the network connection using the SendData Winsock method. In our example we will simply send the text typed into the txtClient TextBox followed by a carriage-return character. The following Click event procedure for the btnSend CommandButton accomplishes that task:

```
Private Sub btnSend_Click()
    ' Send data in the Text1 TextBox
    sckClient.SendData txtCommand.Text & vbCr
End Sub
```

Receiving data using Winsock works a lot like the MSComm control. When data arrive, an event is raised, and the Winsock's DataArrival event procedure is fired with the number of bytes waiting to be retrieved. To copy the data into a variable, use the GetData method. The first argument of GetData is the variable into which data on the port are placed. The second argument is optional and specifies the type of data to be retrieved. An optional third argument is also available for byte arrays and strings. It specifies the maximum length of the data to retrieve. In this case, if more data are available than specified in the maximum length parameter, any remaining data will be lost.

In the following DataArrival event procedure the GetData method retrieves all data into the strData string variable. This is then appended to the contents of the txtResponse TextBox.

```
Private Sub sckClient_DataArrival(ByVal bytesTotal As Long)
    ' Collect data from network connection
    Dim strData As String
    sckClient.GetData strData, vbString
    txtResponse.Text = txtResponse.Text & strData & vbCrLf
End Sub
```

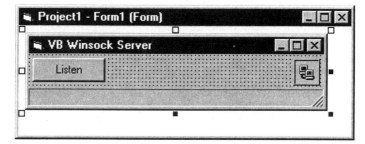

Figure 12-2. *Sample TCP/IP server program form design.*

That's all for the client program. You can find the source code for the client in \Part2\Ex4.vbp of the downloadable software.

Now let's create a simple server. Create a new project and add a CommandButton, a Winsock control, and a StatusBar control to Form1 (see Figure 12-2).

Assign the following property values to your server program controls:

Object Type	Property	Value
Form	Name	frmServer
	Caption	VB Winsock Server
CommandButton	Name	btnListen
	Caption	Listen
Winsock	Name	sckServer
StatusBar	Name	sbrMessage
	Style	1 - sbrSimple

When a program is designated as the server, it listens for a connection request on its assigned port. To cause a program to begin listening for a connection, it is only necessary to set the LocalPort property of the Winsock control and invoke the Listen method. To demonstrate how this is done, in our server we will manually initiate listening from the btnListen CommandButton Click event procedure. The following Click event procedure sets the server port to 1234, and then calls the Listen method to initiate listening. To finish, we put a message in the status bar indicating that listening has been initiated. Listening also can be initiated from the Load event procedure of the main form so that it happens automatically upon startup.

```
Private Sub btnListen_Click()
    ' Initialize the port on which to listen
    sckServer.LocalPort = 1234

    ' Start listening for a client connection request
    sckServer.Listen
    sbrMessage.SimpleText = "Listening ..."
End Sub
```

When a client program executes the Connect method with a Server port number, the listening server's ConnectionRequest event procedure is executed. You can choose to accept the connection in the ConnectionRequest event procedure, or ignore the request. To accept the request, execute the server Winsock control's Accept method with the requestID argument passed to the ConnectionRequest event procedure.

The following ConnectionRequest event procedure first assures that the server Winsock control is closed by checking the State property of the control, then invoking the Close method if necessary. The connection is accepted by invoking the Accept method. A message is placed in the StatusBar before exiting the procedure.

```
Private Sub sckServer_ConnectionRequest(ByVal requestID As Long)
    ' Close the socket if not already closed.
    If sckServer.State <> sckClosed Then sckServer.Close

    ' Accept the connection request
    sckServer.Accept requestID
    sbrMessage.SimpleText = "Connection accepted"
End Sub
```

Receiving and sending data in the server is identical to the client. In this example, we'll just echo anything sent to the server back to the client. The following DataArrival event procedure accomplishes that.

```
Private Sub sckServer_DataArrival(ByVal bytesTotal As Long)
    ' Collect data from network connection
    Dim strData As String
    sckServer.GetData strData, vbString
    sbrMessage.SimpleText = "Received: " & strData

    ' Echo back data sent.
    sckServer.SendData strData
End Sub
```

When the client closes the network connection, the Close event procedure of the server Winsock control is fired. We can use this event to reinitiate listening in case another connection request is made. In the following Close event procedure, the closed state of the server Winsock control is checked, and listening is initiated again by firing the Click event procedure of the btnListen CommandButton.

```
Private Sub sckServer_Close()
    ' Make sure the connection is closed
    If sckServer.State <> sckClosed Then sckServer.Close

    ' Begin listening for another connection
    btnListen_Click
End Sub
```

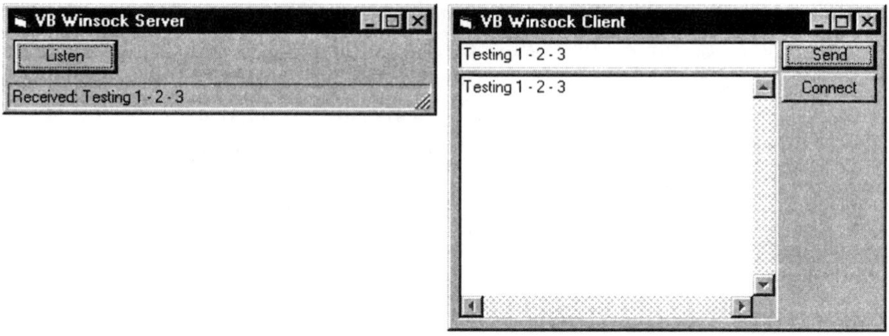

Figure 12-3. The VB TCP/IP client and server programs in action.

To test our new client and server programs, first make sure that TCP/IP networking is set up on your computer. It is not necessary that the computer be connected to a network as long as the localhost IP address is used. Then do the following.

1. Run your server program on the appropriate computer.
2. Click "Listen" to start the server listening to its port.
3. Run your client program on the appropriate computer.
4. Click "Connect" to request a connection with the server. When the connection is established, you'll see the "Connection accepted" message in the server StatusBar.
5. Type a message into the client program's upper TextBox and click "Send." You'll see the message appear in the server StatusBar. The server will then echo your message back to the client and add it to the lower TextBox.
6. Repeat the process as many times as you like.
7. Close the client program to see the server resume listening. You'll see the "Listening . . ." message reappear in the server StatusBar.

That's all there is to it! Figure 12-3 shows the two programs in action. You can find the source code for the server in \Part2\Ex5.vbp of the downloadable software.

MULTICLIENT SERVERS

The server program in the previous example was capable of accepting only a single connection. It was designed to stop listening just before it accepted a connection request. Only after an existing connection is closed can another connection be established. When you are using this technique for controlling an instrument, that's probably exactly what you want.

In a different application you may have a program controlling a long experiment that is continuously collecting and storing data. For example, you may be measuring and storing temperature or pressure data for several days. You can remotely monitor the experiment over a network by building a simple server into your controller. When you connect to the server with your client program, the server accepts the connection and immediately begins mirroring data collected to your client program, in real time.

You can extend this capability to multiple-client programs simultaneously by building a multiclient server. A multiclient server can support multiple simultaneous connections. Most Internet network services, such as E-mail and web servers, are actually multiclient server programs. Your multiclient server-enabled controller can broadcast collected data to all connected clients.

When a connection to a multiclient server is requested, the listening socket does not accept the connection. Instead, another socket is created and directed to accept the connection on a randomly chosen unused port. This way the listening socket can continue to listen for additional connection requests on the same port. We can accomplish this in VB using control arrays. If we change the sckServer Winsock control into a control array, we can easily load, unload, and otherwise track currently loaded Winsock controls.

Let's build a multiclient server program that generates random data every second in order to simulate data collection. Every time a new data point is generated, it will be broadcast to all connected clients.

In a manner similar to the previous project, create a new project and add a CommandButton, a Winsock control, and a StatusBar control to Form1. Also add a Timer control to the Form (see Figure 12-4). Assign the following property values to the new controls.

Object Type	Property	Value
Form	Name	frmServer
	Caption	VB Multiclient Winsock Server
CommandButton	Name	btnListen
	Caption	Listen
Winsock	Name	sckServer
	Index	0
StatusBar	Name	sbrMessage
	Style	1 - sbrSimple
Timer	Name	tmrData
	Interval	1000

It is particularly important that the sckServer Winsock control Index property get the value of 0. This makes it into a control array.

In the declarations section of the frmServer Form we will define a constant that sets the maximum number of connections allowed. This will help prevent the server from becoming overloaded with too many remote connections.

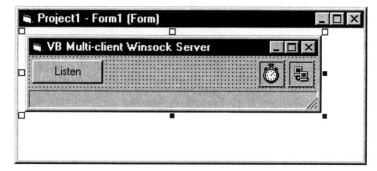

Figure 12-4. Sample TCP/IP multiclient server program form design.

```
' Set the maximum number of allowable connections/controls
Const mConMaxConnections As Integer = 3
```

The Click event procedure of the btnListen button is different from the previous example only in that an index is used to specify the listening Winsock control in the array. We define the Winsock control with an index value of 0 to be the listening control.

```
Private Sub btnListen_Click()
    ' Initialize the port on which to listen
    sckServer(0).LocalPort = 1234

    ' Start listening for a client connection request
    sckServer(0).Listen
    sbrMessage.SimpleText = "Listening ..."
End Sub
```

The DataArrival event procedure also differs from the previous example primarily by the use of an index on the sckServer Winsock control reference. Additionally, we check if data are arriving on the listening socket with an index value of 0. If so, we exit the procedure. Also, when data do arrive on a socket other than the listening socket, we indicate which socket received data in the StatusBar message and echo it back to the same client that sent it.

```
Private Sub sckServer_DataArrival(Index As Integer, ByVal bytesTotal As Long)
    ' Collect data from network connection
    Dim strData As String

    ' Exit if this is the listening socket.
    If Index = 0 Then Exit Sub

    ' Collect data
    sckServer(Index).GetData strData, vbString
    sbrMessage.SimpleText = "Socket " & CStr(Index) & " received: " & strData

    ' Echo back data sent.
    sckServer(Index).SendData strData
End Sub
```

The main difference between the multiclient server and the previous single-client server comes in the ConnectionRequest event procedure listed below. When a connection is requested, the index of the Winsock control on which the request was made is first checked. If it is not the listening socket (index 0), the procedure exits. An available spot in the sckServer Winsock control array is then identified by incrementing the variable intIndex up from an initial value of 1 until an index value is found for which there is no corresponding control in the array. If the index value is greater than the maximum number of allowable connections, then the procedure exits. Otherwise, a new Winsock control is loaded into the sckServer control array at the available location. This new control is then directed to accept the incoming connection request. The user is notified of the accepted connection with a message placed in the StatusBar.

```
Private Sub sckServer_ConnectionRequest(Index As Integer, ByVal requestID As Long)
    ' Accept the connection on the next socket control in the control array
    Dim I As Integer, intIndex As Integer, strMsg As String, sck As Winsock

    ' Ignore request if not the server socket.
    If Index <> 0 Then Exit Sub

    ' Look for an available socket control index
    intIndex = 1
    For Each sck In sckServer
        ' Skip index 0 as this is the listening socket
        If sck.Index > 0 Then
            If intIndex < sck.Index Then Exit For
            intIndex = intIndex + 1
        End If
    Next sck

    ' If exceeded the maximum number of controls then exit.
    If intIndex > mConMaxConnections Then Exit Sub

    ' Load new control and accept connection
    Load sckServer(intIndex)
    sckServer(intIndex).LocalPort = 0
    sckServer(intIndex).Accept requestID
    ' Indicate status
    sbrMessage.SimpleText = "Socket " & CStr(intIndex) & " accepted a connection"

End Sub
```

In the Close event procedure, not only do we make sure that the connection is closed, but we unload the Winsock control in order to free up the spot for another control to be loaded after a future connection request. Unlike the previous server example, listening does not have to be re-established, since the listening socket never closed.

```
Private Sub sckServer_Close(Index As Integer)

    ' If not the listening socket then ...
    If Index > 0 Then
        ' Make sure the connection is closed
        If sckServer(Index).State <> sckClosed Then sckServer(Index).Close
        ' Unload the control
        Unload sckServer(Index)
        sbrMessage.SimpleText = "Socket " & CStr(Index) & " - Connection closed"
    End If

End Sub
```

In this example a Timer control was added and set to fire every second. As you can see in the listing below, when the tmrData Timer fires, a random number is generated and sent to client programs at the other end of all open connections.

```
Private Sub tmrData_Timer()
    ' Broadcast data to all connected clients
    Dim sngData As Single, sck As Winsock

    sngData = Rnd          ' Generate a random number
    For Each sck In sckServer
        ' Send the data to all but the listening socket
        If sck.Index > 0 Then
            sck.SendData CStr(sngData) & vbCr
            DoEvents     ' Allow all clients to get data
        End If
    Next sck
End Sub
```

Source code for the multiclient server can be found in \Part2\Ex6.vbp of the code available online.

We can use the client program developed in Example 4 to test our new multi-client server. To give it a try, do the following:

1. Start up the multiclient server program on your server computer and click "Listen" to initiate listening on port 1234.
2. If you haven't already done so, compile the client program from Example 4 to an executable. Run two or three instances of client program executable on one or more networked client computers.
3. Click "Connect" on each instance of the client program.

In Figure 12-5 we see the multiclient server communicating with three clients. The client programs were started approximately two seconds apart, since the number of data points displayed in each TextBox differs by two and data are generated at a rate of one point per second. Instead of adding each point to a TextBox, it is not hard to imagine adding the point to a strip chart on the client program interface instead. The result would be a program capable

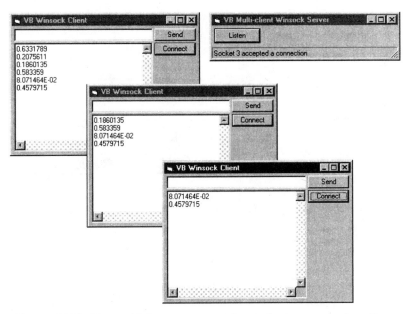

Figure 12-5. The multiclient server and three client programs in action.

of monitoring and graphically displaying the status of an instrument that is being controlled at a remote location.

A VI WINSOCK COMMANDER

When describing the Virtual Instrument in Chapter 6, we mentioned that it is capable of accepting commands over a TCP/IP network connection. We can use the same client program developed in Example 4 to control the VI. Here's how to do it.

1. Start up the VI by running the executable program Vi.exe, or load and run the project \Part2\Vi\Vi.vbp on your server computer.

Figure 12-6. The VI Network Settings dialog.

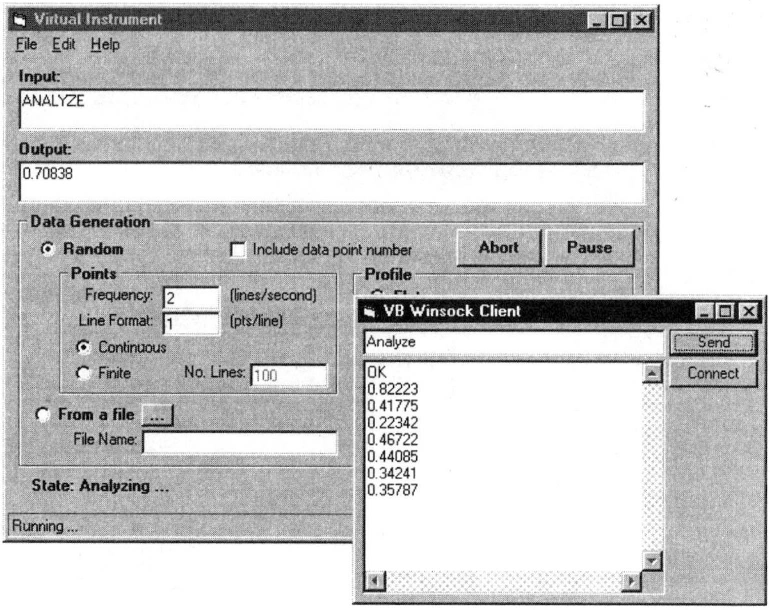

Figure 12-7. The VI under control over a network connection.

2. Select the Network Settings option from the Edit menu to display the Network Settings dialog box. Enter the port number 1234 and make sure the network connection CheckBox is checked. Click "OK" to cause the VI to begin listening on the port (see Figure 12-6).

3. Turn the VI on by clicking "ON."

4. Run the Example 4 executable or load and run the project \Part2\Ex4\Ex4.vbp on a networked client computer.

5. Establish the connection by clicking "Connect" on the client program.

6. Type the command "Analyze" into the client program's upper TextBox and click "Send."

7. To stop the VI from sending data, enter "Abort" into the client program's upper TextBox and click "Send."

The result is shown in Figure 12-7.

13

File Communications

It is not uncommon to be confronted with the need to collect data automatically from a laboratory instrument that offers no capability for remote communications. The only way the instrument can exchange data is by writing to a file, and possibly reading from a file. With careful planning, it is possible to use this capability to develop communication channels with the instrument through files.

A method for successfully implementing a file communications strategy will heavily depend on the details of the situation. The operating system in use and the file access features of the instrument will dictate the extent to which file communications is possible. With creativity and a good understanding of how things work, you will be surprised at what is possible.

A FILE COMMUNICATIONS CLASS

In this section we'll present one approach to communicating through files. The details will be encapsulated in a VB class called *clsFileComm*. The class is designed for bidirectional communications through two files. One file is used for communications in one direction, and a second file for communications in the opposite direction. The two files will be defined as having opposite roles in each program, so the output file in one program will be the input file in the other program. The opposite is the case for the second file. When data are to be sent from one program to the other, the sending program will write the data to its output file. When requested, the receiving program will query its input file (the same file) to see if there are new data to be read. Source for the clsFileComm class can be found in the folder \FileComm of the software distribution.

A signaling mechanism must be devised to indicate that new data exist in a file and therefore should be read by the receiving program. We use an attribute of a file to accomplish this. Windows® files can be marked as Normal, Read Only, Hidden, System, or Archive. VB provides two statements for manipulating the attributes of a file. They are SetAttr and GetAttr. We decided to use the file's Archive attribute to indicate the existence of new data in a file. This was the most compelling choice, since when a file's Archive attribute is set, it implies that the file has been changed since the last time it was backed up. In our case, when the Archive attribute is set it implies that the file has been changed since the last time the receiving program read it. After the receiving program reads the data, it turns the file's Archive attribute off, indicating that the data have been read.

The clsFileComm file communications class is simple. It contains three private variables, the appropriate Property procedures to modify these variables, and two class procedures. The private variables and associated Property procedures are given in the following listing. To create a new clsFileComm class, open a new VB project and add a new class module. Enter all the code listed in this section.

```
Option Explicit
Private mStrOutFile As String    ' Output channel file
Private mStrInFile As String     ' Input channel file
Private mBlnCancel As Boolean    ' True if to cancel an operation

Public Property Let OutFile(strFile As String)
    ' Set the output file name.
    mStrOutFile = strFile
End Property

Public Property Get OutFile() As String
    ' Return the output file.
    OutFile = mStrOutFile
End Property

Public Property Let InFile(strFile As String)
    ' Set the input file name.
    mStrInFile = strFile
End Property

Public Property Get InFile() As String
    ' Return the input file.
    InFile = mStrInFile
End Property

Public Property Let Cancel(blnCancel As Boolean)
    ' Set the local variable indicating that the current operation be cancelled.
    mBlnCancel = blnCancel
End Property
```

The variables mStrOutFile and mStrInFile hold the names of the output and input files to be used for file communications. They are changed using the InFile and OutFile Property procedures. The variable mBlnCancel can be set to True to stop a long read or write that has not terminated. It is set using the Cancel Property procedure.

The two class procedures are called SendData and GetData. As their name implies, they are used to send data by writing to an output file, and to read new data from an input file. Following is a listing of the SendData procedure with each line numbered for convenient reference. Line numbers are not part of the source code. If you are entering this code into VB, leave line numbers out.

```
1.   Public Sub SendData(strData As String)
2.       ' Send data to the output file.
3.       Dim intFileNum As Integer

4.       On Error GoTo SendDataErrorHandler

5.       ' If no output file specified then exit.
6.       If Trim$(mStrOutFile) = "" Then Exit Sub

7.       ' Attempt to open the file locked
8.       intFileNum = FreeFile

9.       ' If the data have been read (archive bit turned off),
10.      ' open the file for Output in order to overwrite existing contents.
11.      ' Otherwise, append data to the file.
12.      mBlnCancel = False
13.  TryToOpenAgain:

14.      If (GetAttr(mStrOutFile) And vbArchive) = 0 Then
15.          Open mStrOutFile For Output Lock Read Write As #intFileNum
16.      Else
17.          Open mStrOutFile For Append Lock Read Write As #intFileNum
18.      End If

19.      Print #intFileNum, strData & vbCr;
20.      Close #intFileNum

21.      ' The archive bit is automatically set,
         ' indicating the file contains new data.
22.      'SetAttr mStrOutFile, vbArchive

23.      Exit Sub
24.  '_____
25.  SendDataErrorHandler:

26.      Select Case Err.Number
27.      Case 53      ' File not found.  Create it and resume.
28.          Open mStrOutFile For Output As #intFileNum
29.          Close intFileNum
30.          Resume
31.      Case 70      ' If the file is locked, release the processor and try again.
32.          DoEvents
33.          ' Check if cancelled
34.          If mBlnCancel = True Then
35.              mBlnCancel = False
36.              Exit Sub
37.          End If
38.          Resume TryToOpenAgain
39.      Case Else
40.          MsgBox "Error (SendData) " & CStr(Err.Number) & ": " & Err.Description
41.      End Select

42.  End Sub
```

The SendData procedure takes a string argument containing the data that are to be communicated through a file. In line 4 we set up the error handler. Lines 5 and 6 check that an output file has been set. If not, the procedure exits. Line 8 gets a free file number. In line 12 the private cancel variable is turned off prior to beginning the sending process. Lines 14 through 18 attempt to open the output file. If the file's Archive attribute is off, the output file is opened for Output. This causes any data in the file to be erased when new data are written. This is exactly what we want, since the receiving program has already read the data in the output file. When Archive is on, we open the file for Append so that new data written to the file do not overwrite data not yet read by the receiving program.

The file is only opened if it can be locked for Read and Write access. An attempt to open the file will fail if another program already has the file open. If the open attempt fails, the procedure will jump to the error handler beginning at line 25. In the case of a "File Not Found" error, a new file is created, and the open attempt is tried again. If the file is currently locked, first the processor is released to keep the application responsive. If the process has not been cancelled, the procedure jumps back to the line labeled TryToOpenAgain, and the attempt is repeated. If the open fails again, the whole process is repeated. This will continue until the output file is opened or the process is cancelled. When the open attempt succeeds, lines 19 and 20 write the data to the file. Line 22 is commented out, but indicates how to set the Archive attribute. Writing new data to a file is all that is needed to set the file's Archive attribute.

The complementary class procedure called GetData is contained in the following listing. Each line is also numbered for convenient referencing. Line numbers are not part of the source code.

```
1.  Public Sub GetData(strData As String)
2.      ' Get data from the input file.
3.      Dim intFileNum As Integer, lngFileLen As Long

4.      On Error GoTo GetDataErrorHandler

5.      ' If no input file specified then exit.
6.      If Trim$(mStrInFile) = "" Then Exit Sub

7.      ' Exit if archive bit is not set, implying file contains no new data.
8.      If (GetAttr(mStrInFile) And vbArchive) = 0 Then Exit Sub
9.   ' Another way to know that the file has changed is to look at
     ' its date and time.
10.  '    Dim datTmp As Date
11.  '    Static datFile As Date
12.  '    datTmp = FileDateTime(mStrInFile)
13.  '    If datTmp <= datFile Then Exit Sub
14.  '    datFile = datTmp        ' Update the latest file date-time stamp
15.      ' Attempt to open the file locked and read all data.
16.      strData = ""             ' Clear data variable
17.      intFileNum = FreeFile
18.      Open mStrInFile For Input Lock Read Write As #intFileNum
```

```
19.       lngFileLen = LOF(intFileNum)
20.       If lngFileLen > 0& Then strData = Input(lngFileLen, #intFileNum)
21.       Close #intFileNum

22.       ' Clear archive bit.
23.       SetAttr mStrInFile, vbNormal

24.       Exit Sub
25. '_____
26. GetDataErrorHandler:

27.       Select Case Err.Number
28.       Case 53      ' If File Not Found, then exit.
29.       Case 70      ' If the file is locked, release the processor
                       ' and try again.
30.           DoEvents
31.           ' Check if cancelled
32.           If mBlnCancel = True Then
33.               mBlnCancel = False
34.               Exit Sub
35.           End If
36.           Resume
37.       Case Else
38.           MsgBox "Error (GetData) " & CStr(Err.Number) & ": " & Err.Description
39.       End Select

40. End Sub
```

GetData will read an entire input file and set the string argument to the contents of the file. In line 4 the error handler is set up. Line 5 exits the procedure if no input file name has been specified. Line 8 looks at the Archive attribute of the input file. If it is not set, the procedure exits, since there are no new data in the file. Lines 10 through 14 are commented out. They were included to demonstrate another way to check if new data exist in a file using the file date and time. If the file date-time approach was being used, the static variable datFile would always hold the last date and time the file was read. When the sending program updated the file, its date and time would also be updated. Line 16 clears the variable to get new data. Line 17 gets a free file number. In line 18 the input file is opened for Input. As with output, an attempt is made to lock the file for Read and Write. If the open attempt fails, the procedure jumps to the error handler starting at line 26. If the error occurred due to the file's not being found, the procedure exits. If the file is locked, the procedure behaves as in SendData. The processor is first released. If not cancelled, the procedure tries to open the file again by resuming with the statement on which the error occurs. This continues until the file can be opened or the process is cancelled. Line 19 gets the length of the file using VB's LOF function. In line 20 the entire contents of the file is read and assigned to the passed string variable. Before exiting, the file is closed in line 21, and the Archive attribute is turned off in line 23.

The resulting class is a handy utility for communicating through files. It encapsulates all the details for accomplishing the basic communications task.

It is very easy to use. Once an instance of the clsFileComm class is created and the input and output file names set, it is only necessary to call SetData to send data and GetData to receive data. The communications files are automatically created if they do not already exist.

COMMUNICATING THROUGH FILES

Let's build an example program that uses our clsFileComm File Communications class. Source code for the following example can be found in the folder \Part2\Ex7 of the code available online.

Create a new VB project and add the clsFileComm class file using the Project | Add File menu option from your Visual Basic® IDE interface. You can also make a local copy of the class file and add that to your project. Add two TextBoxes, four CommandButtons, and a CommonDialog control to Form1 (See Figure 13-1). Make sure that the CommonDialog control is visible in your Toolbox by selecting the "Microsoft Common Dialog Control" option from the Components Dialog, which can be viewed using the Project | Components menu option of the VB IDE. Set the following control properties:

Object Type	Property	Value
Form	Name	frmFileComm
	Caption	File Communications
TextBox	Name	txtOut
	Text	
TextBox	Name	txtIn
	Text	
CommandButton	Name	btnSetInput
	Caption	Set Input
CommandButton	Name	btnSetOutput
	Caption	Set Output
CommandButton	Name	btnSend
	Caption	Send
CommandButton	Name	btnReceive
	Caption	Receive
CommonDialog	Name	cdlFile
	CancelError	True

The btnSetInput and btnSetOutput CommandButtons are used to select the input and output files through which communications will take place. Text entered into the txtOut TextBox will be sent to the other communicating program. Sending is initiated by clicking the btnSend CommandButton. The txtIn TextBox will display a received message.

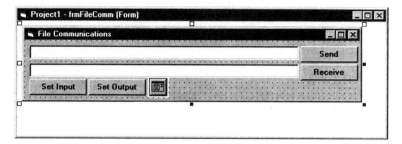

Figure 13-1. Form design for the File Communications example.

Add the following code to the declarations section of the frmFileComm Form. Here we create a new instance of the clsFileComm class and assign it to the newly declared mFileComm variable.

```
Option Explicit

' Instance of file communications class
Private mFileComm As New clsFileComm
```

The Click events of the btnSetInput and btnSetOutput CommandButtons set the names of the input and output files. The cdlFile CommonDialog is used to browse the file hierarchy to either choose existing files or enter the names of new ones. The following listing implements the Click event procedures of the two CommandButtons.

```
Private Sub btnSetInput_Click()
    ' Set the input file.
    On Error GoTo btnSetInput_ClickErrorHandler

    With cdlFile
        .filename = mFileComm.InFile
        .DialogTitle = "Please enter the input file for communications"
        .Filter = "All Files (*.*)|*.*"
        .ShowOpen
        mFileComm.InFile = .filename
    End With

    Exit Sub
'_____
btnSetInput_ClickErrorHandler:
    Select Case Err.Number
    Case cdlCancel
        ' Do nothing if cancelled
    Case Else
        MsgBox "Error (frmFileComm - btnSetInput) " & _
                    CStr(Err.Number) & ": " & Err.Description
    End Select
End Sub
```

```
Private Sub btnSetOutput_Click()
    ' Set the output file.
    On Error GoTo btnSetOutput_ClickErrorHandler

    With cdlFile
        .filename = mFileComm.OutFile
        .DialogTitle = "Please enter the output file for communications"
        .Filter = "All Files (*.*)|*.*"
        .ShowOpen
        mFileComm.OutFile = .filename
    End With

    Exit Sub
'_____
btnSetOutput_ClickErrorHandler:
    Select Case Err.Number
    Case cdlCancel
        ' Do nothing if cancelled
    Case Else
        MsgBox "Error (frmFileComm - btnSetOutput) " & _
                        CStr(Err.Number) & ": " & Err.Description
    End Select
End Sub
```

To send data, we simply use the SendData procedure of the clsFileComm class. The btnSend CommandButton Click event passes the contents of the txtOut TextBox to the SendData procedure of our clsFileComm class instance called mFileComm.

```
Private Sub btnSend_Click()
    ' Send data to the output file.
    mFileComm.SendData txtOut.Text
End Sub
```

We need to initiate the reading of any data sent to a file to be read by the receiving program manually. The GetData method of our mFileComm object is invoked by the btnReceive CommandButton. This method looks for and reads new data from the input file. The string returned is copied into the txtIn TextBox. When no data have been communicated, an empty string is returned, and the TextBox will be cleared.

```
Private Sub btnReceive_Click()
    ' Get data from the communications file.
    Dim strData As String

    mFileComm.GetData strData
    txtIn.Text = strData

End Sub
```

When all the code has been entered, compile the program to an executable, and run two instances of the executable file. The input and output communication files must be assigned for each program. Click "Set Input" on one

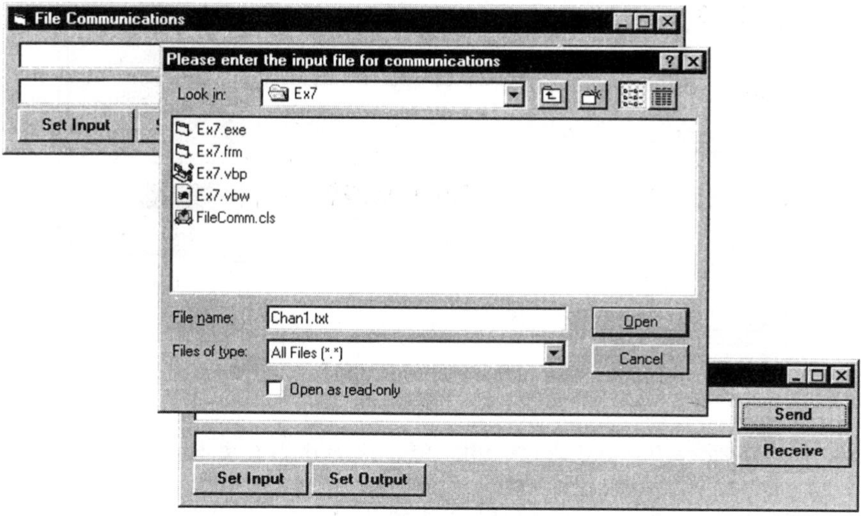

Figure 13-2. *Entering communication file names.*

program and set its input file name to "Chan1.txt" (see Figure 13-2). Click "Set Output" of the same program and set its output file name to "Chan2.txt." Make the complementary assignment to the other example program. Set its input file name to "Chan2.txt" and its output file name to "Chan1.txt." When the assignments are made, you're ready to begin communicating.

Type a message into the txtIn TextBox of one of the programs and click "Send." Go to the other program and click "Receive." The message sent from the first program is received by the second program and displayed in the txtOut TextBox. Try the process in both directions. Send multiple messages from one program before receiving it by the other. All messages will be received at once. Attempt to receive a message before it is sent. An empty string will be returned. Figure 13-3 displays the two programs communicating through files.

WRAPPING UP

In Part 2 we studied four ways to communicate using Visual Basic®. We looked at Dynamic Data Exchange, RS-232 communications, TCP/IP networking, and File Communications. We also created several sample VB programs that employed each of the methods of communication. These techniques and sample programs will be the basis for much of what we will do in Part 3.

It is important to note that there are several other methods of communication available to Visual Basic® that are not covered here. One popular instrument communications standard is IEEE-488, sometimes called the *General*

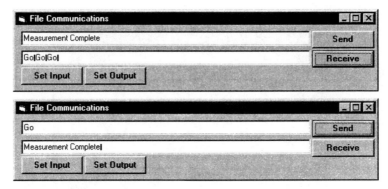

Figure 13-3. File communications in action.

Purpose Interface Bus (GPIB). Unlike RS-232, which transfers data in a serial stream of bits, IEEE-488 employs a high-speed parallel method for data transfer. Data are moved over the IEEE-488 cable 8 bits at a time. Data rates can reach 1 megabyte per second. Communication over an IEEE-488 connection requires a third-party ActiveX control or Dynamic Link Library (DLL) that is specially designed for this purpose. The vendor of your third-party IEEE-488 communication software will provide instructions on how to use it to establish a connection and transfer data.

Several proprietary communication techniques are also available. Fortunately, the flexibility that Visual Basic® provides when interacting with other software brings most communication techniques within our reach. Moreover, instrument vendors are increasingly adopting Microsoft®'s ActiveX standard, producing software modules that can easily be accessed from within Visual Basic®.

PART

3

Device Control and Data Handling

In this section we'll take what we've learned in Part 2 and build on it to produce programs that perform robust device control and data handling. It is important to understand the distinction we make between communication and control. When communicating we move data from place to place over a connection of some type. Using this definition, everything we did in Part 2 falls into the category of communications. By control we are referring to the *coordination of a series of events by interpreting an incoming stream of data from an external device or program and generating an outgoing stream of data that triggers events in a desired fashion.* Communications is the basis upon which control is built. Still, creating robust controllers requires more than reliable communications.

In this part of the book we will review several of the topics that are required for building robust controllers. An informal definition of a robust controller is one that doesn't simply break when a series of events occurs that has never before been encountered. Problems are handled gracefully when they occur. For example, what happens when a message is received that was not expected, or measurements are received in a format that is unusual, but perfectly valid? A robust controller tries to interpret the incoming stream, informs the user when a problem occurs, and points out exactly where the problem occurred and why.

Robust controllers also "know" the behavior of the controlled device or program. They encapsulate a model of the way a controlled entity operates. With this information, it is possible to follow its actions and respond in an appropriate manner.

The result is fantastic! It can be exhilarating when you watch your controller handle difficult situations successfully, and when a problem does occur, error messages are meaningful! Often you can isolate the problem immediately and fix it on the spot. This translates into increased uptime and a real sense of satisfaction.

Before we begin writing controllers, we need to review a few fundamental concepts from the field of Computer Science, and study how they are implemented in Visual Basic®.

14

Multithreading

MULTITASKING VERSUS MULTITHREADING

Microsoft® Windows NT® and UNIX are preemptive multitasking operating systems; each can run several programs or *processes* simultaneously, or at least give the appearance that this is the case by dividing processor time among them. Processes require a fair amount of overhead. Each new process has its own memory space and other resources, but what if you want several things to occur simultaneously within the same process? How can you easily share process resources among simultaneously executing operations? The answer is with *multiple threads*. In other words, by using *multithreading*.

THREADS

Threads are separate simultaneous streams of execution that share resources. A single thread executes one thing at a time, and waits for each to finish before starting the next (see Figure 14-1). When multiple threads exist in a process, they are like processes in that they run separately and simultaneously. They are unlike processes in that they do not incur the same sort of overhead required by a separate process. Instead, threads running in the same process share many resources. The sharing of resources is exactly what makes multithreading so much harder to manage than multitasking. It may be possible for one thread to delete some shared data that another thread is accessing. The result can be catastrophic.

Figure 14-2 illustrates an example where a single process includes multiple simultaneously executing threads. Each thread is indicated with a dotted line. The main thread is on the left of the diagram. It creates several additional threads, which are labeled with a description of their function. Figure 14-2

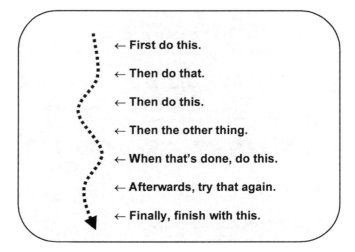

Figure 14-1. A single-threaded process.

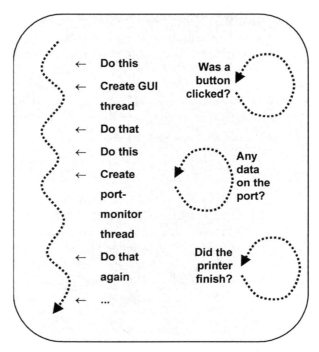

Figure 14-2. A multithreaded process.

demonstrates how multiple threads are often used within the same process. Using a separate thread to monitor the user interface, a communications port, or a print job, can make a program more responsive while utilizing resources more effectively.

15

Multithreading in Visual Basic®

Access to the multithreading capability of an operating system is available through several programming languages like C++ or Java. Visual Basic® does not offer the same flexibility for creating and managing threads that is available in C++ or Java, and for good reason. Writing multithreaded applications can be difficult and error-prone. This is in direct conflict with the philosophy behind Visual Basic® programming—to make Windows® programming easy.

APARTMENT-MODEL THREADING

To address this apparent conflict, Microsoft® has created what is called *apartment-model threading* in Visual Basic®. Apartment-model threading eliminates potential difficulties by executing each thread in a separate "apartment" with a separate copy of global data. Communication between threads is accomplished through a mechanism that provides synchronization called *cross-thread marshaling*. What can be run in separate apartments is constrained, but VB is still evolving. A detailed account of apartment-model threading is beyond the scope of this book. Refer to the documentation provided with Visual Basic® and Microsoft®'s web site (www.microsoft.com) for further details.

VISUAL BASIC® AND THE SINGLE THREAD

In a single VB project, the default behavior is for all your Visual Basic® code to run on a single thread. If you are executing a long procedure and trigger another one through an event, the second event procedure won't begin until the first procedure has finished. This is a critical concept to understand, especially when building controller programs.

You can improve the situation somewhat through the use of a builtin VB function called *DoEvents*. When invoked, DoEvents will yield execution so that

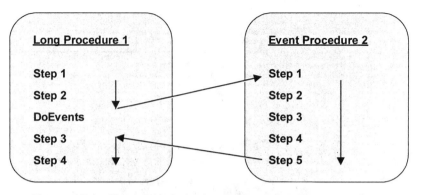

Figure 15-1. Flow of control using DoEvents in a long procedure.

the processor can handle other events that are waiting for the processor. If you periodically call DoEvents during the execution of a long procedure, you give the operating system the opportunity to handle events that are pending. This makes it possible for your user interface to respond and other waiting events to be processed. The net result is that your long process will take even longer to complete since it does not run while other events are being processed, but your application will appear to behave better. If you want to provide users of your software with the option of canceling long procedures, you must periodically call DoEvents so that the Click event procedure of your cancel button is processed. Figure 15-1 illustrates this concept. The long procedure on the left yields the processor to the event procedure on the right. The long procedure does not continue until the event procedure is complete.

Let's create a simple program that demonstrates this concept. Create a new project and add to Form1 a CommandButton, a Timer, two TextBoxes, and two Labels (see Figure 15-2). You can find the source code in \Part3\Ex1 of the downloadable software.

Assign the following property values to the new controls:

Object Type	Property	Value
Form	Name	frmThreadDemo
	Caption	VB Thread Demo
CommandButton	Name	btnTask2
	Caption	Run Task 2
Timer	Name	tmrTask1
	Interval	1000
TextBox	Name	txtOutput1
	Text	
TextBox	Name	txtOutput2
	Text	
Label	Name	lblTask1
	Caption	Task 1
Label	Name	lblTask2
	Caption	Task 2

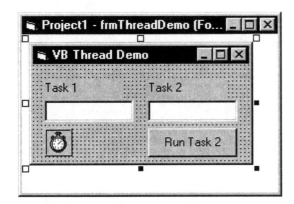

Figure 15-2. *VB single-thread demonstration form design.*

The tmrTask1 Timer control will fire every 1000 milliseconds. When it does, it runs a long procedure, which we'll define as a loop that simply counts from 1 to 10,000. DoEvents is called each time through the loop to process any other pending events. The following Timer event procedure implements the long procedure.

```
Private Sub tmrTask1_Timer()
    Dim I As Integer

    ' Count up to 10000
    For I = 1 To 10000
        txtOutput1.Text = CStr(I)
        DoEvents                    ' Release the processor
    Next I
End Sub
```

The second process is shorter and will be triggered by the btnTask2 CommandButton. The following Click event procedure simply counts from 1 to 500. Within the procedure we call the Refresh method of the TextBox in order to cause its display to update to reflect the changing Text property value. Refresh does not release the processor. It only updates the associated control display. If Refresh is not called from within the loop, you would not see the txtTask2 TextBox update until DoEvents was called again from the Timer event procedure. As a result, the only number you would ever see displayed in the txtTask2 TextBox would be 500.

```
Private Sub btnTask2_Click()
    Dim I As Integer

    ' Count up to 500
    For I = 1 To 500
        txtOutput2.Text = CStr(I)
        txtOutput2.Refresh          ' Refresh the display ...
    Next I                          ' but do not release the processor

End Sub
```

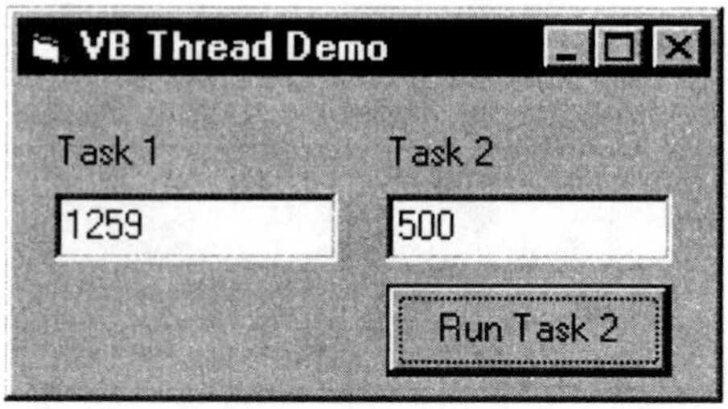

Figure 15-3. *The VB single-thread demo program in action.*

Run the project and wait until you see the Timer trigger its first count from 1 to 10,000. While it's counting, click "Run Task 2." You will see the Timer event procedure stop while the btnTask2 CommandButton Click event procedure runs to completion. When finished, the Timer event procedure will continue counting (see Figure 15-3).

When first confronted with the Timer control, it is not unusual to assume that when the Timer times out, it runs its Timer event procedure on a separate thread. As you can see by the previous example, this is not the case. Unless you create multiple VB executables, or make use of some of the new multithreading features, a single thread executes all the code you ever write. For example, when the OnComm event of the MSComm control fires, it will not execute until the processor is available. If you have a long procedure running that is not periodically calling DoEvents, data coming in to the RS-232 port will not be processed until the long procedure finishes. This is also true for the ConnectionRequest and DataArrival event procedures of the Winsock control. Again, it is important to understand this reality of programming in VB, and to keep it in mind as you move forward.

CHAPTER

16

Concepts of State

A program that controls a device must encapsulate a model of how that device behaves. Without such a model the controller would not know what to expect in response to an issued command. For example, if an instrument is instructed to take a series of ten measurements, the controller will be expecting the ten data values corresponding to the measurements or possibly one of a set of error messages. The expectation of one of several possible responses after a command is issued is part of an encapsulated model of the instrument that is programmed within the controller. If something other than expected is returned, then the controller knows that a serious failure has occurred and the user can be notified. For example, an instrument failure or a faulty connection can cause unexpected or incomplete responses. Of course, the other possibility is that the controller's encapsulated model is wrong.

STATE DIAGRAMS

A model of how an instrument or controlled program functions can be captured in a *state diagram*. State diagrams document all the possible states of an instrument or program that result from a series of commands and events. State diagrams are depicted as a directed graph where nodes represent *states* and directed arcs represent *transitions* between states. Each transition is labeled with the event or command that causes a state transition. States are depicted as rounded boxes and transitions as arrows that connect one state to another. When in a certain state, a command or event that activates an associated outgoing transition will cause a change of state from the current state connected to the tail of the transition arrow to the new state connected to the head of the transition arrow. Figure 16-1 shows a simple state diagram of a program that establishes a remote connection. Before the connection is established, the program is in the *Not Connected* state. After the *open connection* event occurs, the state is changed to *Connected*. When the *close connection* event occurs, the state is moved back to *Not Connected*.

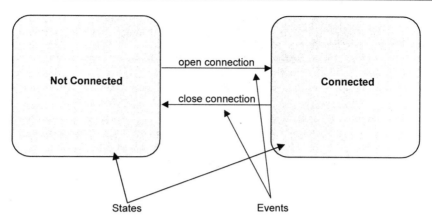

Figure 16-1. A simple state diagram.

A state diagram can be nested within the state of a higher-level state diagram. When this is the case, nested state diagrams are considered *subordinate* to the higher-level state diagram. The state diagram in Figure 16-2 expands the one illustrated in Figure 16-1 by continuing to refine what happens after the *Connected superstate* is entered. You can see now that Figure 16-2 represents a login procedure.

The small solid black circle indicates the initial subordinate state that will be entered by default when the *Connected* state is entered. In this case, immediately after connecting, the initial state subordinate to *Connected* is *Waiting for Username*. The only event that will change this is the submission of a username. Once that is done, the system enters the *Validating Username* state. A username can be accepted or rejected. If rejected the system moves back to *Waiting for Username*. If accepted it moves to the *Waiting for Password*

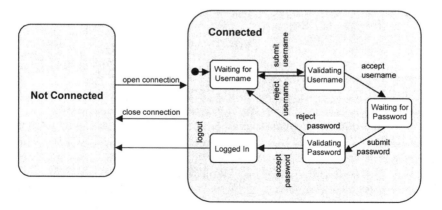

Figure 16-2. Subordinate state diagrams.

state. When a password is submitted the system enters the *Validating Password* state. If the password is accepted the *Logged In* state is entered. If rejected, the system moves back to *Waiting for Username*. Once logged in, if a *logout* event occurs, the system transitions from the *Logged In* subordinate state right to the *Not Connected* state in the higher-level diagram. This is an example of how a state transition can occur directly between lower- and higher-level state diagrams. By contrast, the state transition labeled *close connection* connects the two higher-level states, *Connected* and *Not Connected*. This implies that, regardless of the subordinate state within *Connected*, if a *close connection* event occurs, the system will transition immediately to *Not Connected*.

The notation used here follows Harel [1]. Rumbaugh, Booch, and Jacobson have also adopted it in the definition of the Unified Modeling Language [2]. See these references for much more detail on what is possible using state diagrams.

The Virtual Instrument is itself a kind of instrument and therefore has a well-defined state diagram. Figure 16-3 illustrates the state diagram for the VI.

Similar to the previous example, the VI state diagram also has two high-level states, *Off* and *On*. The *On* state is expanded further within a subordinate state diagram. Transitions are labeled with events that correspond to the VI commands. All commands listed in Table 6-1 are represented in the VI state diagram. Notice that the *Idle* subordinate state has two *self-transitions*. Executing the *Abort* or *Pause* command while the VI is idle is legal, but it will have no effect on the state of the VI. Instead, the transitions leaving *Idle* due to an *Abort* or *Pause* command lead right back to the *Idle* state.

With the state diagram for the VI in hand, we now have a complete understanding of how it operates. By referring to Figure 16-3, we see that the VI can only accept an *On* command when it is off. Immediately after it is turned on it becomes idle. At this point it can accept three commands, "Abort,"

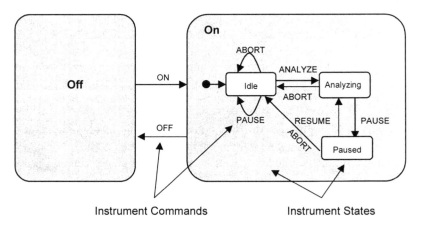

Figure 16-3. The Virtual Instrument state diagram.

"Pause," and "Analyze." The "Analyze" command causes the VI to begin generating data. While analyzing, the VI can be aborted or paused. While paused, it can be resumed or aborted back to the "Idle" state. At any point while on, whether in the *Idle*, *Analyzing*, or *Paused* states, if the VI is turned off, it immediately transitions back to the *Off* state.

State diagrams are used for much more than building controllers. The state diagram is a general-purpose computer science tool. It is also an invaluable tool for building science and engineering applications.

17

State Machines— Implementing State Diagrams in Visual Basic®

The implementation of a state diagram is called a *state machine*. A state machine can be created using VB, and most programming languages, in a relatively straightforward manner. In fact, there are many ways in which to do it, depending on the programming constructs offered by a language. We'll take a simple approach, primarily utilizing conditionals.

To begin, there should be at least one variable defined whose value indicates the current state of the program. With multilevel state diagrams it may be necessary to utilize multiple variables, each indicating the current state of each level. Either these variables must be scoped so as to be available from all locations in the program that refer to the state machine, or appropriate procedures that return the current state must be created. The mechanics behind the state machine can be translated into a series of nested conditional statements with a structure that parallels the structure of the state diagram itself.

AN IMPLEMENTATION OF THE VI STATE DIAGRAM

The best way to demonstrate the concept is with an example. Let's use the VI state diagram in Figure 16-3 to build a state machine with which to interpret VI commands. Create a new VB project and open the code window for Form1. The source code for this example can be found in \Part3\Ex2 of the code available online

We begin by defining a series of constants that represent each state and declaring two variables whose values will change as the current state changes. Two state variables are needed since there are two levels of the state diagram that we wish to represent. Level 1 includes the *On* and *Off* states. Level 2 includes the *Idle*, *Analyzing*, and *Paused* states. A Visual Basic® Enumerated variable is handy as a way to define state constants. The declarations in the following listing satisfy our requirements. Enter the following code into the declarations section of the Form1 code window.

```
' State Variables and Constants
Private Enum enumStateLevel1              ' Level 1 states
    conStateOff
    conStateOn
End Enum

Private Enum enumStateLevel2              ' Level 2 states
    conStateIdle
    conStatePaused
    conStateAnalyzing
End Enum

Private mStateLevel1 As enumStateLevel1   ' Level 1 state variable
Private mStateLevel2 As enumStateLevel2   ' Level 2 state variable
```

One nice aspect about using an Enumerated variable is the Auto List Members feature of VB. When a state variable is declared as an Enum with appropriate constants, entering a line of code to assign a value to the state variable will result in a popup list of options (see Figure 17-1). This is nice, since we won't have to remember the names we used for our Enum constants. Choose from the list and you're guaranteed it's correct.

The next step is to write a procedure that contains a series of nested conditional statements that mirror state transitions defined in the state diagram.

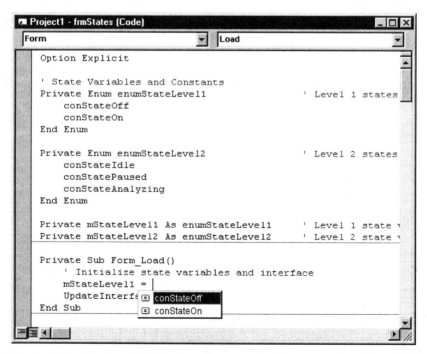

Figure 17-1. The Auto List Members feature using Enumerated variables in VB.

When an event occurs, this procedure will be executed with the event in order to determine how to react. Virtual Instrument events correspond to the commands that are issued to it, which were outlined in Table 6-1. As such, the procedure we define will take the command that has been issued as the event to process. In more realistic examples, this would be expanded to include other events such as read errors, overflows, interrupts, and other appropriate events.

The following listing implements the entire VI state diagram in a procedure called "ProcessCommand." Take a close look at the procedure and explore how it works. Each line in the procedure is preceded with a number. This is not part of the VB code. It has been added in order to improve our ability to refer to particular sections of the procedure. Do not enter these numbers into your VB project.

```
1.    Private Sub ProcessCommand(strCommand As String)
2.        ' Process a command and take appropriate action.

3.        ' Select actions based on Level 1 state
4.        Select Case mStateLevel1

5.      Case conStateOff                    ' When the VI is off ...

6.          Select Case strCommand

7.          Case "ON"                       ' If an ON command is received ...
8.              mStateLevel1 = conStateOn
9.              mStateLevel2 = conStateIdle

10.         ' *** Insert appropriate commands here ***

11.         Case Else
12.             ' Do nothing when anything else is received while the VI is off

13.         End Select

14.     Case conStateOn             ' When the VI is on ...

15.         Select Case strCommand
                            ' No matter what the Level 2 state ...
16.         Case "OFF"              ' if an OFF is received, turn the VI off.
17.             mStateLevel1 = conStateOff

18.         ' *** Insert appropriate commands here ***

19.         Case Else

20.             ' Select actions based on Level 2 state
21.             Select Case mStateLevel2

22.             Case conStateIdle           ' When the VI is idle ...

23.                 Select Case strCommand

24.                 Case "ANALYZE"    ' If an ANALYZE command is received ...
25.                     mStateLevel2 = conStateAnalyzing
```

```
26.                        ' *** Insert appropriate commands here ***

27.                 Case "ABORT", "PAUSE" ' If an ABORT or PAUSE is received ...
28.                     mStateLevel2 = conStateIdle

29.                        ' *** Insert appropriate commands here ***

30.                 Case Else                    ' Otherwise issue an error.
31.                     MsgBox "Invalid command while idle: " & strCommand

32.                 End Select

33.           Case conStateAnalyzing        ' While the VI is analyzing ...

34.                 Select Case strCommand

35.                 Case "ABORT"             ' If an ABORT command is received ...
36.                     mStateLevel2 = conStateIdle

37.                        ' *** Insert appropriate commands here ***

38.                 Case "PAUSE"             ' If a PAUSE command is received ...
39.                     mStateLevel2 = conStatePaused

40.                        ' *** Insert appropriate commands here ***

41.                 Case Else                    ' Otherwise issue an error.
42.                     MsgBox "Invalid command while analyzing: " & strCommand

43.                 End Select

44.           Case conStatePaused           ' While the VI is paused ...

45.                 Select Case strCommand

46.                 Case "ABORT"             ' If an ABORT command is received ...
47.                     mStateLevel2 = conStateIdle

48.                        ' *** Insert appropriate commands here ***

49.                 Case "RESUME"            ' If a RESUME command is received ...
50.                     mStateLevel2 = conStateAnalyzing

51.                        ' *** Insert appropriate commands here ***

52.                 Case Else                    ' Otherwise issue an error.
53.                     MsgBox "Invalid command while paused: " & strCommand

54.                 End Select

55.           Case Else

56.           End Select

57.       End Select
58.   End Select

59.   UpdateInterface                          ' Update the interface

60. End Sub
```

The top-level conditional is a Select statement that determines what section of code to execute based on the value of the first-level state variable called mStateLevel1. This statement begins on line 4. When mStateLevel1 = conStateOff (line 5), the only command that is allowed is *ON*. This is reflected in the statements contained within the conStateOff section of the top-level Select (lines 6-13). When the *ON* command is received, mStateLevel1 is assigned conStateOn, and mStateLevel2 is assigned conStateIdle (lines 8 and 9). This implements the transition in Figure 16-3 labeled "ON" which changes state from *Off* to *On* as well as the default transition which causes the subordinate *On* state to become *Idle*. All other commands are completely ignored. This is an attempt to mimic a real instrument which would have no response whatsoever when it is turned off.

When mStateLevel1 = conStateOn (line 14), the first nested conditional of the statements in that section implements the transition labeled "OFF" in Figure 16-3 (lines 15-19). Recall that the *Off* transition in the VI state diagram will cause the VI to turn off regardless of which subordinate *On* state is occupied. Therefore, when the VI is on, no matter what the value of mStateLevel2, a transition to *Off* will occur. The first nested conditional in the conStateOn section accomplishes exactly that.

If a command other than OFF is received when the VI is on, the action to take depends on the second-level state. This part of the state diagram is implemented in the mStateLevel2 nested conditional (lines 21-56). This conditional tests for the various subordinate *On* states, as indicated by the value of mStateLevel2. The statements within each section of this conditional implement all transitions of the *On* subordinate state diagram.

An invalid command can be trapped using the Case Else part of the Select statement. Examples of this can be seen in lines 30 and 31, 41 and 42, and 52 and 53. In this implementation we pop up a message box indicating the invalid command.

Throughout the procedure you'll find the comment "*** Insert appropriate commands here ***." This is where you would insert code to perform some action in response to the issued command.

TESTING THE VI STATE MACHINE

In order to probe the state machine build the following form interface, which includes three Labels, six CommandButtons, and two TextBoxes (see Figure 17-2).

Assign the properties in the following table to the Form and each control.

Each of the CommandButtons will issue a command to be processed by the state diagram implementation. In the following Click event procedures of each CommandButton we add a call to the ProcessCommand procedure with

Object Type	Property	Value
Form	Name	frmStates
	Caption	VI State Diagram Tester
CommandButton	Name	btnOn
	Caption	On
CommandButton	Name	btnOff
	Caption	Off
CommandButton	Name	btnAnalyze
	Caption	Analyze
CommandButton	Name	btnPause
	Caption	Pause
CommandButton	Name	btnResume
	Caption	Resume
CommandButton	Name	btnAbort
	Caption	Abort
TextBox	Name	txtStateLevel1
	Text	
TextBox	Name	txtStateLevel2
	Text	
Label	Name	lblCommands
	Caption	Commands:
Label	Name	lblStateLevel1
	Caption	State Level 1:
Label	Name	lblStateLevel2
	Caption	State Level 2:

the appropriate command string as the argument. Also, the two TextBoxes will indicate the current first- and second-level state variables.

```
Private Sub btnAbort_Click()
    ProcessCommand "ABORT"
End Sub

Private Sub btnAnalyze_Click()
    ProcessCommand "ANALYZE"
End Sub

Private Sub btnOff_Click()
    ProcessCommand "OFF"
End Sub

Private Sub btnOn_Click()
    ProcessCommand "ON"
End Sub

Private Sub btnPause_Click()
    ProcessCommand "PAUSE"
End Sub

Private Sub btnResume_Click()
    ProcessCommand "RESUME"
End Sub
```

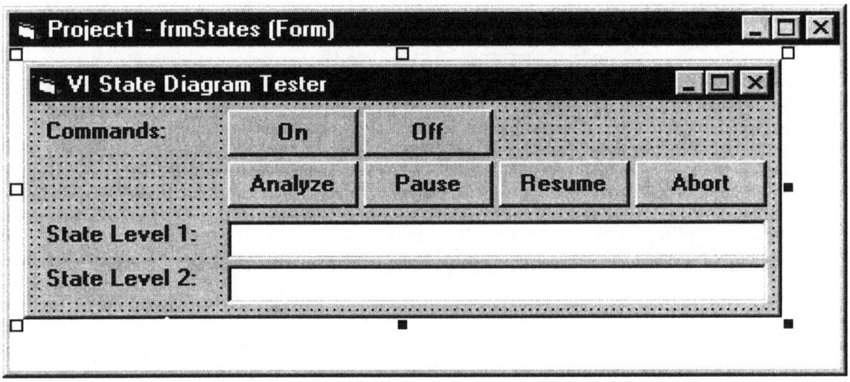

Figure 17-2. VI State Diagram Tester form design.

Remaining details include the initialization of state variables in the Load event procedure of the Form and a procedure for updating the interface when the state changes. Code to perform these tasks follows.

```
Private Sub Form_Load()
    ' Initialize state variables and interface
    mStateLevel1 = conStateOff
    UpdateInterface
End Sub

Private Sub UpdateInterface()
    ' Update the state display on the interface

    Select Case mStateLevel1
    Case conStateOff
        txtStateLevel1.Text = "Off"
        txtStateLevel2.Text = ""

    Case conStateOn
        txtStateLevel1.Text = "On"

        Select Case mStateLevel2
        Case conStateIdle:      txtStateLevel2.Text = "Idle"
        Case conStateAnalyzing: txtStateLevel2.Text = "Analyzing"
        Case conStatePaused:    txtStateLevel2.Text = "Paused"
        End Select

    End Select

End Sub
```

When you initially run the completed project, the state machine is initialized to the *Off* state as indicated by the interface (see Figure 17-3).

Click "On" and begin to explore the way that VI commands cause transitions between states by clicking "Analyze", "Pause", "Resume", and "Abort." Follow the transitions between states using the VI state diagram in Figure 16-3. See if you can execute commands that are invalid for certain states. For example, click "Analyze" to transition into the *Analyzing* state and then click

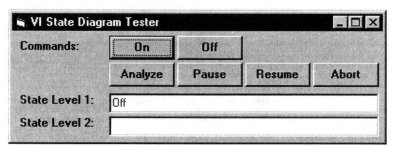

Figure 17-3. Initial appearance of the VI State Diagram Tester form.

"Resume". The Resume command only makes sense after the VI is paused. As a result, this will cause an error.

One of the actions that you can perform when transitioning into a state is to enable only the interface elements that should be available while in that state. The remainder of the interface can be disabled. This would prevent the previous error that occurred when "Resume" was clicked while in the *Analyzing* state. When the *Analyzing* state is entered, since "Resume" is not an available command, the btnResume CommandButton would be disabled, making it impossible to execute the command using the interface. In the interface of the VI, we change the function of a CommandButton to be either Pause or Resume, depending on which option is available in the currently occupied state. Changing the CommandButton Caption indicates the available valid option. Using a state machine to change available options is a common technique for building dynamic graphical user interfaces.

CHAPTER

18

Parsing—Understanding Message Content

Most remotely controllable instruments define their own control languages, which are often composed of a series of two-character commands, occasionally followed by arguments. The complexities of building these command strings can generally be hidden in high-level procedures that encapsulate the details, thereby making the task much easier. No matter how complex a command language gets, sending commands to an instrument is usually not a problem. The real challenge comes when it is time to interpret the returning stream of data, and to do it in a robust manner.

Processing the contents of a data stream presents several challenges. To begin, in a typical situation an issued command results in one of several responses. For example, in response to a command to begin a measurement you may expect either a series of delimited numbers or an error message. The two possible responses can have completely different formats and must be processed separately. How can you gracefully determine which kind of response you have in order to call the correct processing procedure? Another problem arises from the fact that communication channels are not error-proof. It is possible for part of a data stream to be lost or corrupted during transmission. How do you know that something is wrong with a transmission, and how can you respond in a meaningful manner? In a rush to get your controller in operation you may not have accounted for all possible responses. Or, your instrument control language may not be completely documented. What happens when that unexpected error message is returned?

Too often controllers are written in an ad hoc manner. In the absence of a systematic approach to the creation of control programs, a range of peculiar behaviors can result. Error messages are generally not as helpful as they could be, and often point to the wrong problem as the cause of the error. Some poorly written controllers simply crash when confronted with an unexpected response. The worst scenario is when a controller ignores a message and continues to operate, even though an instrument error has occurred and the controller has been notified. Subsequent collected data may be wrong or misinterpreted, but since the controller has ignored the error, the data are stored and presented as valid.

Fortunately, a basic understanding of parsing techniques can solve many of these problems. Your controller will be well organized, substantially more robust, and actually report meaningful error messages. When you are debugging and an error occurs, you will be able to diagnose it right away and possibly fix it on the spot. You get all this by mastering only a few basic ideas. Let's learn how it is done.

PARSING

Parsing is the process of recognizing and translating a linear sequence of data into a suitable format. Parsing is primarily an analytic technique, whose purpose is the recognition of a more complex structure in a one-dimensional stream of data. Once structures in a data stream are recognized, a secondary purpose of parsing is to build a representation of the structures recognized in the incoming data stream so that they can be utilized further. Parsing techniques have been studied and refined over many years by practitioners in the field of computer science. We can benefit tremendously from this body of knowledge.

When you run a Visual Basic® program, the underlying VB engine parses your code into a format that it can execute more efficiently. When VB finds an error it reports it, unless you have trapped it in your code and provided a way to handle the error at run time. A parser is working even when you are typing in a VB Code Window. Each time you enter a line of code, VB parses it to make sure it is syntactically correct. By this time you have no doubt seen the "Compile Error" dialog that indicates that you have an error and turns your line of VB code red. If you have ever wondered how VB knows when something is wrong, you will soon learn the technique.

LEXICAL ANALYSIS VERSUS SYNTACTIC ANALYSIS

Parsing can be logically organized into two tasks. The first is to divide a stream of data into the fundamental syntactic units of a language called its *tokens*. This task is called *lexical analysis*. We'll build a toolkit for performing lexical analysis on a stream of data. The second task is to recognize the structure in the stream of tokens that result from lexical analysis. This task is called *syntactic analysis*. The structure in a stream of tokens is identified by a set of predefined relationships between the tokens called its *grammar*. It is during syntactic analysis that we will be able to generate meaningful error messages and build structures that are represented by the stream of tokens.

Lexical and syntactic analysis can be performed independent of one another. In other words, a stream of data to be parsed can be completely *tokenized* first (divided into a series of tokens) and then syntactically analyzed. It is also possible to perform the two tasks at the same time. That is, if the syntactic analyzer is expecting one of a certain class of tokens, it can ask the lexical analyzer to attempt to recognize a token of that class beginning from the current position in the data stream. In the examples presented here, we will not distinguish between the lexical and syntactic analyzer. Instead, we will use a consistent technique to implement both analysis tasks, thereby blurring the logical division.

GRAMMARS

A *grammar* is the set of rules that defines what constitutes legal combinations of tokens in a stream of data. The rules of a grammar define how each legal structure is decomposed into its parts. The components in a grammar rule are usually defined by other rules in the grammar. In other words, grammars are often recursive by nature. A *context-free grammar* is a special kind of grammar in which each rule can be interpreted independent of the context in which the rule is being applied. For example, if we are parsing VB source code and we are applying the rule for recognizing an IF statement, it does not matter if the IF statement occurs in a subroutine, a function, a DO loop, or another IF statement. The syntax of the IF statement is always the same, regardless of where it is found. The grammar that defines the IF statement is independent of its context. We will only use context-free grammars.

A grammar is often represented using a notation called *Backus-Naur form*, or *BNF*. When the control language of an instrument is documented, it is not uncommon to find the documentation given in BNF. There are many variants of BNF notation. The four grammar rules in Figure 18-1 illustrate the salient points of the flavor of BNF that we will use.

Each element in a grammar rule will be delimited with angle brackets, as is the case with <identifier>, which is the first element in Rule 1. The symbol "::=" in each grammar rule can be read as "is recognized as" or "is defined as," and delimits the left and right sides of a grammar rule. The left side always identifies what is being defined, and the right side identifies how it is defined, or its structure. When two elements on the right-hand side of a rule directly follow one another, it implies that the structure of the element being

Rule 1:   <identifier> ::= <letter> | <letter> <letter_digit_sequence>
Rule 2:   <letter_digit_sequence> ::= (<letter> | <digit>) | (<letter> | <digit>) <letter_digit_sequence>
Rule 3:   <digit> ::= '0' | '1' | '2' | '3' | '4' | '5' | '6' | '7' | '8' | '9'
Rule 4:   <letter> ::= 'A' | 'B' | 'C' | ... | 'x' | 'y' | 'z'

Figure 18-1. *Grammar rules recognizing an identifier.*

defined should also be composed of these two elements in succession. A vertical bar "|" can be read as "or," implying that either the structure to the left or the structure to the right of a "|" symbol can be used to satisfy the rule. Contents within a pair of matching parentheses "( )" should be satisfied before the remainder of an expression. Elements delimited by a pair of single quotes '' identify literal character sequences to be recognized.

With these definitions in mind, Rule 1 can be read as "An identifier is defined as a letter or a letter followed by a letter_digit_sequence." Rule 2 says "A letter_digit_sequence is defined as either a letter or a digit alone, or a letter or digit followed by, a letter_digit_sequence." Note how this rule is defined in terms of itself. Due to the recursive nature of this rule, a letter_digit_sequence can be arbitrarily long. Rule 3 indicates that a digit is the character '0' or '1' or one of the other characters in the set listed on the right-hand side of the rule. Rule 4 defines a letter as one of a set of characters implied as being the upper and lowercase letters. Not all characters were listed in the rule. They are implied by the ellipsis.

PARSE TREES

An inverted tree can be used to represent the result of parsing a string of characters using a particular grammar. Let's expand the grammar defined in Figure 18-1 to include three more rules required to parse a sequence of identifiers. The expanded grammar is represented in Figure 18-2.

Rule 5 gives us the structure of an identifier_sequence, that is, an identifier followed by a terminator or an identifier followed by a separator and another identifier_sequence. Rule 6 defines the possible separators. Here we allow a comma ',' or a semicolon, ';'. Rule 7 defines the possible terminators. Here the symbol <CR> is defined to be carriage return, the character whose decimal code is 13. Similarly, <LF> is defined to be line feed, the character whose decimal code is 10. Refer to the ASCII table and nongraphic control characters table in Appendix A for definitions of these and other nongraphic characters.

As an example, let's consider the character sequence, X1, Y, Z<CR>. Recall that <CR> refers to carriage return, which has no graphic representation.

Rule 1:	<identifier> ::= <letter>	<letter> <letter_digit_sequence>
Rule 2:	<letter_digit_sequence> ::= (<letter> | <digit>)	(<letter> | <digit>) <letter_digit_sequence>
Rule 3:	<digit> ::= '0'	'1'	'2'	'3'	'4'	'5'	'6'	'7'	'8'	'9'
Rule 4:	<letter> ::= 'A'	'B'	'C'	...	'x'	'y'	'z'
Rule 5:	<identfier_sequence> ::= <identifier> <terminator>	<identifier> <separator> <identfier_sequence>
Rule 6:	<separator> ::= ','	';'
Rule 7:	<terminator> ::= <CR>	<LF>

Figure 18-2. *A grammar for recognizing an identifier sequence.*

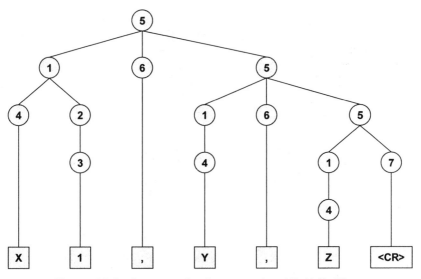

Figure 18-3. *Parse tree for the expression: X1, Y, Z<CR>.*

Figure 18-3 is the parse tree derived by applying the rules in the grammar of Figure 18-2. Circles in the tree are nonterminal nodes that represent an application of a grammar rule. The number in the circle identifies the particular rule applied. Boxes are terminal tree nodes (leaves) that contain a character in the original sequence.

The parse tree makes it clear how the character sequence is interpreted by the grammar. The application of Rule 5 at the root of the tree indicates that the entire character sequence is recognized as an identifier_sequence. The recursive application of grammar rules clearly lays out how that conclusion was drawn. Parse tree nodes labeled as "1" indicate clearly where and how many identifiers are found in the sequence. Character subsequences representing identifiers can be obtained by starting at each of these nodes and proceeding down the tree to the characters at their leaves.

PARSING METHODS

Another way to describe parsing is the successful application of grammar rules that can result in a complete parse tree, even though the tree itself may never actually be represented as a data structure. There are a variety of methods for applying grammar rules to parse an expression. They can be divided into two broad categories, *Top-down* and *Bottom-up*.

19

A Visual Basic®
Parser Class

If you're involved in any form of laboratory programming, parsing is something you're likely to perform over and over again. Whether you are interpreting data coming from an instrument or being read from a data file, parsing techniques are truly general-purpose programming tools. That's why it makes good sense to build a toolkit containing parsing routines that recognize common data types and structures. In this section we'll present and build upon a Visual Basic® parser class that contains many useful parsing routines. The parser class probably won't satisfy all your parsing needs by itself, but it is a good foundation on which to build. Indeed, we've used the code presented in this section for several of our own laboratory programming projects. Source code for the class can be found in the downloadable software in the file \Parser\Parser.cls.

PARSER CLASS DESIGN

The design of our parser class is partially represented in Figure 19-1. The figure does not contain a complete list of class methods. All class methods with descriptions are given in Table 19-1. The name of the parser class is clsParser. It employs the top-down approach to parsing. As you will see, the methods in the class build upon each other. You can extend this for your own purposes. Use the methods of the parser class as a foundation on which to build your own custom parsing methods.

The parser class implements a well-defined grammar, which is given in Figure 19-2. Several of the rules are the same as or similar to previous example grammars.

Table 19-1 lists and describes the parser class methods. Notice the close correspondence between grammar rules and parser class methods. In spite of the similarity between the grammar and class methods, not all methods are implemented in a manner that exactly mimics the grammar definition. There are a few parser class methods that are not reflected in the grammar. They

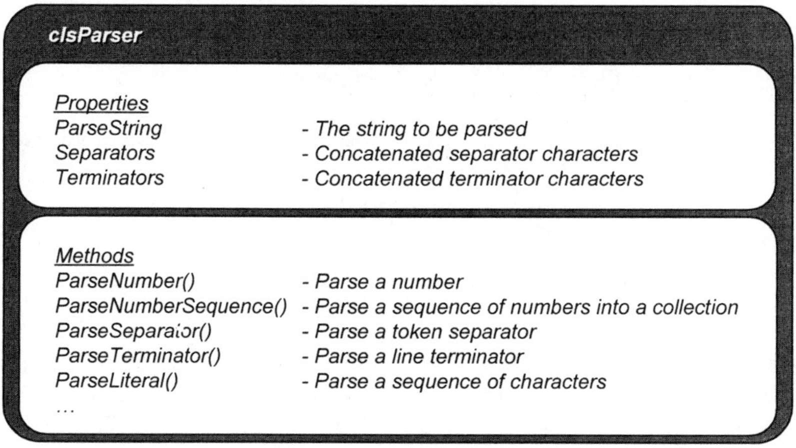

Figure 19-1. Partial representation of clsParser class design.

are: ParseLiteral, ParseDelimitedToken, SyntaxError, and EOF. We'll learn more about these methods in the next section.

HOW THE PARSER CLASS WORKS

The parser class can only parse data that are held by a Visual Basic® string data type. The string to be parsed is assigned to the ParseString property of

TABLE 19-1. clsParser class methods.

clsParser Methods	Description
ParseNumberSequence	Parse a sequence of numbers delimited by a separator. Return numbers in a collection object.
ParseNumber	Parse a number and return it as a double data type.
ParseInteger	Parse a number and return it as a long data type.
ParseDigitSequence	Recognize a contiguous series of digits.
ParseDigit	Recognize a digit in the set {0,1,2,3,4,5,6,7,8,9}.
ParseIdentifier	Parse an identifier. Return it as a string.
ParseLetter	Recognize a letter.
ParseWhitespace	Recognize an arbitrarily long sequence of spaces.
ParseTerminator	Recognize a user-defined terminator character.
ParseSeparator	Recognize a user-defined separator character.
ParseLiteral	Recognize the exact sequence of characters provided.
ParseDelimitedToken	Parse any token delimited by a separator, terminator, or end of parse string. Return it as a string.
SyntaxError	Initiate a syntax error indicating the current parse position.
EOF	Returns True when the current parse position has passed the end of the parse string.

Rule 1:	<number_sequence> ::= <number> | <number> <separator> <number_sequence>
Rule 2:	<number> ::= <integer> | <integer> '.' <digit_sequence>
Rule 3:	<integer> ::= '-' <digit_sequence> | '+' <digit_sequence> | <digit_sequence>
Rule 4:	<digit_sequence> ::= <digit> | <digit> <digit_sequence>
Rule 5:	<digit> ::= '0' | '1' | '2' | '3' | '4' | '5' | '6' | '7' | '8' | '9'
Rule 6:	<identifier> ::= <letter> | <letter> <letter_digit_sequence>
Rule 7:	<letter_digit_sequence> ::= (<letter> | <digit>) | (<letter> | <digit>) <letter_digit_sequence>
Rule 8:	<letter> ::= 'A' | 'B' | 'C' | ... | 'x' | 'y' | 'z'
Rule 9:	<whitespace> ::= ' ' | ' ' <whitespace>
Rule 10:	<separator> ::= (user-defined set of characters)
Rule 11:	<terminator> ::= (user-defined set of characters)

Figure 19-2. clsParser class grammar.

an instance of the parser class. ParseString is actually a Property Let procedure that assigns the given string to the private class variable mStrParseString. The Property Let also resets a private Long variable called mLngPP, which keeps track of the position of the parser in the current ParseString value. The following code shows the class declarations and the ParseString Property Let procedure.

```
' Private class properties
Private mStrSeparators As String        ' A string holding all valid
                                        ' token separators.
Private mStrTerminators As String       ' A string holding all valid
                                        ' line terminators.
Private mStrParseString As String       ' String to parse.
Private mLngPP As Long                  ' Current parser position.

Public Property Let ParseString(str As String)
    ' Reset the parse pointer and set the mStrParseString variable.
    mLngPP = 1
    mStrParseString = str
End Property
```

When parsing is complete, the ParseString property can be assigned to a new string, which can then be parsed from the beginning. As an example, consider a situation in which you want to parse data that are read from a file. One approach is to read the file a line at a time. Each time a line is read, set the value of ParseString in the parser class instance to the newly read line of text. Execute parser class methods in succession to recognize the data represented in the parse string. When finished with that string, read another line from the file and repeat the process. Another approach is to read the entire file into a VB string, assign it to the ParseString property of an instance of the parser class, and process the whole file at once. This can only be done when the file is small enough to store its entire contents in a string variable.

The private variable mLngPP always contains the current position in mStrParseString. When a parser method is called to recognize something in the parse string, the parser begins looking for it at the current position. If found, the mLngPP variable is updated to the position just after the recognized element.

To study how the parser class works, we'll begin with the more specific methods and work our way up to the more general methods. Several parser class methods use a utility called EOF. This is a function that checks if the current parse position is past the end of the parse string.

```
Public Function EOF() As Boolean
    ' True, if past end of ParseString
    EOF = False
    If mLngPP > Len(mStrParseString) Then EOF = True
End Function
```

Several grammar rules require that an exact series of characters be recognized in order for the rule to be successful. We've included a method in the parser class to do just that called ParseLiteral. It takes a string that must be found exactly at the current position on the parse string.

```
Public Function ParseLiteral(strLit As String) As Boolean
    ' Look for an exact match to the given string.
    Dim intLLen As Integer

    ParseLiteral = False        ' Assume failure
    intLLen = Len(strLit)       ' Get the length of the literal string.

    ' Look for the literal string.
    If Mid$(mStrParseString, mLngPP, intLLen) = strLit Then
        mLngPP = mLngPP + intLLen
        ParseLiteral = True
    End If

End Function
```

Another useful method in the parser class is one that simply recognizes and discards an arbitrarily long sequence of space characters. The following ParseWhitespace procedure implements a method in the parser class to do that.

```
Public Sub ParseWhitespace()
    ' Discard any whitespace found.
    Dim strChar As String

    strChar = Mid$(mStrParseString, mLngPP, 1)
    While strChar = " "
        mLngPP = mLngPP + 1
        strChar = Mid$(mStrParseString, mLngPP, 1)
    Wend

End Sub
```

A few of the parser class methods attempt to recognize separator and terminator characters. The parser class is designed to recognize separators and terminators that are composed of only a single character. The separator and terminator characters to use during parsing are set by concatenating them together and assigning the concatenated string of separators to the Separators property of the parser class and the concatenated string of terminators to the Terminators property of the parser class.

Multiple-character separator or terminator tokens can easily be handled in a parsing task using the parser class. If all separator and terminator token characters are included in the Separators and Terminators property strings, multiple-character separator or terminator tokens can be parsed by calling appropriate parsing methods as many times as the length of the separator or terminator token. For example, assume you are parsing responses from an instrument that terminates its communications with the character sequence <CR><LF>, a two-character terminator. This terminator can be recognized using the parser class by assigning the string <CR><LF> to the Terminators property of your parser class instance and calling the ParseTerminator method twice. The first call will recognize the <CR> character and the second call, the <LF> character. The following procedures implement these class methods.

```
Public Function ParseSeparator() As Boolean
    ' Look for the next character to be a valid separator character.
    Dim strChar As String

    ParseSeparator = False
    If EOF() = True Then Exit Function

    strChar = Mid$(mStrParseString, mLngPP, 1)
    If InStr(mStrSeparators, strChar) > 0 Then
        mLngPP = mLngPP + 1
        ParseSeparator = True
    End If

End Function

Public Function ParseTerminator() As Boolean
    ' Look for the next character to be a valid terminator character.
    Dim strChar As String

    ParseTerminator = False
    If EOF() = True Then Exit Function

    ' Match the terminator character
    strChar = Mid$(mStrParseString, mLngPP, 1)
    If InStr(mStrTerminators, strChar) > 0 Then
        mLngPP = mLngPP + 1
        ParseTerminator = True
    End If

End Function
```

High-level parser methods must recognize digits, letters, and their se-quences. We implemented the recognition of digits by searching through the appropriate character set. This is a practical approach since these character sets are small. In the case of a letter, we use ASCII codes to determine if a character is of the appropriate type. Unlike Rule 4 of the grammar in Figure 19-2, sequences of digits are not implemented recursively. It is more efficient simply to recognize as many digits as possible in a contiguous sequence by iterating down the parse string. Procedures implementing these methods are as follows.

```
Public Function ParseDigit() As Boolean
    ' Determine if the current character is a valid digit
    Dim strChar As String

    ParseDigit = False
    If EOF() = True Then Exit Function

    strChar = Mid$(mStrParseString, mLngPP, 1)
    If InStr("0123456789", strChar) Then
        mLngPP = mLngPP + 1
        ParseDigit = True
    End If

End Function

Public Function ParseLetter() As Boolean
    ' Determine if the current character is a valid letter
    Dim intChar As Integer

    ParseLetter = False      ' Assume failure.
    If EOF() = True Then Exit Function

    ' Use the ASCII code to determine if the character is a letter
    intChar = Asc(Mid$(mStrParseString, mLngPP, 1))
    If (intChar >= 65 And intChar <= 90) Or (intChar >= 97 And intChar <= 122) Then
        mLngPP = mLngPP + 1
        ParseLetter = True
    End If

End Function

Public Function ParseDigitSequence(strDigitSequence As String) As Boolean
    ' Parse and return a string of sequential digits.
    Dim lngStartPP As Long, intLen As Integer

    ParseDigitSequence = False          ' Assume failure.
    lngStartPP = mLngPP                 ' Save initial location.

    ' Recognize at least one digit.
    If ParseDigit() = True Then
        ' Recognize additional digits on the sequence.
        While ParseDigit() = True:  Wend

        ' Return the sequence
        intLen = mLngPP - lngStartPP
        strDigitSequence = Mid$(mStrParseString, lngStartPP, intLen)
        ParseDigitSequence = True
    End If

End Function
```

Integers are recognized by looking for an optional leading "+" or "−" character followed by a sequence of digits. VB only provides integer data types that internally store a sign. If a minus sign character is recognized, the sign of the returned long integer argument is adjusted accordingly. The ParseInteger procedure implements this method. The ParseLiteral procedure is used to recognize the sign character, and ParseDigitSequence is used to recognize a sequence of digits.

```
Public Function ParseInteger(lngVal As Long) As Boolean
    ' Parse positive or negative integers.
    Dim lngMultiplier As Long, strDigitSequence As String

    ParseInteger = False                ' Assume failure.
    lngMultiplier = 1&                  ' Assume the integer is positive.

    ' Look for a leading negative or positive sign.
    If ParseLiteral("-") = True Then
        lngMultiplier = -1&
    ElseIf ParseLiteral("+") Then
        ' Do Nothing
    End If

    ' Get a sequence of digits
    If ParseDigitSequence(strDigitSequence) = True Then

        If Not IsNumeric(strDigitSequence) Then Exit Function
        lngVal = CLng(strDigitSequence)

        ' Adjust sign.
        lngVal = lngMultiplier * lngVal
        ParseInteger = True

    End If

End Function
```

Given a way to recognize integers and digit sequences, we can now implement a more general procedure for recognizing numbers. By Rule 2 in the grammar defined in Figure 19-2, a number is composed of a signed integer, possibly followed by a "." character, and a digit_sequence. The following ParseInteger procedure implements a class method that embodies this rule. Additionally, this procedure will recognize as a valid number an integer followed by a "." and no subsequent digit sequence.

```
Public Function ParseNumber(dblVal As Double) As Boolean
    ' Parse a number.  Always returns a double.
    Dim I1 As Long, strDigSeq As String

    ' First look for an integer.
    If ParseInteger(I1) = True Then
        ' If get this far then the procedure is successful.
        ParseNumber = True
```

```
      ' If a decimal place found then look for decimal values as a positive integer.
      ' Build the resulting double.
      If ParseLiteral(".") = True And ParseDigitSequence(strDigSeq) = True Then
            dblVal = CDbl(CStr(I1) & "." & strDigSeq)
      Else
            dblVal = CDbl(I1)
      End If
   End If

End Function
```

To complete the set of number recognition rules, we've included a rule to recognize number sequences in the grammar, and a method in the parser class to do the same. Number sequences are frequently found when processing measured laboratory data. The idea is to recognize a series of numbers delimited by separator tokens. The following ParseNumberSequence procedure implements this method. A number sequence is recognized if at least one number is recognized. If a separator token is recognized after the number, then another number sequence is sought.

Numbers in a number sequence often contain leading spaces. We wanted to allow this possibility, so the procedure begins by discarding all space characters. Since the procedure is called recursively, space characters preceding all numbers in a number sequence are discarded.

Numbers collected by the ParseNumberSequence procedure are returned in a VB collection object, which is passed to the procedure. It is important to create the collection object prior to calling the procedure, since the procedure only adds to the collection; it does not create a new one.

```
Public Function ParseNumberSequence(colNumbers As Collection) As Boolean
   ' Parse a sequence of numbers and store in a collection.
   Dim dblVal As Double

   ParseNumberSequence = False         ' Assume failure.
   ParseWhitespace                     ' Ignore white space at the beginning.

   ' A sequence must begin with at least one number.
   If ParseNumber(dblVal) = True Then
       colNumbers.Add dblVal
       ParseNumberSequence = True

       ' Now look for more elements in the sequence.
       If ParseSeparator() = True Then
           ParseNumberSequence = ParseNumberSequence(colNumbers)
       End If
   End If

End Function
```

The last procedure implementing a grammar rule is called ParseIdentifier. Rule 6 defines an identifier as a letter followed by a sequence of letters or numbers. This is very similar to a digit_sequence, which you will recall is defined as at least one digit followed by a sequence of digits. Implementation of the ParseIdentifier procedure is very similar to ParseDigitSequence.

```
Public Function ParseIdentifier(strIdent As String) As Boolean
    ' Parse an identifier and return it if found.
    Dim lngStartPP As Long, intLen As Integer

    ParseIdentifier = False            ' Assume failure.
    lngStartPP = mLngPP                ' Save initial location.

    ' Identfiers must begin with a letter.
    If ParseLetter() = True Then
        ' Continue incrementing until the next characters is not a digit or letter.
        While ParseLetter() = True Or ParseDigit() = True: Wend

        ' Return the new identfier.
        intLen = mLngPP - lngStartPP
        strIdent = Mid$(mStrParseString, lngStartPP, intLen)
        ParseIdentifier = True
    End If

End Function
```

The ParseDelimitedToken procedure in the parser class is not defined by the grammar, but has been found to be very useful. The procedure returns all characters starting from the current parse string position until a separator or terminator is found, or the end of the parse string is reached. Looking at the implementation below, you'll see that these three cases are handled separately. This was necessary to prevent unwanted behavior. It is possible to group the ParseSeparator and ParseTerminator procedures into the same conditional test. For example, we could have implemented the test as in the following statement:

```
If ParseSeparator() = True or ParseTerminator() = True Then
```

This might seem to be a perfectly acceptible approach, especially since the bodies of both conditionals are identical. But, in this statement, both parse procedures are executed, even if the first returns True. When a separator and a terminator follow the token in a parse string, implementing the test as written above would result in both characters being parsed. This is not the intended behavior. We want only to find the first separator or terminator, and leave the remainder for subsequent parse methods.

```
Public Function ParseDelimitedToken(strToken As String) As Boolean
    ' Get the next token delimited with a separator, terminator
    ' or end of parse string.
    Dim intLen As Integer

    ParseDelimitedToken = False     ' Assume failure

    ' Continue while not the end of the parse string, a separator, or a terminator.
    intLen = 0
    Do
        ' Handle each case separately to prevent unwanted behavior.
        If EOF() = True Then
            strToken = Mid$(mStrParseString, mLngPP - intLen, intLen)
```

```
                ParseDelimitedToken = True
                Exit Do
        ElseIf ParseSeparator() = True Then
                strToken = Mid$(mStrParseString, mLngPP - intLen - 1, intLen)
                ParseDelimitedToken = True
                Exit Do
        ElseIf ParseTerminator() = True Then
                strToken = Mid$(mStrParseString, mLngPP - intLen - 1, intLen)
                ParseDelimitedToken = True
                Exit Do
        End If

        intLen = intLen + 1
        mLngPP = mLngPP + 1
    Loop

End Function
```

The last parser class procedure is a utility to help show useful syntax errors. The SyntaxError procedure takes an error message, and displays it in a MessageBox along with an indication of where the error occurred. The assumption is that the error was encountered at the current parse position. The parse string is included in the error message with the locator string "<here>" inserted just before the next character to be parsed.

```
Public Sub SyntaxError(Msg As String)
    ' Display a syntax error with an indication of the problem.
    Dim strMsg As String

    strMsg = "Syntax Error at position " & CStr(mLngPP) & ".  " & Msg & "." & vbLf
    strMsg = strMsg & Left$(mStrParseString, mLngPP - 1) & "<here>"
    strMsg = strMsg & Right$(mStrParseString, Len(mStrParseString) - mLngPP + 1) & vbLf

    MsgBox strMsg
End Sub
```

These parsing methods are interdependent and reusable. They are ideally suited to be encapsulated together as a class. It is not uncommon to have the need to parse data streams from two sources in the same program. For example, say you are writing an instrument controller that needs to parse data coming from an instrument as well as read and parse settings from an initialization file. It is likely that the two data sources use two entirely different formats. Since the parser toolkit is a class, we can create several instances of the class, each with different separator and terminator character sets. We can then call the methods as necessary without worrying about how each data source separates and terminates its elements.

USING THE PARSER CLASS

More often than not, you will need to extend the parser class to recognize the data elements that exist in your particular application. You can get right into the source code of the parser class and change its behavior. Another

Rule 1:   <response> ::= <measurement> | <error_statement>
Rule 2:   <measurement> ::= <number> <terminator> | <number> <separator> <measurement>
Rule 3:   <error_statement> ::= 'ERROR' <number> <terminator>
Rule 4:   <separator> ::= ',' | '/'
Rule 5:   <terminator> ::= <LF> | ';'

Figure 19-3. *Grammar defining example instrument responses.*

approach is to keep the class intact, but create an instance of the class within another module that defines required extensions.

Once you understand how parser class methods build upon each other, it is an easy task to continue the process by defining new methods that build on that foundation. Continue with the approach used to build parser class methods in order to maintain consistency. None of the parser class methods includes syntax error messages. All syntax errors should be issued from your code, which extends the parser class.

As an example, let's imagine that you want to parse responses that come back from an instrument you are controlling. Assume that in response to a command to measure data, you expect either an error message consisting of an "ERROR" keyword followed by an error code and a terminator, or a series of numbers delimited by separators, followed by a terminator. The grammar that lays out these options is described in Figure 19-3.

Rule 1 of Figure 19-3 indicates that a response can be either a measurement or an error_statement. As defined in Rule 2, a measurement is very similar to the parser class number_sequence, except that a measurement ends with a terminator. Rule 3 defines the error_statement, exactly as we expect. Rules 4 and 5 define possible separators and terminators. To make it interesting, we've included two of each. In real life, chances are good that there will be only a single separator character and a single terminator character specified.

Create a new project and add a ComboBox, a CommandButton, a TextBox, and two Labels to Form1 (see Figure 19-4).

Assign the following properties to the Form and each control:

Object Type	Property	Value
Form	Name	frmParserTest
	Caption	Parser Test
ComboBox	Name	cmbParseString
	Style	0 – Dropdown Combo
	Text	
CommandButton	Name	btnParse
	Caption	Parse
TextBox	Name	txtOutput
	Text	
Label	Name	lblParseString
	Caption	Parse String:
	Alignment	1 – Right Justify
Label	Name	lblOutput
	Caption	Output:
	Alignment	1 – Right Justify

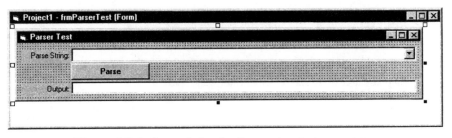

Figure 19-4. Form design for Parser class test program.

We need to do two things in the declarations section of the main form. Since we want the parser class to be available from any point in the form, we need to create the new parser class and a module-level variable to hold a reference to it. Since we will be using the ParseNumberSequence procedure of our parser class instance, we also want to create a new Collection object and a module-level variable to hold a reference to it.

When the main form loads, we will initialize the parser class with appropriate separators and terminators. For convenience, we'll also add a number of sample parse strings to the cmbParseString ComboBox. The following listing achieves all these goals.

```
Dim mParser As New clsParser         ' A new instance of the parser class.
Public mColNumbers As New Collection ' Most recent collection of parsed numbers

Private Sub Form_Load()
    mParser.Separators = ",/"            ' Initialize separators.
    mParser.Terminators = vbCr & ";"     ' Initialize terminators.

    ' Put several examples in the combo box.
    cmbParseString.AddItem "12, -34, 56.7" & vbCr
    cmbParseString.AddItem "12, 34.5, -56; "
    cmbParseString.AddItem "12, 34, 56,-7,8,9     99999; "
    cmbParseString.AddItem "12/-34/56;"
    cmbParseString.AddItem "12/,-34/56.7;"
    cmbParseString.AddItem "ERROR 123" & vbCr
    cmbParseString.AddItem "ERROR " & vbCr
    cmbParseString.AddItem "ERR 123;"
    cmbParseString.AddItem "ERROR 123/" & vbCr
    cmbParseString.AddItem "ERROR -123456789" & vbCr
    cmbParseString.AddItem "ERROR -12345.6789" & vbCr

End Sub
```

To initiate the parse, the btnParse CommandButton is clicked. The Click event procedure of this CommandButton must do a number of things. First the txtOutput TextBox is cleared. Next, the ParserString property of the parser class is set to the contents of the ComboBox. An attempt is made to parse this string using procedures that implement the instrument response grammar defined in Figure 19-3. If successful, a string is constructed to show what was parsed, and the result is displayed in the txtOutput TextBox.

```
Private Sub btnParse_Click()
    Dim strResult As String, strStatement As String
    Dim intCount As Integer, I As Integer

    txtOutput.Text = ""            ' Clear the output TextBox
                                   ' Parse the statement.
    mParser.ParseString = cmbParseString.Text
    If ParseStatement(strStatement) = True Then
                                   ' Collect and display the result.
        strResult = strStatement & " - Values: " & CStr(mColNumbers.Item(1))

        intCount = mColNumbers.Count
        For I = 2 To intCount
            strResult = strResult & "," & CStr(mColNumbers.Item(I))
        Next I

        txtOutput.Text = strResult
    End If

End Sub
```

The core of the example is found in the ParseStatement procedure. Note that this is not a method of the parser class, but a new method that implements the new rules given in the instrument response grammar. We've numbered the lines of code in the following listing as an aid to describe what is happening. These numbers are not part of the source code.

```
1.  Function ParseStatement(strStatement As String) As Boolean
2.      ' Parse the given string.
3.      Dim intErrorCode As Long

4.      ParseStatement = False        ' Assume failure. Clear the collection.
5.      Do While mColNumbers.Count > 0: mColNumbers.Remove 1: Loop

6.      ' Look for an 'ERROR' keyword.
7.      If mParser.ParseLiteral("ERROR") = True Then
8.          ' Skip any white space
9.          mParser.ParseWhitespace

10.         ' Look for an error code.
11.         If mParser.ParseInteger(intErrorCode) = True Then
12.             ' Put the error code on the class number collection.
13.             mColNumbers.Add intErrorCode
14.         Else
15.             mParser.SyntaxError "Expected an Error code"
16.             Exit Function
17.         End If

18.         ' Look for a terminator.
19.         If mParser.ParseTerminator() = False Then
20.             mParser.SyntaxError "Expected a terminator"
21.             Exit Function
22.         End If

23.         ' If all goes well, indicate that an ERROR statement was parsed.
24.         strStatement = "Error"
25.         ParseStatement = True
26.         Exit Function
```

```
27.     ' If an ERROR keyword was not found then look for a number sequence.
28.     ElseIf mParser.ParseNumberSequence(mColNumbers) = True Then
29.         ' Look for a terminator.
30.         If mParser.ParseTerminator() = False Then
31.             mParser.SyntaxError "Expected a terminator"
32.             Exit Function
33.         End If

34.         ' If all goes well, indicate that a measurement was parsed.
35.         strStatement = "Measurement"
36.         ParseStatement = True
37.         Exit Function

38.     ' Otherwise indicate a syntax error.
39.     Else
40.         strStatement = ""
41.         mParser.SyntaxError "Expected a Measurement or Error statement"
42.         Exit Function
43.     End If

44. End Function
```

Lines 4 and 5 prepare for parsing by initializing the return Boolean value to False and clearing anything that is currently in the Collection.

In this implementation, the first thing checked is whether the response is an error statement. This is done in line 7 using the ParseLiteral procedure of the parser class with "ERROR" as the literal string to recognize. If found, all whitespace is skipped in line 9, and an error code is sought in line 11 using the ParseInteger procedure of the parser class. If an integer is found, it is added to the Collection in line 13.

The first syntax error occurs if an error code is not found after an "ERROR" literal. Line 15 calls the SyntaxError procedure of the parser class with the appropriate error message. After displaying the syntax error, there is nothing more to do; so the procedure exits in failure in line 16.

To complete the error statement, a terminator is sought in line 19. If not found, the second syntax error is displayed, and the procedure exits in lines 20 and 21. If the terminator is found, lines 24, 25, and 26 define the statement type returned as "Error," and the procedure exits successfully.

If the "ERROR" literal is not found, a number sequence is sought in line 28. If found, the ParseNumberSequence method will fill the Collection with all numbers parsed from the sequence. Then a terminator is sought in line 30. If the terminator is not found, a syntax error is displayed, and the procedure exits in failure in lines 31 and 32. If a terminator is found, the statement type is set to "Measurement," and the procedure returns successfully in lines 35, 36, and 37.

If neither a measurement nor an error statement is found, the statement type is cleared, the last syntax error is displayed, and the procedure exits in failure in lines 40, 41, and 42.

The ParseStatement procedure is an example of how to extend the functionality of the parser class for your own purposes, as well as how to use the

SyntaxError procedure effectively. The parser class includes other procedures described earlier, which are not demonstrated in this example. Source code for this project can be found in \Part3\Ex3\ of the code available online. Experiment with your own projects to learn how best to utilize the wealth of functionality in this class.

20

Device Monitoring and Control

A unifying theme in laboratory computing is the coordination of an interaction between a piece of software and a device. The device can be an instrument at the other end of an RS-232 cable, a program on the same computer or at the other end of a network, or something completely different. More often than not, this coordinated interaction involves the control of the remote device. In this case, the program is actively initiating a sequence of actions performed by the remote device. Other times a program is created simply to monitor the progress of a remote device of some sort by collecting status messages and generated data. In each case, the program and remote device are interacting with one another to a productive end; they operate in a coordinated fashion. In this section we'll focus on the monitoring and control of remote devices.

Everything we have covered thus far is an important piece of the overall puzzle for building solid device controllers. In Part 2 we studied some of the most popular ways of communicating with remote devices using Visual Basic®. Our examples involved establishing and transmitting data through various kinds of communication channels. We did not refer to these example programs as controllers since communication was either unidirectional or there were no real interactions between the two channels of an example using bidirectional communication. Instead, we used the term *commander*.

Thus far in Part 3 we've discussed a number of additional topics that are necessary as a foundation on which to build solid device controllers. The event-driven nature of VB can make it unclear as to how VB will execute code in different event procedures when their associated events are raised one after another. This is important to understand due to the inevitable need to respond to remote devices in a timely manner. We explored this issue when we discussed Visual Basic®'s behavior from a multithreading perspective.

An ability to track the progress of a remote device is another crucial aspect of building solid controllers. Knowing how to interpret and respond to a received message, or even how to determine if it is valid, is dependent upon knowing what a device currently is or should be doing. The state machine was presented and proposed as a way to manage this problem. We presented a simple technique for implementing state machine in Visual Basic®.

Finally, we addressed the topic of how best to process a stream of data when received from a remote device. Parsing techniques were presented as a solution that offers many benefits. Their rich theoretical basis and countless successful applications to similar problems clearly point to sound parsing techniques as the proper approach. We implemented a Parser class containing many common parsing utilities as a foundation on which to build more customized solutions.

In the following sections we will discuss two approaches for building controllers in Visual Basic®. In the examples we will draw heavily on what we have learned thus far.

The missing piece of the puzzle is a framework in which to close the loop between messages sent and received. We want to be able to:

1. Monitor the input communications channel of one or more remote devices,
2. Process the information received, and
3. Take action to fulfill a predetermined set of tasks or react to dynamically determined conditions.

This will be the topic of the remainder of this part of the book.

MONITORING A DEVICE THROUGH POLLING

The various approaches to monitoring a remote device can be divided into two broad categories, *polling* and *interrupt-driven monitoring*. These are illustrated in Figure 20-1.

With a polling approach, the controller periodically queries connected devices for incoming data, which can then be processed. If the controller does not ask the device whether it has any data to communicate, nothing is received.

The obvious approach to writing a program like this in Visual Basic® is to create a loop that continuously looks at the input communications port for data. Recall that, by default, VB executes all user code on a single thread. If that thread is dedicated to monitoring a communications port, there is nothing left for other tasks, such as responding to button clicks and updating the user interface. It is necessary to invoke DoEvents from within the polling loop if the program is to attend to its other tasks, but this may severely impact the timeliness of subsequent data collection.

Instead of polling continuously, another approach is to poll only when you expect a message. For example, assume you sent a command to an instru-

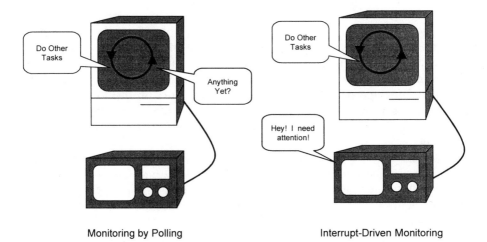

Monitoring by Polling   Interrupt-Driven Monitoring

Figure 20-1. *Polling versus interrupt-driven device monitoring.*

ment connected to your RS-232 port. After sending the message, you can enter a continuous polling loop that looks at the receive buffer of the RS-232 port until the expected message arrives. In this example assume that messages are terminated by <CR><LF> characters. The following function called KeepLooking accomplishes that task.

```
Public Function KeepLooking() As String
    ' Keep looking until able to get a complete message from the input port.
    Dim strInputBuffer As String, intPos As Integer

   ' Clear the receive buffer
   comPort.InBufferCount= 0

   ' Wait until a complete message is found.
   Do
        strInputBuffer = strInputBuffer & comPort.Input
        intPos = InStr(strInputBuffer, vbCrLf)
        If intPos > 0 Then Exit Do
        DoEvents
   Loop

   ' Return the message without the terminator characters.
   KeepLooking = Left$(strInputBuffer, intPos - 1)

End Function
```

The receive buffer of the comPort MSComm control is first cleared by setting the InBufferCount property to a value of zero. Then a series of commands is repeated within a Do Loop. All subsequent contents of the comPort control receive buffer is added to the end of the string variable strInputBuffer. If the <CR><LF> character sequence is found, the Do Loop exits. Otherwise, DoEvents is called to handle other pending events and the loop repeats. After exiting the loop, the intPos integer variable contains the position of <CR> terminator character in the strInputBuffer string variable. The message is copied from the beginning of the string and returned from the function.

This function accomplishes the basic task, but it leaves much to be desired. For example, there is no means for a graceful exit from the function if the complete message never arrives. It can remain stuck in the loop until you terminate the program. Also, anything that arrives after the terminator characters of the message is discarded. Still, the function is simple and may suit your needs.

There are times when continuous polling makes sense. For example, you may have a dedicated process that must respond to a message as fast as possible, or the only way to interact with the process is through the communications channel. We can make substantial improvements to the approach implemented in the previous example.

A better model for device polling is presented as a flow chart in Figure 20-2. In this model, all data on the input port are fetched and added to the end of an input buffer. The buffer is checked to see if a complete command is recognized. If so, it is removed and processed. Either way, the program immediately returns to look for more data on the input buffer, and the process is repeated.

This model assumes that discrete messages and data communicated from a remote device can be recognized. It is often the case that instrument communication protocols require that messages be terminated with a unique character sequence, making a complete message easy to identify.

When messages are short, sent one at a time, and your communications channel is fast, new data on an input port may always represent individual messages that are complete. When this is the case, life is easy. You can collect new data from the input port and process it at the same time as a single message, but it is not uncommon for data to be transmitted more sporadically, introducing a higher degree of complexity. For example, if a device transmits half a message, is delayed for some reason, and completes the message, you may receive the message in two parts. Another difficulty can arise when a device can send more than one message at a time. You may receive two or more messages in one transmission. How can we systematically handle these situations? We need to separate the data collection task from the message-

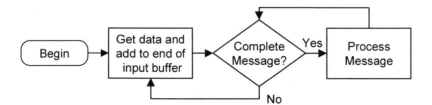

Figure 20-2. Flow chart for monitoring a device by continuous polling.

processing task. The model represented by the flow chart in Figure 20-2 outlines this idea.

The retrieval of data from the input communications port and subsequent message processing are separated in the model. When data arrive, they are added to the end of the input buffer. The first part of a message may already be on the input buffer, and new data may complete the message. Each time new data are collected all complete messages on the input buffer are processed and removed. This continues until a complete message can no longer be recognized on the input buffer. If multiple messages arrive within the same transmission, all are processed before looking for new data.

POLLING AS A "BACKGROUND" TASK

When your application calls for a frequency of polling to be in the range of about 100 milliseconds to 10 seconds, or even longer, it is probably a waste of resources to implement a loop that reads the input port and processes data as fast as the program will run. In this case, the VB Timer ActiveX control offers an excellent alternative to continuous polling. A Timer control can be configured to fire at a predefined frequency using the Interval property. The Interval property takes a value in milliseconds, and can be assigned a value up to 65,535, or about 65 seconds. The Timer control times as cycles are free, leaving your main VB thread available for executing other user code. Performance of your controller can be tuned by adjusting the Interval property value.

A Timer can be used for polling at longer intervals than the maximum value of the Timer's Interval property by adding a static counter variable to the body of the Timer event procedure. Each time the Timer times out, the counter is incremented. When the counter reaches a predefined setpoint, the appropriate polling code is executed, and the counter is reset.

The model for using a Timer to initiate polling is almost identical to continuous polling. The difference occurs when processing is complete; the procedure suspends for a period of time rather than immediately restarting. It is initiated again only when the Timer event procedure is fired. This is illustrated in the flow chart of Figure 20-3.

This model is preferred over continuous polling. Using a Timer, it is possible to have much more control over the performance of your controller program.

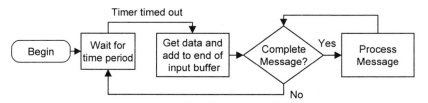

Figure 20-3. Flow chart for polling with a Timer.

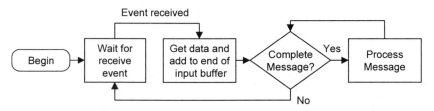

Figure 20-4. Flow chart for interrupt-driven monitoring.

INTERRUPT-DRIVEN DEVICE MONITORING

When available, the preferred method for implementing a controller that monitors an input port is to use an interrupt-driven approach. The model for this approach is represented by the flow chart in Figure 20-4. The only difference between this and previous models is how the core input buffer processing procedure is initiated. Using a polling approach, the controller program must query the device for incoming data. In the interrupt driven approach, the remote device informs the controller that it has data waiting and needs attention.

No matter how it is initiated, we can benefit from using the same core input buffer processing procedure as with previous models. Cases where a message is divided over multiple transmissions, or multiple messages are contained in the same transmission, are all handled gracefully. A shared core procedure also makes it simple to test different models for monitoring a process to identify the best approach.

21

Device Controllers in VB

In this chapter we will present example controllers that implement the models presented in the previous chapter. Each example will share the same device monitoring and input buffer processing framework. Differences will lie mainly in how the input buffer processing procedure is initiated, how input and output ports are addressed, and what is done with a complete message when it is found.

THE CORE INPUT BUFFER PROCESSING PROCEDURE

Since we will share the input buffer processing framework, let's develop that before we present complete examples. The framework encompasses the common parts of flow charts in Figures 20-2, 20-3, and 20-4. That includes the symbols labeled "Get data and add to end of input buffer," "Complete Message?" and "Process Message." The framework includes the functions in Table 21-1.

We will implement the input buffer as a module-level string. This works well when using Parser class procedures to recognize a complete message. After new data are appended to the end of the input buffer string, the entire string can be passed directly to the parser class as the parse string. Input buffers can also be implemented as string arrays or Collection objects.

Of the four functions in Table 21-1, only ProcessInputBuffer and GetMessage are independent of the communications channel and specific application. ProcessInputBuffer is given in the following listing. As stated in its description, it is the procedure that coordinates all the other procedures in the framework. You will notice that it includes calls to the other three functions. It is the procedure that is called when it is time to process data on the input port. In a polling approach, this procedure is fired by a Timer control or in a continuous loop. In an interrupt-driven approach, this procedure is the one that is fired when new data arrive on the input port.

Table 21-1: Input buffer processing functions.

Function Name	Description
FetchInputData	Gets all data from input port and adds to input queue. Returns True if any data are found; False otherwise. Specific to the type of communications channel in use.
GetMessage	Looks for a complete message on the input queue. Removes and returns if found.
ProcessMessage	Processes a message. Actions taken are specific to the application.
ProcessInputBuffer	Coordinates the whole process. This is the procedure that is called to initiate input buffer processing.

```
Private Sub ProcessInputBuffer()
    Dim strMessage As String

    ' Get any new data
    If FetchInputData() = False Then Exit Sub

    ' Process all complete messages.
    strMessage = GetMessage()
    Do While strMessage <> ""
        ProcessMessage strMessage
        strMessage = GetMessage()
    Loop

End Sub
```

The first step is to pull any data off the input port and append them to the input buffer string. That is accomplished by the FetchInputData procedure. If no new data are found, FetchInputData will return False, and ProcessInputBuffer exits. There is no need to continue when there are no new data to process. When new data are added to the input buffer, the GetMessage procedure is called to look for a complete message. If one is found, it returns the message as a string; otherwise it returns an empty string. The new message is processed with the ProcessMessage procedure. This is repeated until there are no further complete messages on the input buffer.

GetMessage is implemented in the following listing. The input buffer is represented as the module-level string variable named mStrInputBuffer. A line termination character identifies a complete message. In this example we are looking for a carriage-return character. When found, the message is removed from the left of the input buffer and returned.

```
Private Function GetMessage() As String
    ' Get an entire message.
    Dim intPosition As Integer        ' Line termination character(s) position
    Dim strMessage As String          ' Store a message
                                      ' Error handler
    On Error GoTo GetMessageErrorHandler
```

```
    strMessage = ""                         ' Look for line termination characters
    intPosition = InStr(mStrInputBuffer, vbCr)
    If intPosition > 0 Then               ' If found then remove the command
        strMessage = Left$(mStrInputBuffer, intPosition - 1)
                                          ' Keep any remaining data
        mStrInputBuffer = Right$(mStrInputBuffer, Len(mStrInputBuffer) - intPosition)
    End If

    GetMessage = strMessage               ' Return message
    Exit Function
'_____
GetMessageErrorHandler:
    Select Case Err.Number
    Case Else
        MsgBox "Error (GetMessage) " & CStr(Err.Number) & ": " & Err.Description
    End Select
End Function
```

IMPLEMENTING DEVICE POLLING IN VB

As the available toolkit for communicating with external devices improves, the need to implement controllers using polling decreases. Modern communication software almost exclusively employs more powerful interrupt, or event-driven, approaches. Even so, there are still situations where polling is the only option.

Recall the File Communications example of Chapter 13. We had to initiate the receiving of data manually from an input communication file. To improve the way that this example operates, we can check for new data on a regular basis using a polling approach. Periodically, the GetData method of the clsFileComm file communications class can be invoked to check the input file for new data.

If you recall how the SendData and GetData methods of clsFileComm class were implemented, you may recognize that they use a continuous polling approach. In each case continuous polling occurs when an attempt is made to open input and output communication files. If a file cannot be locked as it is opened, the procedure repeats the attempt continuously until it is successful or terminated by invoking the class's Cancel method.

DEVICE COMMUNICATIONS THROUGH FILE POLLING

Let's use the clsFileComm file communication class to build an application that polls for new data using a Timer control. The example application will use the previously defined ProcessInputBuffer and GetMessage procedures, and will define the application specific ProcessMessage and FetchInputData procedures. It will also demonstrate how to embed these procedures within an application. The completed example project can be found in the folder \Part3\Ex4 of the code available online.

Create a new project and add two TextBox controls, three CommandButtons, a StatusBar control, a CommonDialog control, and a Timer control to Form1 (see Figure 21-1). Also add to your project the file in which you saved the clsFileComm class, or a copy.

Assign the following properties to the Form and each control:

Object Type	Property	Value
Form	Name	frmFileComm
	Caption	File Communications Client
TextBox	Name	txtOut
	Text	
TextBox	Name	txtIn
	Text	
	MultiLine	True
	ScrollBars	3 – Both
CommandButton	Name	btnSend
	Caption	Send
	Default	True
CommandButton	Name	btnSetInput
	Caption	Set Input
CommandButton	Name	btnSetOutput
	Caption	Set Output
StatusBar	Name	sbrStatus
	Style	1 – sbrSimple
CommonDialog	Name	cdlFile
	CancelError	True
Timer	Name	tmrFileComm
	Enabled	True

As was the case with the example in Chapter 13 that introduced the clsFileComm class, the btnSetInput and btnSetOutput CommandButtons are

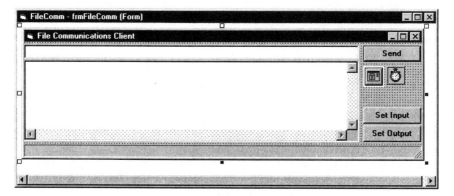

Figure 21-1. Form design for the File Communications example with polling.

used to select the input and output files through which communications will take place. Text entered into the txtOut TextBox will be sent to the other communicating program. Sending is initiated by clicking the btnSend CommandButton. In this example, anything received will automatically be added to the txtIn TextBox.

Add the following code to the frmFileComm Form. Declare a string variable to act as the input buffer and create a new instance of the clsFileComm class. Upon loading the form, initialize the tmrFileComm Timer control.

```
Option Explicit

' Instance of file communications class
Private mFileComm As New clsFileComm

' Buffer to hold data received on input channel
Private mStrInputBuffer As String

Private Sub Form_Load()
    ' Init timer parameters
    tmrFileComm.Interval = 2000
    tmrFileComm.Enabled = True
End Sub
```

As before, the Click event procedures of the btnSetInput and btnSetOutput CommandButtons set the names of the input and output files. The cdlFile CommonDialog is used to set these names. The following listing implements the Click events of the two CommandButtons.

```
Private Sub btnSetInput_Click()
    ' Set the input file.
    On Error GoTo btnSetInput_ClickErrorHandler

    With cdlFile
        .filename = mFileComm.InFile
        .DialogTitle = "Please enter the input file for communications"
        .Filter = "All Files (*.*)|*.*"
        .ShowOpen
        mFileComm.InFile = .filename
    End With

    Exit Sub
'   _____
btnSetInput_ClickErrorHandler:
    Select Case Err.Number
    Case cdlCancel
        ' Do nothing if cancelled
    Case Else
        MsgBox "Error (btnSetInput) " & CStr(Err.Number) & ": " & Err.Description
    End Select
End Sub

Private Sub btnSetOutput_Click()
    ' Set the output file.
    On Error GoTo btnSetOutput_ClickErrorHandler
```

```
With cdlFile
    .filename = mFileComm.OutFile
    .DialogTitle = "Please enter the output file for communications"
    .Filter = "All Files (*.*)|*.*"
    .ShowOpen
    mFileComm.OutFile = .filename
End With

Exit Sub
'_____
btnSetOutput_ClickErrorHandler:
    Select Case Err.Number
    Case cdlCancel
        ' Do nothing if cancelled
    Case Else
        MsgBox "Error (btnSetOutput) " & CStr(Err.Number) & ": " & Err.Description
    End Select
End Sub
```

To send data, the SendData method of the mFileComm object is invoked with the contents of the txtOut TextBox. The btnSend CommandButton Click event procedure initiates the process.

```
Private Sub btnSend_Click()
    ' Send data to the output file.
    sbrStatus.SimpleText = "Sending to " & mFileComm.OutFile & " ..."
    mFileComm.SendData txtOut.Text
    sbrStatus.SimpleText = ""
End Sub
```

We use the tmrFileComm Timer control to poll periodically for any input data. When the Timer times out, we need to process the input buffer as outlined in the device monitoring model of Figure 20-3. We have already listed the ProcessInputBuffer and GetMessage procedures that make up a portion of this device monitoring model. Make sure that these procedures are included in the frmFileComm Form code. It is only necessary to call the ProcessInputBuffer procedure when the Timer times out, as follows:

```
Private Sub tmrFileComm_Timer()
    ' Check input file at predetermined time intervals.
    ProcessInputBuffer
End Sub
```

To complete the polling model implementation, we need to define the FetchInputData and ProcessMessage procedures. To get data from the file communications input file we use the clsFileComm GetData procedure. If data are found on the input channel, they are appended to the end of the input buffer. When a complete message is found on the input buffer, we simply append it to the txtIn TextBox contents. These two procedures are given in the following listing.

```
Private Function FetchInputData() As Boolean
    ' Get any new data from the input port and append to Input Queue.
    ' Return true if any found.
    Dim strData As String

    FetchInputData = False                    ' Assume no new data.

    mFileComm.GetData strData
    If strData <> "" Then
        mStrInputBuffer = mStrInputBuffer & strData
        FetchInputData = True
    End If

End Function

Private Sub ProcessMessage(strMessage As String)
    ' Process received message by appending to TextBox
    If strMessage <> "" Then txtIn.Text = txtIn.Text & strMessage & vbCrLf
End Sub
```

When all the code has been entered, compile the program and run two instances of the executable (see Figure 21-2). Set the input and output communications files so that the input file of the first executable is the output file of the second, and vice versa. Type a message into the txtIn TextBox of one of the programs and click "Send." Within two seconds the message will appear in the output TextBox of the other program. Type a response into the other program and click "Send." The response will appear at the first program.

This message-processing model will handle both the situation where a message is transmitted partially and completed at a later time, and the situa-

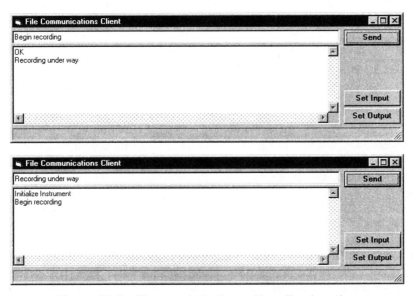

Figure 21-2. File communications with polling in action.

tion where multiple messages are included in the same transmission. To see how multiple messages from one transmission are processed, type in a message and click the send button of one of the programs several times. The same message will be written to the output file several times before the receiving program has a chance to read it. When the receiving program Timer fires, it will read the whole transmission and process each message separately. If only a partial message was written to a file, the terminating carriage-return character would not be written, and therefore a complete message would not be found. No action would be taken until the remaining portion of the message was communicated through the file, including the carriage-return character.

THE MSCOMM ONCOMM EVENT

It is more efficient to process the input buffer of a controller only when new data arrive. The MSComm control has a single event called OnComm, which will fire whenever the CommEvent property changes its value. CommEvent will change for a number of reasons, including the arrival of new data on the input port. One of the most powerful features of the MSComm control is an ability to program it based on the occurrence of specific related events. We will use the OnComm event as the signal indicating that the input buffer should be processed.

The MSComm control behaves a little differently than many other controls that react to events. More often than not, a control will have a separate event procedure for each type of event that can occur. The OnComm event of MSComm is a general-purpose event that fires for a wide variety of reasons, including changes in the status of the RS-232 port or various communications errors. In Table 10-5 we listed several common predefined constants that can be used to compare with the current value of the CommEvent property in order to determine the event that has occurred. See the CommEvent property of the MSComm control in VB Help for a complete listing of CommEvent constants.

We are mainly interested in the predefined MSComm constant named comEvReceive. When OnComm is fired and the CommEvent property holds a value equal to the value of this constant, it indicates that the number of characters in the MSComm's receive buffer is equal to or greater than the value of its Rthreshold property. We will use this event to fire our input buffer processing procedure in the following MSComm VI controller example.

AN EVENT-DRIVEN RS-232 CONTROLLER FOR THE VI

Let's take the next step and build a simple controller for the Virtual Instrument using the interrupt-driven model for device monitoring outlined in Figure 20-4. The structure for this example is similar to the previous one, but it will include many more of the concepts that we have covered in this part of the book. In this example we will communicate with an RS-232 port and trigger input buffer processing using the MSComm OnComm event rather than a Timer. We will track the state of the controller and use it to determine how to process messages received from the VI. We will use procedures of the clsParser class to interpret and react to VI messages. All the code for the RS-232 VI Controller example can be found in the folder \Part3\RS232Ctrl of the downloadable software. As in the RS-232 example of Part 2, to run this example you'll need two available RS-232 ports connected together with a null-modem cable. The two ports can be on the same computer or on different computers (see Figure 10-3).

To begin, create a new VB project. Include the file \Parser\Parser.cls in the new project by adding it directly into the project, or copying it into a new folder and adding it from the new location. Add a ComboBox, CommandButton, and MSComm control to Form1. Modify their properties as follows:

Object Type	Property	Value
Form	Name	frmRS232Ctrl
	Caption	RS232 VI Controller
ComboBox	Name	cmbSend
	Style	0 – Dropdown Combo
	Text	
CommandButton	Name	btnSend
	Caption	Send
	Default	True
MSComm	Name	comVI

Note there is no reason to set the properties of the MSComm since we will do this in code. The frmRS232Ctrl Form should look like the form shown in Figure 21-3.

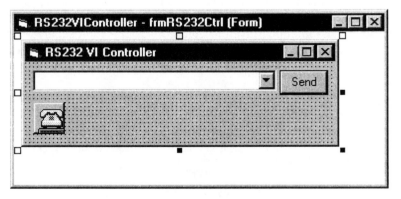

Figure 21-3. Form design for the RS-232 VI Controller.

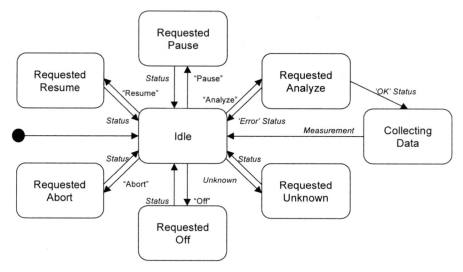

Figure 21-4. State diagram for the RS-232 VI Controller.

The state diagram to be implemented by the controller is given in Figure 21-4. The controller will begin in the *Idle* state and change depending on the VI command issued. Transitions out of the *Idle* state are labeled with the VI command that causes the transition. Most commands cause the controller to wait in a *Requested* state until a Status message is returned. When an "OK" status message is returned from an "Analyze" command, the controller goes into the *Collecting Data* state. If an "Error" status is returned, the controller goes back to *Idle*. Transition from *Collecting Data* back to *Idle* occurs when the controller receives a Measurement message, which contains measured data.

The grammar for VI responses is given in Figure 21-5. The two main types of messages are Status and Measurement. A Measurement message is not expanded since it is defined to be a number_sequence, which is expanded in the clsParser class grammar given in Figure 19-2. The valid separator character is defined to be a comma, ",", and the terminator character to be a carriage return.

Rule 1:	<status> ::= 'OK' | <error_statement>
Rule 2:	<measurement> ::= <number_sequence>
Rule 3:	<error_statement> ::= 'ERROR' <number> <terminator>
Rule 4:	<separator> ::= ','
Rule 5:	<terminator> ::= <CR>

Figure 21-5. Grammar defining VI responses.

We need to declare a number of variables and constants in the controller example. Add the following code to the declarations section of the frmRS232Ctrl Form.

```
Option Explicit

' The state of the Controller
Private mIntState  As Integer

' State constants
Const conIdle As Integer = 0                ' Controller is idle
Const conRequestedAnalyze As Integer = 1   ' Controller requested the VI to Analyze
Const conRequestedPause As Integer = 2     ' Controller requested the VI to Pause
Const conRequestedResume As Integer = 3    ' Controller requested the VI to Resume
Const conRequestedAbort As Integer = 4     ' Controller requested the VI to Abort
Const conRequestedOff As Integer = 5       ' Controller requested the VI to turn Off
Const conRequestedUnknown As Integer = 6   ' Controller requested an unknown task
Const conCollectingData As Integer = 7     ' Controller is collecting data from the VI

' Buffer to hold RS-232 input
Private mStrInputBuffer As String

' Object variable for Parser class instance
Private mParser As clsParser
```

The private module-level variable mIntState will be used to hold a constant that indicates the current state of the controller. The eight constants following this declaration define the possible states. These correspond to the states in Figure 21-4. We could have equally well used an Enum here to define state constants instead of declaring them explicitly. For input buffer processing we need a module-level string to act as the input buffer. The private variable mStrInputBuffer is declared to serve that purpose. Finally, we need to declare a module-level reference to a clsParser object, which we have done with the mParser variable.

Upon loading the frmRS232Ctrl Form, we will initialize the comVI MSComm control, create and initialize the mParser clsParser class, fill the cmbSend ComboBox, and initialize the state of the controller. The following listing accomplished these tasks.

```
Private Sub Form_Load()

    With comVI          ' Set up the comm control
        .CommPort = 2
        .Settings = "19200,N,8,1"
        .RThreshold = 1
        .PortOpen = True
    End With
                        ' Create and setup new clsParser class
    Set mParser = New clsParser
    mParser.Separators = ","
    mParser.Terminators = vbCr
```

```
                                ' Fill the combobox
        cmbSend.AddItem "Analyze"
        cmbSend.AddItem "Pause"
        cmbSend.AddItem "Resume"
        cmbSend.AddItem "Abort"
        cmbSend.AddItem "Off"

                                ' Initialize the controller state
        mIntState = conIdle
    End Sub
```

We have set the value of the comVI MSComm control's CommPort property to 2 since by default the VI used CommPort = 1. You may have to change the CommPort property of this example to another value depending on the ports that are available on the computer that you are using to run this example. We also set the RThreshold property of the comVI MSComm control to 1 in order to cause it to fire its OnComm event whenever there is one or more characters waiting to be retrieved from the input buffer.

A new clsParser class is created and a reference to it assigned to the mParser variable. Its Separators property is initialized to the string "," and Terminators property to the predefined constant vbCr, which holds the carriage-return character. These are the separator and terminator characters used by the VI. If you change these values in the VI, make sure you also change them in the example, otherwise the controller will not work properly.

Finally, the cmbSend ComboBox is initialized with the five VI commands for convenience, and the mIntState variable is initialized to conIdle, the constant defining the default controller state.

To send a command to the VI, add the following code to the btnSend CommandButton Click event procedure.

```
    Private Sub btnSend_Click()
        Dim strCommand As String

            On Error GoTo btnSendErrorHandler

            ' Massage the command string
        strCommand = UCase(Trim(cmbSend.Text))

            ' Send contents of the text box out the RS-232 port
        comVI.Output = strCommand & vbCr

            ' Change state based on command to be issued
        If Left$(strCommand, 7) = "ANALYZE" Then
            mIntState = conRequestedAnalyze
        ElseIf strCommand = "PAUSE" Then
            mIntState = conRequestedPause
        ElseIf strCommand = "RESUME" Then
            mIntState = conRequestedResume
        ElseIf strCommand = "ABORT" Then
            mIntState = conRequestedAbort
        ElseIf strCommand = "OFF" Then
            mIntState = conRequestedOff
        Else
            mIntState = conRequestedUnknown
        End If

        Exit Sub
```

```
'   _____
btnSendErrorHandler:

    Select Case Err.Number
    Case Else
        MsgBox "Error " & CStr(Err.Number) & ": " & Err.Description
    End Select

End Sub
```

In this event procedure, we copy the text from the cmbSend ComboBox and process it to remove unwanted spaces and to make it case insensitive by changing to upper case. We add a carriage return to the end and set the Output property of the comVI MSComm control to the result. This is all we need to do to send the command over the RS-232 port to the VI. Before completing the event procedure, the state of the controller is changed. The state transition implemented here is a function of the command that has been issued.

We use the OnComm event of the MSComm control to determine when to initiate input buffer processing. When OnComm is fired, we will check the CommEvent property of the comVI MSComm control to determine if the event is a receive event. As described previously, comparing it to the predefined comEvReceive constant accomplishes this. When the OnComm event is a receive event, we call the ProcessInputBuffer procedure to initiate input buffer processing. The following listing is the complete OnComm event.

```
Private Sub comVI_OnComm()
    ' Process data received on RS-232 port

    ' Check for a receive event
    If comVI.CommEvent = comEvReceive Then
        ' Get any new data on input
        ProcessInputBuffer

    End If
End Sub
```

For processing data received by the controller, the ProcessInputBuffer and GetMessage procedures are the same as given previously. They are repeated in the following listing:

```
Private Sub ProcessInputBuffer()
    Dim strMessage As String

    ' Get any new data
    If FetchInputData() = False Then Exit Sub

    ' Process all complete messages.
    strMessage = GetMessage()
    Do While strMessage <> ""
        ProcessMessage strMessage
        strMessage = GetMessage()
    Loop

End Sub
```

```vb
Private Function GetMessage() As String
    ' Get an entire message
    Dim intPosition As Integer              ' Position of line term character(s)
    Dim strMessage As String                ' Store a message
                                            ' Error handler
    On Error GoTo GetMessageErrorHandler

    strMessage = ""                         ' Look for line termination characters
    intPosition = InStr(mStrInputBuffer, vbCr)
    If intPosition > 0 Then                 ' If found then remove the message
      strMessage = Left$(mStrInputBuffer, intPosition - 1)
                                            ' Keep any remaining data
      mStrInputBuffer = Right$(mStrInputBuffer, Len(mStrInputBuffer) - intPosition)
    End If

    GetMessage = strMessage                 ' Return message
    Exit Function
'_____
GetMessageErrorHandler:
    Select Case Err.Number
    Case Else
      MsgBox "Error (GetMessage) " & CStr(Err.Number) & ": " & Err.Description
    End Select
End Function
```

The remaining two procedures used in device monitoring, FetchInputData and ProcessMessage, must be customized to the particular situation. The following listing demonstrates how to implement FetchInputData for an RS-232 port. We use the InBufferCount property of the comVI MSComm control to determine if there actually is anything in the receive buffer. If so, we use the Input property to add the contents of the buffer to the controller's input buffer, stored in the mStrInputBuffer string variable.

```vb
Private Function FetchInputData() As Boolean
    ' Get any new data from the input port and append to Input Queue.
    ' Return true if any found.

    FetchInputData = False                  ' Assume no new data.

    If comVI.InBufferCount > 0 Then
        mStrInputBuffer = mStrInputBuffer & comVI.Input
        FetchInputData = True
    End If

End Function
```

Complete messages received from the VI are processed with the ProcessMessage procedure, which is contained in the following listing. The VI message is immediately set to the mParser ParseString property in preparation for parsing.

```vb
Private Sub ProcessMessage(strMessage As String)
    ' Process Message from a command
    Dim strStatus As String, colData As New Collection
```

```
    mParser.ParseString = strMessage          ' Set the statement to parse

    Select Case mIntState                     ' Switch on the state of the controller
    Case conIdle                              ' When idle, indicate unexpected commun
       MsgBox "Unexpected communication: " & strMessage

    Case conRequestedAnalyze                  ' Controller requested VI to Analyze
       If ParseStatus(strStatus) = True Then  ' Expecting a status line
           mIntState = conCollectingData      ' Change state to collecting data
       End If

    Case conCollectingData                    ' Controller is collecting data
                                              ' Expecting a sequence of data
       If mParser.ParseNumberSequence(colData) = True Then
          MsgBox "Collected " & CStr(colData.Count) & " data points"
          mIntState = conIdle                 ' Change state back to idle
       End If

    Case Else                                 ' Anything else returns a status line
       If ParseStatus(strStatus) = True Then  ' Expecting a status line
           If Left(strStatus, 5) = "ERROR" Then MsgBox "Command failed: " & strStatus
           mIntState = conIdle                ' Change state back to idle
       End If
    End Select

End Sub
```

Processing steps depend on the state of the controller. When the controller is *Idle*, no responses are expected. An "Unexpected communication" error message is displayed in a Message Box if something shows up on the input port when the controller is Idle.

After an "Analyze" command is issued, the Status message is parsed with the ParseStatus procedure. When the status is "OK," the ParseStatus procedure returns True, otherwise False is returned. If ParseStatus returns True while the controller is in the *Requested Analyze* state, the controller is transitioned into the *Collecting Data* state. When a message is received while the controller is in the *Collecting Data* state, it is expected to be a Measurement, which is defined as a number_sequence. In this case the ParseNumberSequence procedure of the clsParser class is used to process the message, and the controller is transitioned back to Idle. The number of data points successfully collected from the VI is displayed in a Message Box.

While the controller is in any other state, all messages from the VI are expected to be Status messages. The ProcessMessage procedure will use ParseStatus to process any other message and transition the controller state back to *Idle*. Error messages are displayed in a Message Box.

The last procedure to add to the RS-232 VI Controller example is ParseStatus, which implements the portion of the grammar in Figure 21-5 that defines status messages. The following listing implements this procedure.

```
Private Function ParseStatus(strStatus As String) As Boolean
    ' Parse a status line
    Dim lngCode As Long
```

```
With mParser
    ' Look for an "OK"
    If .ParseLiteral("OK") = True Then
            strStatus = "OK"
            ParseStatus = True

    ' Look for an error status line, get and return code
    ElseIf .ParseLiteral("Error") = True Then
        .ParseWhitespace
        If .ParseInteger(lngCode) = True Then
            strStatus = "ERROR " & CStr(lngCode)
            ParseStatus = True
        End If
    Else
        ParseStatus = False
    End If

End With

End Function
```

To test the example controller, run the VI and turn it on. Make sure that the two RS-232 ports to be used are connected with a null-modem cable. Run the example controller program. Select or type "Analyze 10" into the ComboBox and click "Send." You will see something like that shown in Figure 21-6.

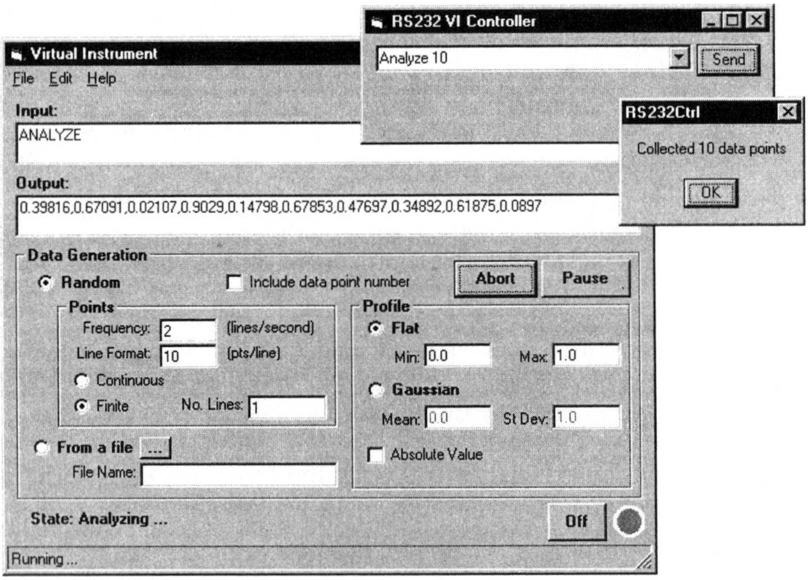

Figure 21-6. The RS-232 VI Controller in action.

SIMILARITIES BETWEEN MSCOMM AND WINSOCK

The MSComm control and Winsock control are very similar in the way they operate. Their property and procedure names are different, but the model by which each operates is enough alike to make it relatively easy to convert an application that communicates over an RS-232 port to one that communicates over a TCP/IP network. The most important similarity between the two controls is the way each triggers notification that data have arrived. We saw how the OnComm event of the MSComm control is fired when new data are available in the receive buffer of the RS-232 port. Similarly, the Winsock control fires its DataArrival event when new data arrive on the socket connection. Let's compare the procedures of the two controls that are necessary to perform the four basic functions: establishing a connection, sending data, receiving data, and closing a connection.

When communicating over an RS-232 port, no real connection is made between your program and the device at the other end of the cable. The only real connection that is made is between your program and the RS-232 port. That is, your program opens the port. You can send data out the RS-232 port, even if there is nothing on the other end that is listening. We've seen that to open an RS-232 port using an MSComm control, you must identify the port number by setting the CommPort property, specify communications parameters using the Setting property, and set the PortOpen property to True. For example, consider the following code fragment:

```
With MSComm1
    .CommPort = 2
    .Settings = "19200,N,8,1"
    .PortOpen = True
End With
```

A Winsock control can be used to establish two types of network conversations. One requires that a connection is made, and the other one doesn't. By definition, a TCP conversation is a connection-oriented communications protocol. There must be something at the other end of the connection to accept a connection request, otherwise a connection cannot be established. This is the default protocol used by a Winsock control. The alternative is to use the UDP protocol. UDP is a connectionless protocol. Similar to an RS-232 connection, you can send data out a port using UDP, even if there is nothing listening on the other end.

The following code fragment requests a TCP network connection. The RemoteHost and RemotePort properties of the Winsock control are set, and the Connect procedure is executed to request a connection.

```
With Winsock1
    .RemotePort = 1234
    .RemoteHost = "127.0.0.1" ' ... or enter a name
    .Connect
End With
```

If the connection request is accepted, the Winsock control's Connect event will fire.

```
Private Sub Winsock1_Connect()
    MsgBox "A connection has been established!"
End Sub
```

If you need to communicate with a device that can accept TCP network connections, you can clearly see that establishing the connection is as easy as opening an RS-232 port.

A single statement is all that is required to send data using either the MSComm or Winsock controls. As we have seen, the MSComm control sends data when its Output property is set to a value. In the following code fragment, the strCommand variable holds string data to be transmitted out the RS-232 port by the MSComm1 control.

```
MSComm1.Output = strCommand
```

The Winsock control sends data using its SendData method, as in the following example.

```
Winsock1.SendData strCommand
```

Both controls use an event-based approach to receiving data. When something new arrives in the RS-232 receive buffer or at the connected network port, each control fires an event. We've seen how the MSComm control fires the OnComm event to indicate that any one of a number of events has occurred. We need to test the value of the MSComm CommEvent property to discover what has caused the event to occur.

```
Private Sub MSComm1_OnComm()
    Dim strData As String
    If MSComm1.CommEvent = comEvReceive Then
        strData = MSComm1.Input
        mStrInputBuffer = mStrInputBuffer & strData
    End If
End Sub
```

When new data arrive on the local port of a network connection, the Winsock control DataArrival event occurs. Use the GetData method to retrieve new data into a local variable.

```
Private Sub Winsock1_DataArrival(ByVal bytesTotal As Long)
    Dim strData As String
    Winsock1.GetData strData, vbString
    mStrInputBuffer = mStrInputBuffer & strData
End Sub
```

Closing connections is accomplished in each case using a single statement. To close an open RS-232 port, set the MSComm control PortOpen property to False.

```
MSComm1.PortOpen = False
```

A TCP network connection can be closed using the Close method of the Winsock control.

```
Winsock1.Close
```

Even though their methods of communicating are very different, the manners in which the MSComm and Winsock controls are used are quite similar. In fact, there is enough similarity to make it relatively easy to convert a VB program that uses one form of communications to the other. In the next section we will demonstrate this by converting the RS-232 VI Controller example to a Winsock VI Controller.

AN EVENT-DRIVEN WINSOCK CONTROLLER FOR THE VI

The Virtual Instrument can accept TCP connection requests and respond to commands over the network connection as if they were received on an RS-232 port. We can convert the RS-232 VI controller example to one that controls the VI over a network using the similarities outlined in the previous section. The framework used to build the example controller can remain the same. The only changes required involve communication issues. In this section we will only present portions of the Winsock VI Controller example that were changed from the RS-232 VI Controller. The completed Winsock VI Controller can be found in the folder \Part3\WinsockCtrl of the code available online.

To begin the conversion process, make a copy of the frmRS232Ctrl Form from the previous example and place it in a new folder. It's not a bad idea to rename the file, as we will be changing it. Create a new VB project and include the copied form file by selecting it from the menu option Project | Add File from the VB development environment. Delete the default Form1 from the project by clicking on it and selecting the Project | Remove Form1 menu option. You'll also need to include the Parser class in the new project. Add the file to the project from a common location, or copy the Parser.cls class file to your new folder and include it in the project from that location.

Delete the MSComm control on the frmRS232Ctrl Form and replace it with a new Winsock control. Don't forget to add the Winsock control to your toolbox first. To do this, select the Microsoft Winsock Control CheckBox from the Components dialog, which you can display by selecting the Project | Components menu option from the VB development environment menu bar.

Set the following Form and Winsock properties values. Your Form will look
like Figure 21-7.

Object Type	Property	Value
Form	Name	frmWinsockCtrl
	Caption	Winsock VI Controller
Winsock	Name	sckVI

Now let's make the necessary code changes. We initialized the MSComm
control in the Form_Load event procedure of the RS-232 controller example.
We need to change that to initialize the Winsock control.

Replace the code fragment

```
With comVI          ' Set up the comm control
    .CommPort = 1
    .Settings = "19200,N,8,1"
    .RThreshold = 1
    .PortOpen = True
End With
```

in the Form_Load event procedure with

```
If sckVI.State <> sckClosed Then sckVI.Close
With sckVI            ' Set up the Winsock control
    .RemoteHost = "127.0.0.1" ' ... or enter a name
    .RemotePort = 1234
    .Connect          ' Connect
End With
```

We have used the loopback IP address 127.0.0.1, which assumes that the
VI and controller program will be running on the same computer. If you are
going to run the VI on a different computer from the one that will run the
controller, enter the IP address or name of that computer in place of
"127.0.0.1."

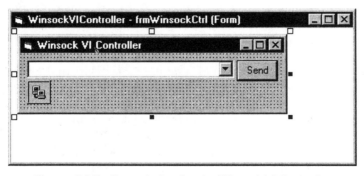

Figure 21-7. Form design for the Winsock VI Controller.

Next let's change the Click event procedure of the btnSend CommandButton. Only one line needs to be removed from the RS-232 controller example. The code that we will replace it with also checks that a connection has been established as a precaution.

Replace the code fragment

```
' Send contents of the text box out the RS-232 port
comVI.Output = strCommand & vbCr
```

in the btnSend_Click event procedure with

```
' Send contents of the text box over the network connection.
If sckVI.State <> sckConnected Then
    MsgBox "Error. Connection is not open! (State=" & CStr(sckVI.State) & ")"
    Exit Sub
Else
    sckVI.SendData strCommand & vbCr
End If
```

We need to change the way that arrival of new data initiates input buffer processing. Delete the comVI_OnComm event procedure entirely, and add a call to the ProcessInputBuffer procedure in the DataArrival event procedure of the sckVI Winsock control.

```
Private Sub sckVI_DataArrival(ByVal bytesTotal As Long)
    ' Process data received over the network connection.
    ProcessInputBuffer

End Sub
```

The last procedure to modify is FetchInputData. The way new data are retrieved must be changed from the RS-232 port to the network connection.

Replace the code fragment …

```
If comVI.InBufferCount > 0 Then
    mStrInputBuffer = mStrInputBuffer & comVI.Input
    FetchInputData = True
End If
```

in the FetchInputData procedure to

```
If sckVI.BytesReceived > 0 Then
    sckVI.GetData strData, vbString
    mStrInputBuffer = mStrInputBuffer & strData
    FetchInputData = True
End If
```

The procedures ProcessInputBuffer, GetMessage, ProcessMessage, and ParseStatus can all remain unchanged. That's it!

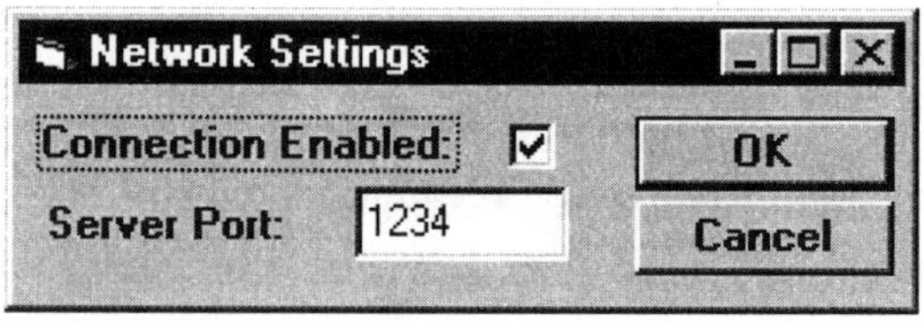

Figure 21-8. The VI Network Settings dialog.

Now we can test the new program. Follow these steps.

1. Run the VI on the computer whose IP address or name you entered in the example code.
2. Enable the network connection by selecting the Connection Enabled CheckBox from the Network Settings dialog, which can be opened by selecting the Edit | Network Settings menu option on the VI (see Figure 21-8).
3. Make sure that the network port number in the Network Settings dialog is the same as the one you entered in the example and close the dialog.
4. Turn the VI on by clicking "On."
5. Start the Winsock VI Controller example program. Note that as soon as the example program is started, it will attempt to establish a connection with the VI.
6. Enter a VI command, such as "Analyze 23," into the cmbSend ComboBox and click "Send."

The resulting behavior should be identical to the RS-232 VI Controller example (see Figure 21-9). The only difference is that now the VI is being controlled over a network. With VB, controlling devices on the other end of network is as easy as controlling them through an RS-232 port. Think of the possibilities for your laboratory!

WRAPPING UP

We covered a wide range of topics in this part of the book, all with the ultimate goal of developing device controllers. Early on we discussed multithreading in Visual Basic®, state machines, and parsing techniques. Methods for implementing state diagrams and parsing in VB were presented. A general-purpose Parser class was also developed. An understanding of each of these topics and device communications is necessary background for robust controller development.

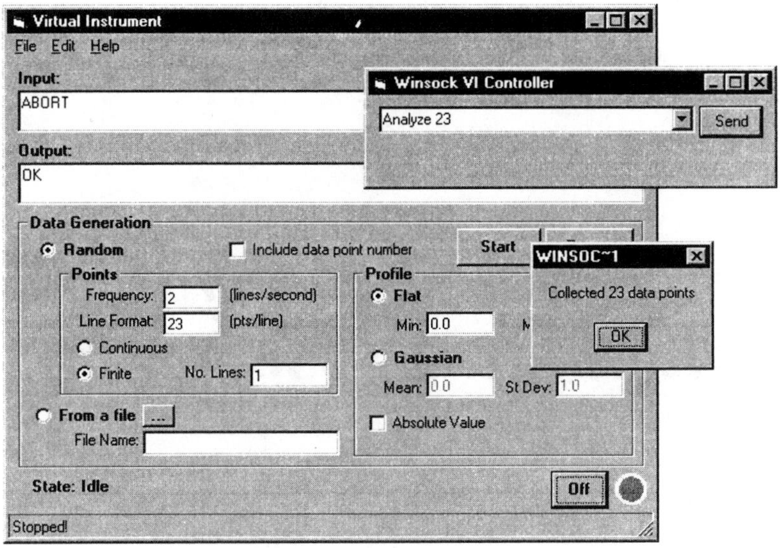

Figure 21-9. The Winsock VI Controller in action.

Two models were introduced for device monitoring. In the polling model the controller program has the responsibility to check for incoming data on a communications port. Polling can be programmed to occur as fast as possible, or on a less frequent basis, depending on the needs of the controlled device. A Timer control was proposed for controlling the frequency of device polling. In the interrupt-driven model for device monitoring the controller doesn't look for new data, but waits until it is notified that new data have arrived. We used the appropriate events of two communication controls to indicate to the controller program that new data were waiting on a communications port.

A general-purpose framework was proposed for organizing the acquisition, interpretation, and reaction to device messages. It accounts for the variety of ways that data can be transmitted. The framework gracefully handles the receipt of partial messages or multiple messages in the same transmission. A state diagram is used to track the operation of the controlled device, and is critical for determining when a valid message has been received and how to respond. Dropped data due to transmission errors or other malformed messages are recognized and flagged with useful error messages using parsing techniques. The controller program is kept responsive with a good understanding of multithreading and how VB executes user code. Brought together and seamlessly integrated, the result is a robust device controller written in Visual Basic®.

At this stage of the game we are experts at interacting with a wide variety of devices. Sooner or later a human is involved. Interacting with humans is a different thing altogether. That is the topic of Part 4.

4

Graphical Interfaces and Data Presentation

Communicating with and controlling devices is only part of the story. In the end, people are always involved. Therefore, the human interface is another critical component of the laboratory computing story. Controller settings must be conveniently entered and modified. Collected data must be presented in tabular and graphical formats. A glance at a control panel should be sufficient to convey the status of one or more monitored devices. The graphical display of data and creation of virtual control panels are two areas in which VB excels.

In this final part of the book we will investigate various techniques for building interfaces for scientific and engineering laboratory applications. We will investigate ways to use existing tools in Visual Basic® for a variety of purposes. We will also spend significant time on building custom graphical displays, both active and interactive. You'll be surprised at how simple it can be to build sophisticated displays using the toolkit provided by VB.

CHAPTER

22

Scientific Plotting with MSChart

A chart is perhaps the most common method used to present scientific and engineering data. VB's MSChart control has remarkably powerful capabilities. It provides the most common business and scientific plotting options. It even includes an ability to generate 3D plots with interactive features, including dynamic rotation!

On the down side, the power of the MSChart control translates into increased complexity. It is relatively easy to create a simple chart, but customizing further can be a frustrating endeavor. The MSChart control's object model includes more than 44 separate object classes! That's not the number of objects in the model—that's the number of object types. There can be more object instances depending on the complexity of your chart.

We'll begin this chapter by first introducing the MSChart control. Then we'll describe it in more detail in what follows. We'll have a look at many of the object types that are included in the object model, and investigate the main objects in depth. We will demonstrate the various ways that you can specify the data to be charted, and the options available for customizing the way a chart appears. Let's get started.

INTRODUCING THE MSCHART CONTROL

The MSChart control is highly versatile, providing a wide range of options for displaying your data. It can chart data in 2D and 3D formats, including those listed in Table 22-1.

To get an idea for what these chart types look like, Figure 22-1 is a gallery of charts created using the MSChart control.

Each instance of an MSChart control is associated with a DataGrid object. The DataGrid holds data and labels that make up the current chart. Editing the properties and calling the methods of the DataGrid object is one of the easiest ways to specify MSChart control data.

TABLE 22-1. MSChart Types.

MSChart Type	Dimensions Available
Bar Chart	2D or 3D
Line Chart	2D or 3D
Area Chart	2D or 3D
Step Chart	2D or 3D
Pie Chart	2D Only
XY (Scatter) Plot	2D only
Combination of styles	2D or 3D

While the MSChart control is quite versatile, it does not offer a complete scientific plotting toolkit. If you are looking for sophisticated data plotting or statistical features, you had better look elsewhere. But for the more common charting needs, the MSChart control is much more than adequate.

A QUICK START

Let's get started with a simple demonstration of how to use the MSChart control. Create a new VB project. Make sure that the project includes the Microsoft Chart Control by verifying that the CheckBox that contains this name is selected in the VB Components dialog. This can be displayed by selecting the menu option Project | Components from the VB menu bar. Sketch a new MSChart control and a CommandButton on Form1 (see Figure 22-2). The source code for the completed project can be found in the folder \Part4\Ex1 of the code available online.

Set the following control properties.

Object Type	Property	Value
Form	Name	frmPlot
	Caption	Test Plot
MSChart	Name	chtPlot
CommandButton	Name	btnPlotIt
	Caption	Plot It

Add the following code to the Click event procedure of the btnPlotIt CommandButton:

```
Private Sub btnPlotIt_Click()
    ' Add data to a plot one point at a time
    Dim I As Integer, X As Single
    Const conPi As Single = 3.14159
```

```
With chtPlot
    .chartType = VtChChartType2dXY   ' Set chart type
    .RowCount = 100                  ' Set number of data points
    .ColumnCount = 2                 ' A column for X and Y

    For I = 1 To 100                 ' Generate points
        .Row = I
        .Column = 1                  ' X column
        X = CSng(I - 1) * 0.05 * conPi
        .Data = 10# * Sin(X)
        .Column = 2                  ' Y column
        .Data = 10# * Sin(X) * Sin(X * 0.6)
    Next I

End With
End Sub
```

When the btnPlotIt CommandButton is clicked, the chtPlot MSChart control will be configured with chart properties and chart data. The event procedure sets the MSChart type to be a 2D X-Y chart with a table containing 100 X-Y points. The data table is filled by looping over the rows of the table while calculating X and Y values using trigonometric functions. Calculated values are saved in the table.

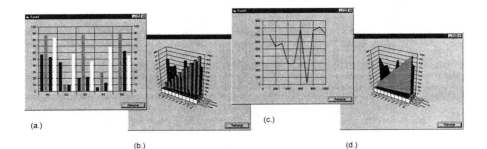

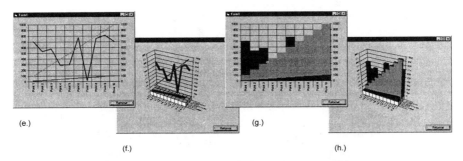

Figure 22-1. An MSChart Gallery: (a) 2D Bar Chart, (b) 3D Bar Chart, (c) 2D XY Chart, (d) 3D Area Chart, (e) 2D Line Chart, (f) 3D Line Chart, (g) 2D Step Chart, (h) 3D Step Chart.

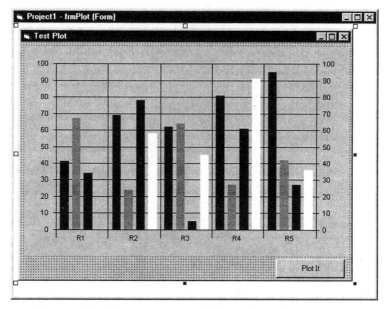

Figure 22-2. Form design for MSChart Quick Start example.

Run the project and click "Plot It." The result will look like that shown in Figure 22-3. The best way to investigate the various properties of the chtPlot MSChart control is to change property values in the example and rerun the project. The design of the MSChart control makes it easy to get started quickly.

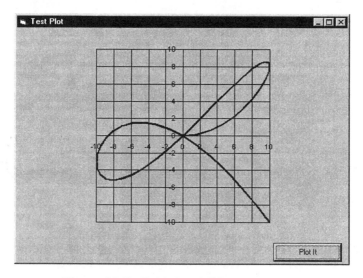

Figure 22-3. Quick Start MSChart example.

TABLE 22-2. Some properties of the MSChart control.

Property	Data Type	Description
ChartType	Enum	Determines the type of chart
ChartData	Variant	Returns or sets the chart data as a two-dimensional array
RandomFill	Boolean	Determines if data will be generated randomly
ShowLegend	Boolean	Determines if the chart legend will be displayed
Row	Integer	The current data grid row
Column	Integer	The current data grid column
Data	String	Data value at the current row and column
DataGrid	DataGrid	Object that holds/describes chart data
Footnote	Footnote	Object that holds/describes text beneath a chart
Legend	Legend	Object that holds/describes the chart legend
Plot	Plot	Object that holds/describes the actual plot
Title	Title	Object that holds/describes the title above the chart

Now let's take a closer look at the features of the MSChart control.

MSCHART PROPERTIES

Charts created using the MSChart control can be complex. They can include several data series, several axes, titles, footnotes, a legend, and more. This complexity is directly reflected in the object model defined by the control. Access to objects contained within an MSChart control begins with the control's properties. Table 22-2 displays several of the more important MSChart control properties. We will see how these are used in the following examples.

The last five properties given in Table 22-2 provide references to objects in an MSChart control. We will need to navigate through one of these references to objects farther down the object hierarchy to gain access to many of the more obscure properties of an MSChart control.

MSCHART METHODS

The MSChart control only has a few methods worth pointing out. They are described in Table 22-3. The EditCopy and EditPaste methods give you a way

TABLE 22-3. Some methods of the MSChart control.

Method	Description
EditCopy	Copies the current chart and its data to the clipboard. The chart is copied as a Windows® Metafile and the data coped as tab-delimited text
EditPaste	Pastes the Windows Metafile or tab-delimited data on the Clipboard into the current selected item
Layout	Causes a chart to lay itself out by recalculating automatic chart parameters

to move data to and from the MSChart control through the Clipboard. An image of the chart can also be copied or pasted as a Windows® Metafile using these same methods. The Layout method will reformat a chart by automatically calculating chart formatting parameters.

Objects further down the MSChart object hierarchy also provide methods for manipulating their own data. We will investigate methods of other MSChart objects as we encounter them.

MSCHART EVENTS

The most interesting and powerful feature of the MSChart control is the collection of events to which you can attach code. In addition to a few events that are common to many controls, MSChart also has three categories of events that are associated with major MSChart objects. The event categories are *Selected* events, *Activated* events, and *Updated* events. Table 22-4 lists MSChart objects that have events in these categories.

Selected events occur when an object is clicked. Activated events occur when an object is double-clicked. Updated events occur when an object has changed. The name of an event associated with a particular object is the name of the event category appended to the object name. For example, when a chart axis is clicked, the AxisSelected event occurs. In a few cases there are multiple MSChart objects of a given type. For example, there is more than one Axis object. To distinguish between multiple objects of the same type, each event procedure is passed a set of arguments that identify the particular object to which the event refers. The arguments are different for each event procedure and depend on the type of object that needs to be identified.

Three categories of events for 11 objects results in 33 different event procedures to which you can add VB code that reacts to user interaction with

TABLE 22-4. MSChart objects that have Selected, Activated, and Updated events.

Object	Description
Axis	A chart axis
AxisLabel	Text labeling a tick or category
AxisTitle	Text labeling an entire axis
Chart	The chart itself
Footnote	Floating text that can be placed on a chart
Legend	A box that describes data series
Plot	The plot itself
Point	A point that makes up one of the curves on a plot
PointLabel	Text that labels a point
Series	A collection of related points that are charted together
Title	Text labeling the entire chart

an MSChart control. The result is a very high degree of control and customizability. You can use an MSChart control as a very sophisticated interface to a set of underlying computational methods.

There are two additional MSChart events worth mentioning. The DataUpdated event occurs when a data point changes. Arguments passed to this event procedure identify the particular data point that has changed and the data series in which it occurs. The DonePainting event occurs after a chart determines that it needs to repaint itself. Repainting is necessary when the visual format of a chart changes.

SPECIFYING AN MSCHART TYPE

We opened this chapter with a discussion of the range of chart types that can be created using the MSChart control. To specify the chart type in code, you simply set the ChartType property of an MSChart control to the proper constant. The ChartType property is an Enum, implying that you can take advantage of VB's Automatic Code Completion feature to discover constant names. Table 22-5 lists the available chart types and the associated ChartType property constant.

SPECIFYING MSCHART DATA

There are two ways to specify the data that are to be displayed in an MSChart control. You can add data one point at one at a time to the DataGrid object. Or you can fill an array and pass the whole thing to the MSChart control's DataGrid. Let's take a look at these two approaches in more detail.

The Quick Start example in this chapter demonstrates how to add data to an MSChart DataGrid object one point at a time. The procedure involves first

TABLE 22-5. MSChart type constants.

ChartType	Enum Constant
3D Bar	VtChChartType3dBar
2D Bar	VtChChartType2dBar
3D Line	VtChChartType3dLine
2D Line	VtChChartType2dLine
3D Area	VtChChartType3dArea
2D Area	VtChChartType2dArea
3D Combination	VtChChartType3dCombination
2D Combination	VtChChartType2dCombination
2D Pie	VtChChartType2dPie
2D XY	VtChChartType2dXY
3D Step	VtChChartType3dStep
2D Step	VtChChartType2dStep

specifying the size of the DataGrid using the MSChart RowCount and ColumnCount properties. Once this is done, the current row and column in the DataGrid are set by assigning values to the MSChart Row and Column properties. You can then set or retrieve the associated data value using the Data property. In the Quick Start example we created a loop that iterated 100 times. During each pass through the loop, the current row and column were changed, and X and Y data were calculated and saved in the DataGrid.

The purpose of each column of data in the DataGrid depends on the type of chart specified. For an X-Y plot, column 1 should contain X data and column 2 should contain Y data. Additional pairs of columns indicate additional sets of X-Y data to plot. For example, columns 3 and 4 should contain X and Y data values for an additional curve. A bar chart would plot each column in the table as a separate series of bars.

MSChart controls also allow you to specify a label for each series of data, and each point in a series. Labels can also be specified one at a time using the MSChart ColumnLabelCount, ColumnLabelIndex, and ColumnLabel properties for data series labels, and the RowLabelCount, RowLabelIndex, and RowLabel properties for point labels.

Data points and data series can have multiple label levels. The number of levels is determined by the ColumnLabelCount and RowLabelCount properties. For a given row or column, an individual data point or data series label level is selected by setting the ColumnLabelIndex or RowLabelIndex properties. To specify a label for a given data point, set the Row property of an MSChart control to the data point and the RowLabelIndex property to the label level. Then assign a label to the RowLabel property. If you want one label to be assigned to a set of contiguous points, only set the label for the first point in the set. Leave the remaining labels unspecified. The MSChart control will handle the formatting. The case is similar for multiple level data series labels. Set the Column property of an MSChart control to the appropriate data series and the ColumnLabelIndex to the data series label level. Then assign a label to the ColumnLabel property.

To demonstrate this, let's begin with the Quick Start example from this chapter. The following modified Click event procedure adds two data point label levels for a 2D bar chart.

```
Private Sub btnPlotIt_Click()
    ' Add data to a plot one point at a time
    Dim I As Integer, X As Single
    Const conPi As Single = 3.14159

    With chtPlot
        .chartType = VtChChartType2dBar ' Set chart type

        .RowCount = 10                  ' Set number of data points
        .ColumnCount = 2                ' Two series of data

        .RowLabelCount = 2              ' Two levels of point labels
```

```
            For I = 1 To 10                    ' Generate points
               .Row = I
               .Column = 1                     ' X column
               X = CSng(I - 1) * 0.05 * conPi
               .Data = 10# * Sin(X)

               .RowLabelIndex = 1              ' First level point label
               .RowLabel = "Point " & CStr(I)
               If (I - 1) Mod 5 = 0 Then       ' Second level point label
                   .RowLabelIndex = 2          ' for every five points
                   .RowLabel = "Group " & CStr(I \ 5 + 1)
               End If

               .Column = 2                     ' Y column
               .Data = 10# * Sin(X) * Sin(X * 0.6)
            Next I
        End With
    End Sub
```

In this modified procedure, we changed the chart type to a 2D bar chart. The number of data points was reduced to 10 by changing the RowCount property of the MSChart control. The RowLabelCount property is set to 2, indicating that there will be two levels of data point labels. Labels are set in the loop that assigns data to the DataGrid object. The level-one row label for each data point is set by first assigning the RowLabelIndex property for the current row to 1, and then the RowLabel property to the string "Point #," where "#" is replaced with the index of the loop. The second-level label is set for data points 1 and 6 only. This is accomplished by first checking if (I-1) Mod 5 = 0, which is satisfied when I equals 1 or 6. If this condition is true, the RowLabelIndex is set to 2 and the RowLabel is set to the string "Group #," where "#" is replaced with the result of the calculation I \ 5 + 1. Figure 22-4

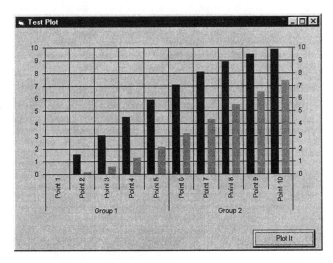

Figure 22-4. Modified Quick Start example demonstrating multiple label levels.

is the chart that results from these changes. The completed project can be found in \Part4\Ex2 of the code available online.

The SetSize method of the DataGrid object can be used in place of the ColumnCount, RowCount, ColumnLabelCount and RowLabelCount properties of the MSChart or DataGrid objects. Refer to VB Help for more details.

Another approach to setting the data and labels for a chart is to fill a two-dimensional Variant array with the appropriate data points and labels, and assign it to the MSChart control ChartData property. This approach can be a little more convenient since you can assign values to elements of the array in any way that is most appropriate to your application. When it is in the format you desire, pass it to the MSChart control for charting.

The array must contain the numeric data to be charted. The layout of the data in the Variant array is the same as the DataGrid object; data series or X-Y pairs are stored in consecutive columns. Data points are stored in consecutive rows. The array can also contain data series and data point labels. Data series labels are placed in the first row and data point labels in the first column of the array. Figure 22-5 demonstrates what a Variant array to be charted might look like. It is also possible to specify multiple levels of labels in the array. For example, if you wanted two levels of data point labels, the first two columns of the Variant array should contain the appropriate labels exactly as it would be in the DataGrid object of the MSChart control.

Once the Variant array is set up, you can hand the entire array to an MSChart control by assigning it to the MSChart ChartData property. The MSChart control determines how to interpret the data in the array by the data types of the array elements. For example, if all elements in the first column in the array cannot be interpreted as numeric data, the MSChart assumes it is a label and assigns it to the appropriate data point label properties.

To demonstrate this, let's create a chart and populate it with data in the format specified by the Variant array in Figure 22-5. Create a new project and add an MSChart control and a CommandButton to Form1. Set the control properties as follows:

Add the following code to the btnPlotIt CommandButton Click event procedure. The Variant array called vrnData is filled with data similar to those shown in Figure 22-5. Random data are generated in the example instead of predetermined data points. Bounds of the vrnData array are not important.

Object Type	Property	Value
Form	Name	frmPlot
	Caption	Patient Data
MSChart	Name	chtPlot
CommandButton	Name	btnPlotIt
	Caption	Plot It

	Column 0	Column 1	Column 2	Column 3
Row 0		"Patient 1"	"Patient 2"	"Patient 3"
Row 1	"Week 1"	0.72	0.91	0.86
Row 2	"Week 2"	0.64	0.80	0.66
Row 3	"Week 3"	0.37	0.32	0.87
Row 4	"Week 4"	0.50	0.33	0.99
Row 5	"Week 5"	0.64	0.05	0.59

Figure 22-5. A sample Variant array to be assigned to an MSChart's ChartData property.

We declared the array so that the first column and row are accessed using a zero index. This was done for convenience. The zeroth row and zeroth columns in the array contain labels. Data begin with row 1, column 1. Figure 22-6 shows the resulting chart. The completed example can be found in the folder \Part4\Ex3 of the code available online.

```
Private Sub btnPlotIt_Click()
    ' Generate a bar chart using a variant array
    Dim vrnData(0 To 5, 0 To 3) As Variant
    Dim I As Integer
```

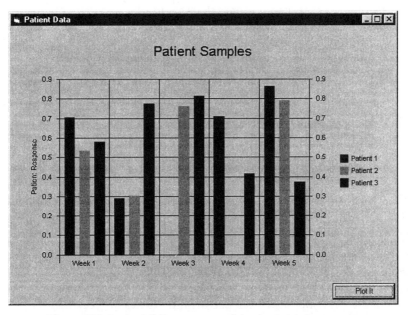

Figure 22-6. An MSChart generated using a Variant array.

```
' Specify data series labels
vrnData(0, 1) = "Patient 1"
vrnData(0, 2) = "Patient 2"
vrnData(0, 3) = "Patient 3"

' Specify data and data point labels
For I = 1 To 5
    vrnData(I, 0) = "Week " & CStr(I)
    vrnData(I, 1) = Rnd          ' Generate random data
    vrnData(I, 2) = Rnd
    vrnData(I, 3) = Rnd
Next I

' Set up the chart
With chtPlot
    .chartType = VtChChartType2dBar          ' Set the chart type

    .TitleText = "Patient Samples"           ' Set the chart titles
    .Title.VtFont.Size = 16
    .Plot.Axis(VtChAxisIdY).AxisTitle = "Patient Response"
    .ShowLegend = True
    .ChartData = vrnData                     ' Assign data to chart
End With

End Sub
```

TITLES AND LEGENDS

Charts can be annotated with various titles. You can specify a title for the entire
chart, titles for axes, and a footnote title. Text for the main chart title and footnote can be specified directly using properties of MSChart. To change the
format of these titles such as font or location, or to specify axis titles and their
formats, you must move down the MSChart object hierarchy and directly
manipulate the properties of the appropriate objects. We'll talk more about
this shortly.

To set the main chart title, assign a string to the TitleText property of the
MSChart control. Assigning a string to the FootnoteText property will set the
chart's footnote. In the previous example we set the main title of the chart
and formatted it with the following line of code, which was executed within
the scope of the MSChart control.

```
.TitleText = "Patient Samples"             ' Set the chart titles
.Title.VtFont.Size = 16
```

Assigning a string to TitleText sets the main title for the chart. To increase the
font size of the title we needed to set the Size property of the VtFont object,
which belongs to the Title object of the MSChart control.

The Y axis was assigned a title as well. This was accomplished with the
following line of code, also executed with the MSChart control's scope:

```
.Plot.Axis(VtChAxisIdY).AxisTitle = "Patient Response"
```

In this case, we assigned a title string to the AxisTitle property of the Plot's Y-axis object, which is owned by the MSChart control. The Plot object holds a collection of Axis objects. To refer to the Y axis we needed to use the proper index, which is held in the predefined VtChAxisIsY constant.

In the previous example we also displayed a legend with data series labels. This is easily accomplished by setting the ShowLegend property of the MSChart control to True. To format the Legend further, you'll have to refer to the Legend object, its subobjects, and their properties.

SERIES STATISTICS

The MSChart control offers a few built-in features for calculating and displaying statistics that describe a data series. For certain chart types it will automatically calculate the maximum, minimum, mean, or standard deviation of a particular series of data, or it will fit a straight line through the series data using linear regression. The maximum, minimum, and mean are displayed as a horizontal line that is added to the chart. The standard deviation is displayed as a pair of horizontal lines drawn at one standard deviation above the mean, and one below the mean. The regression line is also straight and is drawn through the data with the appropriate slope and y intercept. You can add only one, or any combination, of the lines that describe these statistics to an MSChart.

The MSChart control contains a Plot object, which describes the actual data plot. Plot has a Collection called the SeriesCollection, which contains a set of Series objects. A Series object describes one series of data that is currently being plotted. Each Series object has a StatLine object, which governs the subset of five statistics lines that are drawn and how they are formatted. To determine which of the five lines are drawn on a chart, the Flag property of the StatLine object must be set appropriately. To access the Flag property you must successfully navigate down the MSChart object hierarchy. As an example, let's say that we want to draw a line at the mean of the second series of data on a Plot. To navigate to the desired StatLine Flag property, use a line of code like the following:

```
MyChart.Plot.SeriesCollection.Item(2).StatLine.Flag = VtStatsMean
```

We picked the second series in the SeriesCollection using the Item property with an index of 2. The StatLine Flag property was set to a predefined constant, which indicates that a mean line should be drawn on the chart's plot. Other Flag property constants are given in Table 22-6. This set of constants is determined by the VtChStats Enum, which is predefined in VB.

Multiple statistics lines can be drawn for a single Series by setting the StatLine Flag property to the value that results from "Or-ing" the associated constants together. For example, if we wanted to display the mean and stan-

TABLE 22-6. VtChStats Enum constants to be used to assign values to the StatLine Flag property.

StatLine Flag Constant	Description
VtStatsMaximum	Draws a line at the maximum series value
VtStatsMinimum	Draws a line at the minimum series value
VtStatsMean	Mean of all values in the series
VtStatsRegression	Fits and draws a straight line through the series values
VtStatsStddev	Draws horizontal lines at the upper and lower standard deviation of the series values

dard deviation for the first series, we would execute a line of code like the following.

```
MyChart.Plot.SeriesCollection.Item(1).StatLine.Flag = VtStatsMean Or VtStatsStddev
```

Additional properties of the StatLine object are used to modify the format of statistics lines. The Style and Width properties are used to set the line style and width. The Style property should be set to an appropriate VtPenStyle Enum constant. Width takes a single-precision number. The VtColor property returns a reference to a VtColor object whose properties can be modified to set the color of the statistics line. Refer to VB Help or the Object Browser for further details.

To demonstrate statistics lines, create a new project and sketch an MSChart control and a CommandButton onto Form1. Set the following control properties:

Object Type	Property	Value
Form	Name	frmPlot
	Caption	Series Statistics
MSChart	Name	chtPlot
CommandButton	Name	btnPlotIt
	Caption	Plot It

Add the following code to the btnPlotIt CommandButton Click event procedure:

```
Private Sub btnPlotIt_Click()
    ' Create a line chart
    Dim vrnData(0 To 100, 1 To 2) As Variant, I As Integer

    ' Create the data
    vrnData(0, 1) = "Random Data"                 ' Data Set Label
    For I = 1 To 100
```

```
            vrnData(I, 1) = I * 100                    ' Generate data
            vrnData(I, 2) = Rnd * 5000#
        Next I

        ' Set up the chart
        With chtPlot
            .chartType = VtChChartType2dXY          ' Set the chart type
            .TitleText = "Series Statistics"        ' Set the chart titles
            .Title.VtFont.Size = 16
            .FootnoteText = "* Regression line and Standard Deviation are shown"
            .Footnote.Location.LocationType = VtChLocationTypeBottomLeft
            .Plot.Axis(VtChAxisIdX).AxisTitle = "X Data"
            .Plot.Axis(VtChAxisIdY).AxisTitle = "Y Data"
                                                    ' Set up statistics lines
            With .Plot.SeriesCollection.Item(1).StatLine
                .Flag = VtChStatsRegression Or VtChStatsStddev
                .Style(VtChStatsStddev) = VtPenStyleDashed
            End With

            .ShowLegend = True
            .ChartData = vrnData                    ' Assign data to chart
        End With
    End Sub
```

Scanning through the procedure, you will see that several chart titles are set. Also, a regression line and standard deviation line have been added to the first (and only) chart series. The two standard deviation lines are changed to dashed lines in order to distinguish them from the regression line. The resulting chart is displayed in Figure 22-7. The complete project can be found in \Part4\Ex4 of the code available online.

INTERACTIVE FEATURES OF MSCHART

In additional to a powerful charting facility, the MSChart control provides flexible methods for enabling user interaction. Earlier we discussed how several MSChart objects have Selected, Activated and Updated events, which occur when a user interacts with an MSChart. A Selected event occurs when an MSChart object is clicked, an Activated event occurs when an object is double-clicked, and an Updated event occurs when an object's data are changed. Procedures associated with these events allow you to respond by performing any action that you can program.

Disallowing interactive selections can effectively disable Selected and Updated events. The MSChart control has a property called AllowSelections, which can be set to False to disable the selection of MSChart objects. Make sure that AllowSelections is set to True if you want the user to be able to select or activate MSChart objects. A single MSChart data point or an entire data series can be selected. The first time a data point is clicked, the entire series is selected. The second click causes only the point to be selected. To turn data series selection off, set the AllowSeriesSelection MSChart control property to False. When this is the case, the first click will only select a single data point.

Another powerful interactive feature of the MSChart control is the ability to rotate a 3D chart interactively. Holding down the control key while your cursor is over an activated MSChart control will cause it to change to the rotation cursor. While the rotation cursor is visible, you can click on the chart and dynamically drag it around to change the viewpoint. This feature can be enabled by setting the AllowDynamicRotation MSControl property to True, and disabled by setting it to False.

Let's demonstrate some of these features with an example. We will build a simple program that displays data associated with a 96-well microtiter plate. A 96-well microtiter plate is an 8 by 12 array of small vessels called wells that can hold substances. These plates are often used to perform tests on substance samples, 96 at a time. The data to be charted in this example will be stored as an 8 by 12 array of numbers.

Create a new VB project. On Form1 sketch a new MSChart control, two TextBoxes, two Labels, and a CommandButton. Refer to Figure 22-8 for the form design. A completed version of the project can be found in the folder \Part4\PlateBrowser of the code available online.

Set control properties as follows:

Object Type	Property	Value
Form	Name	frmBrowser
	Caption	Microplate Data Browser
MSChart	Name	chtPlate
CommandButton	Name	btnNewData
	Caption	New Data
Label	Name	lblWell
	Caption	Well:
Label	Name	lblValue
	Caption	Value:
TextBox	Name	txtWell
	Text	
TextBox	Name	txtDataValue
	Text	

We want to declare a form-level two-dimensional Variant array to hold microplate data so that it can be filled and accessed by different procedures in the Form module. The lower bounds of the array are each declared as 0. Zeroth-array row and column will be used for data point and data series labels. Upper bounds are 8 and 12 to accommodate one data point for each well in a microtiter plate. Enter the following code into the declarations section of the frmBrowser Form.

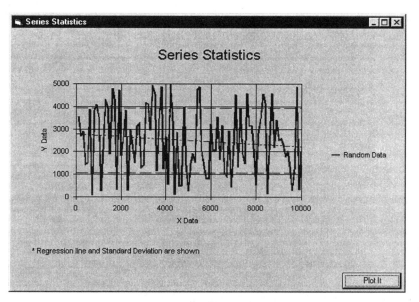

Figure 22-7. An MSChart with regression and standard deviation lines.

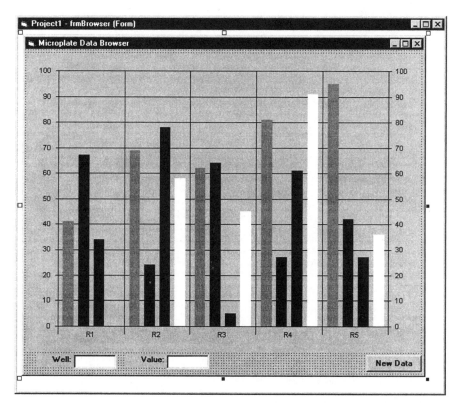

Figure 22-8. Form design for the Microplate Data Browser.

223

```
Option Explicit

' A module level variant array to hold data and labels
Private mVrnData(0 To 8, 0 To 12) As Variant
```

Upon loading the Form, we will assign data point and data series labels to appropriate elements of the mVrnData array. We will also initialize the chtPlate MSChart by setting its chart type, axis label formats, and interactive features. The MSChart property AllowSelections is set to True, but AllowSeriesSelection is set to False. This combination of settings lets the user select a plotted data point by clicking on it once. If AllowSeriesSelection was set to True, the first mouse click would select the entire series. Two clicks would be required to select a single data point. To give the user the ability to rotate the chart dynamically, the MSChart property AllowDynamicRotation is set to True. Finally, the btnNewData CommandButton Click event procedure is called to initialize stored data to random numbers. Following is the frmBrowser Form's Load event procedure:

```
Private Sub Form_Load()
    ' Set up the chart properties
    Dim I As Integer

    ' Set data point and data series labels
    For I = 1 To 8
        mVrnData(I, 0) = Chr$(I + 64)
    Next I
    For I = 1 To 12         ' Add a space so MSChart interprets the number as a label
        mVrnData(0, I) = " " & CStr(I)
    Next I

    ' Set up the chart
    With chtPlate
        ' Set chart type
        .chartType = VtChChartType3dBar

        ' Set axis label formats
        .Plot.Axis(VtChAxisIdX).Labels(1).VtFont.Size = 14
        .Plot.Axis(VtChAxisIdX).Labels(1).VtFont.Style = VtFontStyleBold
        .Plot.Axis(VtChAxisIdY).Labels(1).VtFont.Size = 14
        .Plot.Axis(VtChAxisIdY).Labels(1).VtFont.Style = VtFontStyleBold
        .Plot.Axis(VtChAxisIdZ).Labels(1).VtFont.Size = 14
        .Plot.Axis(VtChAxisIdZ).Labels(1).VtFont.Style = VtFontStyleBold

        ' Enable chart components to be selected
        .AllowSelections = True

        ' Disable series selection so that point selection occurs on first click
        .AllowSeriesSelection = False

        ' Allow the chart to be rotated
        .AllowDynamicRotation = True

    End With
```

```
    ' Initially fill with random data
    btnNewData_Click
End Sub
```

The btnNewData CommandButton Click event procedure contains the code to generate a new set of random data and assign it to the chtPlate MSChart control for demonstration purposes. It also increments the chart number displayed in its title. Chart data are produced by generating random numbers between 0 and 1 and raising them to the power of 20. This tends to produce numbers that are skewed torward zero. Relatively few get near a value of 1, making them easier to select with the mouse.

```
Private Sub btnNewData_Click()
    ' Regenerate random data and chart
    Dim I As Integer, J As Integer
    Static intPlateNum As Integer

    ' Generate data so only a few numbers are much greater than 0
    For I = 1 To 8
        For J = 1 To 12
            mVrnData(I, J) = Rnd ^ 20
        Next J
    Next I

    ' Assign data to the chart
    chtPlate.ChartData = mVrnData

    ' Create a new title
    intPlateNum = intPlateNum + 1
    chtPlate.TitleText = "Plate " & CStr(intPlateNum)
    chtPlate.Title.VtFont.Size = 20
End Sub
```

The chtPlate MSChart PointSelected event procedure provides the interactive capabilities for the example. When a data point is selected on the chart, the PointSelected event procedure is executed with the data necessary to identify the selected point. The Series argument is the index of the data series, and the DataPoint argument is the index of the data point in the series. We use these arguments to retrieve the data point from the mVrnData array, and to build a string that identifies the associated position in the microtiter plate. The MouseFlags argument provides information for determining if any key was also held down while the mouse was clicked.

```
Private Sub chtPlate_PointSelected(Series As Integer, DataPoint As Integer, _
                        MouseFlags As Integer, Cancel As Integer)
    ' Set the text box values
    txtWell.Text = Chr$(DataPoint + 64) & CStr(Series)
    txtDataValue.Text = Format(mVrnData(DataPoint, Series), "0.###")
End Sub
```

Run the completed example program. Click a bar on the chart to display its location and data value (see Figure 22-9). Hold the control key down to

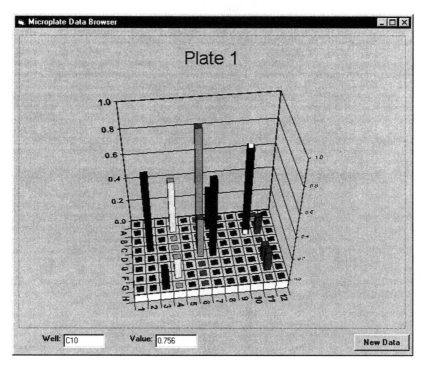

Figure 22-9. Interacting with the Microplate Data Browser.

change the mouse pointer to the rotation cursor. While continuing to hold the control key down, press and hold the left mouse button down on any part of the plot and move it to rotate the plot (Figure 22-10).

THE MSCHART OBJECT MODEL

We have referred to quite a few objects contained in the object model of the MSChart control. On occasion it was necessary to traverse the object hierarchy through a number of objects before gaining access to an object or property of interest. It can be very frustrating when you are trying to set something specific and you can't seem to find the object and property that you need to set. For example, you need to traverse at least five objects in order to get to the property that lets you change the style of an axis label. The following line of code adapted from the previous example illustrates this point:

```
chtPlate.Plot.Axis(VtChAxisIdZ).Labels(1).VtFont.Style = VtFontStyleBold
```

Learning how to traverse and manipulate the object hierarchy can be time consuming. In this section we will try to make the process a little easier by

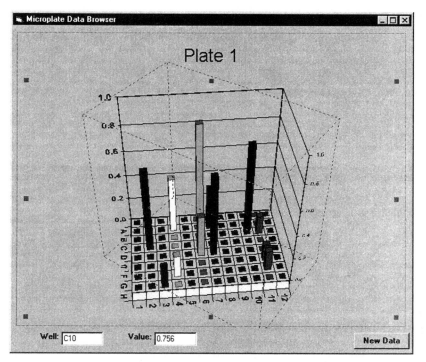

Figure 22-10. Interactively rotating an MSChart plot.

looking at the MSChart object model more closely, and demonstrating how to discover every detail.

As we mentioned at the beginning of this chapter, there are more than 44 separate object classes that are used to make up the MSChart object model. The majority of these objects are listed alphabetically in Table 22-7. Along with the name of each object is a brief description as well as the higher-level object that contains it. Several objects listed have multiple instances located at various places in the MSChart object model. When this is the case, no single higher-level container object can be identified, and is therefore listed as "(various)."

Table 22-7 can be handy when trying to determine how to traverse the MSChart object hierarchy to access a certain object. Once you have identified the object you wish to access, you can find it in the table, then find its container. Next find the container's container, and so on, until you have reached the MSChart control at the root of the hierarchy. Using dot-notation, you can traverse the path identified in the reverse direction to access the object nested within the hierarchy.

Another helpful tool for understanding and navigating the MSChart object model is the diagram in Figure 22-11. This shows the MSChart object model as a containment hierarchy. It illustrates the main MSChart objects and how they are contained within other objects of the overall MSChart object model.

TABLE 22-7. Objects in the MSChart Object Model

MSChart Object	Description	Container
1. Axis	An axis of the plot	Plot
2. AxisGrid	The area around an axis	Axis
3. AxisScale	Describes the scale of an axis	Axis
4. AxisTitle	The title of an axis	Axis
5. Backdrop	The background area of an object	(various)
6. Brush	Sets the graphic fill for an object	(various)
7. CategoryScale	Describes the grid of a category (X) Axis	Axis
8. Coor	An X-Y pair of single-precision numbers	(various)
9. DataGrid	Holds data to be charted	MSChart
10. DataPoint	Describes a single data point	DataPoints
11. DataPoints	A collection of related DataPoint objects	Series
12. DataPointLabel	A label for a data point	DataPoint
13. Fill	Describes the backdrop of an object	Backdrop
14. Footnote	Text that appears beneath a plot	MSChart
15. Frame	Describes how the chart backdrop is filled	Backdrop
16. IFontDisp	Describes font characteristics	(various)
17. Intersection	Describes the point at which two axes cross	Axis
18. Label	Describes an axis label	Labels
19. Labels	A collection of axis label objects	Axis
20. Lcoor	An X-Y pair of long integers	(various)
21. Legend	Key describing chart data	MSChart
22. Light	Describes the way a plot is lighted	Plot
23. LightSource	Describes a single source of light illuminating a chart	LightSources
24. LightSources	A collection of LightSource objects	Light
25. Location	Describes the position of a chart label	(various)
26. Marker	Describes the marker for a particular DataPoint object	DataPoint
27. Pen	Describes the color and style of the way an object is drawn	(various)
28. Plot	Portion of an MSChart that displays data	MSChart
29. PlotBase	The area underneath the plot on a chart	Plot
30. Rect	Describes a rectangular region	Location
31. Series	A collection of data points and formatting	SeriesCollection
32. SeriesCollection	A collection of Series objects	Plot
33. SeriesMarker	Describes a data point marker for an entire series	Series
34. SeriesPosition	Describes the position of a Series in a chart	Series
35. Shadow	Describes the shadow displayed for a Backdrop object	Backdrop
36. StatLine	Describes a Series statistic lines	Series
37. TextLayout	Describes the position and orientation of a label	(various)
38. Tick	Describes positional markers that appear along an axis	Axis
39. Title	Describes the main title for a chart	MSChart

(continued)

TABLE 22-7. Continued

MSChart Object	Description	Container
40. ValueScale	Formats the grid of a value (Y) axis	Axis
41. VtFont	Describes the font of chart text	(various)
42. VtColor	Describes a color used to display a chart object	(various)
43. Wall	Describes 3D chart value axis background formatting	Plot
44. Weighting	Describes the size of a pie slice on a pie chart	Plot

It is interesting to note that several MSChart control properties exist just to make it easier to access a property of an object that can be found deeper in the hierarchy. For example, accessing the TitleText property of MSChart is the same as accessing the Text property of the Title object contained by an MSChart control. In other words, the following two statements are equivalent for a hypothetical MSChart control called MyChart.

```
MyChart.TitleText = "This is the Title"
MyChart.Title.Text = "This is the Title"
```

You can prove it to yourself by making the change in one of the example projects. The same is the case for the FootnoteText property and the Footnote.Text reference from an MSChart control. A few of the DataGrid properties are the same as MSChart control properties. For example, the ColumnCount property of the DataGrid object is the same as the ColumnCount property of the MSChart control. The same is the case for ColumnLabelCount,

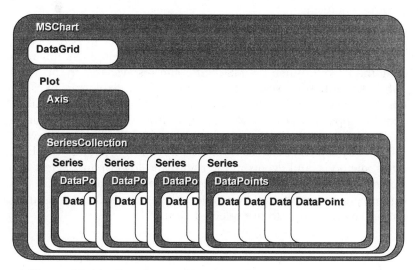

Figure 22-11. *Containment hierarchy of the main MSChart objects.*

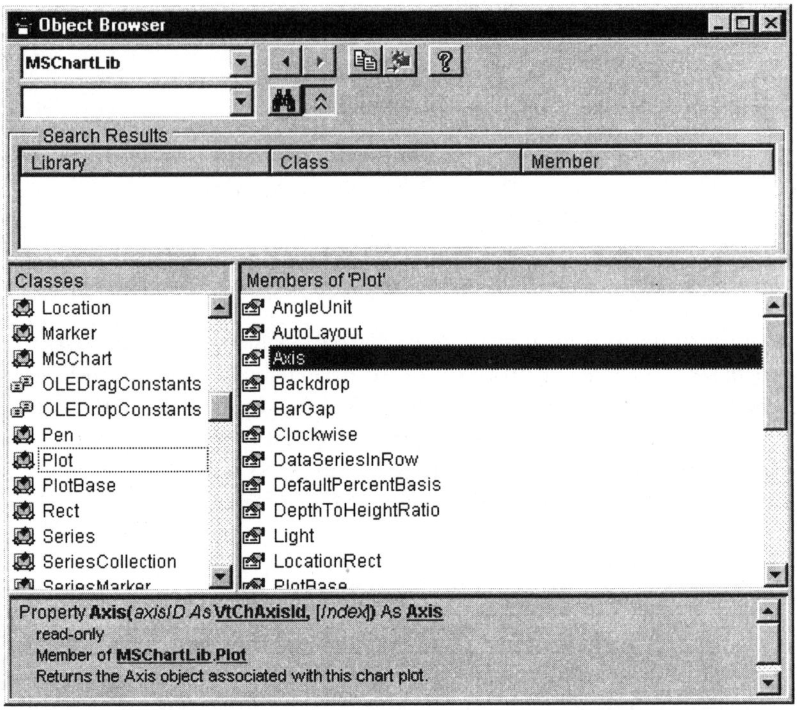

Figure 22-12. Object Browser investigating the MSChartLib library.

RowCount, and RowLabelCount properties. Providing multiple ways to set MSChart properties may make it easier to access commonly used properties, but it can be confusing.

The best way to get all the details of the MSChart object model is to use the Object Browser. We introduced the Object Browser in Part 1. You can display the Object Browser from the VB Integrated Development Environment by hitting the F2 key. When the MSChart control is available in the Toolbox, either the MSChartLib or MSChart20Lib library is available for investigating through the Object Browser. Selecting one of these libraries from the drop-down in the upper left portion of the Object Browser window will limit the classes displayed to those in that library (Figure 22-12). Navigate the MSChart object model by selecting classes in the left-hand lower pane to display class properties, methods, and events in the right-hand lower pane. Select a property method or event to see more details in the bottom pane. Follow links in the bottom pane to jump to different object classes, predefined constants, and other information relating to the selected item.

CHAPTER

23

Tabular Data Display and Editing

The simplest way to present data is in a table. We've used tables time and time again in this book. VB ships with a super grid control for displaying tabular data called MSFlexGrid. If displaying data in a table is what you need, then MSFlexGrid can do a lot for you. The MSFlexGrid control will display text and/or graphics in the cells of a grid. Cell text color, size, style, and other formatting options can be set on a cell-by-cell basis. Column and row alignment, size, and visibility can also be set. When configured properly an MSFlexGrid control can also retrieve and display data from a database.

The MSFlexGrid control has several expected methods and events. Methods include AddItem for adding a new row to the grid and Clear for clearing the grid contents. Events include Click, which occurs when the grid is clicked with a mouse, and Scroll, which occurs when the grid view is changed using a ScrollBar. We'll investigate MSFlexGrid control features further in the following sections.

It is important to point out that the MSFlexGrid control is not a spreadsheet. It provides no mechanism for interactively editing cell contents. This might catch the first-time grid control user off-guard. It looks like a spreadsheet; why doesn't it act like one? Spreadsheets are much more complex than a simple grid control. Furthermore, different spreadsheet applications behave differently. If you need a full-featured spreadsheet control to embed in your VB application, you are probably better off buying one of the many commercially available third-party spreadsheet controls. On the other hand, if you want a lightweight spreadsheet that has custom editing features, it is relatively easy to build it using MSFlexGrid. Later on in this chapter we will demonstrate how to build a basic spreadsheet using the MSFlexGrid control. The good news is that MSFlexGrid provides all the necessary hooks to get the job done.

A QUICK START

Let's build a simple example to demonstrate some of the features of the
MSFlexGrid Control. In the example we will build an interface that displays
communication options in a table, and allows the options to be toggled on
or off individually. Create a new VB project and make sure that the "Microsoft®
FlexGrid Control" option is selected in the Components dialog, which can be
displayed by selecting the Project | Components menu option from the IDE.
Sketch a new MSFlexGrid control onto Form1 and set the following control
properties.

Object Type	Property	Value
Form	Name	frmTable
	Caption	Communication Options
MSFlexGrid	Name	grdTable
	AllowUserResizing	3 - flexResizeBoth

This example uses several icon files that are distributed with the Professional
Edition of VB. For convenience, we've included copies of these files with the
completed example in the folder \Part4\Ex5 of the online code.

Enter the following code into the declarations section of the frmTable Form.
Here we've declared one module-level string variable called mStrAppPath that
will be initialized with the startup path of the application. This is where the
example will look for graphics files.

```
Option Explicit

Private mStrAppPath As String          ' Path of application
```

Upon loading the application we initialize the MSFlexGrid control. This
includes setting cell formats, setting row and column sizes, and initializing
textual and graphic cell contents. The following Load event procedure of the
frmTable Form does the initialization.

```
Private Sub Form_Load()
    ' Initialize the table
    Dim I As Integer

    mStrAppPath = App.Path & "\"        ' Save the initial application path

    With grdTable                       ' Format the grid
        .FixedRows = 0                  ' Fixed rows and columns
        .FixedCols = 1
        .Rows = 5                       ' Rows and columns
        .Cols = 4
        .WordWrap = True                ' Wrap text
        .RowHeight(-1) = 600            ' Set row and column sizes
        .ColWidth(0) = 1000
        .ColWidth(1) = 600
        .ColWidth(2) = 600
        .ColWidth(3) = 1000
```

```
            .Col = 0                          ' Set column 0 labels and formats
            .Row = 0
            .CellFontBold = True
            .Text = "Serial Port"
            .Row = 1
            .CellFontBold = True
            .Text = "Parallel Port"
            .Row = 2
            .CellFontBold = True
            .Text = "Network"
            .Row = 3
            .CellFontBold = True
            .Text = "Wireless"
            .Row = 4
            .CellFontBold = True
            .Text = "File"

            .Col = 1                          ' Set column 1 pictures
            .Row = 0
            Set .CellPicture = LoadPicture(mStrAppPath & "Phone01.ico")
            .Row = 1
            Set .CellPicture = LoadPicture(mStrAppPath & "Net06.ico")
            .Row = 2
            Set .CellPicture = LoadPicture(mStrAppPath & "Net01.ico")
            .Row = 3
            Set .CellPicture = LoadPicture(mStrAppPath & "Phone14.ico")
            .Row = 4
            Set .CellPicture = LoadPicture(mStrAppPath & "Disk04.ico")

            .Col = 2                          ' Initialize the selection display
            For I = 0 To 4
                .Row = I
                Set .CellPicture = LoadPicture(mStrAppPath & "Misc13.ico")
                .TextMatrix(I, 3) = "Inactive"
            Next I

        End With
    End Sub
```

Finally, we want to make it possible to toggle an option on or off when the user clicks on column two of the grid. This column contains one of two icons that indicate the selection state of the row. The option is on when column two contains a red light icon and column three contains the text "Active." The option is off when column two contains a white circle icon and column three contains the text "Inactive." The red light and white circle icon files are also distributed with VB and included in the completed project folder. The following Click event procedure of the grdTable MSFlexGrid control toggles a particular row option on or off.

```
Private Sub grdTable_Click()
    ' Toggle selection
    Dim intRow As Integer

    With grdTable
        If .Col <> 2 Then Exit Sub      ' Only react to mouse clicks on column 2
        intRow = .Row                   ' Save the row
```

```
                                  ' If option is on - turn it off

    If .TextMatrix(intRow, 3) = "Active" Then
       Set .CellPicture = LoadPicture(mStrAppPath & "Misc13.ico")
       .Col = 3                        ' Change column 3 text
       .CellForeColor = vbBlack        ' Change text color
       .CellFontBold = False           ' Turn bold off
       .Text = "Inactive"              ' Set text
       .Col = 2
    Else                               ' If option is off - turn it on
       Set .CellPicture = LoadPicture(mStrAppPath & "Misc15.ico")
       .Col = 3                        ' Change column 3 text
       .CellForeColor = vbRed          ' Change text color
       .CellFontBold = True            ' Turn bold on
       .Text = "Active"                ' Set text
       .Col = 2
    End If

  End With

End Sub
```

Once all the code is entered, run the example program. Click on the grid cell containing the white circle icon to change it to the red light and to activate the option. Clicking a second time will disable the option. Figure 23-1 shows the example in action. Since Figure 23-1 is not printed in color, the red "light" shows up as more of a dark gray circle.

MSFLEXGRID PROPERTIES

The previous Quick Start example demonstrates a number of the properties of MSFlexGrid. Table 23-1 lists several properties with their data types and a brief description.

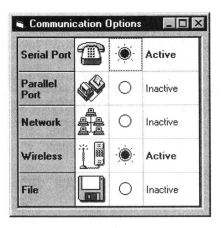

Figure 23-1. An example program using the MSFlexGrid control.

TABLE 23-1. Some properties of the MSFlexGrid control.

Property	Data Type	Description
AllowUserResizing	Integer	Determines whether rows and/or columns can be resized by the user
Rows	Long	Sets or returns the number of grid rows
Cols	Long	Sets or returns the number of grid columns
FixedRows	Long	Sets or returns the number of fixed grid rows
FixedCols	Long	Sets or returns the number of fixed grid columns
ColWidth(*col*)	Long	Sets or returns the width of a column
RowHeight(*row*)	Long	Sets or returns the height of a row
Row	Long	Sets or returns the active grid row
Col	Long	Sets or returns the active grid column
RowSel	Long	Sets or returns bounding row in current selection
ColSel	Long	Sets or returns bounding column in current selection
CellFontBold	Boolean	Sets or returns the bold state of the active cell
CellForeColor	Integer	Sets or returns the text color of the active cell
Text	String	Sets or returns the text contained in the active cell
TextMatrix(*row, col*)	String	Sets or returns the text in the cell at location row, col without it being active
CellPicture	(graphic)	Sets the graphic that is currently displayed in the active cell
Sort	Integer	Determines the style of sorting rows in the grid; rows are sorted using data in the columns selected at the time of assignment
Wordwrap	Boolean	Determines whether the text in the active cell is to be wrapped

The size of an MSFlexGrid control is set using the Cols and Rows properties. MSFlexGrid controls can also have fixed rows and columns, which are set using the FixedRows and FixedCols properties. If the number of fixed rows is greater than zero, then the number of rows in an MSFlexGrid control must be at least one greater than the number of fixed rows. The same is the case for the number of columns and fixed columns. The width of a column can be set using the ColWidth property and the height of a row set using the RowHeight property. ColWidth and RowHeight take an argument that identifies the row or column. If the argument to either property is set to −1, the size setting applies to all rows or columns.

The MSFlexGrid control offers a wide range of display formatting options. Almost all formatting options are applied to the active cell, which is set using the Row and Col properties. Row and column indexes begin with 0. Refer to VB Help for a complete listing of cell formatting options.

Other properties, such as Text and CellPicture, also apply to the active cell. The Text property sets or returns the text contained in the active cell, and the CellPicture property sets the picture contained in the active cell. CellPicture takes a reference to a graphic object; it must be assigned using the Set keyword.

It can be unnecessarily time-consuming and visually unattractive to require that a cell be active before its contents can be set. Initializing the contents of a large grid would require that each cell be activated and set, one-by-one. Fortunately the TextMatrix property of the MSFlexGrid control provides direct access to the text contents of a grid cell without requiring that the cell be active. TextMatrix takes a row and column index argument. Using TextMatrix to set or retrieve cell contents can be much more visually attractive and not require that the active cell location be saved and reset after updating a grid.

The rows of an MSFlexGrid control can be sorted by selecting the columns that contain data to sort on, and setting the Sort property appropriately. Only rows selected using the Row and RowSel MSFlexGrid properties are sorted. Data to use to determine the sort order are determined by the MSFlexGrid Col and ColSel properties. If more than one column of data is selected, sorting begins with the leftmost column and proceeds to the right. The style of sorting to perform is determined by the constant assigned to the MSFlexGrid Sort property. Table 23-2 lists the predefined Sort constants with a description of each. The last option in the table with a value of 9 has no associated constant. Assigning the Sort property to a value of 9 indicates that the sort algorithm should use a custom comparison procedure to determine how to sort the rows. The MSFlexGrid Compare event procedure is where this comparison algorithm is defined. Compare receives the indexes for the two rows of data to be compared and an Integer variable called cmp that is to be assigned to a value indicating how the rows compare. The variable cmp is assigned

TABLE 23-2. MSFlexGrid Sort constants.

Sort Constant	Value	Description
flexSortNone	0	No sort
flexSortGenericAscending	1	Sorts ascending; guesses how to interpret sort column data
flexSortGenericDescending	2	Sorts descending; guesses how to interpret sort column data
flexSortNumericAscending	3	Sorts ascending; interprets sort column data as numeric
flexSortNumericDescending	4	Sorts descending; interprets sort column data as numeric
flexSortStringAscending	7	Sorts ascending; interprets sort column data as a string
flexSortStringDescending	8	Sorts descending; interprets sort column data as a string
flexSortStringNoCaseAsending	5	Sorts ascending; ignores case
flexSortStringNoCaseDescending	6	Sorts descending; ignores case
(no constant)	9	Uses user-defined Compare Event procedure to determine sort order

to a value of –1 if the first row precedes the second, a value of 1 if the second row precedes the first, and 0 if the two rows are equivalent. The built-in sort feature of the MSFlexGrid control is quite handy; it saves you from writing your own sort.

MSFLEXGRID METHODS

Table 23-3 lists a few MSFlexGrid methods that are worth mentioning. Rows can be programmatically added or removed using the AddItem and RemoveItem methods. The AddItem method takes a string argument that indicates the contents of the newly added row. Multiple cell contents are delimited in the string argument with a tab character. An optional integer argument passed to AddItem indicates where the new row should be inserted. Leaving out the optional argument causes the new row to be added to the end of the grid. The RemoveItem method takes an integer that identifies the row to be deleted from the grid. The Clear method of the MSFlexGrid control clears the contents and formatting of the entire control. This includes text and graphic cell content. Refer to VB Help for more detail on these and other MSFlexGrid methods.

MSFLEXGRID EVENTS

The MSFlexGrid control has a full complement of event procedures to which you can add your own code. The first seven MSFlexGrid events listed and briefly described in Table 23-4 (Click, DblClick, GotFocus, LostFocus, KeyDown, KeyUp, KeyPress) are all the standard events that are shared by many other controls. The last six events are specific to the MSFlexGrid control.

We have already seen the MSFlexGrid Compare event procedure, which is used when the Sort property is set to a value of 9, indicating that a custom sort is to be performed. The LeaveCell event occurs immediately before the active cell is about to change. The EnterCell event occurs immediately after the active cell has changed. And the RowColChange event occurs after the active cell is changed.

TABLE 23-3. Some MSFlexGrid methods.

Method	Description
AddItem	Adds a new row to an MSFlexGrid; takes a string indicating row contents and an optional index where the row is to be added
RemoveItem	Removes a row identified by an index argument
Clear	Clears the contents of an MSFlexGrid

TABLE 23-4. Some MSFlexGrid events.

Event	Description
Click	Occurs when an MSFlexGrid is clicked with the mouse
DblClick	Occurs when an MSFlexGrid is double-clicked with the mouse
GotFocus	Occurs when the MSFlexGrid becomes the control with focus.
LostFocus	Occurs when the MSFlexGrid loses focus
KeyDown	Occurs when any key is pressed while the MSFlexGrid has focus
KeyUp	Occurs when any key is released while the MSFlexGrid has focus
KeyPress	Occurs when an ANSI character key is pressed while the MSFlexGrid has focus
Compare	Compares the data in two rows and returns a value indicating their sort order
LeaveCell	Occurs just before a cell loses its active status
EnterCell	Occurs just after a cell becomes active
RowColChange	Occurs when the active cell changes
SelChange	Occurs when the current set of selected cells changes
Scroll	Occurs when the MSFlexGrid is scrolled

To understand the difference between the LeaveCell, EnterCell, and RowColChange events, consider a situation where the current active cell, which is in row 1, is changed to a cell in row 3. Popping up a MessageBox from each of these three event procedures reveals what is actually happening. The contents of each MessageBox should contain the event procedure that initiated it and the current Row property value. When the active cell changes, three MessageBoxes will appear. The first will be displayed by the LeaveCell event procedure, which indicates that the current active cell is in row 1. The second will be displayed by the EnterCell event procedure, which indicates that the active cell is in row 3. The third will be displayed by the RowColChange event procedure. The LeaveCell event procedure lets you perform an action before the active cell is changed, such as saving changes made to the data stored in the cell. The EnterCell event procedure allows you to perform an action just as a new cell becomes active, such as backing up the contents of the new cell in case an edit is cancelled. It is convenient to use the RowColChange event procedure only when a single action must be performed as the active cell changes, such as updating a related display.

The SelChange MSFlexGrid event occurs when the currently selected range of cells is changed. This event is handy when an action must be performed as the current selection changes, such as temporarily storing the selection or calculating a statistic that summarizes selected data. The Scroll event occurs when the current view of the grid is scrolled programmatically or using the ScrollBars. We will make heavy use of MSFlexGrid events in the next section, where we will build a simple spreadsheet.

A VB SPREADSHEET

We now know how to display data in an MSFlexGrid control. But how can we provide for interactive editing of the grid cell contents? After becoming accustomed to the way spreadsheets operate, it seems natural simply to click on a cell and start editing its contents. Unfortunately, as we mentioned earlier, interactive editing is not something that is provided with the MSFlexGrid control. In this section we will build our own VB spreadsheet using an MSFlexGrid control, a TextBox control, and some VB code to weave them together. What's even better is that since we will be defining the spreadsheet editing behavior ourselves, we can customize it in any way we like to suit the needs of our application.

We want to be able to use the VB Spreadsheet in multiple projects, as well as multiple times within the same project. For that reason all the code defining the spreadsheet behavior is encapsulated within a class that we've called clsSheet. Figure 23-2 illustrates the relationship among our clsSheet class, an MSFlexGrid and TextBox control, external application code, and the user. The

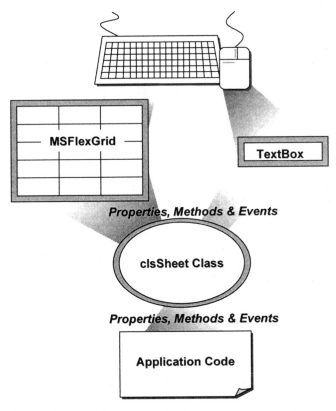

Figure 23-2. Relationship of objects in the VB Spreadsheet.

application creates an instance of the clsSheet class and interacts with it through its properties, methods, and events. In turn, the clsSheet class coordinates the MSFlexGrid and the TextBox controls through their properties, methods, and events. The user interacts with the clsSheet object through the MSFlexGrid and TextBox controls using the mouse and keyboard. The result is an interface whose collective behavior is that of a spreadsheet.

Let's first take a look at the properties, methods, and events of the clsSheet class and how to use the class in your own project. We'll close this chapter with an in-depth look at how the clsSheet class is implemented.

CREATING AN INSTANCE OF THE CLSSHEET CLASS

The clsSheet class is a custom VB object. You must include the class file in your project so that VB can make use of it. You can find the class file, called Sheet.cls, in the folder \Sheet of the code available online. You can create a new instance of the clsSheet class as you would any other object in VB. For example, the following lines of code declare a new variable of type clsSheet and create a new instance of the class.

```
Dim WithEvents mSheet as clsSheet
Set mSheet = New clsSheet
```

The clsSheet class has an event that will fire an event procedure when it occurs. To have the opportunity to program the event procedure, the WithEvents keyword must be used when declaring the new clsSheet variable. After declaring a new object variable using WithEvents, the object's name will appear in the upper left-hand dropdown box of the Code Editor window in the VB IDE along with the other objects in your project. Selecting the new object in the Code Editor window will reveal all available event procedures in the upper right-hand dropdown.

Before proceeding further, it is critical that the MSFlexGrid and TextBox controls you plan to use as the clsSheet class's interface be hooked up to the class. You can accomplish this by assigning the clsSheet's Grid property to the MSFlexGrid control and the EditBox property to the TextBox control. Assume that your MSFlexGrid is called grdSheet and your TextBox is called txtEdit. The following two lines of code will associate these controls with the clsSheet instance stored in mSheet:

```
Set mSheet.Grid = grdSheet
Set mSheet.EditBox = txtEdit
```

The clsSheet class does not check that these variables have been assigned. Using an instance of the class without assigning these variables will result in run-time errors. One possible enhancement to the class is to make sure that the MSFlexGrid and TextBox controls are assigned to the Grid and EditBox clsSheet properties before the class attempts to access them. We'll point out other potential enhancements as we go along.

After the instance is created and the Grid and EditBox properties are assigned, you are ready to begin using the spreadsheet.

PROPERTIES OF CLSSHEET CLASS

Table 23-5 lists all properties of the custom clsSheet class along with property data types and a brief description.

Grid and EditBox, the two most important clsSheet properties, were described in the previous section. These must be set appropriately before an instance of the class will behave correctly. The remaining class properties are what you would expect in a typical spreadsheet object.

The Cols and Rows properties are used to set or return the number of grid columns and row. By definition the clsSheet class has one visible fixed column and one visible fixed row. The location of the active cell can be set or returned using the Col and Row properties. These four clsSheet properties,

TABLE 23-5. Properties of the clsSheet spreadsheet class.

Property	Data Type	Description
Grid	MSFlexGrid	Sets the MSFlexGrid to use as its interface
EditBox	TextBox	Sets the TextBox to use as its interface
Cell	Variant	Sets or returns the contents of a cell given a row and column
Col	Integer	Sets or returns the active column index
Cols	Integer	Sets or returns the number of non-fixed columns in the grid
ColTitle	String	Sets the title for the given column index
ColWidth	Integer	Sets the width for the given column index
ColAlign	Integer	Sets the alignment for the given column index
ColFormat	String	Sets the column format string for the given column index
ColChanged	Boolean	Sets or returns a Boolean indicating that data for the given column index have changed
Row	Integer	Sets or returns the active row index
Rows	Integer	Sets or returns the number of nonfixed rows
RowTitle	String	Sets the title for the given row index
RowHeight	Integer	Sets the height for the given row index
RowData	Long	Sets or returns a long integer associated with the given row index
RowChanged	Boolean	Sets or returns a Boolean indicating that data for the given row index have changed

Cols, Rows, Col, and Row, behave in a manner that is very similar to the MSFlexGrid control.

There a number of properties that set row and column style. Using appropriate properties, you can set the title and width of a column, as well as the alignment and format of data in cells of a column. Row title and height can also be set using clsSheet properties. The MSFlexGrid control can store a long integer along with each row in the grid. This feature was passed along through the RowData property of the clsSheet class. Refer to Table 23-5 for details.

Something not found in the MSFlexGrid control is the pair of properties called ColChanged and RowChanged. These properties will return True when a given index refers to a column or row whose data have changed. This is useful when trying to decide whether or not to update a file or a database that stores the grid data. ColChanged and RowChanged properties can be set to True or False as needed. For example, when a row of data is saved, you can reset the RowChanged property to False. When data in the row change again, it will automatically be set back to True.

METHODS OF THE CLSSHEET CLASS

Methods provided by the clsSheet class implement some basic spreadsheet functions. They are listed and briefly described in Table 23-6.

The ClearSelectedCells method simply enters an empty string into all cells in the current selection. CancelEdit will stop an editing session and leave the contents of a cell unchanged. CopyToClipboard copies the contents of selected cells to the ClipBoard in a format that is compatible with Microsoft® Excel. PasteFromClipboard updates the contents of selected cells with the ClipBoard contents. Unlike Microsoft® Excel, only cells that are selected are updated

TABLE 23-6. Methods of the clsSheet spreadsheet class.

Method	Description
ClearSelectedCells	Clear the contents of selected cells
CancelEdit	Stop editing and leave cell contents unchanged
CopyToClipboard	Copy contents of selected cells to the ClipBoard
PasteFromClipboard	Paste contents of the ClipBoard into the cell selection
FillDown	Copy the contents of the topmost row in a selection to all other rows
FillRight	Copy the contents of the leftmost column in a selection to all other columns
Find	Find a cell containing a given string; find again when no string is passed
MakeCellVisible	Scroll to make the cell at the given row and column indexes visible
SelectRow	Select the entire row with the given index and scroll to make it visible

when this method is executed. FillDown and FillRight implement some very basic cell-filling manipulations. The Find method takes a string argument and searches the grid for a cell whose contents include the passed string. If Find is called a second time without a string argument, searching picks up where it left off. This is similar to the Find Again option found in Microsoft® Excel.

MakeCellVisible and SelectRow are a couple unique methods. When manipulating a spreadsheet programmatically, it is usually not very useful to make a cell active without being able to see it from the user interface. MakeCellVisible takes row and column indexes of a cell and scrolls the grid in order to bring the cell into view. SelectRow automatically selects all the cells in the row identified by the given row index and scrolls to bring at least part of the row into view.

EVENTS OF THE CLSSHEET CLASS

We have implemented only one event in the clsSheet class. This event is called CellChanged, and occurs when data change in a cell. Arguments passed to the event procedure are the row and column indexes of the cell that has changed. Remember that in order to gain access to this event, the clsSheet object variable must be declared using the WithEvents keyword in the application that creates an instance of the class.

A single event may seem a little paltry, but don't forget that you have the source code for this class and can change it in any way that suits your application. You can modify the event procedure to include an argument that contains the new contents of the changed cell or the old contents of the cell before it was changed. You can add new events or delete all the events. It is entirely up to you. A pair of missing methods will save the contents of the grid to a file and load the contents of a file back into the grid. You may want to add these methods to the class as an exercise. In any case, clsSheet provides a good starting point from which to work.

USING THE CLSSHEET CLASS

Let's demonstrate how to use the clsSheet class with an example. The completed example can be found in the folder \Part4\Ex6 of the code available online.

Create a new VB project and sketch an MSFlexGrid and TextBox control on Form1. Make sure to add the Sheet.cls file to your project using the Project | Add File menu option from the VB IDE. Set the following control properties. It is important to set the BorderStyle property of the TextBox manually to a value of None. This property cannot be set at run time. The spreadsheet will function even if the TextBox BorderStyle property is not set, but it will not look as good during cell editing.

Object Type	Property	Value
Form	Name	frmSheet
	Caption	VB Spreadsheet
MSFlexGrid	Name	grdSheet
TextBox	Name	txtEdit
	BorderStyle	0 - None

In the declarations section of the frmSheet Form module add the following two lines of code. The declaration will properly create a new module-level variable called mSheet of type clsSheet. The new variable is declared using the WithEvents keyword to assure that we will have access to clsSheet event procedures.

```
Option Explicit

Private WithEvents mSheet As clsSheet
```

Add the following code to the frmSheet Form_Load event procedure. In the body of the procedure the clsSheet object is created and assigned to the mSheet variable. The Grid and EditBox properties of mSheet are also set to the new MSFlexGrid and TextBox controls. The remainder of the procedure formats the new spreadsheet to have eight rows and twelve columns. Row and column titles are assigned, column formatting is specified, and the grid is filled with random data values.

```
Private Sub Form_Load()
    ' Create and initialize the Sheet object.
    Dim I As Integer, J As Integer

    Set mSheet = New clsSheet        ' Create the new class

    With mSheet
        Set .Grid = grdSheet         ' Assign MSFlexGrid and TextBox controls
        Set .EditBox = txtEdit

        .Rows = 8                    ' Set the sheet size
        .Cols = 12

        For I = 1 To 8               ' Set row titles
            .RowTitle(I) = Chr$(I + 64)
        Next I

        For J = 1 To 12              ' Set column titles
            .ColTitle(J) = CStr(J)
            .ColWidth(J) = 600
            .ColFormat(J) = "0.000"
        Next J

        For I = 1 To 8               ' Initialize to random data
            For J = 1 To 12
                .Cell(I, J) = Rnd
            Next J
        Next I

    End With
End Sub
```

What we've done thus far in this example is more than enough to get it working. You may want to run it now to see how it works. Let's continue adding to the example by building a set of menus and tying them to mSheet object methods.

Open the Menu Editor by selection the Tools | Menu Editor menu option from the VB IDE while the frmSheet Form window is active. Create two new top-level menu options with submenus as outlined in Table 23-7. Figure 23-3 shows the Menu Editor while creating the menu for this example.

Add the following procedures to the frmSheet Form module. Except for the Click event procedure of the mnuFileExit submenu, each of these procedures simply ties a menu option to the appropriate mSheet object method. Have a closer look at these procedures to see how they operate. A few mSheet method calls were embedded within mouse pointer changes. If the spreadsheet is large, some of the methods may take more than a fraction of a second. By changing the mouse pointer to an hourglass while the method is executing, the user is reassured that something is happening.

```
Private Sub mnuEditUndo_Click()
    mSheet.CancelEdit
End Sub
Private Sub mnuEditCut_Click()
    mSheet.CopyToClipboard
    mSheet.ClearSelectedCells
End Sub

Private Sub mnuEditCopy_Click()
    mSheet.CopyToClipboard
End Sub
```

TABLE 23-7. clsSheet example Menu Editor settings.

Menu Caption	Parent Menu Caption	Name	Shortcut
&File		mnuFile	(None)
E&xit	&File	mnuFileExit	(None)
&Edit		mnuEdit	(None)
&Undo	&Edit	mnuEditUndo	Ctrl+Z
-	&Edit	mnuEditSep1	(None)
Cu&t	&Edit	mnuEditCut	Ctrl+X
&Copy	&Edit	mnuEditCopy	Ctrl+C
&Paste	&Edit	mnuEditPaste	Ctrl+V
Cl&ear	&Edit	mnuEditClear	(None)
-	&Edit	mnuEditSep2	(None)
&Find	&Edit	mnuEditFind	Ctrl+F
Find &Again	&Edit	mnuEditFindAgain	Ctrl+G
-	&Edit	mnuEditSep3	(None)
Fill &Down	&Edit	mnuEditFillDown	Ctrl+D
Fill &Right	&Edit	mnuEditFillRight	Ctrl+R

```
Private Sub mnuEditPaste_Click()
    mSheet.PasteFromClipboard
End Sub

Private Sub mnuEditClear_Click()
    Screen.MousePointer = vbHourglass
    mSheet.ClearSelectedCells
    Screen.MousePointer = vbDefault
End Sub

Private Sub mnuEditFillDown_Click()
    Screen.MousePointer = vbHourglass
    mSheet.FillDown
    Screen.MousePointer = vbDefault
End Sub

Private Sub mnuEditFillRight_Click()
    Screen.MousePointer = vbHourglass
    mSheet.FillRight
    Screen.MousePointer = vbDefault
End Sub

Private Sub mnuFileExit_Click()
    Unload Me
End Sub
```

The following Click event procedures for the mnuEditFind and mnuEditFindAgain submenus are a bit more involved. Selecting the Find op-

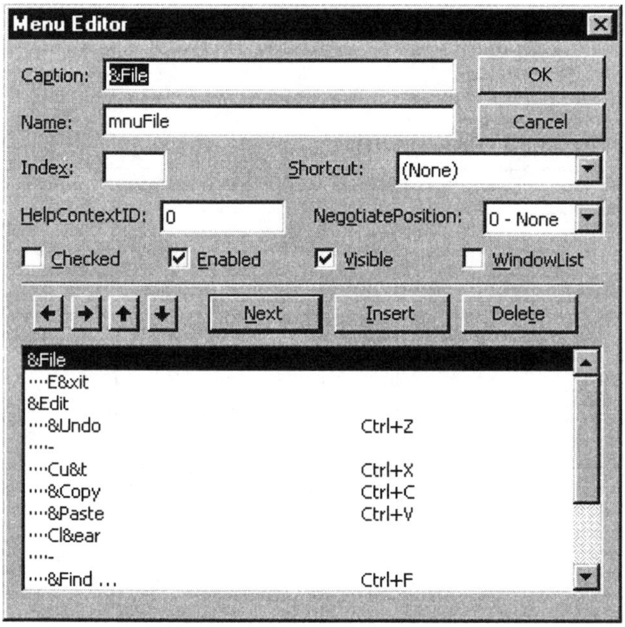

Figure 23-3. Setting up a menu for the clsSheet example.

tion from the Edit menu will pop up an InputBox requesting a string to find in the spreadsheet. If the string is not empty then the mSheet Find method is called with the entered string as its argument. The Find method will return true if the string is found, activate the cell in which it was found, and scroll the grid to make it visible. The Click event procedure executed when the Find Again menu option is selected is the same as Find, except no search string is requested or passed to the mSheet Find method. This will cause the mSheet class to pick up searching where it previously left off. If no cell is found containing the search string, a MessageBox is displayed indicating that result.

```
Private Sub mnuEditFind_Click()
    ' Find the given substring
    Dim strValue As String

    strValue = Trim(InputBox("Find what: ", "Find", strValue))
    If strValue = "" Then Exit Sub

    Screen.MousePointer = vbHourglass
    If mSheet.Find(strValue) = False Then
        Screen.MousePointer = vbDefault
        MsgBox "Not found", vbOKOnly, "Find"
    End If
    Screen.MousePointer = vbDefault

End Sub

Private Sub mnuEditFindAgain_Click()
    ' Find the given pattern again.

    Screen.MousePointer = vbHourglass
    If mSheet.Find() = False Then
        Screen.MousePointer = vbDefault
        MsgBox "Not Found", vbOKOnly, "Find"
    End If
    Screen.MousePointer = vbDefault

End Sub
```

The last bit of code in the example demonstrates the use of the CellChanged mSheet event. In the following event procedure we simply print the changed cell row and column index to the Immediate Window of the IDE.

```
Private Sub mSheet_CellChanged(intRow As Integer, intCol As Integer)
    Debug.Print "Cell Changed: Row=" & CStr(intRow) & ", Col=" & CStr(intCol)
End Sub
```

When you run the example, you will see a form that looks like the one in Figure 23-4. Keep your eye on the Immediate Window to see the messages printed when a cell changes its contents. Double-click on a cell to edit it. Navigate around the spreadsheet using the tab, return, shift, and arrow keys. Begin an edit and cancel it by hitting the escape key, selecting the Edit | Undo menu option, or typing Ctrl+Z. Try the other Edit menu options to see how they work as well.

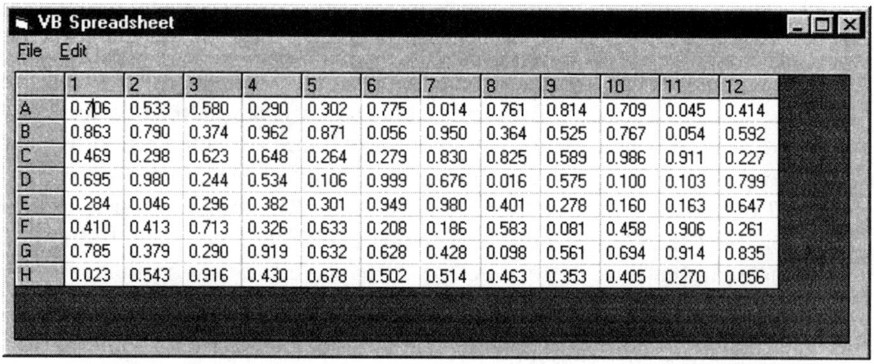

	1	2	3	4	5	6	7	8	9	10	11	12
A	0.706	0.533	0.580	0.290	0.302	0.775	0.014	0.761	0.814	0.709	0.045	0.414
B	0.863	0.790	0.374	0.962	0.871	0.056	0.950	0.364	0.525	0.767	0.054	0.592
C	0.469	0.298	0.623	0.648	0.264	0.279	0.830	0.825	0.589	0.986	0.911	0.227
D	0.695	0.980	0.244	0.534	0.106	0.999	0.676	0.016	0.575	0.100	0.103	0.799
E	0.284	0.046	0.296	0.382	0.301	0.949	0.980	0.401	0.278	0.160	0.163	0.647
F	0.410	0.413	0.713	0.326	0.633	0.208	0.186	0.583	0.081	0.458	0.906	0.261
G	0.785	0.379	0.290	0.919	0.632	0.628	0.428	0.098	0.561	0.694	0.914	0.835
H	0.023	0.543	0.916	0.430	0.678	0.502	0.514	0.463	0.353	0.405	0.270	0.056

Figure 23-4. The clsSheet spreadsheet example in action.

Other controls can be added to the Form that contains the MSFlexGrid and TextBox controls used for the clsSheet object interface. Indeed, this is one perfectly acceptable way to use the spreadsheet. Be aware that in this case there is one potential conflict that may cause unexpected behavior. It occurs while navigating a clsSheet grid using the tab key. If any TabStop property of an additional control is set to True, the tab key will not cause the clsSheet MSFlexGrid column to be changed. Instead, focus will be changed from the grid to one of the controls with a True-valued TabStop property. To assure that the tab key will work correctly for spreadsheet navigation, make sure to set the TabStop property to False for all other controls on the same form.

CLSSHEET CLASS IMPLEMENTATION

Implementation of the clsSheet class is lengthy, but not complex. If you are satisfied with using the class the way it is, you can safely skip this section and move on to the next, but if you'd like to learn how to modify the way the spreadsheet behaves, it is essential to understand how the clsSheet class works. Source code for the clsSheet class can be found in the file named Sheet.cls in the \Sheet folder of the online code.

The following listing is the declarations section of the clsSheet class. Similar to the way we declared the mSheet variable in the preceding example using the WithEvents keyword, we want access to the events of the MSFlexGrid and TextBox controls used as the clsSheet object interface. Therefore, we also declare the private class variables to hold references to the MSFlexGrid and TextBox controls using the WithEvents keyword. Remaining declarations include a few integers to hold the location of the current cell being edited and some constants, which we will describe shortly. The last declaration is for the event that the clsSheet class can raise. To modify the event you can make changes in this event declaration and reflect your changes in each place where the event is raised in the class implementation.

```
Option Explicit

Private WithEvents mGrd As MSFlexGrid   ' Private reference to an MSFlexGrid control
Private WithEvents mTxt As TextBox      ' Private reference to a TextBox control

Private mIntEditRow As Integer          ' The row being edited
Private mIntEditCol As Integer          ' The column being edited

Private Const mConRowOffset As Integer = 2 ' Row and column offsets to account for
Private Const mConColOffset As Integer = 1 ' fixed rows and columns
                                           ' Default column width and alignment
Private Const mConDefaultWidth As Integer = 1000
Private Const mConDefaultAlign As Integer = 0 ' flexAlignLeft

Public Event CellChanged(intRow As Integer, intCol As Integer)
```

Once a clsCheet object is created, the very next step is to assign the
MSFlexGrid and TextBox control to the clsSheet object Grid and EditBox properties. From the user's perspective this appears to be a simple assignment, but
as you can see in the following two Property Set procedures, much more
happens. Storing a reference to each control is only the beginning. The
MSFlexGrid and TextBox controls are also formatted and initialized.

Most of what happens in these Property Set procedures is due to the way
certain column and row properties are stored. Most clsSheet column and row
property values are passed along to MSFlexGrid properties directly. Others
have no equivalent in MSFlexGrid and must be accommodated specially. A
convenient place to store new column and row properties is in hidden rows
and columns of MSFlexGrid. Setting a column's width or row's height to a
value of 0 will hide it. In this implementation we have two fixed columns and
three fixed rows. The first fixed column is hidden, and used to store the
changed state of each row. The second fixed column displays the title for each
row. The first two fixed rows are hidden. The first fixed row holds the changed
state for each column. The second fixed row holds a format string for the data
stored in the cells of each column. The third fixed row displays each column's
title. The following Grid Property Set procedure creates, hides, and initializes
the required fixed columns and rows. The difference between the number of
actual rows and columns and the number that you see when using the clsSheet
class is reflected in the mConColOffset and mConRowOffset constants that
were defined in the declarations section of the class. These constants are used
throughout this implementation to map a given grid location to the actual
MSFlexGrid location. By defining the offsets as constants, we can easily add
or remove fixed rows or columns by simply changing the constant values
without having to scour the code for hard-coded offsets.

```
Public Property Set EditBox(txtEdit As TextBox)
    ' Set the private TextBox variable
    Set mTxt = txtEdit
```

```
      ' Set some properties
      With mTxt
         .Visible = False
         .Text = ""
         .TabStop = False

         ' Note - This properties must be set at design time.
         '.BorderStyle = vbBSNone
      End With
End Property

Public Property Set Grid(grdFlex As MSFlexGrid)
      Dim I As Integer

      ' Set the private MSFlexGrid variable
      Set mGrd = grdFlex

      ' Set some properties
      With mGrd
         .Appearance = flexFlat
         .FocusRect = flexFocusHeavy
         .TabStop = False
         .ScrollBars = flexScrollBarBoth

         ' Check for proper size and format
         If .Cols < mConColOffset + 2 Then .Cols = mConRowOffset + 2
         If .Rows < mConRowOffset + 2 Then .Rows = mConRowOffset + 2
         If .FixedCols < mConColOffset + 1 Then .FixedCols = mConColOffset + 1
         If .FixedRows < mConRowOffset + 1 Then .FixedRows = mConRowOffset + 1

         .ColWidth(0) = 0    ' Hide column dedicated to saving changed row state.
         .ColWidth(1) = 500  ' Set first fixed column width.
         .RowHeight(0) = 0   ' Hide row dedicated to saving changed column state.
         .RowHeight(1) = 0   ' Hide row dedicated to saving the column format.

         ' Initialize column formats and changed state to false
         For I = 1 To Cols
               ColChanged(I) = False
               ColAlign(I) = mConDefaultAlign
               ColWidth(I) = mConDefaultWidth
               ColTitle(I) = "Column " & CStr(I)
         Next I

         ' Initialize the row title and change state to false
         For I = 1 To Rows
               RowChanged(I) = False
               RowTitle(I) = CStr(I) & "."      ' Row Title
         Next I

      End With

End Property
```

The following Property Get and Property Let procedures are used to set and return the number of rows and columns in the spreadsheet. Returning the Rows and Cols properties of a clsSheet object is simply a matter of adjusting the MSFlexGrid Rows and Cols property values by the number of fixed rows and columns. When setting the Rows and Cols clsSheet object properties, any new rows or columns must be formatted and initialized in a manner similar to what was done in the Grid Property Set procedure.

```
Public Property Get Cols() As Integer
    ' Return the number of columns.  Actual minus number fixed.
    Cols = mGrd.Cols - mConColOffset - 1
End Property

Public Property Let Cols(intCols As Integer)
    ' Sets the number of available grid columns.
    Dim I As Integer, intCurrCols As Integer

    ' Set the number of columns in the sheet.  Enforce a minimum of 1.
    If intCols < 1 Then intCols = 1
    intCurrCols = Cols        ' Actual grid columns are greater by fixed columns
    mGrd.Cols = intCols + mConColOffset + 1

    ' Set default formats for any new columns.
    For I = intCurrCols + 1 To intCols
        ColChanged(I) = False
        ColAlign(I) = mConDefaultAlign
        ColWidth(I) = mConDefaultWidth
        ColTitle(I) = "Column " & CStr(I)
    Next I

End Property

Public Property Get Rows() As Integer
    ' Return the number of sheet rows.  Actual minus fixed rows.
    Rows = mGrd.Rows - mConRowOffset - 1
End Property

Public Property Let Rows(intRows As Integer)
    ' Set the number of available grid rows.
    Dim I As Integer, intCurrRows As Integer

    ' Set the number of rows in the sheet.  Minimum of 1.
    If intRows < 1 Then intRows = 1
    intCurrRows = Rows                        ' Increase actual rows by fixed rows
    mGrd.Rows = intRows + mConRowOffset + 1

    ' Initialize rows
    For I = intCurrRows + 1 To intRows
        RowChanged(I) = False              ' Not changed
        RowTitle(I) = CStr(I) & "."        ' Row Title
    Next I

End Property
```

A series of row and column properties are implemented by either passing properly adjusted values between the clsSheet object and the MSFlexGrid control, or by setting or returning values in hidden MSFlexGrid rows and columns. Study the following listing to discover how each clsSheet object property is implemented. Each of these procedures involves a straightforward exchange of data.

```
Public Property Let Col(intCol As Integer)
    ' Set the active column

    ' Check for a valid column
    If intCol < 1 Or intCol > Cols Then Exit Property

    mGrd.Col = intCol + mConColOffset
End Property

Public Property Get Col() As Integer
    ' Get the active column
    Col = mGrd.Col - mConColOffset
End Property

Public Property Let Row(intRow As Integer)
    ' Set the active row

    ' Check for valid row
    If intRow < 1 Or intRow > Rows Then Exit Property

    mGrd.Row = intRow + mConRowOffset
End Property

Public Property Get Row() As Integer
    ' Get the active row
    Row = mGrd.Row - mConRowOffset
End Property

Public Property Let ColAlign(intCol As Integer, intAlign As Integer)
    ' Save the column alignment

    ' Check for a valid column
    If intCol < 1 Or intCol > Cols Then Exit Property

    ' Set alignment
    mGrd.ColAlignment(intCol + mConColOffset) = intAlign
End Property

Public Property Let ColTitle(intCol As Integer, strTitle As String)
    ' Save the column title

    ' Check for a valid column
    If intCol < 1 Or intCol > Cols Then Exit Property

    ' Set title
    mGrd.TextMatrix(mConRowOffset, intCol + mConColOffset) = strTitle
End Property

Public Property Let ColWidth(intCol As Integer, intWidth As Integer)
    ' Set the column width

    ' Check for a valid column
    If intCol < 1 Or intCol > Cols Then Exit Property

    ' Set the width
    mGrd.ColWidth(intCol + mConColOffset) = intWidth
End Property
```

```
Public Property Let ColFormat(intCol As Integer, strFormat As String)
    ' Set the column format string
    ' Check for a valid column
    If intCol < 1 Or intCol > Cols Then Exit Property

    ' Column formats are stored in row 1
    mGrd.TextMatrix(1, intCol + mConColOffset) = strFormat
End Property

Public Property Let RowData(intRow As Integer, lngValue As Long)
    ' Set the row's long data

    ' Check for valid row
    If intRow < 1 Or intRow > Rows Then Exit Property

    ' Set data value
    mGrd.RowData(intRow + mConRowOffset) = lngValue
End Property

Public Property Get RowData(intRow As Integer) As Long
    ' Get the row's long data

    ' Check for valid row
    If intRow < 1 Or intRow > Rows Then Exit Property

    ' Get data value
    RowData = mGrd.RowData(intRow + mConRowOffset)
End Property

Public Property Let RowTitle(intRow As Integer, strTitle As String)
    ' Save the row title

    ' Check for a valid row
    If intRow < 1 Or intRow > Rows Then Exit Property

    ' Set title
    mGrd.TextMatrix(intRow + mConRowOffset, mConColOffset) = strTitle
End Property

Public Property Let RowHeight(intRow As Integer, intHeight As Integer)
    ' Set the row height

    ' Check for a valid row
    If intRow < 1 Or intRow > Rows Then Exit Property

    ' Set the height
    mGrd.RowHeight(intRow + mConRowOffset) = intHeight
End Property

Public Property Get ColChanged(intCol As Integer) As Boolean
    ' Return contents of hidden 'column changed' row.

    ' Check for valid column
    If intCol < 1 Or intCol > Cols Then Exit Property
    ColChanged = CBool(mGrd.TextMatrix(0, intCol + mConColOffset))
End Property
```

```
Public Property Let ColChanged(intCol As Integer, blnChanged As Boolean)
    ' Set the contents of hidden 'column changed' row.
        ' Check for valid column
    If intCol < 1 Or intCol > Cols Then Exit Property

    mGrd.TextMatrix(0, intCol + mConColOffset) = blnChanged
End Property

Public Property Get RowChanged(intRow As Integer) As Boolean
    ' Return contents of hidden 'row changed' column.

    ' Check for valid row
    If intRow < 1 Or intRow > Rows Then Exit Property

    RowChanged = CBool(mGrd.TextMatrix(intRow + mConRowOffset, 0))
End Property

Public Property Let RowChanged(intRow As Integer, blnChanged As Boolean)
    ' Set the contents of hidden 'row changed' column.

    ' Check for valid row
    If intRow < 1 Or intRow > Rows Then Exit Property

    mGrd.TextMatrix(intRow + mConRowOffset, 0) = blnChanged
End Property
```

The following pair of Cell Property procedures provides access to the contents of a cell in the MSFlexGrid control. The Cell Property Get procedure simply returns the contents of the appropriate MSFlexGrid cell. But the Cell Property Let procedure does more. When a cell is edited, we indicate that the cell contents have changed by setting the RowChanged and ColChanged properties of the cell's row and column. Also, this is the place where the clsSheet object's CellChanged event is raised.

```
Public Property Let Cell(intRow As Integer, intCol As Integer, vrnCellVal As Variant)
    ' Set the contents of a cell.
    ' Take a variant so that it can accept most data types.

    ' Check for out-of-range
    If intRow < 1 Or intRow > Rows Then Exit Property
    If intCol < 1 Or intCol > Cols Then Exit Property

    ' Assign value
    mGrd.TextMatrix(intRow + mConRowOffset, intCol + mConColOffset) = _
                Format(vrnCellVal, mGrd.TextMatrix(1, intCol + mConColOffset))

    ' Mark row and column as changed
    RowChanged(intRow) = True
    ColChanged(intCol) = True

    RaiseEvent CellChanged(intRow, intCol)
End Property

Public Property Get Cell(intRow As Integer, intCol As Integer) As Variant
    ' Return the contents of a cell.
    ' Returns a variant so that the cell data can automatically be converted to
    ' receiving variable type.
```

```
    ' Check for out-of-range
    If intRow < 1 Or intRow > Rows Then Exit Property
    If intCol < 1 Or intCol > Cols Then Exit Property

    Cell = mGrd.TextMatrix(intRow + mConRowOffset, intCol + mConColOffset)
End Property
```

The next three procedures are the basis for interactive editing of the spread-sheet. At last we see where the TextBox control comes into play.

The BeginEdit procedure initiates editing of the currently active cell. The manner in which editing is initiated depends on the optional character code that is passed to the procedure. If no character is passed, the TextBox is initialized with the contents of the cell being edited. If the passed character is backspace or delete, the TextBox is initialized with an empty string. The TextBox will be initialized with any other character passed to the procedure. This mimics the editing behavior of Microsoft® Excel. The TextBox is then sized to match the edited cell, positioned exactly over the cell, and made visible. The result is the appearance that the contents of the cell is being edited when actually it is the contents of the TextBox.

When editing is completed, the CommitEdit procedure is called. CommitEdit copies the contents of the TextBox into the cell being edited using the clsSheet class Cell Property Let procedure to ensure proper bookkeeping. The TextBox is hidden again, and the Grid gets focus.

Editing can be cancelled at any point by calling the CancelEdit procedure. This procedure clears the contents of the TextBox and hides it. No change is made to the contents of the cell. Of the previous three procedures, only CancelEdit is declared as Public. CancelEdit can be invoked from outside the clsSheet class effectively to "undo" an edit that is currently in progress. In practice, public access to the other two editing procedures has not been found to be useful.

You can modify these procedures to add your own custom behavior. For example, use a ComboBox control in place of the TextBox to offer the user a selection of valid options. Fill the ComboBox from the BeginEdit procedure before making it visible. Options can depend on the column and/or row being edited.

```
Private Sub BeginEdit(Optional KeyAscii As Integer)
    ' Begin editing the currently selected cell.
    Dim intOffset As Integer

    intOffset = 30          ' Tweakable parameter adjusting for lack of border.
    mIntEditRow = Row       ' Save the position of the cell being edited.
    mIntEditCol = Col

    With mTxt        ' Configure the edit TextBox
        ' Process the passed key to create familiar spreadsheet behavior.
        Select Case KeyAscii
```

```
                ' If no key passed, copy current cell contents into edit text box.
                Case 0
                    .Text = mGrd.Text

                ' Clear cell contents.
                Case vbKeyBack, vbKeyDelete
                    .Text = ""

                ' Otherwise, replace current text in cell.
                Case Else
                    .Text = Chr$(KeyAscii)
                    .SelStart = 1

                End Select

                ' Size and show the edit text box.
                .Left = mGrd.Left + mGrd.ColPos(mIntEditCol + mConColOffset) + 2 * intOffset
                .Top = mGrd.Top + mGrd.RowPos(mIntEditRow + mConRowOffset) + intOffset
                .Width = mGrd.ColWidth(mIntEditCol + mConColOffset) - (2 * intOffset)
                .Height = mGrd.RowHeight(mIntEditRow + mConRowOffset) - intOffset
                .Visible = True
                .SetFocus

            End With

    End Sub

    Private Sub CommitEdit()
        ' Update the currently edited cell.
        If mTxt.Visible <> True Then Exit Sub

        ' Copy text back into cell, and hide edit box.
        Cell(mIntEditRow, mIntEditCol) = mTxt.Text
        mTxt.Visible = False

        ' Cancel edit location.
        mIntEditRow = -1
        mIntEditCol = -1
        ' Make sure focus is on grid
        mGrd.SetFocus
    End Sub

    Public Sub CancelEdit()
        ' Cancel the current edit.
        mTxt.Text = ""
        mTxt.Visible = False

        ' Cancel edit location.
        mIntEditRow = -1
        mIntEditCol = -1

        ' Make sure focus is on grid
        mGrd.SetFocus
    End Sub
```

We've seen the procedures for implementing cell editing. But when are these procedures called? The answer is another important element that defines the behavior of spreadsheet editing. The following five MSFlexGrid and TextBox event procedures are the beginning. One way to initiate editing of a cell is to double-click it. The MSFlexGrid DblClick event procedure calls BeginEdit to initiate cell editing. Editing is committed whenever a cell is exited, the MSFlexGrid is scrolled, and the MSFlexGrid or TextBox loses focus.

```
Private Sub mGrd_DblClick()
    ' Begin editing a cell when it is double-clicked.
    BeginEdit
End Sub

Private Sub mGrd_LeaveCell()
    ' Commit an edit when leaving a cell.
    CommitEdit
End Sub

Private Sub mGrd_GotFocus()
    ' Commit an edit when the grid gets focus.
    CommitEdit
End Sub

Private Sub mGrd_Scroll()
    ' Commit an edit when the grid is scrolled.
    CommitEdit
End Sub

Private Sub mTxt_LostFocus()
    ' Commit any changes if the edit box loses focus.
    CommitEdit
End Sub
```

The following six procedures couple editing with spreadsheet navigation. KeyDown event procedures of the MSFlexGrid and TextBox controls can result in spreadsheet navigation, cell editing, or both. When the MSFlexGrid has focus, the return, tab, and shift keys will navigate up, down, left, or right. The MSFlexGrid control already responds to arrow keys by changing the active cell. We don't have to trap and respond to these keys. A TextBox KeyDown event will result in spreadsheet navigation or cancellation of editing. The return, tab, shift, and arrow keys trigger navigation. The escape key cancels editing. Again, the behavior defined here mimics Microsoft® Excel for consistency.

The four navigation methods defined below are MoveDown, MoveUp, MoveLeft, and MoveRight. Before navigating, each method checks to see if there is a place to go, or if it is at the boundary of the spreadsheet. Any attempt to navigate the spreadsheet will cause an edit to be committed. When navigation is possible, the MSFlexGrid active cell will change, causing the LeaveCell event procedure to fire, which calls CommitEdit. If navigation is not possible since the active cell is at the edge of a spreadsheet, the navigation method will itself call the CommitEdit procedure.

```
Private Sub mGrd_KeyDown(KeyCode As Integer, Shift As Integer)
    ' Override certain keycode processing for enhanced navigation.
    Dim blnShift As Boolean, blnCtrl As Boolean, blnAlt As Boolean
    ' Save the state of combination keys.
    blnShift = (Shift And vbShiftMask) > 0
    blnAlt = (Shift And vbAltMask) > 0
    blnCtrl = (Shift And vbCtrlMask) > 0
```

```
    With mGrd
        Select Case KeyCode
        ' Move up or down with the return key
        Case vbKeyReturn
            If blnShift = True Then
                MoveUp
            Else
                MoveDown
            End If
        ' Move left or right with the tab key
        Case vbKeyTab
            If blnShift = True Then
                MoveLeft
            Else
                MoveRight
            End If
        End Select
    End With

End Sub

Private Sub mTxt_KeyDown(KeyCode As Integer, Shift As Integer)
    ' React to editing keys pressed while in edit text box.
    Dim blnShift As Boolean, blnCtrl As Boolean, blnAlt As Boolean

    ' Save the state of comination keys.
    blnShift = (Shift And vbShiftMask) > 0
    blnAlt = (Shift And vbAltMask) > 0
    blnCtrl = (Shift And vbCtrlMask) > 0

    ' Move the current cell or cancel edit.
    With mGrd
        Select Case KeyCode
        ' Move up or down on return or down arrow
        Case vbKeyReturn, vbKeyDown
            If blnShift = True Then
                MoveUp
            Else
                MoveDown
            End If
        ' Move up or down on up arrow
        Case vbKeyUp
            If blnShift = True Then
                MoveDown
            Else
                MoveUp
            End If
        ' Move left or right on tab
        Case vbKeyTab
            If blnShift = True Then
                MoveLeft
            Else
                MoveRight
            End If
        ' Cancel editing in escape
        Case vbKeyEscape
            CancelEdit
        End Select
    End With

End Sub
```

```
    Private Sub MoveDown()
        ' Attempt to move the current cell to the one below.
        With mGrd

            If Row < Rows Then
                ' Edit is committed when row is changed
                Row = Row + 1
                ' Make sure the new row is visible
                If mGrd.RowIsVisible(Row + mConRowOffset) = False Then _
                                    mGrd.TopRow = mGrd.TopRow + 1
            Else
                CommitEdit
            End If

        End With

    End Sub

    Private Sub MoveUp()
        ' Attempt to move the current cell to the one below.
        With mGrd

            If Row > 1 Then
                ' Edit is committed when row is changed
                Row = Row - 1
                ' Make sure the new row is visible
                If mGrd.RowIsVisible(Row + mConRowOffset) = False Then _
                                    mGrd.TopRow = mGrd.TopRow - 1
            Else
                CommitEdit
            End If

        End With
    End Sub

    Private Sub MoveRight()
        ' Attempt to move the current cell to the one to the right.
        With mGrd
            If Col < Cols Then
                ' Edit is committed when column is changed
                Col = Col + 1
                ' Make sure the new col is visible
                If mGrd.ColIsVisible(Col + mConColOffset) = False Then _
                                    mGrd.LeftCol = mGrd.LeftCol + 1
            Else
                CommitEdit
            End If
        End With
    End Sub

    Private Sub MoveLeft()
        ' Attempt to move the current cell to the one to the left.
        With mGrd
            If Col > 1 Then
                ' Edit is committed when column is changed
                Col = Col - 1
                ' Make sure the new col is visible
                If mGrd.ColIsVisible(Col + mConColOffset) = False Then _
                                    mGrd.LeftCol = mGrd.LeftCol - 1
```

```
        Else
            CommitEdit
        End If
    End With
End Sub
```

The following two KeyPress event procedures of the MSFlexGrid and TextBox controls are used to cancel any further propagation of the tab, carriage return, and escape characters. This prevents the MSFlexGrid from beeping as well. When the MSFlexGrid KeyPress event procedure gets a key other than tab, carriage return, or escape, it initiates editing with that key by calling BeginEdit.

```
Private Sub mGrd_KeyPress(KeyAscii As Integer)
    ' React to pressed keys.
    Select Case KeyAscii
    Case 9, 13, 27              ' Cancel Tab, CR and Esc
        KeyAscii = 0
    Case Else                   ' Pass other characters to cell editing.
        BeginEdit KeyAscii
    End Select

End Sub

Private Sub mTxt_KeyPress(KeyAscii As Integer)
    ' React to pressed keys.
    Select Case KeyAscii
    Case 9, 13, 27              ' Cancel Tab, CR and Esc
        KeyAscii = 0
    End Select
End Sub
```

The MSFlexGrid control has a Clear method that wipes out all cell contents and formatting for the entire grid. We need a more limited clear method that only erases the contents of selected cells. The following clsSheet ClearSelectedCells method accomplishes that. Within the procedure the corners of the selected region are first sorted. Then the procedure loops over all the cells in the selected region, setting the contents of each to an empty string.

```
Public Sub ClearSelectedCells()
    ' Clear the selected cells
    Dim intR1 As Integer, intR2 As Integer, intC1 As Integer, intC2 As Integer
    Dim I As Integer, J As Integer

    ' Sort the corners of the selection region.
    With mGrd
        If .Row > .RowSel Then
            intR1 = .RowSel - mConRowOffset
            intR2 = .Row - mConRowOffset
        Else
            intR1 = .Row - mConRowOffset
            intR2 = .RowSel - mConRowOffset
        End If
```

```
            If .Col > .ColSel Then
        intC1 = .ColSel - mConColOffset
        intC2 = .Col - mConColOffset
    Else
        intC1 = .Col - mConColOffset
        intC2 = .ColSel - mConColOffset
    End If

    ' Clear all cells
    For I = intR1 To intR2
        For J = intC1 To intC2
            Cell(I, J) = ""
        Next J
    Next I

  End With
End Sub
```

MSFlexGrid has a built-in procedure for accessing the ClipBoard. The following clsSheet CopyToClipboard and PasteFromClipboard methods are merely wrappers for the predefined MSFlexGrid ClipBoard methods.

```
Public Sub CopyToClipboard()
    ' Copy the selected cells to the clipboard.
    Clipboard.SetText mGrd.Clip
End Sub

Public Sub PasteFromClipboard()
    ' Paste text on clipboard into sheet
    mGrd.Clip = Clipboard.GetText
End Sub
```

The following FillDown and FillRight methods of clsSheet are implemented in an obvious manner. Each procedure loops over selected cells. In the case of FillDown, cell contents are copied when in the topmost row and written to a cell when in any other row. FillRight copies cell contents when in the leftmost column and writes it to a cell for any other column.

```
Public Sub FillDown()
    ' Copy the contents of the first row in the selection
    ' down to subsequent rows.
    Dim I As Integer, J As Integer, intStart As Integer
    Dim strVal As String

    intStart = mGrd.Row
    For I = mGrd.Col To mGrd.ColSel
        For J = mGrd.Row To mGrd.RowSel
            If J = intStart Then
                ' Save first value
                strVal = Cell(J - mConRowOffset, I - mConColOffset)
            Else
                ' Set values below
                Cell(J - mConRowOffset, I - mConColOffset) = strVal
            End If
        Next J
    Next I

End Sub
```

```
Public Sub FillRight()
    ' Copy the contents of the first column in the selection
    ' across to subsequent columns.
    Dim I As Integer, J As Integer, intStart As Integer
    Dim strVal As String

    intStart = mGrd.Col
    For I = mGrd.Row To mGrd.RowSel
        For J = mGrd.Col To mGrd.ColSel
            If J = intStart Then
                ' Save first value
                strVal = Cell(I - mConRowOffset, J - mConColOffset)
            Else
                ' Set values across
                Cell(I - mConRowOffset, J - mConColOffset) = strVal
            End If
        Next J
    Next I

End Sub
```

The MSFlexGrid control includes properties to determine if a row or column is visible, and methods to scroll the grid automatically to bring a row or column into view. The RowIsVisible and ColIsVisible properties of MSFlexGrid return True if a row or column corresponding to a given index is currently within view. The TopRow and LeftCol methods of MSFlexGrid bring a row or column with a given index into view by appropriately scrolling the grid. We use these members of MSFlexGrid to create a clsSheet method called MakeCellVisible, which will scroll the spreadsheet as needed in order to cause the cell identified by a given row and column index to come into view. The following listing is the implementation of that procedure.

```
Public Sub MakeCellVisible(intRow As Integer, intCol As Integer)
    ' Make the given cell visible by scrolling as necessary

    ' Check for out-of-range
    If intRow < 1 Or intRow > Rows Then Exit Sub
    If intCol < 1 Or intCol > Cols Then Exit Sub

    ' Select the cell
    Row = intRow
    Col = intCol
    ' If the row or column is not visible then make it visible
    If mGrd.RowIsVisible(intRow + mConRowOffset) = False Then _
                            mGrd.TopRow = intRow + mConRowOffset
    If mGrd.ColIsVisible(intCol + mConColOffset) = False Then _
                            mGrd.LeftCol = intCol + mConColOffset
    ' Make sure grid has the focus
    mGrd.SetFocus

End Sub
```

Another clsSheet method we've found to be useful is one that selects an entire row and scrolls the row into view. The following clsSheet SelectRow method takes the index of a spreadsheet row, selects all the cells in the row, and scrolls the spreadsheet in an attempt to move the row to the top of the visible portion of the spreadsheet.

```
Public Sub SelectRow(intRow As Integer)
    ' Select the given row and make it visible

    ' Check for valid row
    If intRow < 1 Or intRow > Rows Then Exit Sub

    Row = intRow                        ' Set starting selection position
    Col = 1

    With mGrd                           ' Set ending selection position
        .RowSel = intRow + mConRowOffset
        .ColSel = Cols + mConColOffset

        .TopRow = intRow + mConRowOffset  ' Make the row visible
        .SetFocus                         ' Make sure the grid has focus
    End With

End Sub
```

The clsSheet Find method takes an optional string argument that specifies the string to search for in the cells of the spreadsheet. When a string argument is provided, the string is stored in a static procedure variable and the static search position variable is initialized. Both the search string and search position variables are static, so that if the method is called again with no argument, the search can pick up where it left off.

Cells of the MSFlexGrid control are searched using TextArray. The MSFlexGrid TextArray property is similar to TextMatrix, only it takes a single sequential index instead of both row and column indexes. Fixed rows and columns are eliminated in the search by converting a sequential index to the row and column indexes of the spreadsheet. Only if both the row and column indexes are greater than zero is the cell contents searched. The VB InStr function is used to determine if the contents of each cell contain the search string. When found, the cell is made visible using the MakeCellVisible clsSheet method and the procedure returns True. If the spreadsheet is exhausted without finding a matching cell, the procedure returns false. A more sophisticated Find procedure can be implemented by using VB's Like operator in place of InStr.

```
Public Function Find(Optional strString As Variant) As Boolean
    ' Search through the grid starting at the current location and look
    ' for cell contents matching the given string.
    Static strSearch As String, lngPos As Long
    Dim I As Long, lngCells As Long, intRow As Integer, intCol As Integer
    Dim intCols As Integer

    Find = False        ' Assume not found
```

```
    ' If search string is given then assume the search is starting new
    If Not IsMissing(strString) Then
        strSearch = strString              ' Store search string and initial
        lngPos = 0&                        ' position in static variables
    End If

    lngCells = mGrd.Rows * mGrd.Cols - 1&       ' Calculate the upper bound
    intCols = mGrd.Cols                         ' Save the number of columns
    ' Loop over all cells searching for the string
    For I = lngPos To lngCells - 1&             ' Loop over all cells
        intRow = (I \ intCols) - mConRowOffset  ' Calculate row and column
        intCol = (I Mod intCols) - mConColOffset ' from sequential index
        If intRow > 0 And intCol > 0 Then       ' Exclude fixed rows and columns
            If InStr(mGrd.TextArray(I), strSearch) Then      ' Look for string
                MakeCellVisible intRow, intCol  ' Make cell visible when found
                lngPos = I + 1                  ' Store next starting position
                Find = True                     ' Return success
                Exit Function
            End If
        End If
    Next I

End Function
```

Wow! We've covered every line of code that defines the clsSheet class. I think you'll agree that while there is a healthy number of procedures, the complexity is minimal. Along the way we've pointed out a number of places where you might want to modify the behavior of the class. It is easy to come up with many more ideas as well. For example, you could easily inhibit editing of certain rows or columns by preventing BeginEdit from being executed from the appropriate cell locations. You could add color properties that set cell foreground or background colors. You could create a Cell Property Set procedure that assigns a graphic to a cell. Since you have the source code for the class, limitations are dictated by your imagination and programming abilities.

24

Visual Basic® Graphics Fundamentals

One way to add new functionality to your interface is to weave together ActiveX Controls that are provided with Visual Basic® so that they function in a coordinated fashion. For example, a ScrollBar and TextBox can be linked so that a change in the ScrollBar's position will be reflected in the numeric value displayed by the TextBox. Likewise, a numeric value entered into the TextBox can update the position of the ScrollBar. The two controls are woven together through their event procedures. In this example, the ScrollBar's Change event procedure will update the TextBox Text property, and the TextBox Change event procedure will update the ScrollBar's Value property. By weaving existing controls together in this manner you can build powerful new user interface functionality with minimal investment of effort. We leave it to the reader to investigate ways to use the standard VB toolkit to build customized interfaces to their applications. But when the standard suite of controls runs out of gas, what options are left?

Beginning with this section, and for the remainder of Part 4, we will discuss ways to build your own active and interactive graphical interfaces using VB. Since you will programmatically draw the interface yourself, you are free to make it appear any way you like. This opens up a whole range of new possibilities. For example, your interface can be an exact replica of an instrument front panel, or perhaps with new features that you feel were left out by the instrument manufacturer. Of course, drawing a completely new interface will require a bit more work than simply using one of the standard controls. But you'll be surprised at how easy it is, and you'll benefit tremendously from an ability to customize your user interface to a particular application.

Starting with Version 5 of Visual Basic®, you can actually build and distribute your own ActiveX controls, and while you can use the methods described here as the basis for new ActiveX controls, we won't cover that topic. There are many good references on how to build your own ActiveX controls using VB. Instead, we'll use a different approach for building interfaces in an object-oriented fashion.

In our approach the drawing surface is separate from the underlying code that displays itself on the surface. As you'll discover, VB provides three objects that can act as drawing surfaces and have enough commonality to make them largely interchangeable. By encapsulating the code that generates a display in one object, and identifying the display as another object, we gain significant flexibility. We will be able to change dynamically where an object draws itself, direct it to draw itself on multiple surfaces, or have it draw itself on a series of drawing surfaces in order to capture snapshots of its state over time. This approach is very similar to the one used to build the VB spreadsheet in Chapter 23. The difference between this approach and the one taken to build the VB Spreadsheet object is that the features of existing VB controls were used for spreadsheet editing and display. In what follows we will be drawing the graphical interface from scratch. Using this approach to distribute your code you'll probably have to hand over the source and a few instructions for use. When you want to distribute without revealing your source code, wrap it up in an ActiveX control first.

A QUICK START

Let's begin our exploration of Visual Basic®'s drawing capabilities with an example. The completed example can be found in the folder \Part4\Ex7 of the online code. Create a new VB project and sketch a CommandButton on Form1. Set the following properties.

Object Type	Property	Value
Form	Name	frmCanvas
	Caption	Drawing Canvas
CommandButton	Name	btnDraw

Add the following btnDraw CommandButton Click event procedure:

```
Private Sub btnDraw_Click()
    ' Draw on the form
    frmCanvas.Line (100, 100)-(2000, 2000)   ' Draw a line
    frmCanvas.CurrentX = 1000                 ' Change the current position
    frmCanvas.CurrentY = 500
    frmCanvas.Print "Hello World"             ' Print some text
    frmCanvas.DrawWidth = 4                   ' Draw a thick red box
    frmCanvas.Line (500, 1000)-(2000, 2000), vbRed, B

End Sub
```

Run the example and click the btnDraw CommandButton. On the frmCanvas Form will appear a line, a box, and some text (see Figure 24-1). It's that simple!

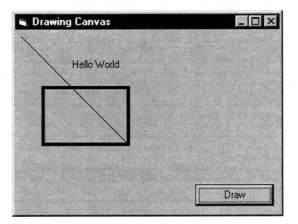

Figure 24-1. A Quick Start example demonstrating a few of Visual Basic®'s drawing capabilities.

Let's look at what occurred. A Form is one of the objects that can act as a drawing surface. In this example we used the frmCanvas Form's Line method first to draw a thin black line. The CurrentX and CurrentY properties were used to move the current drawing position to a new location on the Form. The Form's Print method was used to transfer text onto the Form. Its DrawWidth property value was increased and the Line method called again to draw a thicker red box.

A PictureBox control and a Printer object can also act as drawing surfaces. We'll cover the Printer object in more detail later, but it is worth noting here that the Printer object has no real graphical interface unless you call the sheet of paper that emerges from a printer a graphical interface. As we'll see, the Printer object shares graphics methods with Forms and PictureBox controls. This implies that generating a hard copy of your drawing can amount simply to redirecting your program to draw on the Printer object instead of a Form or PictureBox.

Many other controls can display graphic images but do not act as drawing surfaces. We've already seen that the MSFlexGrid control can display graphic images within a cell. Other controls that can display graphic images include the Image control, CommandButton, OptionButton, CheckBox, Toolbar, TabStrip, and so on.

GRAPHICS METHODS

Visual Basic® includes only the most basic drawing capabilities, but this is all we'll need to accomplish a diverse range of sophisticated custom graphical interfaces. Table 24-1 lists available graphics methods along with a brief description of each. We will cover the syntax for each of these methods with

TABLE 24-1. Graphics methods of Visual Basic® drawing surfaces.

Graphics Method	Description
Line	Draws a line on a drawing surface
Circle	Draws a circle, ellipse, arc, or pie slice on a drawing surface
PSet	Draws a single point on a surface or drawing surface
Point	Returns an RGB value of a point (not available with Printer object)
Cls	Clears the entire drawing surface (not available with Printer object)
Print	Prints a list of elements to a drawing surface
PaintPicture	Draws the contents of a graphic file on a drawing surface

plenty of examples. Give the examples a try by modifying the Quick Start example project. Change parameters and observe how the drawn graphic changes to get a full appreciation for how they work.

The Line method draws a line or a box on a drawing surface; Circle draws a circle, arc, pie slice, or ellipse on a drawing surface; and PSet draws a single point. The syntax for these methods is a little unusual. We'll describe the main features of each. Refer to VB Help for details.

The Line method takes two points on a drawing surface as a minimum set of arguments. Syntactically, the two points are specified as in the following statement:

```
MyDrawingSurface.Line (X1, Y1)-(X2, Y2)
```

MyDrawingSurface is an object that implements a Line method. X1,Y1 and X2,Y2 are the X and Y coordinates of the two point arguments. Point arguments are enclosed within parentheses and separated by a dash. Point coordinates are separated with a comma.

Adding a color constant to the list of Line method arguments will set the color of a line. For example, the following statement will draw a green line between the points (500, 500) and (900, 900) on the frmCanvas drawing surface:

```
frmCanvas.Line (500, 500)-(900, 900), vbGreen
```

Table 24-2 lists predefined Visual Basic® color constants. Color constants are stored as Long integers. You can generate any color that can be represented using the RGB function in VB. Refer to VB Help for more details.

The Line method can also be used to draw a box. Add a "B" as the argument after color to the Line method argument list in order to cause the method to draw a box using point arguments as the opposing corners of the box instead of line endpoints. Add a "BF" argument if you would like the box to be filled with the color indicated by the color argument. For example, the

TABLE 24-2. Predefined color constants in VB.

Color	Predefined Constant
Black	vbBlack
Red	vbRed
Green	vbGreen
Yellow	vbYellow
Blue	vbBlue
Magenta	vbMagenta
Cyan	vbCyan
White	vbWhite

following statement will draw a green-filled box with corners at the points (500, 500) and (900, 900):

```
frmCanvas.Line (500, 500)-(900, 900), vbGreen, BF
```

The Circle method can be used to draw a circle, ellipse, arc, or pie slice on a drawing surface. At a minimum, the arguments to the Circle method are the center point of a circle and its radius. The following statement will draw a circle on the frmCanvas Form that is centered at the point (500, 500) with a radius of 400:

```
frmCanvas.Circle (500, 500), 400
```

The next Circle argument specifies the circle color. The following statement will draw the same circle, only with a blue outline:

```
frmCanvas.Circle (500, 500), 400, vbBlue
```

You cannot fill a circle using the Circle method. You need to set the FillColor and FillStyle properties of the drawing surface object in order to fill a circle. We will describe these and other graphics properties in the next section.

The next two circle method arguments after color specify the start and end angles to use when you want to draw an arc instead of a circle. These arguments are given in radians. Arcs are drawn in a counter-clockwise direction with angles measured in relation to a vector extending from the center of the circle to the right. The following statements draw a blue arc that bounds the upper right quadrant of a circle:

```
Const pi As Single = 3.14159
frmCanvas.Circle (500, 500), 400, vbBlue, 0, 0.5 * pi
```

The arc is turned into a pie slice by changing the angle arguments to negative numbers. Since 0 cannot be negative, we need to replace the 0-angle argument with a small negative number. The next two statements will draw a pie slice that bounds the upper right quadrant of a circle with a radius of 400:

```
Const pi As Single = 3.14159
frmCanvas.Circle (500, 500), 400, vbBlue, -0.0001, -0.5 * pi
```

The last Circle method argument is an aspect ratio that turns a circle, arc, or pie slice into an ellipse, or portion thereof. The aspect ratio argument is a single-precision number that represents the height of the ellipse over its width. An aspect ratio greater than 1 will result in an ellipse that is tall and thin. A value less than 1 will produce a short and wide ellipse. The following statements flatten the previous pie slice:

```
Const pi As Single = 3.14159
frmCanvas.Circle (500, 500), 400, vbBlue, -0.0001, -0.5 * pi, 0.5
```

The PSet method sets the color of a single point on a drawing surface. It takes a single point as a required argument and a color constant as an optional argument. The following statement will set the color of the point at the coordinates (500, 500) to magenta:

```
frmCanvas.PSet (500, 500), vbMagenta
```

The Point method takes the coordinates of a location on a drawing surface and returns a long integer that corresponds to the point color value. After setting the point at 500, 500 to magenta using the PSet method, the following statement will show that the color value at that point is 16711935, which is the long integer representation of magenta:

```
MsgBox CStr(frmCanvas.Point(500, 500))
```

The Print graphics method takes a comma-separated list of elements to be printed on a drawing surface. The Print method renders its arguments in a manner similar to the way that the Print # statement would write them to a file.

The Cls graphics method clears a drawing surface of all graphics and restores its original image. The original image need not be the default battleship gray background color of most controls. We will use this feature to our benefit when designing more sophisticated graphical interfaces.

The PaintPicture graphics method transfers a graphic image to a drawing surface. It is quite flexible, taking up to 10 different arguments. Required arguments include the graphic to draw and the coordinates at which to draw it. The graphic must be passed as a Picture object or transferred from the Picture property of another control.

Let's demonstrate Cls and PaintPicture with an example. The completed example can be found in the folder \Part4\Ex8 of the code available online. Create a new project and sketch a CommandButton on Form1. Set the following properties.

Object Type	Property	Value
Form	Name	frmCanvas
	Caption	Swimming Fish
CommandButton	Name	btnSwim

Add the following btnSwim CommandButton Click event procedure.

```
Private Sub btnSwim_Click()
    ' Paint a graphic onto a form
    Dim dblX As Double, dblY As Double, I As Integer
    Dim pct As Picture
    Const pi = 3.1415926

    ' Load the graphic file into a Picture object
    Set pct = LoadPicture(App.Path & "\" & "fish.bmp")

    ' Make the fish swim
    For I = 0 To 3600
        dblX = 2000# * (1# + Cos((pi / 180#) * 0.2 * CDbl(I)))
        dblY = 500# * (1# + Sin((pi / 180#) * CDbl(I)))
        Cls
        PaintPicture pct, dblX, dblY
    Next I
End Sub
```

This procedure loads a fish bitmap from the file named fish.bmp using the LoadPicture function and stores it in the pct variable, declared as a Picture object. To make the fish "swim" a series of X-Y locations is computed within a loop. Each time through the loop the Form is cleared using the Cls method and the fish picture is drawn on the form at the new location using the PaintPicture method. Run the example and click "Swim" to start the fish swimming. The result will appear like that shown in Figure 24-2.

GRAPHICS PROPERTIES

Graphics properties work hand-in-hand with graphics methods to generate a graphical display. Many of the graphics methods described in the previous section do not offer the breadth of formatting options that are possible. In this chapter's Quick Start example the thickness of the red box was not determined

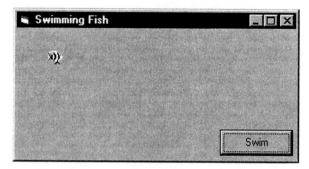

Figure 24-2. The "Swimming Fish" example in action.

by an argument to the Line method. It was determined by the DrawWidth property value of the Form, which was set prior to executing the Line method. Table 24-3 lists graphics properties with the data type and a brief description for each. Graphics properties include formatting options, drawing position, background graphics, and repaint options for the drawing surface object.

The DrawWidth property is used to set or return the width of lines drawn on the drawing surface object. DrawStyle determines the pattern used to draw lines that have a width equal to 1. When visible, lines with widths greater than 1 are all drawn solid. Table 24-4 lists and describes predefined constants that can be used to set or test a DrawStyle property.

FillStyle and FillColor properties are used to set or return the pattern and color used to fill a closed object drawn on a drawing surface. FillColor takes a predefined color constant (see Table 24-2), or the long integer returned from

TABLE 24-3. Visual Basic® graphics properties.

Graphics Property	Data Type	Description
DrawWidth	Integer	Sets or returns line width
DrawStyle	Integer	Sets or returns line style
DrawMode	Integer	Sets or returns pen style
FillStyle	Integer	Sets or returns the pattern used to fill a closed graphic
FillColor	Long	Sets or returns the color used to fill a graphic
BackColor	Long	Sets or returns background color
ForeColor	Long	Sets or returns foreground color
CurrentX	Integer	Sets or returns the current drawing surface horizontal position
CurrentY	Integer	Sets or returns the current drawing surface vertical position
AutoRedraw	Boolean	True if to repaint a drawing surface using persistent graphics; False if to repaint by calling the Paint event procedure
Picture	Picture	Sets or returns the current graphic of an object
Image	Picture	Returns an object's persistent graphic

TABLE 24-4. Graphic draw styles and predefined constants.

Drawing Style	Predefined Constant
Solid line	vbSolid
Dashed line	vbDash
Dotted line	vbDot
Dash-dot alternate line	vbDashDot
Dash-dot-dot alternating line	vbDashDotDot
Transparent line	vbInvisible
Line drawn on inside of a closed shape	vbInsideSolid

a call to the RGB function. Table 24-5 lists the available fill styles along with predefined constants that you can use to set or test the FillStyle property of a drawing surface object.

BackColor and ForeColor properties of a drawing surface specify colors used to produce graphics. Both properties take predefined color constants or color integers created with the RGB function. BackColor sets the color that fills the drawing surface before any drawing begins. ForeColor determines the color for all subsequent drawn graphics, unless the color is overridden by a graphic method color argument, such as that available in Line and Circle methods. Changing the ForeColor property does not affect the color of existing graphics. It only determines the color of graphics that are drawn after the property is changed.

The CurrentX and CurrentY properties determine where the next graphic element will be drawn, unless overridden by graphic method arguments. For example, to print text at a certain place on a drawing surface, you must set the CurrentX and CurrentY properties prior to executing the Print method. When printing is complete, CurrentX and CurrentY values are changed to the next logical place for printing to begin.

The Picture graphic property sets or returns a graphic that is displayed on the drawing surface. The graphic can be set at design time or run time with a string that locates a graphic file. At run time the property can also be assigned from another control's Picture property, or any Image property. One

TABLE 24-5. Graphic fill styles and predefined constants.

Fill Style	Predefined Constant
Solid Fill	vbFSSolid
Transparent Fill	vbFSTransparent
Horizontal Line Fill	vbHorizontalLine
Vertical Line Fill	vbVerticalLine
Upward Diagonal Line Fill	vbUpwardDiagonal
Downward Diagonal Line Fill	vbDownwardDiagonal
Cross Fill	vbCross
Diagonal Cross Fill	vbDiagonalCross

TABLE 24-6. A few graphics drawing modes with predefined constants.

Draw Mode	Predefined Constant
Draw in black	vbBlackness
Draw in color specified by ForeColor	vbCopyPen
Draw by inverting pixel values	vbInvert

important aspect that should be understood about a drawing surface object's Picture property is that the graphic it stores is copied to the drawing surface when the Cls method is invoked. We will use this feature extensively to restore an unchanging graphic backdrop when we begin to build our own graphic interfaces.

Proper use of a drawing surface's DrawMode property makes it possible to do some interesting things. DrawMode determines how a graphic element will be transferred to the drawing surface. How many different ways can you draw something on a drawing surface? You may be surprised to find out that there are 16 different ways! Table 24-6 lists perhaps the most common modes with predefined constants. You can have a look at all the options by searching for "Drawing Constants" in VB Help.

The default DrawMode property is equal to the predefined constant vbCopyPen. In this case, the color specified by the ForeColor property is used to draw anything new on the drawing surface. When DrawMode is equal to vbBlackness, all graphics are drawn in black. A DrawMode equal to vbInvert does something altogether different.

Rather than drawing something with a known color, when a drawing surface DrawMode property is equal to vbInvert, the pixel colors on the drawing surface are inverted where the graphic element is drawn. The interesting aspect about inverting a pixel color is that, if you invert it a second time, it returns to the original color. This implies that if you draw the same thing twice on a drawing surface object with a DrawMode property equal to vbInvert, the first time it is drawn it will appear, and the second time it is drawn it will disappear. How is this useful? The next example lets you select a whole range of CheckBoxes on a Form using a graphic lasso. The completed example can be found in the folder \Part4\Ex9 of the code available online.

Create a new VB project and sketch 12 or so CheckBox controls on Form1. Assign properties as given in the following table. We want all the CheckBoxes to be part of a single control array. The easiest way to accomplish this is to sketch the first CheckBox on the form, set its properties to those of the CheckBox with Index=0 in the following table, copy the CheckBox, and paste it 11 times. The Form design will appear as in Figure 24-3.

Enter the following code in to the declarations section of the frmSelect Form module. Four module-level integers are declared to hold the current corners of the lasso. A module-level boolean called mBlnDrawing is declared to hold the current drawing state. When mBlnDrawing is True, the program is in the

Object Type	Property	Value
Form	Name	frmCanvas
	Caption	CheckBox Lasso
CheckBox	Name	chkSelect
	Caption	
	Index	0
CheckBox	Name	chkSelect
	Caption	
	Index	1
CheckBox	Name	chkSelect
	Caption	
	Index	2
CheckBox	Name	chkSelect
	Caption	
	Index	3
CheckBox	Name	chkSelect
	Caption	
	Index	4
CheckBox	Name	chkSelect
	Caption	
	Index	5
CheckBox	Name	chkSelect
	Caption	
	Index	6
CheckBox	Name	chkSelect
	Caption	
	Index	7
CheckBox	Name	chkSelect
	Caption	
	Index	8
CheckBox	Name	chkSelect
	Caption	
	Index	9
CheckBox	Name	chkSelect
	Caption	
	Index	10
CheckBox	Name	chkSelect
	Caption	
	Index	11

process of drawing the lasso. When mBlnDrawing is False, the lasso is not being drawn.

```
Option Explicit

' Variables to hold lasso coordinates
Private mIntX1 As Integer, mIntY1 As Integer, mIntX2 As Integer, mIntY2 As Integer

Private mBlnDrawing As Integer          ' Current drawing mode
```

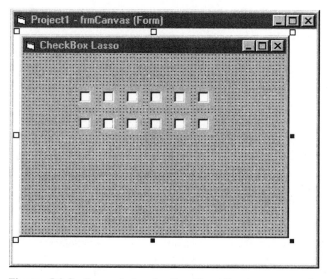

Figure 24-3. Form design for the CheckBox lasso example.

When the frmCanvas Form is loaded, set its graphics property values. We want the Form to have a white background, draw dotted lines, and draw in Invert mode. To accomplish this, in the following Form Load event procedure the frmCanvas BackColor property is set to vbWhite, the DrawMode property to vbInvert, and the DrawStyle property to vbDot. We also change the BackColor property of all CheckBoxes in order to help them better blend in with the Form background.

```
Private Sub Form_Load()
    Dim I As Integer

    ' Initialize Form graphics properties
    With frmCanvas
        .BackColor = vbWhite
        .DrawMode = vbInvert
        .DrawStyle = vbDot
    End With

    ' Set CheckBox background color to blend in with form
    For I = 0 To 11
        chkSelect(I).BackColor = vbWhite
    Next I
End Sub
```

When the mouse is pressed down on the form, we set the drawing mode variable to True, save the current mouse position in module-level integer variables, and draw the first lasso. Since the coordinates of the opposite corners of the lasso are the same, the lasso will be quite small. The following frmCanvas MouseDown event procedure implements this.

```
Private Sub Form_MouseDown(Button As Integer, Shift As Integer, X As Single, Y As Single)
    mBlnDrawing = True                          ' Initialize drawing
    mIntX1 = X: mIntY1 = Y                       ' Initialize points
    mIntX2 = X: mIntY2 = Y
    Line (mIntX1, mIntY1)-(mIntX2, mIntY2), , B ' Draw first lasso
End Sub
```

When the mouse moves, if drawing has been initiated, we want to erase the previous lasso and draw a new lasso with the new mouse coordinates. Recall that to erase a graphic element while in Invert drawing mode, you draw it a second time. The following frmCanvas MouseMove event procedure erases the current lasso by drawing it with the currently saved coordinates, updates the lasso coordinates, and draws it again.

```
Private Sub Form_MouseMove(Button As Integer, Shift As Integer, X As Single, Y As Single)
    If mBlnDrawing = False Then Exit Sub         ' If not drawing then exit
    Line (mIntX1, mIntY1)-(mIntX2, mIntY2), , B ' Erase the last lasso
    mIntX2 = X: mIntY2 = Y                        ' Update saved points
    Line (mIntX1, mIntY1)-(mIntX2, mIntY2), , B ' Draw the new lasso
End Sub
```

When the mouse is released, we want to erase the last lasso and cancel our custom drawing mode. The following frmCanvas MouseUp event procedure accomplished that. Before exiting this procedure, we invoke another procedure called SelectItems.

```
Private Sub Form_MouseUp(Button As Integer, Shift As Integer, X As Single, Y As Single)
    Line (mIntX1, mIntY1)-(mIntX2, mIntY2), , B ' Erase the last lasso
    mBlnDrawing = False                          ' Exit drawing mode
    SelectItems
End Sub
```

Even though the last lasso has been erased, its coordinates are still saved in module-level integer variables. The SelectItems procedure first sorts these coordinate values, and then loops over all CheckBoxes to see if any are contained within the last lasso. If so, they are checked.

```
Private Sub SelectItems()
    Dim I As Integer, intLeft As Integer, intTop As Integer
    Dim X1 As Integer, Y1 As Integer, X2 As Integer, Y2 As Integer

    If mIntX1 < mIntX2 Then                       ' Sort corners of lasso
        X1 = mIntX1:  X2 = mIntX2
    Else
        X1 = mIntX2:  X2 = mIntX1
    End If

    If mIntY1 < mIntY2 Then
        Y1 = mIntY1:  Y2 = mIntY2
    Else
        Y1 = mIntY2:  Y2 = mIntY1
    End If
```

```
' Select all CheckBoxes that fall in lasso
For I = 0 To 11
    intLeft = chkSelect(I).Left                    ' Save position of CheckBox
    intTop = chkSelect(I).Top
                                                   ' Set CheckBox value
    If X1 < intLeft And X2 > intLeft And Y1 < intTop And Y2 > intTop Then
            chkSelect(I).Value = vbChecked
    End If
Next I

End Sub
```

Run the program and give it a try. Click on the form and sweep out a range of CheckBoxes. All CheckBoxes that fall within the lasso will be checked when the mouse is released. Figure 24-4 shows the example program being used.

AUTOREDRAW, PERSISTENT GRAPHICS, AND THE PAINT EVENT

When a drawing surface object such as a Form or PictureBox is resized, or obscured by another window and then revealed, the object must repaint itself. VB offers two methods for handling this task. In the first method a memory buffer is automatically created that stores and maintains a copy of the screen image. This memory buffer is called a persistent graphic. When the drawing surface needs to be repainted, VB uses the persistent graphic to repaint the screen. All this is done for you by setting the AutoRedraw graphic property to True. Figure 24-5 illustrates the idea. You can access a persistent graphic through the Image graphic property.

The down side of AutoRedraw becomes obvious when you have one or more large drawing surfaces to maintain. Keeping a copy of each as a persistent graphic can eat up memory quickly.

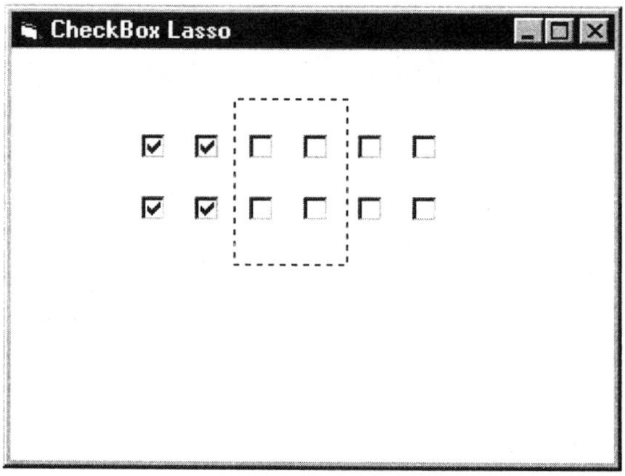

Figure 24-4. The CheckBox Lasso example in action.

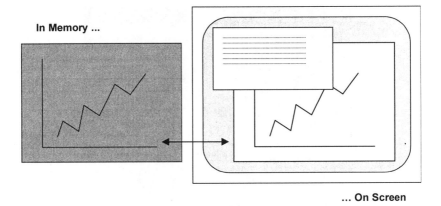

In Memory ...

... On Screen

Figure 24-5. A persistent graphic automatically generated using AutoRedraw.

An alternative to using AutoRedraw is the Paint event. When AutoRedraw is False, no persistent graphic is maintained, and the drawing surface object will receive Paint events whenever it needs to be repainted. VB will invoke the Paint event procedure when it receives a Paint event. You can regenerate an image using graphic methods called from within the Paint event procedure.

Use AutoRedraw when you can afford the memory and the screen image is dynamic or time consuming to recreate. Regenerate the screen image from the Paint event procedure when it is static and quick to recreate.

COORDINATE SYSTEMS

In the last section of this introductory chapter we discuss drawing surface coordinate systems. We have referred many times to the coordinates of the screen. The coordinate system is used by several graphic methods, such as Line and Circle, to determine where graphic elements are to be drawn. VB allows you to change the coordinate system of a drawing surface to suit your needs.

The default coordinate system of a drawing surface defines its origin as the uppermost left-hand point with length measured in a unit called *twips*. There are approximately 1440 twips in an inch. Everything we've drawn to this point has been done in twips. To create Figure 24-6 we added the following two lines of code to the frmCanvas Load event procedure of a new project and ran the program. A line is drawn beginning in the upper left-hand corner of the form and ending somewhere in the middle. The statement that generated the line is then printed at the current coordinates.

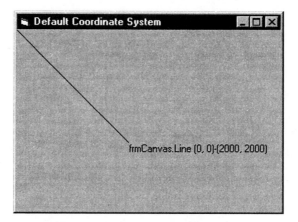

Figure 24-6. *A line drawn in a Form's default coordinate system.*

```
frmCanvas.Line (0, 0)-(2000, 2000)
frmCanvas.Print "frmCanvas.Line (0, 0)-(2000, 2000)"
```

Measurement units of a drawing surface object can be changed by setting the ScaleMode graphic property. Table 24-7 lists ScaleMode constants along with a description of the associated unit of measurement. For example, if we wanted to draw everything on the frmCanvas Form in pixels, the following line of code would make the necessary change:

```
frmCanvas.ScaleMode = vbPixels
```

TABLE 24-7. Units of measurement, ScaleMode constants, and a brief description of each.

Measurement Unit	ScaleMode Constant	Screen Dependent?	Description
Twips	vbTwips	No	There are 1440 twips per logical inch
Points	vbPoints	No	There are 72 points per logical inch
Pixels	vbPixels	Yes	The smallest unit of screen resolution
Characters	vbCharacters	No	A character has about 240 twips vertically and 120 twips horizontally
Inches	vbInches	No	A logical inch
Millimeters	vbMillimeters	No	A logical millimeter
Centimeters	vbCentimeters	No	A logical centimeter
User-defined	vbUser	No	Custom coordinates system, defined by the user

Note that all units of measurement, except pixels, are independent of screen resolution. A pixel (picture element) is the smallest dot that can be created using a particular screen driver and computer monitor. The number of pixels that can be displayed defines screen resolution. Using a screen-independent unit of measure will help your drawing appear the same when created on separate computer monitors with different screen resolutions.

When drawing an object of known dimensions, it can be a real advantage to use a custom coordinate system. With custom coordinate systems, you get to set how distance is measured in the horizontal and vertical dimensions on a drawing surface. When you have the actual dimensions of an object that you are about to draw, it is much easier to change the coordinate system of the drawing surface to match object dimensions instead of converting every point of every graphic element before you paint it. Table 24-8 lists the drawing surface properties that can be used to customize the coordinate system of a drawing surface.

The ScaleWidth property sets the number of units that span the horizontal dimension and ScaleHeight sets the number of units that span the vertical dimension. ScaleLeft sets the leftmost coordinate value and ScaleTop sets the topmost coordinate value.

The Scale method can be used as an alternative to these four properties. Arguments passed to the Scale method are the upper left-hand and lower right-hand coordinates that define the corners of a custom coordinate system. The argument format is similar to the Line method; corner point arguments are enclosed within parentheses and separated by a dash. By way of demonstration we executed the following lines of code from the Load event procedure of a Form called frmCanvas. The result is given in Figure 24-7.

```
frmCanvas.Scale (-1#, 1#)-(1#, -1#)
frmCanvas.CurrentX = -0.5
frmCanvas.CurrentY = -0.5
frmCanvas.Print "+ (-0.5, -0.5)"
frmCanvas.CurrentX = 0.5
frmCanvas.CurrentY = 0.5
frmCanvas.Print "+ (0.5, 0.5)"
```

TABLE 24-8. Properties for setting a user-defined coordinate system on a drawing surface.

Property	Data Type	Description
ScaleWidth	Single	Sets or returns the number of units in the horizontal dimension
ScaleHeight	Single	Sets or returns the number of units in the vertical dimension
ScaleLeft	Single	Sets or returns the coordinate value for leftmost point
ScaleTop	Single	Sets or returns the coordinate value for topmost point

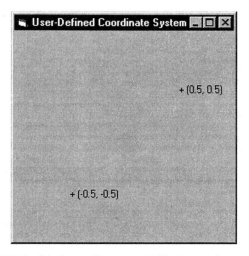

Figure 24-7. Printing with a user-defined coordinate system.

First a user-defined coordinate system for the Form was established using the Scale method. It was defined to have a horizontal range of [–1, 1] and a vertical range of [1, -1]. Then we printed two strings that roughly identify the positions (–0.5, –0.5) and (0.5, 0.5) on the Form using the new coordinate system. The point (–0.5, –0.5) is located in the lower-left quadrant of the Form and (0.5, 0.5) in the upper-right quadrant of the Form. But wait! Previously we indicated that length in the vertical dimension was measured beginning from the top and increasing downward. This result indicates that vertical length is being measured from the bottom and increasing upward! If you take a close look at the arguments of the previous Scale method, you'll discover that the Y coordinate in each point has been swapped. That is, the coordinate value was set to be 1.0 at the top of the vertical dimension and –1.0 at the bottom of the vertical dimension. The effect is to flip the default way distance is measured in the vertical dimension to something more natural.

CHAPTER

25

Active Graphic Displays

In this chapter we will present a method for building your own *active graphic displays*. When we use the term *active graphics*, we are referring to graphical displays that automatically change to reflect changes in associated data. A real-life analogy to an active graphic is a control panel readout. In fact, this is exactly the kind of display that we want to build using active graphic techniques. Don't confuse active graphics with ActiveX. Active graphics is merely an informal technique for graphical representing dynamic data.

A MODEL FOR ACTIVE GRAPHIC DISPLAYS

We will present two examples of active graphic displays. Both examples utilize the same underlying model (see Figure 25-1). All the code that manages the display will be encapsulated within a VB class. One of the properties of the class will be a reference to a drawing surface on which the graphic display will be generated. This is similar to the way in which the clsSheet spreadsheet class was designed in Chapter 23. The clsSheet class includes two properties that hold references to an MSFlexGrid and TextBox control, which are used to orchestrate the spreadsheet interface. Our graphic display classes will each have a property that holds a reference to a PictureBox control. This property declaration could easily be changed to a Form or Printer object, or it could be declared as type Object and accept any of the three drawing surface objects.

To use an active graphic class, you will have to create a new instance of the class and set its drawing surface property to a reference to an appropriate control. Again, in all our examples we will use the PictureBox control. The act of assigning the PictureBox will invoke a Property Set procedure in the object that will configure it appropriately. Each active graphic class will have one or more properties, which, when assigned a value, will automatically result in a change of the display. In summary, to use an active graphic object, you only need to create an instance of the class, assign a drawing surface, and set its properties. The object handles all the rest.

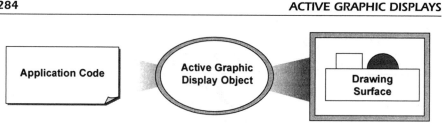

Figure 25-1. A model for Active Graphic Display objects.

AN ACTIVE STRIPCHART GRAPHIC DISPLAY OBJECT

The first active graphic object that we will build is a strip chart. The StripChart object will be designed to plot a series of values that scrolls from the right side of the display to the left as new values are added. The StripChart class will have one property and one method. The PictureBox property is used to set the PictureBox control on which the StripChart will draw itself. The AddPoint method will take a single-precision number, which will be added dynamically to the StripChart display and cause it to scroll to the left. You can find the complete example code that follows in the folder \Part4\StripChart of the code available online.

To define the new StripChart class, create a new VB project and add a new class module. Set the Name property of the class module to StripChart. Add the following code to the declarations section of the StripChart Class module. We declare a number of items in the declarations section. The mConNumPoints constant defines the number of values that can be held by the StripChart at any one time. The mSngChartVals array is used to hold the values that will be displayed by the StripChart. The mIntStartIndex Integer variable identifies the rotating array index that locates the value used to begin the StripChart display. The StripChart will be drawn in the PictureBox whose reference is held by the mPct PictureBox variable.

```
Option Explicit

' A constant defining the number of points the class should plot
Const mConNumPoints As Integer = 101

' Array that holds StripChart values
Private mSngChartVals(0 To mConNumPoints - 1) As Single

' Index in the array that is the current starting point
Private mIntStartIndex As Integer

' A reference to the PictureBox on which to draw the StripChart
Private WithEvents mPct As PictureBox
```

Add the following PictureBox Property Set procedure to the StripChart class module. This procedure assigns and causes the initialization of the PictureBox drawing surface. The procedure copies the given PictureBox reference argument to the private mPct class variable and initializes a custom coordinate system. The PictureBox drawing surface coordinate system will always be the same regardless of its actual size. This will assure that the StripChart drawing will fill the PictureBox no matter how the PictureBox is sized on a Form. Invoking the SetBackground procedure sets the StripChart background, and the StripChart is drawn using initial array values by invoking DrawChart.

```
Public Property Set PictureBox(pctBox As PictureBox)
    ' Set and configure the PictureBox on which the strip chart will be drawn.
    Set mPct = pctBox

    ' Set the coordinates of the PictureBox.
    With mPct
        .ScaleLeft = -0.2
        .ScaleWidth = 1.4
        .ScaleTop = 1.2
        .ScaleHeight = -1.4
    End With

    ' Draw the axes and save background.  Draw initial chart.
    SetBackground
    DrawChart

End Property
```

Add the following SetBackground procedure to the class module. The majority of this procedure calls graphics methods in order to draw the StripChart outline, ticks, and labels. One thing to point out about this procedure is that it stores the resulting graphic in the Picture property of the PictureBox. By doing this we can use the PictureBox Cls method to restore the static background image without having to redraw it. To store a background image the AutoRedraw property is initially set to True so that, in addition to drawing on the PictureBox, a copy of the drawing is maintained in a persistent graphic behind the scenes. When the background image is finished, it is stored by assigning the Picture property of the PictureBox to its own Image property. We then disable AutoRedraw by setting the property to False since we will no longer need this feature. We'll use this same technique in all examples in this chapter and the one that follows.

```
Private Sub SetBackground()
    ' Draw the axes and save in the PictureBox Picture property
    mPct.AutoRedraw = True       ' Begin persistent graphic
    mPct.BackColor = vbWhite     ' Clear

    ' Draw outline
    mPct.Line (0, 0)-(1#, 1#), vbBlack, B

    ' Draw ticks and labels
    mPct.Line (0#, 0#)-(-0.02, 0#), vbBlack
```

```
    mPct.FontSize = 12
    mPct.CurrentX = -2# * mPct.TextWidth("0.0")
    mPct.CurrentY = -mPct.TextHeight("0.0") * 0.5
    mPct.Print "0.0"

    mPct.Line (0#, 1#)-(-0.02, 1#), vbBlack
    mPct.CurrentX = -2# * mPct.TextWidth("1.0")
    mPct.CurrentY = 1# - mPct.TextHeight("1.0") * 0.5
    mPct.Print "1.0"

    ' Store the background image in the Picture property
    mPct.Picture = mPct.Image
    mPct.AutoRedraw = False

End Sub
```

Add the following DrawChart procedure to the class module. DrawChart first calls the PictureBox's Cls method to restore the saved background. Then it loops over the array of stored values and generates the bars that represent the StripChart data.

```
Private Sub DrawChart()
    ' Draw the StripChart
    Dim I As Integer, sngX As Single, sngXIncrement As Single

    ' Reset the background
    mPct.Cls

    ' Draw chart values
    sngX = 0#
    sngXIncrement = 1# / CSng(mConNumPoints - 1)
    mPct.DrawWidth = 3

    For I = mIntStartIndex To mConNumPoints - 1
        mPct.Line (sngX, 0#)-(sngX, mSngChartVals(I)), vbRed
        sngX = sngX + sngXIncrement
    Next I

    For I = 0 To mIntStartIndex - 1
        mPct.Line (sngX, 0#)-(sngX, mSngChartVals(I)), vbRed
        sngX = sngX + sngXIncrement
    Next I

End Sub
```

Add the following AddPoint method to the class module. A new value is added to the StripChart array using the AddPoint method. AddPoint saves the passed value to the array at the rotating index, increments the index in preparation for the next point to be added, and redraws the StripChart to reflect the change.

```
Public Sub AddPoint(sngPoint As Single)
    ' Add a point to the rotating point array
```

```
' Add point to next position in array
mSngChartVals(mIntStartIndex) = sngPoint

' Update starting point for drawing the chart
mIntStartIndex = mIntStartIndex + 1
If mIntStartIndex > mConNumPoints - 1 Then mIntStartIndex = 0
' Redraw the StripChart
DrawChart

End Sub
```

The final required addition to the class module is a call to redraw the StripChart from the PictureBox Paint event procedure. Since we will not be using the AutoRedraw feature, the StripChart must be redrawn manually whenever the PictureBox receives a Paint event.

```
Private Sub mPct_Paint()
    DrawChart          ' Redraw the StripChart when needed
End Sub
```

Now that the StripChart class is defined, let's use it. Sketch a PictureBox and a CommandButton on Form1. Set the following property values.

Object Type	Property	Value
Form	Name	frmStripChart
	Caption	StripChart
PictureBox	Name	pctCanvas
CommandButton	Name	btnAddPoint
	Caption	Add Point

Add the following lines of code to the declarations section of the frmStripChart Form module. The only module-level declaration we need here is for a new StripChart object.

```
Option Explicit

' Module-level variable to hold a reference to the StripChart object
Private mChart As StripChart
```

Add the following frmStripChart Form_Load event procedure, which creates a new instance of the StripChart class and assigns its PictureBox property to the pctCanvas PictureBox Control upon loading the form.

```
Private Sub Form_Load()
    ' Create and initialize the new StripChart class
    Set mChart = New StripChart
    Set mChart.PictureBox = pctCanvas

End Sub
```

Add the following btnAddPoint CommandButton Click event procedure, which uses the mChart StripChart object's AddPoint method to add a randomly generated value to the StripChart display.

```
Private Sub btnAddPoint_Click()
    ' Add a random point to the StripChart
    mChart.AddPoint Rnd
End Sub
```

When all your code is entered, run the program and give it a try. Click "Add Point" several times and watch the StripChart display scroll (see Figure 25-2). You can easily use the StripChart class in your own VB project by including the StripChart.cls file, and creating and initializing the object as in this example. Call the StripChart object AddPoint method whenever you want to add a new point to the display. In fact, you can create several instances of the StripChart class and display them simultaneously on different PictureBox controls in your program.

Before moving to the next example, we simply couldn't resist going back to one of the examples in Part 3 and adding a StripChart object to display data collected from the Virtual Instrument. Here's what we did:

- We copied the Winsock VI Controller example project in the folder \Part3\WinsockCtrl to the new folder \Part4\WinsockCtrl.
- We copied the StripChart.cls class file into the new folder as well.
- After opening the WinsockCtrl.vbp project file, we added the StripChart.cls file to the project.
- We enlarged the main frmWinsockCtrl Form, sketched a new PictureBox, and named it pctCanvas.
- In a manner identical to the previous example, we declared a new StripChart object variable in the declarations section of the main frmWinsockCtrl form, assigned it to a new StripChart object, and initialized its PictureBox property in the Form_Load event procedure.

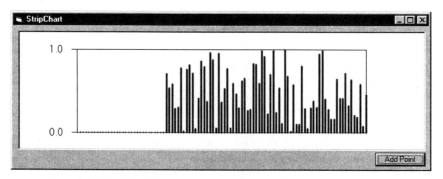

Figure 25-2. The StripChart Active Graphic Display class in action.

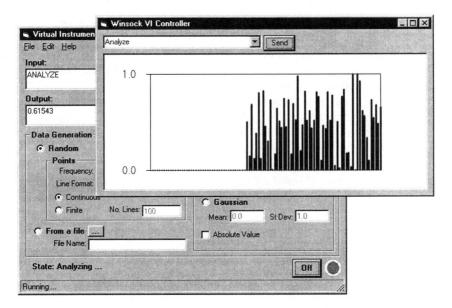

Figure 25-3. *The modified Winsock VI Controller with an active display of collected data using a StripChart object.*

- Finally, we commented out two lines in the ProcessMessage procedure that displayed the number of points collected and changed state back to idle, and inserted a line of code that added the first point collected to the StripChart.

The result is a program that controls the VI over a network, and automatically charts collected data as they arrive. To demonstrate it, we ran the VI and set it up for network communications. Then we started up the new controller program, selected the "Analyze" option, and sent the command to the VI. Figure 25-3 shows the new controller program with a StripChart object displaying collected data. You can find the source code for the new Winsock VI Controller in the folder \Part4\WinsockCtrl of the code available online.

AN ACTIVE GASGAUGE GRAPHIC OBJECT

As a second example of an active graphic display object, let's create a semicircular gauge with a needle that actively rotates to display the gauge's current Value property. The semicircular background of the gauge is divided into a red and green pie slice. Assigning a value to the class's SetPoint property determines the boundary between the two pie slices. Since the gauge will imitate something you'd see on a gas tank, we named the class GasGauge.

You will find that the construction of the GasGauge class is very similar to StripChart, even though their graphical displays have no similarity. The most significant difference between the StripChart and GasGauge classes is the way the stored data are drawn. You will find the following completed example program in the folder \Part4\GasGauge of the code online.

To build the GasGauge class, create a new VB project and insert a new class module. Set the class module's name to GasGauge. Add the following code to the declarations section of the class module. We declare an mPct private PictureBox variable. We also declare two Private single-precision variables called mSngValue and mSngSetPoint, which will be used to store the Value and SetPoint property values of a GasGauge object. Finally, we define the constant Pi for convenience.

```
Option Explicit

' A reference to the PictureBox on which top draw the gauge
Private WithEvents mPct As PictureBox

' The value currently displayed on the gauge [0, 100]
Private mSngValue As Single

' The value that divides the red and green area [0, 100]
Private mSngSetPoint As Single
Const Pi As Single = 3.14159           ' The constant Pi
```

Add the following Property Set procedure to the class module. Similar to the Property Set procedure in StripChart, this new PictureBox Property Set procedure assigns the mPct private class variable and sets up a custom coordinate system for the PictureBox. Before finishing, it invokes the SetBackground procedure and draws the initial gauge by invoking DrawGauge.

```
Public Property Set PictureBox(pctBox As PictureBox)
    Dim sngHeight As Single, sngWidth As Single, sngNewHeight As Single

    ' Set the PictureBox on which the gauge should be drawn
    Set mPct = pctBox

    ' Get PictureBox dimensions
    sngWidth = mPct.Width
    sngHeight = mPct.Height

    ' Set the coordinates of the PictureBox.
    ' The x-dimension is always constraining when drawing a circle.
    sngNewHeight = 2.8 * (sngHeight / sngWidth) - 0.8
    With mPct
        .ScaleLeft = -1.4
        .ScaleWidth = 2.8
        .ScaleTop = sngNewHeight + 0.4
        .ScaleHeight = -(sngNewHeight + 0.8)
    End With
```

```
            ' Set the background and draw the gauge
            SetBackground
            DrawGauge

    End Property
```

Add the following SetBackground procedure to the class module. SetBackground draws the gauge background using the initial SetPoint property on the PictureBox while maintaining a persistent graphic. The persistent graphic image is then stored in the mPct PictureBox's Picture property.

```
Private Sub SetBackground()
 ' Draw the background and save in PictureBox
Dim sngX As Single, sngY As Single, sngX2 As Single, sngY2 As Single
Dim I As Integer

mPct.AutoRedraw = True            ' Initiate the persistent graphic
mPct.BackColor = vbWhite          ' Clear

mPct.DrawWidth = 2                ' Set graphic properties
mPct.FillStyle = 0 ' solid

mPct.FillColor = vbGreen
mPct.Circle (0#, 0#), 1, vbBlack, -0.00001, -0.01 * (100# - mSngSetPoint) * Pi
mPct.FillColor = vbRed
mPct.Circle (0#, 0#), 1#, vbBlack, -0.01 * (100# - mSngSetPoint) * Pi, -Pi

For I = 0 To 100 Step 25          ' Draw ticks
    sngX = Cos((100# - I) * 0.01 * Pi)
    sngY = Sin((100# - I) * 0.01 * Pi)
    sngX2 = 0.9 * Cos((100# - I) * 0.01 * Pi)
    sngY2 = 0.9 * Sin((100# - I) * 0.01 * Pi)
    mPct.Line (sngX, sngY)-(sngX2, sngY2), vbBlack
Next I

mPct.Font.Size = 18              ' Draw the 'E' and 'F' indicators
mPct.CurrentX = -1.3
mPct.CurrentY = 0.3
mPct.Print "E"

mPct.CurrentX = 1.1
mPct.CurrentY = 0.3
mPct.Print "F"

mPct.Picture = mPct.Image    ' Store persistent graphic in the Picture property
mPct.AutoRedraw = False
End Sub
```

Add the following DrawGauge procedure to the class module. A gauge display is updated by first restoring the saved background image using the mPct Cls method, and then drawing the gauge needle at an angle consistent with the gauge Value property.

```
    Private Sub DrawGauge()
        ' Draw the gauge on the PictureBox
        Dim sngX As Single, sngY As Single
```

```
' Restore the background
mPct.Cls

' Draw the needle
sngX = 0.95 * Cos((100# - mSngValue) * 0.01 * Pi)
sngY = 0.95 * Sin((100# - mSngValue) * 0.01 * Pi)
mPct.DrawWidth = 4
mPct.Line (0#, 0#)-(sngX, sngY), vbBlack

End Sub
```

Add the following pair of Value Property procedures to the class module.
The Value Property Get simply returns the value stored in the private
mSngValue variable. The Value Property Let procedure first clips the given
value to the restricted range [0, 100], sets the mSngValue private variable, and
redraws the gauge.

```
Public Property Get Value() As Single
    ' Return the gauge Value property value
    Value = mSngValue
End Property

Public Property Let Value(sngValue As Single)
    ' Set the value to be displayed by the needle on the gauge.

    ' Clip to the range [0, 100]
    If sngValue < 0# Then
        mSngValue = 0#
    ElseIf sngValue > 100# Then
        mSngValue = 100#
    Else
        mSngValue = sngValue
    End If

    ' Redraw the gauge
    DrawGauge

End Property
```

Add the following pair of SetPoint Property procedures to the class module. Again, the SetPoint Property Get procedure simply returns the value of
the private mSngSetPoint variable. The SetPoint Property Let procedure clips
the passed value to the range [0, 100], assigns the value to the private
mSngSetPoint variable, regenerates and stores the gauge background, and
redraws the gauge.

```
Public Property Get SetPoint() As Single
    ' Return the gauge SetPoint property value
    SetPoint = mSngSetPoint
End Property

Public Property Let SetPoint(sngSetPoint As Single)
    ' Set the value that marks the separation between the green and red areas.
```

```
    ' Clip to the range [0, 100]
    If sngSetPoint < 0# Then
        mSngSetPoint = 0#
    ElseIf sngSetPoint > 100# Then
        mSngSetPoint = 100#
    Else
        mSngSetPoint = sngSetPoint
    End If

    ' Reset the new background and redraw the gauge
    SetBackground
    DrawGauge

End Property
```

We need to define a couple more procedures to complete the class. Since we are not using the AutoRedraw feature, we need to redraw the gauge from the PictureBox's Paint event procedure. Also, we want the SetPoint property to be initialized to something other than 0. To accomplish this, we initialize the private mSngSetPoint and mSngValue properties from the Class's Initialize event procedure. Add the following two procedures to the class module.

```
Private Sub mPct_Paint()
    ' Redraw the gauge
    DrawGauge
End Sub

Private Sub Class_Initialize()
    ' Initialize GasGauge class property values
    mSngSetPoint = 25#
    mSngValue = 0#
End Sub
```

As with StripChart, using the GasGauge class is simple. Sketch a PictureBox, two CommandButtons, and two TextBoxes on Form1. Set the following property values:

Object Type	Property	Value
Form	Name	frmGauge
	Caption	GasGauge
PictureBox	Name	pctCanvas
CommandButton	Name	btnValue
	Caption	Value
CommandButton	Name	btnSetPoint
	Caption	SetPoint
TextBox	Name	txtValue
	Text	
TextBox	Name	txtSetPoint
	Text	

Add the following lines of code to the declarations section of the frmGauge Form module. The only form-level variable declared is mGauge, which will hold a reference to a new GasGauge object.

```
Option Explicit

' Module-level variable to hold a reference to the GasGauge object
Private mGauge As GasGauge
```

Add the following Load event procedure to the frmGauge module. When the form loads, the new GasGauge object is created and initialized with a reference to the pctCanvas PictureBox control.

```
Private Sub Form_Load()
    ' Create and initialize the new GasGauge class
    Set mGauge = New GasGauge
    Set mGauge.PictureBox = pctCanvas
End Sub
```

Add the following btnValue and btnSetPoint Click event procedures. In each case, text in the associated Textbox is checked to be numeric, converted, and assigned to the corresponding mGauge property.

```
Private Sub btnValue_Click()
   ' Change the needle property value
   If IsNumeric(txtValue.Text) Then mGauge.Value = CSng(txtValue.Text)
End Sub

Private Sub btnSetPoint_Click()
   ' Change the setpoint property value
   If IsNumeric(txtSetpoint.Text) Then mGauge.SetPoint = CSng(txtSetpoint.Text)
End Sub
```

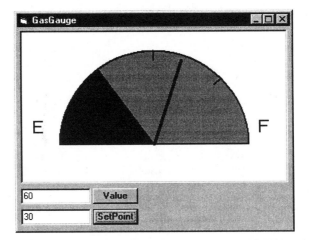

Figure 25-4. The GasGauge Active Graphic Display class in action.

Run the program and give it a try (see Figure 25-4). Enter a new gauge value and click "Value" to see the needle move. Enter a new setpoint and click "SetPoint" to see the gauge background change.

In practice you could use one or more instances of the GasGauge object for a variety of purposes. For example, you may have an A/D board hooked up to a level sensor. A Timer control can be configured to poll the level value at a convenient interval, convert the level reading, and assign the result to the GasGauge Value property. The GasGauge object updates its own display.

CHAPTER

26

Interactive Graphic Displays

Active graphic displays are great. But what would be really useful is if, in addition to responding to changes in associated data values, we had the ability to interact with the display using the mouse as well as have it raise its own events when its internal data satisfy predefined conditions. You may have seen ActiveX controls for sale that let you sketch something like a rotary knob or slider onto your form, and manipulate it at run time using your mouse. The control's display changes as you interact with its interface in order to let you know what is happening. Other controls produce a graphical display of data that changes to reflect the changing data. Behind the scenes the control is firing events, such as Change or Threshold, when internal values change or when certain conditions are satisfied.

We can expand upon the model for active graphic displays in order to build in features such as these to produce what we'll call *interactive graphic displays*. Interactivity occurs in two directions. The user interacts with the object through its display using the mouse, and the object interacts with the application program through its events. We can easily add both styles of interactivity to an active graphic display object. We saw exactly how to accomplish the first kind of interactivity with the CheckBox Lasso example in Chapter 24. The basic idea is the same. The value of a module-level variable is used to indicate when the user is interacting with the interface, and the MouseDown, MouseMove, and MouseUp PictureBox event procedures are used to modify private object variables and update the interface. We also saw how to accomplish the second kind of interactivity when we declared and generated our own events as part of the VB Spreadsheet example. We'll collect these techniques together and apply them to the creation of new interactive graphic display objects.

AN INTERACTIVE KNOB GRAPHIC OBJECT

In this example we'll build a graphic rotary-action knob that can be rotated using the mouse. Each time its value changes it will raise a custom Change event. We'll use its event procedure to update a readout indicating the current setting. You can find the following example in its entirety in the folder \Part4\Knob of the code available online.

To build the new Knob class, create a new VB project and insert a new class module. Set the Name property of the class module to Knob. Add the following code to the declarations section of the class module. Here we declare the familiar mPct PictureBox private class variable, making sure to use the WithEvents keyword. We also declare the mSngValue private variable to hold the current Knob setting. The mBlnSelecting variable will be used to determine when the user is interacting with the Knob interface. The constant Pi is defined for convenience. Finally, we declare a new event called Change. The object will raise the Change event whenever the Knob object setting is changed.

```
Option Explicit

Private WithEvents mPct As PictureBox   ' The PictureBox on which to draw the knob
Private mSngValue As Single             ' Value of the knob [0, 100]
Private mBlnSelecting As Boolean        ' Interactive state variable
Const Pi As Single = 3.14159            ' The constant Pi

' Declare the change event which is raised when the knob value changes.
Public Event Change(ByVal sngValue As Single)
```

The idea behind the following PictureBox Property Set, SetBackground, and DrawKnob procedures is identical to that of the previous chapter. The PictureBox Property Set procedure assigns the private PictureBox variable and initializes the PictureBox coordinate system. Before finishing it invokes SetBackground to generate and save the background image, and draws the initial knob image with DrawKnob. The only real difference between these procedures and what we saw previously is that a rotary action knob is being drawn instead of a gas gauge or strip chart. Add the following three procedures to the class module.

```
Property Set PictureBox(pctBox As PictureBox)
    Dim sngWidth As Single, sngHeight As Single, sngAspect As Single

    ' Set the PictureBox on which the gauge should be drawn
    Set mPct = pctBox

    ' Get PictureBox dimensions
    sngWidth = mPct.Width
    sngHeight = mPct.Height
    sngAspect = sngWidth / sngHeight
```

```
        ' Set the coordinates of the PictureBox.
    If sngAspect > 1# Then
        With mPct
            .ScaleLeft = -1.4 * sngAspect
            .ScaleWidth = 2.8 * sngAspect
            .ScaleTop = 1.4
            .ScaleHeight = -2.8
        End With

    Else
        With mPct
            .ScaleLeft = -1.4
            .ScaleWidth = 2.8
            .ScaleTop = 1.4 * sngAspect
            .ScaleHeight = -2.8 * sngAspect
        End With
    End If

    ' Save the background image and initially draw the knob.
    SetBackground
    DrawKnob

End Property

Private Sub SetBackground()
    ' Set the knob background
    Dim sng As Single, sngAngle As Single
    Dim sngX1 As Single, sngY1 As Single, sngX2 As Single, sngY2 As Single

    mPct.AutoRedraw = True          ' Begin to maintain a persistent graphic
    mPct.BackColor = vbButtonFace   ' Erase all and set the background color
    mPct.FillStyle = 0 ' solid
    mPct.DrawWidth = 2

    ' Draw the circle
    mPct.FillColor = vbWhite
    mPct.Circle (0#, 0#), 1, vbGrayText

    ' Draw the tick marks
    mPct.DrawWidth = 4
    For sng = -45# To 225# Step 45#
        sngAngle = sng * (Pi / 180#)
        sngX1 = 1.1 * Cos(sngAngle)
        sngY1 = 1.1 * Sin(sngAngle)
        sngX2 = 1.2 * Cos(sngAngle)
        sngY2 = 1.2 * Sin(sngAngle)
        mPct.Line (sngX1, sngY1)-(sngX2, sngY2), vbRed
    Next sng

    ' Label the first and last tick
    mPct.Font.Size = 16
    mPct.CurrentX = -1#
    mPct.CurrentY = -1#
    mPct.Print "0"

    mPct.CurrentX = 0.7
    mPct.CurrentY = -1#
    mPct.Print "100"
```

```
        ' Save the generated background image
        mPct.Picture = mPct.Image ' Copy the persistent graphic to the Picture property
        mPct.AutoRedraw = False   ' Turn off the persistent graphic
End Sub                           ' for better performance

Public Sub DrawKnob()
        Dim sng As Single, sngAngle As Single
        Dim sngX1 As Single, sngY1 As Single, sngX2 As Single, sngY2 As Single

        ' Reset the background
        mPct.Cls

        ' Draw the knob mark
        mPct.DrawWidth = 2
        sngAngle = (225# - (mSngValue * 2.7)) * (Pi / 180#)
        sngX1 = 0.6 * Cos(sngAngle)
        sngY1 = 0.6 * Sin(sngAngle)
        sngX2 = 1# * Cos(sngAngle)
        sngY2 = 1# * Sin(sngAngle)
        mPct.Line (sngX1, sngY1)-(sngX2, sngY2), vbBlack

End Sub
```

Add the following pair of Property procedures to the class module. The Value Property Get procedure simply returns the current Knob setting. The Value Property Let procedure clips the passed value to the range [0, 100], saves the new Knob setting in the private object variable, redraws the Knob, and raises the Change event indicating that the Knob value has changed.

```
Public Property Get Value() As Single
        ' Return the knob Value property
        Value = mSngValue
End Property

Public Property Let Value(sngValue As Single)
        ' Set the value to be displayed by the knob.

        ' Clip to the range [0, 100]
        If sngValue < 0# Then
            mSngValue = 0#
        ElseIf sngValue > 100# Then
            mSngValue = 100#
        Else
            mSngValue = sngValue
        End If

        ' Redraw the knob
        DrawKnob

        ' Raise an event indicating that the value has changed
        RaiseEvent Change(mSngValue)

End Property
```

To build interactivity into the Knob object, we follow the ideas presented in the Lasso CheckBox example and program the MouseDown, MouseMove, and MouseUp events of the PictureBox. When the user presses the mouse down on the PictureBox, the mBlnSelection object variable is set to True to indicate that the user is selecting the Knob value. The current Knob Value property is also set to a value that is computed based on the mouse position using the custom CPositionToValue function. The Knob's Value property is continuously updated in the MouseMove event procedure as the mouse is being moved over the PictureBox while still in the proper mode. When the mouse is released, mBlnSelecting is set to False to cancel any updating.

Add the following MouseDown, MouseMove, and MouseUp event procedures, and the CPositionToValue function to the class module.

```
Private Sub mPct_MouseDown(Button As Integer, Shift As Integer, X As Single, Y As Single)
    ' Change the knob setting to appropriate value
    mBlnSelecting = True
    Value = CPositionToValue(X, Y)
End Sub

Private Sub mPct_MouseMove(Button As Integer, Shift As Integer, X As Single, Y As Single)
    ' Change the knob setting to appropriate value
    If mBlnSelecting = False Then Exit Sub    ' If not setting then exit
    Value = CPositionToValue(X, Y)
End Sub

Private Sub mPct_MouseUp(Button As Integer, Shift As Integer, X As Single, Y As Single)
    ' Exit setting state
    mBlnSelecting = False
End Sub

Private Function CPositionToValue(X As Single, Y As Single) As Single
    ' Convert the X-Y mouse position to a knob value
    Dim sngValue As Single

    If X > 0# Then
        sngValue = Atn(Y / X)
    ElseIf X < 0# Then
        sngValue = Atn(Y / X) + 3.1416
    End If

    CPositionToValue = 100# - ((sngValue * (180# / 3.1416)) + 45#) / 2.7

End Function
```

Finally, add the following Paint event procedure to the Knob class module to assure that the Knob display will be updated as needed.

```
Private Sub mPct_Paint()
    ' Regenerate the knob image
    DrawKnob
End Sub
```

We can use a Knob object in a manner that is almost identical to the objects presented in the previous chapter. The only significant differences are that you must declare the Knob object variable using the WithEvents keyword in order to have access to its events. Also, we get to program its events by adding code to its event procedures.

Add a PictureBox, CommandButton, TextBox, and Label to Form1. Assign the following property values:

Object Type	Property	Value
Form	Name	frmKnob
	Caption	Knob
PictureBox	Name	pctCanvas
CommandButton	Name	btnSet
	Caption	Set
TextBox	Name	txtValue
	Text	
Label	Name	lblValue
	Caption	Value

Add the following code to the declarations section of the frmKnob Form. The mKnob Knob object variable must be declared using the WithEvents keyword.

```
Option Explicit

' Module-level variable to hold reference for Knob object
Private WithEvents mKnob As Knob
```

Initialize the mKnob object upon loading the form. Also, set the mKnob object Value property using the contents of the txtValue TextBox when the btnSet button is clicked. Add the following lines of code to the frmKnob module.

```
Private Sub Form_Load()
    ' Create and initialize the new knob class
    Set mKnob = New Knob
    Set mKnob.PictureBox = pctCanvas
End Sub

Private Sub btnSet_Click()
    ' Change the knob setting to appropriate value
    If IsNumeric(txtValue.Text) Then mKnob.Value = CSng(txtValue.Text)
End Sub
```

This time we get to add code to the mKnob Change event procedure. Whenever the mKnob value changes and the Change event procedure fires, update the txtValue TextBox to reflect the change. By doing this, not only will the Knob rotate when we drag it with the mouse, but its new value will continuously be displayed. Add the following mKnob Change event procedure to the frmKnob module:

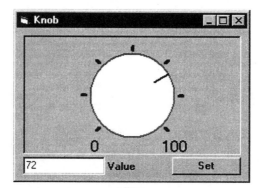

Figure 26-1. *The interactive graphic Knob object in action.*

```
Private Sub mKnob_Change(ByVal sngValue As Single)
    ' When the value changes, automatically reflect in the text box
    txtValue.Text = CInt(sngValue)
End Sub
```

Try out your new interactive graphic knob (see Figure 26-1). Run the program and change the Knob's value by dragging it around with the mouse. You also have the option of programmatically setting the Knob by entering a value into the txtValue TextBox and clicking "Set."

Modify the Knob class to suit your needs. You can change its color, size, range, or whatever else you decide is useful. Since it is a class, you can create as many instances of Knob objects as you need. Lay out a series of Knob objects along the bottom of a Form and add several modified GasGauge objects to build a sound mixing board style interface. Since you have the source code, you can modify these classes as you like.

AN INTERACTIVE THERMOMETER GRAPHIC OBJECT

As the last example in this series, let's build an interactive Thermometer graphic display class. In addition to using a Thermometer object to display temperature, we'll design the class to allow the user to drag the mercury meniscus up and down so that it can be used to set a temperature value as well. The Thermometer class will have a Temperature property and a Threshold property. The Temperature property will be used to set or return the current temperature value of the Thermometer object. The Threshold property is a settable temperature boundary. A notification will occur when the Thermometer's temperature crosses its Threshold. Whenever the Thermometer's Temperature property value changes, it will raise a Change event. When Temperature crosses a Thermometer's Threshold in the upward direction, an OverThreshold event will be raised. When crossing in the downward direction, an UnderThreshold event will be raised. You will find the

Thermometer class and a complete example in the folder \Part4\Thermometer of the code available online.

Let's build the Thermometer class. Create a new VB project and insert a new class module. Set the Name property of the class module to Thermometer. Add the following code to the class module's declarations section. Here we see the private mPct PictureBox variable and the mBlnSelecting variable, which is used to indicate the interactive state of the object. The two private variables mSngTemp and mSngThreshold are used to store the object's current temperature and threshold. The three events described previously are also declared. Each passes a single-precision number, which is the temperature value at the time the event is raised.

```
Option Explicit

Private WithEvents mPct As PictureBox      ' Reference to PictureBox object
Private mBlnSelecting As Boolean           ' Selection state

Private mSngTemp As Single                 ' Internal store of temperature value
Private mSngThreshold As Single            ' Internal store of threshold value

' Change event raised each time temperature changes.
Public Event Change(ByVal sngTemperature As Single)

' OverThreshold event raised when the threshold is crossed in an upward direction.
Public Event OverThreshold(ByVal sngTemperature As Single)

' UnderThreshold event raised when the threshold is crossed in a downward direction.
Public Event UnderThreshold(ByVal sngTemperature As Single)
```

Add the following PictureBox Property Set, SetBackground, and DrawThermometer procedures to the class module. By now you'll find no surprises. The PictureBox Property Set procedure assigns the given PictureBox reference to the private mPct class variable. SetBackground generates and saves the Thermometer background image in the PictureBox's Picture property. The background image is composed of a red circular bulb, a white vertical stem, and a blue region at the top of the stem whose size is determined by the Thermometer's Threshold property. DrawThermometer resets the background image and updates the displayed meniscus to reflect the current temperature value.

```
Public Property Set PictureBox(pctBox As PictureBox)
    ' Set up the PictureBox on which to draw the Thermometer
    Dim sngHWidth As Double, I As Integer

    Set mPct = pctBox             ' Set the internal picture box on which to draw
                                  ' Set the coordinate system
    sngHWidth = (mPct.Width / mPct.Height) * 70#
    With mPct
        .ScaleLeft = -sngHWidth
        .ScaleWidth = 2 * sngHWidth
        .ScaleTop = 110#
        .ScaleHeight = -140#
    End With
```

```
        ' Create and save the background.  Initially draw the thermometer.
        SetBackground
        DrawThermometer

End Property

Private Sub SetBackground()
        ' Draw and save the background
        Dim I As Integer

        mPct.AutoRedraw = True          ' Initiate persistent graphic
        mPct.BackColor = vbWhite

        ' Draw background
        mPct.FillStyle = vbSolid
        mPct.FillColor = vbRed               ' Draw Bulb
        mPct.Circle (0, -8), 10, vbBlack

        mPct.FillColor = vbWhite             ' Draw Stem
        mPct.Line (-5, 0)-(5, 100), vbWhite, B  ' Fill Stem
        mPct.Line (-5, 0)-(-5, 100), vbBlack   ' Draw sides
        mPct.Line (5, 0)-(5, 100), vbBlack

        mPct.FillColor = vbBlue              ' Draw Threshold region
        mPct.Line (-5, mSngThreshold)-(5, 100), vbBlack, B

        For I = 0 To 100 Step 20             ' Draw Temperature Scale
            mPct.Line (5, I)-(8, I), vbBlack
            mPct.Print I
        Next I

        ' Save background
        mPct.Picture = mPct.Image
        mPct.AutoRedraw = False
End Sub

Private Sub DrawThermometer()
        ' Draw the thermometer on the PictureBox

        ' Restore the background
        mPct.Cls

        ' Redraw the stem of the thermometer.
        mPct.FillColor = vbRed                       ' Fill with mercury
        mPct.Line (-5, 0)-(5, mSngTemp), vbRed, B
        mPct.Line (-5, 0)-(-5, mSngTemp), vbBlack    ' Draw sides
        mPct.Line (5, 0)-(5, mSngTemp), vbBlack

End Sub
```

Add the following pair of Threshold Property procedures to the class module. These procedures set and return the current Thermometer object Threshold property. The Property Get procedure simply returns the threshold value. The Property Let procedure first clips the given value to the valid threshold range of [0, 100] and then sets the private mSngThreshold variable to the new value. This procedure then regenerates and saves the new background image with a call to SetBackground, and redraws the Thermometer by invoking DrawThermometer.

```
Public Property Get Threshold() As Single
    ' Return the thermometer threshold
    Threshold = mSngThreshold
End Property

Public Property Let Threshold(sngNewThresh As Single)
    ' Set the Threshold property value

    ' Clip threshold to reasonable values
    If sngNewThresh < 0# Then sngNewThresh = 0#
    If sngNewThresh > 100# Then sngNewThresh = 100#

    ' Set the new value
    mSngThreshold = sngNewThresh

    ' Reset the new background and redraw the Thermometer
    SetBackground
    DrawThermometer

End Property
```

Add the following pair of Temperature Property procedures to the class module. The Temperature Property Get procedure simply returns the current temperature value stored in the object. The Temperature Property Let procedure clips the new temperature value to the valid range of [0, 100], sets the internal mSngTemp variable to the result, redraws the Thermometer, and raises the Change event. In addition, if the old Temperature value is less than or equal to the current Threshold, and the new Temperature value is greater than the current Threshold, then the OverThreshold event is raised. On the other hand, if the old Temperature value is greater than or equal to the current Threshold, and the new Temperature value is less than the current Threshold, then the UnderThreshold event is raised.

```
Public Property Get Temperature() As Single
    Temperature = mSngTemp            ' Return internal temperature value
End Property

Public Property Let Temperature(sngNewTemp As Single)
    ' Set the Thermometer's temperature
    Dim sngOldTemp As Single
                                      ' Clip temperature to reasonable values
    If sngNewTemp < 0# Then sngNewTemp = 0#
    If sngNewTemp > 100# Then sngNewTemp = 100#

    sngOldTemp = mSngTemp             ' Save old temperature
    mSngTemp = sngNewTemp             ' Set new temperature

    DrawThermometer                   ' Update the drawing

    RaiseEvent Change(mSngTemp)       ' Raise the Change event
    If sngOldTemp <= mSngThreshold And sngNewTemp > mSngThreshold Then _
                                RaiseEvent OverThreshold(mSngTemp)
    If sngOldTemp >= mSngThreshold And sngNewTemp < mSngThreshold Then _
                                RaiseEvent UnderThreshold(mSngTemp)

End Property
```

Since we don't want the initial Threshold value to be zero, add the following Initialize event procedure to the class module. This procedure arbitrarily initializes Threshold to a value of 70 and Temperature to a value of 0.

```
Private Sub Class_Initialize()
    ' Initialize object properties
    mSngTemp = 0#
    mSngThreshold = 70#
End Sub
```

Add the following MouseDown, MouseMove, and MouseUp PictureBox event procedures to make it possible for the user to set Temperature by dragging the meniscus with the mouse. The MouseDown event procedure puts the Thermometer object in selecting mode by assigning the private mBlnSelecting class variable to True. The object's Temperature value is updated in the MouseDown and MouseMove event procedures using the current value of the mouse's Y coordinate. We can do this because we defined the Y dimension of the PictureBox's coordinate system to follow the tick marks on the side of the Thermometer. In other words, the coordinate system is designed so that the Thermometer's Temperature property value is identical to the Y coordinate of the top of the Thermometer's meniscus. MouseUp cancels the Thermometer object's selecting mode by assigning mBlnSelection to False.

```
Private Sub mPct_MouseDown(Button As Integer, Shift As Integer, X As Single, Y As Single)
    mBlnSelecting = True            ' Enter selecting state
    Temperature = Y                 ' Set temperature
End Sub

Private Sub mPct_MouseMove(Button As Integer, Shift As Integer, X As Single, Y As Single)
    If mBlnSelecting = False Then Exit Sub
    Temperature = Y                 ' Update temperature
End Sub

Private Sub mPct_MouseUp(Button As Integer, Shift As Integer, X As Single, Y As Single)
    mBlnSelecting = False           ' Exit selecting state
End Sub
```

To try out the Thermometer class, add a PictureBox, two CommandButtons, and two TextBoxes to Form1. Set property values as follows.

Object Type	Property	Value
Form	Name	frmThermometer
	Caption	Thermometer
PictureBox	Name	pctCanvas
CommandButton	Name	btnTemperature
	Caption	Temperature

continued

Object Type	Property	Value
TextBox	Name	txtTemperature
	Text	
CommandButton	Name	btnThreshold
	Caption	Threshold
TextBox	Name	txtThreshold
	Text	

Add the following lines of code to the declarations section of the frmTemperature Form module. Make sure to use the WithEvents keyword when declaring the mThermometer variable.

```
Option Explicit

Private WithEvents mThermometer As Thermometer        ' Create Thermometer object
```

Add the following Form Load event procedure, btnTemperature CommandButton Click event procedure, and btnThreshold CommandButton Click event procedure to the frmTemperature Form module. The Form_Load event procedure creates the new Thermometer object and initializes it. The btnTemperature and btnThreshold Click event procedures attempt to assign Temperature or Threshold property values using text entered into txtTemperature or txtThreshold TextBoxes.

```
Private Sub Form_Load()
    ' Create and initilize the Thermometer class
    Set mThermometer = New Thermometer
    Set mThermometer.PictureBox = pctCanvas
End Sub

Private Sub btnTemperature_Click()
    ' Reset the Temperature.
    If IsNumeric(txtTemperature.Text) Then _
              mThermometer.Temperature = CSng(txtTemperature.Text)
End Sub

Private Sub btnThreshold_Click()
    ' Reset the Threshold.
    If IsNumeric(txtThreshold.Text) Then _
              mThermometer.Threshold = CSng(txtThreshold.Text)
End Sub
```

Add the following three event procedures to the frmThermometer Form module. The Thermometer object Change event procedure updates the displayed Temperature value in the txtTemperature TextBox. When an OverThreshold Thermometer object event occurs, we change the frmThermometer background color to red, and ring the computer's bell in an attempt to draw attention to the event. When an UnderThreshold event oc-

curs, we change the frmThermometer's background color back to the default
gray.

```
Private Sub mThermometer_Change(ByVal sngTemperature As Single)
    ' Update the TextBox value
    txtTemperature.Text = Format(sngTemperature, "0.0")
End Sub

Private Sub mThermometer_OverThreshold(ByVal sngTemperature As Single)
    ' Turn the form background red when the threshold is exceeded
    frmThermometer.BackColor = vbRed
    Beep
End Sub

Private Sub mThermometer_UnderThreshold(ByVal sngTemperature As Single)
    ' Restore the form color when under threshold
    frmThermometer.BackColor = vbButtonFace
End Sub
```

Run the example program and give it a try. Use the mouse to drag the
Thermometer's meniscus and watch the Temperature display change. Pull
the meniscus over the Threshold value into the blue region and watch the
Form background color turn red. Pull the meniscus down below the
Threshold, out of the blue region and watch the Form background turn
back to battleship gray. Figure 26-2 shows the example in an
UnderThreshold and OverThreshold condition. Since the figure is not
printed in color, the red and blue regions appear to be dark gray.

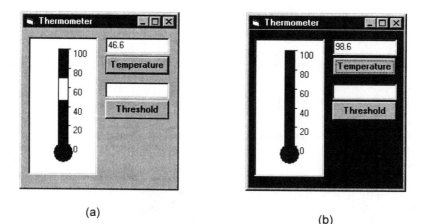

(a)   (b)

Figure 26-2. The interactive graphic Thermometer object in action: (a) before crossing
the threshold value; (b) after an OverThreshold event.

WRAPPING UP

In this final part of the book we investigated a variety of methods for presenting and manipulating science and engineering data. In Chapter 22 the MSChart ActiveX control was covered in detail. MSChart is a convenient and powerful tool for generating plots of data. Tabular data display and manipulation was discussed in Chapter 23, with an emphasis on the MSFlexGrid control. A new class called clsSheet was constructed that extends the capabilities of the MSFlexGrid control so as to create a functional spreadsheet. Spreadsheet style interfaces are ubiquitous in science and engineering software applications. The MSFlexGrid control and the clsSheet class provide spreadsheet functionality with the option to customize its interactive behavior for your own needs.

While the graphics capabilities of VB are really very basic, they are by no means insignificant. In Chapter 24 we covered the fundamentals of graphics in Visual Basic®. This is only the beginning of what is possible. VB offers more in the graphics arena, and when you hit the bottom of what VB has to offer, it's a short step to the Windows® API, where you have access to almost any graphics method available in Windows®.

VB graphics fundamentals were covered in preparation for the last two chapters, which use what was learned to build custom active and interactive graphical interfaces with a focus on the presentation of science and engineering data. Active display objects present their data graphically, and automatically update their displays to reflect changing data. Active displays provide functionality that mimics a control panel, with buttons, gauges, and other similar devices designed to present measured data. Interactive graphic display objects extend this concept by building in more opportunities for direct manipulation through a graphical interface. With interactive graphic displays, not only is it possible to update a display by programmatically changing associated data, but interaction with the object through its graphical display is possible using the mouse and keyboard. The addition of custom events also makes it possible for the object to interact with the application by firing appropriate events when associated data satisfy certain predefined conditions.

The techniques presented in these chapters are easily reused to build graphic displays of almost any sort. The examples presented share a significant amount in terms of their underlying organization. It is easy to see how these ideas can be used to build your own active and interactive graphic display classes that are customized to the needs of your particular application.

REFERENCES

1. D. Harel, "Statecharts: A visual formalism for complex systems," *Science of Computer Programming.* **8**, 231-274 (1987).

2. J. Rumbaugh, G. Booch, and I. Jacobson, *Unified Modeling Language Reference Manual*, Addison-Wesley Publishing Company, New York, 1998.

A:

ASCII Character Set and Code Table

ASCII is an acronym for the standard called: American Standard Code for Information Interchange. The ASCII standard maps the numbers 0 through 127 to a set of printable, and some nonprintable, characters. The American National Standard Institute (ANSI) was responsible for creating the ASCII standard. The standard is extremely important and used by almost all major computer manufacturers as the basis of their character set encoding. The following table lists the numbers 0 through 127 in decimal and hexadecimal, and gives the character corresponding to each number, as defined by the ASCII standard.

Dec	Hex	Char	Dec	Hex	Char	Dec	Hex	Char	Dec	Hex	Char
0	0	\<NUL>	32	20	*space*	64	40	@	96	60	'
1	1	\<SOH>	33	21	!	65	41	A	97	61	a
2	2	\<STX>	34	22	"	66	42	B	98	62	b
3	3	\<ETX>	35	23	#	67	43	C	99	63	c
4	4	\<EOT>	36	24	$	68	44	D	100	64	d
5	5	\<ENQ>	37	25	%	69	45	E	101	65	e
6	6	\<ACK>	38	26	&	70	46	F	102	66	f
7	7	\<BEL>	39	27	'	71	47	G	103	67	g
8	8	\<BS>	40	28	(	72	48	H	104	68	h
9	9	\<HT>	41	29	)	73	49	I	105	69	i
10	A	\<LF>	42	2A	*	74	4A	J	106	6A	j
11	B	\<VT>	43	2B	+	75	4B	K	107	6B	k
12	C	\<FF>	44	2C	,	76	4C	L	108	6C	l
13	D	\<CR>	45	2D	-	77	4D	M	109	6D	m
14	E	\<SO>	46	2E	.	78	4E	N	110	6E	n
15	F	\<SI>	47	2F	/	79	4F	O	111	6F	o
16	10	\<DLE>	48	30	0	80	50	P	112	70	p
17	11	\<DC1>	49	31	1	81	51	Q	113	71	q
18	12	\<DC2>	50	32	2	82	52	R	114	72	r
19	13	\<DC3>	51	33	3	83	53	S	115	73	s
20	14	\<DC4>	52	34	4	84	54	T	116	74	t
21	15	\<NAK>	53	35	5	85	55	U	117	75	u
22	16	\<SYN>	54	36	6	86	56	V	118	76	v
23	17	\<ETB>	55	37	7	87	57	W	119	77	w
24	18	\<CAN>	56	38	8	88	58	X	120	78	x
25	19	\<EM>	57	39	9	89	59	Y	121	79	y
26	1A	\<SUB>	58	3A	:	90	5A	Z	122	7A	z
27	1B	\<ESC>	59	3B	;	91	5B	[	123	7B	{
28	1C	\<FS>	60	3C	<	92	5C	\	124	7C	|
29	1D	\<GS>	61	3D	=	93	5D	]	125	7D	}
30	1E	\<RS>	62	3E	>	94	5E	^	126	7E	~
31	1F	\<US>	63	3F	?	95	5F	_	127	7F	\<DEL>

Common designations for nongraphic control characters are listed in the following table with a brief definition of each.

Character	Description
<NUL>	Null
<SOH>	Start of Header
<STX>	Start of Text
<ETX>	End of Text
<EOT>	End of Transmission
<ENQ>	Enquiry
<ACK>	Acknowledge
<BEL>	Bell
<BS>	Backspace
<HT>	Horizontal Tab
<LF>	Line Feed
<VT>	Vertical Tab
<FF>	Form Feed
<CR>	Carriage Return
<SO>	Shift In
<SI>	Shift Out
<DLE>	Data Link Escape
<DC1>	Device Control 1
<DC2>	Device Control 2
<DC3>	Device Control 3
<DC4>	Device Control 4
<NAK>	Negative Acknowledge
<SYN>	Synchronous Idle
<ETB>	End of Transmission Block
<CAN>	Cancel
<EM>	End of Medium
<SUB>	Substitute
<ESC>	Escape
<FS>	File Separator
<GS>	Group Separator
<RS>	Record Separator
<US>	Unit Separator
<DEL>	Delete

B:

Descriptions of Example Problems

This appendix lists all example VB projects included in this book and the accompanying software available online from Wiley's web site. Use your web browser to visit the URL ftp://ftp.wiley.com/public/sci_tech_med/labvb and download the file labvb6.zip for examples written in version 6.0 of Visual Basic®, or labvb5.zip for examples written in version 5.0 of Visual Basic®.

Chapter 2: IDE Fundamentals

1. \Part1\Ex1\Ex1.vbp

   This is a Quick Start example that demonstrates the fundamentals of building applications in Visual Basic®.

Chapter 6: Introducing the Virtual Instrument

2. \Vi\Vi.vbp

   This is the source code for the Virtual Instrument. It can be used to modify the functionality of the VI and make new VI executables.

Chapter 8: Using Dynamic Data Exchange in Visual Basic®

3. \Part2\Ex1.vbp

   First example of initiating a DDE conversation. An Automatic DDE link is created with Microsoft® Excel.

4. \Part2\Ex2\Destntn.vbp

   A sample VB program that acts as a Destination in a DDE conversation. This program is designed to communicate with the example Source.vbp.

5. \Part2\Ex2\Source.vbp

   A sample VB program that acts as a Source in a DDE conversation. This program is designed to communicate with the example program defined in Destntn.vbp.

6. \Part2\DDECmdr\DDECmdr.vbp

   A program that sends commands to the Virtual Instrument over a DDE link.

Chapter 10: RS-232C Communications in Visual Basic®

7. \Part2\Ex3\Ex3.vbp

   A Quick Start example illustrating RS-232 communications using the MSComm ActiveX control and a loopback plug.

8. \Part2\RS232Cmdr\RS232Cmdr.vbp

   This program is designed to send commands to the Virtual Instrument over an RS-232 connection. It illustrates how simple it is to use the MSComm ActiveX control for RS-232 communications.

Chapter 12: TCP/IP Networking in Visual Basic®

9. \Part2\Ex4\Ex4.vbp

   A simple TCP/IP client program created using the Winsock ActiveX control. This program demonstrates how to program the essential functions necessary for a TCP/IP client.

10. \Part2\Ex5\Ex5.vbp

    A single-client TCP/IP server program. That accepts a connection request from a client and echoes anything sent over the network connection back to the client.

11. \Part2\Ex6\Ex6.vbp

    A multi-client TCP/IP server program. Demonstrates how to accept and manage multiple connections from client programs. Generates random data every second and sends data to all connected clients.

Chapter 13: File Communications

12. \FileComm\FileComm.cls

    Defines a general-purpose class called clsFileComm that can be used to implement communications between programs through files.

13. \Part2\Ex7\Ex7.vbp

An example program that uses the clsFileComm file communications class.

Chapter 15: Multithreading in Visual Basic®

14. \Part3\Ex1\Ex1.vbp

This example demonstrates that Visual Basic® offers only a single thread of execution for all user code by default. The example program attempts to run two processes simultaneously.

Chapter 17: State Machines—Implementing State Diagrams in Visual Basic®

15. \Part3\Ex2\Ex2.vbp

This program illustrates a method for implementing a state machine in Visual Basic®. It implements the Virtual Instrument state machine as an example.

Chapter 19: A Visual Basic® Parser Class

16. \Parser\Parser.cls

Defines a class that implements a variety or parsing functions.

17. \Part3\Ex3\Ex3.vbp

An example program that demonstrates the use of the Parser class.

Chapter 21: Device Controllers in VB

18. \Part3\Ex4\Ex4.vbp

This is an example program that improves upon the File Communications example given in Chapter 13 through the use of polling.

19. \Part3\RS232Ctrl\RS232Ctrl.vbp

This example implements a program that controls the Virtual Instrument over an RS-232 port. It uses a state machine to track the VI and the Parser class to interpret returned data.

20. \Part3\WinsockCtrl\WinsockCtrl.vbp

This example program controls the Virtual Instrument over a TCP/IP network connection. It is obtained by exchanging the MSComm control in the RS-232 controller program with a Winsock control and making the necessary code changes.

Chapter 22: Scientific Plotting with MSChart

21. \Part4\Ex1\Ex1.vbp

    This is a quick start example demonstrating how to create a basic chart using the MSChart control with minimal effort.

22. \Part4\Ex2\Ex2.vbp

    A modification of the previous example demonstrating how to set multiple levels of axis labels and how they appear on an MSChart plot.

23. \Part4\Ex3\Ex3.vbp

    An example of how to assign chart data to an MSChart control using a Variant array.

24. \Part4\Ex4\Ex4.vbp

    This example demonstrates how to add statistics lines to a chart and format their appearance.

25. \Part4\PlateBrowser\PlateBrowser.vbp

    Interactive features of the MSChart control are utilized in this example to provide the user with an ability to click on a bar in a 3D chart to display associated data.

Chapter 23: Tabular Data Display and Editing

26. \Part4\Ex5\Ex5.vbp

    This Quick Start example demonstrates how to get started right away using the MSFlexGrid control. It also shows how to display graphics as well as text in an MSFlexGrid cell

27. \Part4\Ex6\Ex6.vbp

    This example demonstrates how to use the custom clsSheet object with an MSFlexGrid and TextBox to add a spreadsheet to an application.

Chapter 24: Visual Basic® Graphics Fundamentals

28. \Part4\Ex7\Ex7.vbp

    This Quick Start example demonstrates a few of the basic VB drawing functions.

29. \Part4\Ex8\Ex8.vbp

    A method for reading a graphic from a file and transferring it to a drawing surface is illustrated in this example.

30. \Part4\Ex9\Ex9.vbp

    This example provides the essential components for building a lasso in VB. The use of a lasso is demonstrated by providing a series of CheckBoxes that can be selected all at once with a lasso.

Chapter 25: Active Graphic Displays

31. \Part4\StripChart\StripChart.vbp

    A class that displays a strip chart is demonstrated. As new data are added to a StripChart object, the display automatically updates.

32. \Part4\WinsockCtrl\WinsockCtrl.vbp

    This example is a modification of the example by the same name from Part 3. A StripChart object is added to the example that automatically updates as new data are received from the Virtual Instrument.

33. \Part4\GasGauge\GasGauge.vbp

    The GasGauge class is demonstrated in this example. GasGauge displays a typical semicircular gas tank style gauge with a needle that automatically updates as its associated Value property changes.

Chapter 26: Interactive Graphic Displays

34. \Part4\Knob\Knob.vbp

    This example demonstrates the first interactive graphic class called Knob. A Knob object displays a typical rotary-action knob that can be interactively set using the mouse or programmatically. It also includes a Change event that is used to update other portions of the display when a Knob's Value property changes.

35. \Part4\Thermometer\Thermometer.vbp

    The Thermometer class is demonstrated in this example. A Thermometer object displays a Temperature property value as a traditional glass thermometer with mercury meniscus. Dragging the mercury meniscus with the mouse sets the Temperature property value. The class also has two events that indicate when the Temperature value passes over and under a threshold.

APPENDIX

C:

Instructions for Building the Virtual Instrument

This apppendix gives specifications for all forms and lists all source code used to implement the Virtual Instrument. By following the instructions the Virtual Instrument can be built starting with a completely new Visual Basic® project.

The Virtual Instrument program is composed of a main Form and three additional Forms used for data-entry dialog boxes. We will take each of these Forms one at a time, and present the Form design, control properties and source code for each.

To begin, create a new VB project and make sure that the following components are included in the project.

1. Microsoft® Comm Control
2. Microsoft® Common Dialog Control
3. Microsoft® Windows® Common Controls
4. Microsoft® Winsock Control

THE MAIN FORM

Create the following controls on a new form and assign given property values. Refer to Figure C-1 for control placement and sizing. The two Image controls included on the form contain bitmaps that implement the On and Off "lights" on the VI front panel. To create these bitmaps we used the Microsoft® Paint program that comes with most versions of the Windows® operating system. We created two bitmap files called "on.bmp" and "off.bmp." Each file is 28 pixels wide by 28 pixels high. The "on.bmp" file contains a green circle with a gray background, and the "off.bmp" file contains a red circle with a gray background.

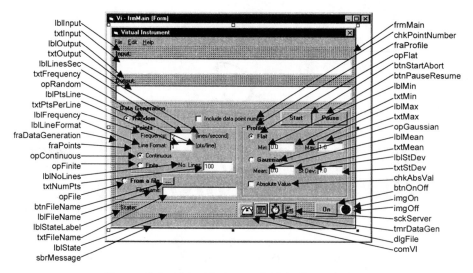

lblInput
txtInput
lblLinesSec
txtFrequency
opRandom
lblPtsLine
txtPtsPerLine
lblFrequency
lblLineFormat
fraDataGeneration
fraPoints
opContinuous
opFinite
lblNoLines
txtNumPts
opFile
btnFileName
lblFileName
lblStateLabel
txtFileName
lblState
sbrMessage

frmMain
chkPointNumber
fraProfile
opFlat
btnStartAbort
btnPauseResume
lblMin
txtMin
lblMax
txtMax
opGaussian
lblMean
txtMean
lblStDev
txtStDev
chkAbsVal
btnOnOff
imgOn
imgOff
sckServer
tmrDataGen
dlgFile
comVI

Figure C-1. Virtual Instrument Main Form design.

Object Type	Property	Value
Form	Name	frmMain
	Caption	Virtual Instrument
	BorderStyle	1 – Fixed Single
	LinkMode	1 – Source
	LinkTopic	VI
Label	Name	lblInput
	Caption	Input:
TextBox	Name	txtInput
	Text	
	MultiLine	True
Label	Name	lblOutput
	Caption	Output:
TextBox	Name	txtOutput
	Text	
Label	Name	lblLinesSec
	Caption	(lines/second)
TextBox	Name	txtFrequency
	Text	2
OptionButton	Name	opRandom
	Caption	Random
	Value	True
Label	Name	lblPtsLine
	Caption	(pts/line)

Object Type	Property	Value
TextBox	Name	txtPtsPerLine
	Text	1
Label	Name	lblFrequency
	Caption	Frequency:
Label	Name	lblLineFormat
	Caption	Line Format:
Frame	Name	fraDataGeneration
	Caption	Data Generation
	Enabled	False
Frame	Name	fraPoints
	Caption	Points
OptionButton	Name	opContinuous
	Caption	Continuous
	Value	True
OptionButton	Name	opFinite
	Caption	Finite
	Value	False
Label	Name	lblNoLines
	Caption	No. Lines:
TextBox	Name	txtNumPts
	Text	100
OptionButton	Name	opFile
	Caption	From a file
	Value	False
CommandButton	Name	btnFileName
	Caption	…
Label	Name	lblFileName
	Caption	File Name:
Label	Name	lblStateLabel
	Caption	State
TextBox	Name	txtFileName
	Text	
Label	Name	lblState
	Caption	
	BorderStyle	0 - None
StatusBar	Name	sbrMessage
	Style	1 - sbrSimple
CheckBox	Name	chkPointNumber
	Caption	Include data point number
	Value	0 - Unchecked
Frame	Name	fraProfile
	Caption	Profile
OptionButton	Name	opFlat
	Caption	Flat
	Value	True

(continued)

Object Type	Property	Value
CommandButton	Name	btnStartAbort
	Caption	Start
CommandButton	Name	btnPauseResume
	Caption	Pause
Label	Name	lblMin
	Caption	Min:
TextBox	Name	txtMin
	Text	0.0
Label	Name	lblMax
	Caption	Max:
TextBox	Name	txtMax
	Text	1.0
OptionButton	Name	opGaussian
	Caption	Gaussian
	Value	False
Label	Name	lblMean
	Caption	Mean:
TextBox	Name	txtMean
	Text	0.0
Label	Name	lblStDev
	Caption	St Dev.
TextBox	Name	txtStDev
	Text	1.0
CheckBox	Name	chkAbsVal
	Caption	Absolute Value
	Value	0 - Unchecked
CommandButton	Name	btnOnOff
	Caption	On
Image	Name	imgOn
	BorderStyle	0 - None
	Picture	On.bmp
Image	Name	imgOff
	BorderStyle	0 - None
	Picture	Off.bmp
Winsock	Name	sckServer
	Protocol	0 - sckTCPProtocol
Timer	Name	tmrDataGen
	Enabled	False
	Interval	500
CommonDialog	Name	dlgFile
	CancelError	True
	Filter	Text (*.txt)|*.txt|All (*.*)|*.*
MSComm	Name	comVI
	RThreshold	1

The VI also has menus. Open the Menu Editor while the frmMain Form window is active. Create three new top-level menu options with submenus as follows:

Menu Caption	Parent Menu Caption	Name	Shortcut
&File		mnuFile	(None)
E&xit	&File	mnuFileExit	(None)
&Edit		mnuEdit	(None)
&Transmission Formats ...	&Edit	mnuEditXmitFormat	(None)
&RS232 Port Settings ...	&Edit	MnuEditRS232PortSettings	(None)
&Network Settings ...	&Edit	mnuEditNetworkSettings	(None)
&Help		mnuHelp	(None)
&About the Virtual Instrument	&Help	mnuHelpAbout	(None)

The following listing is all the code that should be entered into the frmMain Code Window.

```
Option Explicit

' Version and date of the VI
Const gVIVersion As Single = 1.3
Const gVIDate As Date = #6/12/98#

' State Variables and Constants
Private Enum enumState
    conStateOff
    conStateIdle
    conStatePaused
    conStateAnalyzing
End Enum
Private mStateOperate As enumState      ' Operating state of the VI

' Serial Port Settings
Private mBlnCommEnabled As Boolean      ' True if the serial port to be enabled
Private mIntCommPort As Integer         ' The serial port number
Private mStrCommSettings As String      ' Serial port settings
Private mStrInputBuffer As String       ' The accumulate buffer

' Network Connection Settings
Private mBlnNetworkEnabled As Boolean   ' True if the network to be enabled
Private mIntServerPort As Integer       ' Port on which VI server listens.

' Data Transmission Formatting Characters
Private mStrTokenSep As String              ' Token separator
Private mStrLineTerm As String              ' Line terminator

' Command Processor Result Codes
Const conResultSuccess As Integer = 0       ' Command successful
Const conResultFail As Integer = 1          ' Command failed
Const conResultIllegalCommand As Integer = 2  ' Command not legal at this point
```

```
' Data Generation Parameters
Private mLngPointNumber As Long          ' The number of the generated point

Private mIncludePointNum As Boolean      ' Whether point number in data gen.
Private mDataSource As Integer           ' Source of data
Const conSourceRandom As Integer = 1     ' Randomly generated
Const conSourceFile As Integer = 2       ' Obtained from a file

Private mRandomStyle As Integer                   ' Style of random data generation
Const conRandomStyleContinuous As Integer = 1 ' Continuous data generation
Const conRandomStyleFinite As Integer = 2     ' Finite data generation
Private mRandomNumLines As Integer            ' Number of random points to generate
Private mRandomPtsPerLine As Integer          ' Number of random points per line

Private mSourceFileName As String             ' Data file source
Private mSourceFileNum As Integer             ' Source file number

Private mRandomProfile As Integer
Const conRandomProfileGaussian As Integer = 1 ' Generate a gaussian profile
Const conRandomProfileFlat As Integer = 2     ' Generate a flat profile

Private mProfileGaussianMean As Single        ' Parameters characterizing
Private mProfileGaussianVar As Single         ' Gaussian profile

Private mProfileFlatMin As Single             ' Range of flat profile
Private mProfileFlatMax As Single

Private Function CommandPauseAnalysis() As Integer
    ' Pause data generation
    btnPauseResume.Caption = "Resume"
    sbrMessage.SimpleText = "Paused!"
    CommandPauseAnalysis = conResultSuccess
End Function

Private Function CommandResumeAnalysis() As Integer
    ' Resume data generation
    btnPauseResume.Caption = "Pause"
    sbrMessage.SimpleText = "Resumed!"
    CommandResumeAnalysis = conResultSuccess

End Function

Private Function CommandAbortPause() As Integer
    ' Abort from the pause state
    tmrDataGen.Enabled = False               ' Disable data generation
    Close                                    ' Close any open files
    btnStartAbort.Caption = "Start"
    btnPauseResume.Caption = "Pause"
    sbrMessage.SimpleText = "Aborted!"
    CommandAbortPause = conResultSuccess
End Function

Private Function CommandAbortAnalysis() As Integer
    ' Abort from the data generation state
    tmrDataGen.Enabled = False               ' Disable data generation
    Close                                    ' Close any open files
    btnStartAbort.Caption = "Start"
    sbrMessage.SimpleText = "Stopped!"
    CommandAbortAnalysis = conResultSuccess
End Function
```

```
Private Function CommandStartAnalysis() As Integer
    ' Initiate data generation
    UpdateDataGenParameters              ' Update data generation params
    If mDataSource = conSourceFile Then  ' If data from a file then open the file
        mSourceFileNum = FreeFile
        Open mSourceFileName For Input As mSourceFileNum
    End If
    tmrDataGen.Enabled = True              ' Enable data generation timer
    sbrMessage.SimpleText = "Running ..."
    btnStartAbort.Caption = "Abort"
    CommandStartAnalysis = conResultSuccess
End Function

Private Function CommandInstrumentOn() As Integer
    ' Turn the instrument on
    fraDataGeneration.Enabled = True       ' Enable data generation section
    imgOn.Visible = True                   ' Make the green light visible
    imgOff.Visible = False
    btnOnOff.Caption = "Off"               ' Change the On/Off button caption
    ResetRS232Port                         ' Begin processing RS232 port commands
    ResetNetworkConnection                 ' Begin processing network commands
    CommandInstrumentOn = conResultSuccess
End Function

Private Function CommandInstrumentOff() As Integer
    ' Turn the instrument off
    tmrDataGen.Enabled = False             ' Disable data generation
    TerminateRS232Port                     ' Disable RS232 command processing
    TerminateNetworkConnection             ' Disable network connection
    frmMain.LinkMode = vbLinkNone          ' Shut down any DDE links
    Close                                  ' Close any open files
    btnStartAbort.Caption = "Start"        ' Reset all button captions
    btnPauseResume.Caption = "Pause"
    btnOnOff.Caption = "On"
    imgOff.Visible = True                  ' Make the red light visible
    imgOn.Visible = False
    fraDataGeneration.Enabled = False      ' Disable data generation frame

    sbrMessage.SimpleText = ""             ' Clear status bar
    CommandInstrumentOff = conResultSuccess
End Function

Private Function GetNetworkCommand() As String
    ' Get an entire command line from the network connection.
    Dim intPosition As Integer     ' Position of the line term character(s)
    Dim intTermLen As Integer      ' Number of chars in line terminator string
    Dim strCommand As String       ' Store a command
    Dim strData As String
                                   ' Error handler
    On Error GoTo GetNetworkCommandErrorHandler

    intTermLen = Len(mStrLineTerm)
    strCommand = ""                ' Grab anything on network connection
    sckServer.GetData strData, vbString
    mStrInputBuffer = mStrInputBuffer & strData
                                   ' Look for line termination characters
    intPosition = InStr(mStrInputBuffer, mStrLineTerm)
```

```
    While intPosition > 0                     ' If found then remove the command
        strCommand = Left(mStrInputBuffer, intPosition - 1)
        txtInput.Text = strCommand            ' Keep any remaining data
        mStrInputBuffer = Right(mStrInputBuffer, Len(mStrInputBuffer) - _
                                            (intPosition + intTermLen - 1))
        intPosition = InStr(mStrInputBuffer, mStrLineTerm)
    Wend

    GetNetworkCommand = strCommand            ' Return command
    Exit Function
'_____
GetNetworkCommandErrorHandler:
    Select Case Err.Number
    Case Else
        MsgBox "Error (frmMain - GetNetworkCommand) " & _
                            CStr(Err.Number) & ": " & Err.Description
    End Select
End Function

Private Function ProcessCommand(strCommand As String) As String
    ' Process a command.
    ' State changes are confined to this procedure.
    ' Result is returned as a string.
    Dim intResultCode As Integer, strResult As String
    Dim intPos As Integer, intArg As Integer, strArg As String

    intResultCode = conResultSuccess          ' Begin assuming successful
    strCommand = UCase(Trim(strCommand))      ' Make case insensitive
    If strCommand = "" Then Exit Function     ' Do nothing with an empty command

    ' If there is an integer argument, parse it out.
    intArg = 0
    intPos = InStr(strCommand, " ")
    If intPos > 0 Then
        strArg = Right(strCommand, Len(strCommand) - intPos)
        If IsNumeric(strArg) Then intArg = CInt(strArg)
        strCommand = Left(strCommand, intPos - 1)
    End If

    ' Put command in Input box
    txtInput.Text = strCommand

    Select Case mStateOperate                 ' Switch on the state of the VI
    Case conStateIdle                         ' When VI is idle
        Select Case strCommand

        Case "ANALYZE"                        ' Start analysis (data generation)
            If intArg > 0 Then                ' If the num of pts was passed to the VI,
                opFinite.Value = True         ' set the data generation to be finite,
                txtNumPts.Text = "1"          ' set the number of lines to 1
                txtPtsPerLine.Text = CStr(intArg)   ' and set the num of points passed.
            End If

            intResultCode = CommandStartAnalysis
            If intResultCode = conResultSuccess Then mStateOperate = conStateAnalyzing

        Case "ABORT", "PAUSE"                 ' Abort or Pause operation
            ' No state change required
```

```
        Case "OFF"
            intResultCode = CommandInstrumentOff
            If intResultCode = conResultSuccess Then mStateOperate = conStateOff

        Case Else                              ' Illegal command
            intResultCode = conResultIllegalCommand
        End Select

    Case conStateAnalyzing                     ' Analyzing
        Select Case strCommand

        Case "PAUSE"                           ' Pause analysis
            intResultCode = CommandPauseAnalysis
            If intResultCode = conResultSuccess Then mStateOperate = conStatePaused

        Case "ABORT"                           ' Abort the analysis
            intResultCode = CommandAbortAnalysis
            If intResultCode = conResultSuccess Then mStateOperate = conStateIdle

        Case "OFF"
            intResultCode = CommandInstrumentOff
            If intResultCode = conResultSuccess Then mStateOperate = conStateOff

        Case Else                              ' Illegal command
            intResultCode = conResultIllegalCommand
        End Select

    Case conStatePaused                        ' Paused
        Select Case strCommand
        Case "RESUME"                          ' Resume analysis
            intResultCode = CommandResumeAnalysis
            If intResultCode = conResultSuccess Then mStateOperate = conStateAnalyzing

        Case "ABORT"                           ' Abort a paused state
            intResultCode = CommandAbortPause
            If intResultCode = conResultSuccess Then mStateOperate = conStateIdle

        Case "OFF"
            intResultCode = CommandInstrumentOff
            If intResultCode = conResultSuccess Then mStateOperate = conStateOff

        Case Else                              ' Illegal command
            intResultCode = conResultIllegalCommand
        End Select

    Case conStateOff                           ' When the VI is off
        Select Case strCommand

        Case "ON"                              ' Turn the VI on
            intResultCode = CommandInstrumentOn     ' Set the state variable
            If intResultCode = conResultSuccess Then mStateOperate = conStateIdle
        Case Else                              ' Illegal command
            intResultCode = conResultIllegalCommand

        End Select

End Select
```

```
     ' Update the state display
     Select Case mStateOperate
     Case conStateOff:       lblState.Caption = "Off"
     Case conStateIdle:      lblState.Caption = "Idle"
     Case conStateAnalyzing: lblState.Caption = "Analyzing ..."
     Case conStatePaused:    lblState.Caption = "Paused"
     End Select

     ' Process result code
     strResult = ProcessResultCode(intResultCode, strCommand)

     ProcessCommand = strResult

End Function

Private Sub UpdateDataGenParameters()
     ' Update all stored data generation parameters

     mLngPointNumber = 0&                    ' Initialize point number to 0

     ' Set variable indicating whether to include a point number
     If chkPointNumber.Value = vbChecked Then
         mIncludePointNum = True
     ElseIf chkPointNumber.Value = vbUnchecked Then
         mIncludePointNum = False
     End If

     ' Set data source and parameters
     If opRandom.Value = True Then
         mDataSource = conSourceRandom
         If IsNumeric(txtFrequency.Text) Then
             tmrDataGen.Interval = CInt(1000# / CSng(txtFrequency.Text))
         End If
         If IsNumeric(txtPtsPerLine.Text) Then
             mRandomPtsPerLine = CInt(txtPtsPerLine.Text)
         End If

         ' Update data generation style
         If opContinuous.Value = True Then
             mRandomStyle = conRandomStyleContinuous
         ElseIf opFinite.Value = True Then
             mRandomStyle = conRandomStyleFinite
             If IsNumeric(txtNumPts.Text) Then mRandomNumLines = CInt(txtNumPts.Text)
         End If

         ' Update data generation profile
         If opGaussian.Value = True Then
             mRandomProfile = conRandomProfileGaussian
             If IsNumeric(txtMean.Text) Then mProfileGaussianMean = CSng(txtMean.Text)
             If IsNumeric(txtStDev.Text) Then
                 mProfileGaussianVar = CSng(txtStDev.Text)
                 mProfileGaussianVar = mProfileGaussianVar * mProfileGaussianVar
             End If

         ElseIf opFlat.Value = True Then
             mRandomProfile = conRandomProfileFlat
             If IsNumeric(txtMin.Text) Then mProfileFlatMin = CSng(txtMin.Text)
             If IsNumeric(txtMax.Text) Then mProfileFlatMax = CSng(txtMax.Text)

         End If
```

```vb
            ' Randomize random number generator
            Randomize

        ' Data obtained from a file
        ElseIf opFile.Value = True Then
            mDataSource = conSourceFile
            mSourceFileName = txtFileName.Text

        End If

End Sub

Public Property Let CommPort(intPort As Integer)
    ' Set the comm port
    If intPort = 1 Or intPort = 2 Then mIntCommPort = intPort
End Property

Public Property Let CommSettings(strSettings As String)
    ' Set the comm settings string
    mStrCommSettings = strSettings
End Property

Public Property Let CommEnabled(blnEnabled As Boolean)
    ' Enable or disable the comm port
    mBlnCommEnabled = blnEnabled
End Property

Public Property Let NetworkEnabled(blnEnabled As Boolean)
    ' Enable or disable the network connection
    mBlnNetworkEnabled = blnEnabled
End Property

Public Property Get NetworkEnabled() As Boolean
  ' Return a boolean indicating whether or not the network connection is to be enabled.
    NetworkEnabled = mBlnNetworkEnabled
End Property

Public Property Let ServerPort(intPort As Integer)
    ' Set the port on which the server socket should listen.
    mIntServerPort = intPort
End Property

Public Property Get ServerPort() As Integer
    ' Return the current server port setting
    ServerPort = mIntServerPort
End Property

Public Property Let TokenSep(strSep As String)
    ' Set the token separator character(s)
    mStrTokenSep = strSep
End Property

Public Property Let LineTerm(strTerm As String)
    ' Set the liner termination character(s)
    mStrLineTerm = strTerm
End Property


Public Sub ResetNetworkConnection()
```

```
    ' Reset the parameters of the network connection
    mStrInputBuffer = ""                    ' Clear the accumulating input buffer
                                            ' Close the port
    If sckServer.State <> sckClosed Then sckServer.Close
    DoEvents
    sckServer.LocalPort = mIntServerPort  ' Set the port on which to listen
    If mBlnNetworkEnabled = True Then
        sckServer.Listen                    ' Begin listening
        sbrMessage.SimpleText = "Listening ..."
    Else
        sbrMessage.SimpleText = ""
    End If
End Sub

Public Sub TerminateNetworkConnection()
    ' Close network connection
    mStrInputBuffer = ""                    ' Clear the accumulating input buffer
    sckServer.Close                         ' Close the port
End Sub

Public Sub ResetRS232Port()
    ' Reset the command processor for the RS-232 port
    mStrInputBuffer = ""                    ' Clear the accumulating input buffer
                                            ' If open then close the serial port.
    If comVI.PortOpen = True Then comVI.PortOpen = False
    comVI.CommPort = mIntCommPort         ' Configure the serial port
    comVI.Settings = mStrCommSettings
                                            ' If enabled then open the serial port.
    If mBlnCommEnabled = True Then comVI.PortOpen = True

End Sub

Private Sub TerminateRS232Port()
    ' Terminate processing of commands
    mStrInputBuffer = ""                    ' Clear the accumulate buffer
                                            ' Close the serial port if open
    If comVI.PortOpen = True Then comVI.PortOpen = False
End Sub

Private Function GetRS232Command() As String
    ' Get an entire command line
    Dim intPosition As Integer            ' Position of the line term character(s)
    Dim intTermLen As Integer             ' Number of chars in line term string
    Dim strCommand As String              ' Store a command
                                          ' Error handler
    On Error GoTo GetRS232CommandErrorHandler

    intTermLen = Len(mStrLineTerm)
    strCommand = ""                           ' Grab anything on input buffer
    mStrInputBuffer = mStrInputBuffer & comVI.Input
                                          ' Look for line termination characters
    intPosition = InStr(mStrInputBuffer, mStrLineTerm)
    While intPosition > 0                   ' If found then remove the command
        strCommand = Left(mStrInputBuffer, intPosition - 1)
        txtInput.Text = strCommand          ' Keep any remaining data
        mStrInputBuffer = Right(mStrInputBuffer, Len(mStrInputBuffer) - _
                                        (intPosition + intTermLen - 1))
        intPosition = InStr(mStrInputBuffer, mStrLineTerm)
    Wend
```

```
        GetRS232Command = strCommand                ' Return command
        Exit Function
'_____
GetRS232CommandErrorHandler:
    Select Case Err.Number
    Case Else
        MsgBox "Error (frmMain - GetRS232Command) " & CStr(Err.Number) & _
                                        ": " & Err.Description
    End Select

End Function

Private Sub ReturnRS232Result(strMessage As String)
    ' Return the result string on the RS232 port.
    On Error GoTo ReturnRS232ResultErrorHandler

    If comVI.PortOpen = True Then comVI.Output = strMessage & mStrLineTerm

    Exit Sub
'_____
ReturnRS232ResultErrorHandler:

    Select Case Err.Number
    Case Else
        MsgBox "VI Error (frmMain - ReturnRS232Result) " & CStr(Err.Number) & _
                                        ": " & Err.Description
    End Select

End Sub

Private Sub ReturnNetworkResult(strMessage As String)
    ' Return the result string on the network connection.
    On Error GoTo ReturnNetworkResultErrorHandler

    If sckServer.State <> sckClosed Then sckServer.SendData strMessage & mStrLineTerm

    Exit Sub
'_____
ReturnNetworkResultErrorHandler:

    Select Case Err.Number
    Case Else
        MsgBox "VI Error (frmMain - ReturnNetworkResult) " & CStr(Err.Number) & _
                                        ": " & Err.Description
    End Select

End Sub

Private Function ProcessResultCode(intResult As Integer, Optional strData As Variant) _
                                                    As String
    ' Process the result code from a command process and react appropriately
    Dim strResultMsg As String

    Select Case intResult
    Case conResultSuccess                ' On a successful result code
        strResultMsg = "OK"
    Case conResultIllegalCommand
        strResultMsg = "Error " & CStr(intResult) & ": "
        If IsMissing(strData) Then strData = "(Unknown)"
        strResultMsg = strResultMsg & "Illegal Command - " & strData
```

```
    Case Else
        strResultMsg = "Error " & CStr(intResult) & ": "
        strResultMsg = strResultMsg & "Result code not understood"
    End Select

    txtOutput.Text = strResultMsg               ' Put message in output text box
    ProcessResultCode = strResultMsg
End Function

Private Sub btnFileName_Click()
    ' Open File dialog and get data file name
    On Error GoTo btnFileName_ClickErrorHandler
    With dlgFile
        .filename = ""
        .ShowOpen
        mSourceFileName = .filename
        txtFileName.Text = .FileTitle
    End With
    Exit Sub
'_____
btnFileName_ClickErrorHandler:
    Select Case Err.Number
    Case cdlCancel   ' User cancelled
        ' Do nothing
    Case Else
        MsgBox "Error (frmMain - btnFileName_Click) " & CStr(Err.Number) & _
                                      ": " & Err.Description
    End Select
End Sub

Private Sub btnOnOff_Click()
    ' Turn the Virtual Instrument on or off
    Select Case mStateOperate
    Case conStateOff                    ' If the Instrument is Off, then turn it on
        ProcessCommand "ON"
    Case Else                           ' If in any other state then turn it off
        ProcessCommand "OFF"
    End Select

End Sub

Private Sub btnPauseResume_Click()
    ' Pause or Resume data generation
    If mStateOperate = conStatePaused Then  ' Resume
        ProcessCommand "Resume"
    Else                                ' Pause
        ProcessCommand "Pause"
    End If

End Sub

Private Sub btnStartAbort_Click()
    ' Start or Abort data generation
    If mStateOperate = conStateIdle Then   ' Begin data generation
        ProcessCommand "Analyze"
    Else                                   ' Abort operation
        ProcessCommand "Abort"
    End If

End Sub
```

```
Private Sub comVI_OnComm()
    ' Whenever RThreshold number of characters are received, process input
    Dim strCommand As String, strResult As String

    If comVI.CommEvent = comEvReceive Then
        strCommand = GetRS232Command()
        If strCommand <> "" Then
            strResult = ProcessCommand(strCommand)
            ReturnRS232Result strResult
        End If
    End If
End Sub

Private Sub Form_LinkClose()
    ' The DDE link has terminated.
    sbrMessage.SimpleText = "DDE Link Terminated"
End Sub

Private Sub Form_LinkExecute(CmdStr As String, Cancel As Integer)
    ' Process commands that come on a DDE link
    If ProcessCommand(CmdStr) = "OK" Then
        Cancel = False
    Else
        Cancel = True
    End If

End Sub

Private Sub Form_LinkOpen(Cancel As Integer)
    ' If the VI is off then refuse the connection.
    If mStateOperate = conStateOff Then Cancel = True
    sbrMessage.SimpleText = "DDE Link Initiated"
End Sub

Private Sub Form_Load()
    ' Initialize the application
    SetDefaultCommParameters          ' Default communication parameters
    SetDefaultNetworkParameters       ' Default network connection parameters
    SetDefaultFormatParameters        ' Default data format parameters
    SetDefaultDataGenParameters       ' Default data generation parameters
    mStateOperate = conStateOff       ' Initial state is off

End Sub

Private Sub SetDefaultCommParameters()
    mIntCommPort = 1                  ' Default settings
    mStrCommSettings = "19200,N,8,1"
    mBlnCommEnabled = True
    mStrLineTerm = vbCr               ' Carriage Return
End Sub

Private Sub SetDefaultNetworkParameters()
    NetworkEnabled = False            ' Default network parameters
    ServerPort = 1234
End Sub

Private Sub SetDefaultFormatParameters()
    TokenSep = ","                    ' Default transmission formats
    LineTerm = vbCr
End Sub
```

```
Private Sub SetDefaultDataGenParameters()
    ' Set the default data generation parameters
    mLngPointNumber = 0&                    ' The number of the generated point
    mIncludePointNum = False                ' Do not include a point number
    chkPointNumber.Value = mIncludePointNum

    mDataSource = conSourceRandom           ' Random source of data
    opRandom.Value = True
    tmrDataGen.Interval = 500               ' 2 lines per second
    txtFrequency.Text = "2"
    txtPtsPerLine.Text = "1"

    mRandomStyle = conRandomStyleContinuous ' Continuous data generation
    opContinuous.Value = True

    mRandomProfile = conRandomProfileFlat   ' Generate a flat profile
    opFlat.Value = True
    mProfileFlatMin = 0#                    ' In a range of [0, 1)
    mProfileFlatMax = 1#
    txtMin.Text = "0.0"
    txtMax.Text = "1.0"
    txtMean.Text = "0.0"
    txtStDev.Text = "1.0"

End Sub

Private Sub Form_QueryUnload(Cancel As Integer, UnloadMode As Integer)
    ' Unload any other forms first
    Dim frm As Form
    For Each frm In Forms
        If frm.Name <> "frmMain" Then Unload frm
    Next frm
End Sub

Private Sub mnuEditNetworkSettings_Click()
    frmNetworkSettings.Show
End Sub

Private Sub mnuEditRS232PortSettings_Click()
    frmCommSettings.Show
End Sub

Private Sub mnuEditXmitFormat_Click()
    frmXmitFormats.Show
End Sub

Private Sub mnuFileExit_Click()
    Unload Me
End Sub

Private Sub mnuHelpAbout_Click()
    Dim strMessage As String

    strMessage = "Virtual Instrument - Version " & Format(gVIVersion, "0.0") & _
                        ", Date " & Format(gVIDate, "mm/dd/yyyy") & vbCrLf
    strMessage = strMessage & _
        "Copyright 1996, 1997, 1998, 1999 Mark F. Russo and Martin M. Echols"
    MsgBox strMessage

End Sub
```

```vb
Private Sub opContinuous_Click()
    txtNumPts.Enabled = False          ' Enable/disable options
End Sub

Private Sub opFile_Click()
    txtFileName.Enabled = True          ' Enable/disable options
    btnFileName.Enabled = True
    fraPoints.Enabled = False
    fraProfile.Enabled = False
End Sub

Private Sub opFinite_Click()
    txtNumPts.Enabled = True            ' Enable/disable options
End Sub

Private Sub opFlat_Click()
    txtMin.Enabled = True               ' Enable/disable options
    txtMax.Enabled = True
    txtMean.Enabled = False
    txtStDev.Enabled = False

End Sub

Private Sub opGaussian_Click()
    txtMean.Enabled = True              ' Enable/disable options
    txtStDev.Enabled = True
    txtMin.Enabled = False
    txtMax.Enabled = False
End Sub

Private Sub opRandom_Click()
    fraPoints.Enabled = True            ' Enable/disable options
    fraProfile.Enabled = True
    txtFileName.Enabled = False         ' Disable other options
    btnFileName.Enabled = False
End Sub

Private Sub sckServer_ConnectionRequest(ByVal requestID As Long)
    ' Accept or reject a connection
    Dim strMsg As String

    ' If the VI is off then simply exit with no response.
    If mStateOperate = conStateOff Then Exit Sub

    ' If the server socket is not listening, refuse the connection request.
    If sckServer.State <> sckListening Then Exit Sub

    ' Close the listening socket and accept a connection from a client
    sckServer.Close
    DoEvents
    sckServer.Accept requestID

    ' Init application
    sbrMessage.SimpleText = "Network connection accepted!"
End Sub

Private Sub sckServer_Close()
    ' Close the connect and resume listening
    ResetNetworkConnection
End Sub
```

```vb
Private Sub sckServer_DataArrival(ByVal bytesTotal As Long)
    ' Process commands that arrive on the socket
    Dim strCommand As String, strResult As String

    strCommand = GetNetworkCommand()
    If strCommand <> "" Then
        strResult = ProcessCommand(strCommand)
        ReturnNetworkResult strResult
    End If

End Sub

Private Sub sckServer_Error(ByVal Number As Integer, Description As String, _
                    ByVal Scode As Long, ByVal Source As String, _
                    ByVal HelpFile As String, ByVal HelpContext As Long, _
                    CancelDisplay As Boolean)
    MsgBox "sckServer Error: " & CStr(Number) & " " & Description
End Sub

Private Sub tmrDataGen_Timer()
    ' When data generating timer times out, generate more data and send
    Dim dblData As Double
    Dim strOutput As String, strLine As String
    Dim I As Integer

    strOutput = ""

    ' If paused or off then exit
    If mStateOperate = conStatePaused Or mStateOperate = conStateOff Then Exit Sub

    ' Increment point number and check for overflow
    mLngPointNumber = mLngPointNumber + 1
    If mLngPointNumber >= 2147483646 Then mLngPointNumber = 1

    ' Add point number if required
    If mIncludePointNum = True Then _
                strOutput = strOutput & CStr(mLngPointNumber) & mStrTokenSep

    ' If generating random numbers ...
    If mDataSource = conSourceRandom Then

        ' If a finite number of points then check for completion
        If mRandomStyle = conRandomStyleFinite And _
                                    mLngPointNumber > mRandomNumLines Then
            ProcessCommand "Abort"
            Exit Sub
        End If

        For I = 1 To mRandomPtsPerLine
            ' If generating a gaussian profile ...

            If mRandomProfile = conRandomProfileGaussian Then
                ' Number from Gaussian profile
                dblData = GaussianDeviate
                dblData = mProfileGaussianVar * dblData + mProfileGaussianMean

            ' If generating a flat profile ...
            ElseIf mRandomProfile = conRandomProfileFlat Then
                dblData = (mProfileFlatMax - mProfileFlatMin) * Rnd + mProfileFlatMin
            End If
```

```
                    ' Take absolute value if necessary
                    If chkAbsVal.Value = vbChecked Then dblData = Abs(dblData)

                    strOutput = strOutput & Format(dblData, "0.0####")
                    If I < mRandomPtsPerLine Then strOutput = strOutput & mStrTokenSep

            Next I

      ' Data obtained from a file
      ElseIf mDataSource = conSourceFile Then
            If EOF(mSourceFileNum) = True Then
                ProcessCommand "Abort"
                Exit Sub
            Else
                Line Input #mSourceFileNum, strLine
                strOutput = strOutput & strLine
            End If
      End If

      ' Return generated data to appropriate connected ports and the interface.
      txtOutput.Text = strOutput
      If mBlnCommEnabled = True Then ReturnRS232Result strOutput
      If sckServer.State <> sckClosed Then ReturnNetworkResult strOutput

End Sub

Private Function GaussianDeviate() As Single
      ' Returns an approprimation to a normally distributed deviate
      ' with zero mean and unit variance
      Dim sngSum As Single, I As Integer

      sngSum = 0#
      For I = 1 To 12
            sngSum = sngSum + Rnd()
       Next I
      GaussianDeviate = ((sngSum / 6#) - 1#) * 6#

End Function
```

TRANSMISSION FORMATS DIALOG

To create the Transmission Formats dialog, add another new form to the project and add two Labels, two ComboBoxes, and two CommandButtons (see Figure C-2). Assign control properties as follows.

Object Type	Property	Value
Form	Name	frmXmitFormats
	Caption	Transmission Formats
	Border Style	3 – Fixed Dialog
Label	Name	lblTokenSep
	Caption	Token Separator:

(continued)

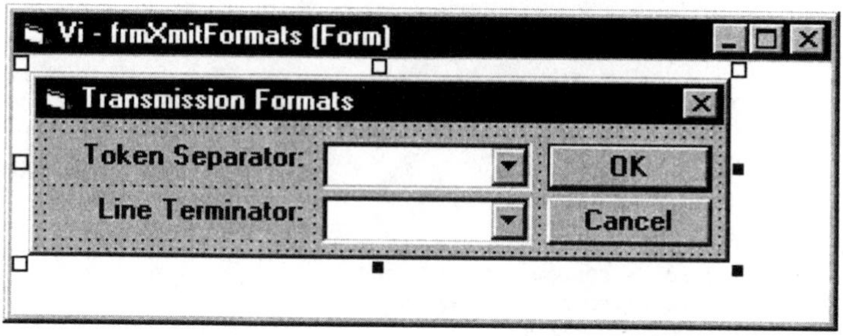

Figure C-2. Virtual Instrument Transmission Formats Dialog Form design.

Object Type	Property	Value
Label	Name	lblLineTerminator
	Caption	Line Terminator:
ComboBox	Name	cmbTokenSep
	Text	
ComboBox	Name	cmbLineTerm
	Text	
CommandButton	Name	btnOK
	Caption	OK
CommandButton	Name	btnCancel
	Caption	Cancel

Enter the following code into the frmXmitFormats From Code Window:

```
Option Explicit

' Transmission start/end constants
Const mNone As Integer = 1
Const mSTX As Integer = 2            ' Start of text
Const mETX As Integer = 3            ' End of text
Const mEOT As Integer = 4            ' End of transmission
Const mSpace As Integer = 5          ' Space
Const mComma As Integer = 6          ' Comma
Const mTab As Integer = 7            ' Tab
Const mCRLF As Integer = 8           ' Carriage Return, Linefeed
Const mCR As Integer = 9             ' Carriage Return
Const mLF As Integer = 10            ' Linefeed

Private Sub InitializeForm()
    ' Initialize the combo boxes
```

```
        ' Token Separators
        With cmbTokenSep
            .Clear
            .AddItem "<Comma>":        .ItemData(.NewIndex) = mComma
            .AddItem "<Tab>":          .ItemData(.NewIndex) = mTab
            .AddItem "<Space>":        .ItemData(.NewIndex) = mSpace
            .ListIndex = 0             ' Default to <Comma>
        End With

        ' Line Terminators
        With cmbLineTerm
            .Clear
            .AddItem "<CR>":           .ItemData(.NewIndex) = mCR
            .AddItem "<LF>":           .ItemData(.NewIndex) = mLF
            .AddItem "<CR><LF>":       .ItemData(.NewIndex) = mCRLF
            .ListIndex = 0             ' Default to <CR><LF>
        End With

End Sub

Private Sub ResetFormatEffectors()
        ' Reset Main Form Transmission Format Effectors
        ' Token Separators
        With cmbTokenSep
            If .ListIndex < 0 Then      ' Not selected or new entry
                frmMain.TokenSep = Trim(.Text)

            Else                        ' Provided option selected
                Select Case .ItemData(.ListIndex)
                Case mComma             ' Comma
                    frmMain.TokenSep = ","
                Case mTab               ' Tab
                    frmMain.TokenSep = vbTab
                Case mSpace             ' Space
                    frmMain.TokenSep = " "
                End Select

            End If
        End With

        ' Line Terminators
        With cmbLineTerm
            If .ListIndex < 0 Then      ' Not selected or new entry
                frmMain.LineTerm = Trim(.Text)

            Else                        ' Provided option selected
                Select Case .ItemData(.ListIndex)
                Case mCRLF              ' <CR><LF>
                    frmMain.LineTerm = vbCrLf
                Case mCR                ' <CR>
                    frmMain.LineTerm = vbCr
                Case mLF                ' <LF>
                    frmMain.LineTerm = vbLf
                End Select

            End If
        End With
End Sub
```

```
Private Sub btnCancel_Click()
    Hide
End Sub

Private Sub btnOK_Click()
    ' Reset Format Effectors strings in Main Form
    ResetFormatEffectors
    Hide
End Sub

Private Sub Form_Load()
    InitializeForm
End Sub
```

COMMUNICATION SETTINGS DIALOG

To create the Communication Settings Formats dialog, add a third new form to the project and add a CheckBox, five Labels, five ComboBoxes, and two CommandButtons (see Figure C-3). Assign control properties as follows:

Object Type	Property	Value
Form	Name	frmCommSettings
	Caption	Communication Settings
	Border Style	3 – Fixed Dialog
CheckBox	Name	chkEnabled
	Caption	Port Enabled:
	Value	1 - Checked
Label	Name	lblPortNumber
	Caption	Port Number:
Label	Name	lblBaudRate
	Caption	Baud Rate:
Label	Name	lblParity
	Caption	Parity:
Label	Name	lblDataBits
	Caption	Data Bits:
Label	Name	lblStopBits
	Caption	Stop Bits:
ComboBox	Name	cmbCommPort
	Text	
	Style	2 – Dropdown List
ComboBox	Name	cmbBaudRate
	Text	
	Style	2 – Dropdown List
ComboBox	Name	cmbParity
	Text	
	Style	2 – Dropdown List
ComboBox	Name	cmbDataBits
	Text	
	Style	2 – Dropdown List

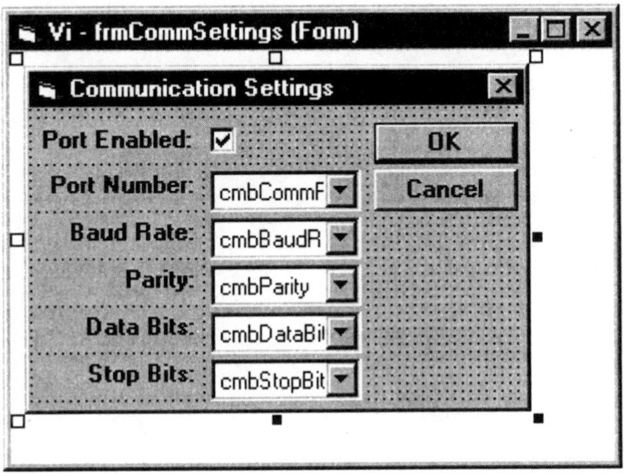

Figure C-3. Virtual Instrument Communication Settings Form design.

ComboBox	Name	cmbStopBits
	Text	
	Style	2 – Dropdown List
CommandButton	Name	btnOK
	Caption	OK
CommandButton	Name	btnCancel
	Caption	Cancel

Enter the following code into the frmCommSettings from Code Window.

```
Option Explicit

Private Sub ResetCommSettings()
    ' Build the Comm Settings string based on selections
    Dim strTmp As String, lngTmp As Long

    strTmp = ""

    ' Reset the flag indicating whether or not the port is to be enabled
    If chkEnabled.Value = vbChecked Then
        frmMain.CommEnabled = True
    Else
        frmMain.CommEnabled = False
    End If

    ' Reset Comm port parameter
    frmMain.CommPort = cmbCommPort.ItemData(cmbCommPort.ListIndex)

    ' Baud Rate
    strTmp = strTmp & CStr(cmbBaudRate.ItemData(cmbBaudRate.ListIndex))

    ' Parity
    strTmp = strTmp & "," & Chr$(cmbParity.ItemData(cmbParity.ListIndex))
```

```
    ' Data Bits
    strTmp = strTmp & "," & CStr(cmbDataBits.ItemData(cmbDataBits.ListIndex))

    ' Stop Bits
 strTmp = strTmp & "," & CStr(CSng(cmbStopBits.ItemData(cmbStopBits.ListIndex)) * 0.5)

    ' Reset Main Form settings parameter
    frmMain.CommSettings = strTmp

    ' Cause changes to take effect
    frmMain.ResetRS232Port

End Sub

Private Sub InitializeForm()
    ' Initialize the dropdown lists

    ' RS-232 Port
    With cmbCommPort
        .Clear
        .AddItem "Port 1":    .ItemData(.NewIndex) = 1
        .AddItem "Port 2":    .ItemData(.NewIndex) = 2
        .ListIndex = 0        ' Default to Port 1
    End With

    ' Baud Rate
    With cmbBaudRate
        .Clear
        .AddItem "1200":      .ItemData(.NewIndex) = 1200
        .AddItem "2400":      .ItemData(.NewIndex) = 2400
        .AddItem "9600":      .ItemData(.NewIndex) = 9600
        .AddItem "14400":     .ItemData(.NewIndex) = 14400
        .AddItem "19200":     .ItemData(.NewIndex) = 19200
        .ListIndex = 4        ' Default to 19200 BAUD
    End With

    ' Parity
    With cmbParity
        .Clear
        .AddItem "Even":      .ItemData(.NewIndex) = Asc("E")
        .AddItem "Mark":      .ItemData(.NewIndex) = Asc("M")
        .AddItem "None":      .ItemData(.NewIndex) = Asc("N")
        .AddItem "Odd":       .ItemData(.NewIndex) = Asc("O")
        .AddItem "Space":     .ItemData(.NewIndex) = Asc("S")
        .ListIndex = 2        ' Default to No Parity
    End With

    ' Data Bits
    With cmbDataBits
        .Clear
        .AddItem "4":         .ItemData(.NewIndex) = 4
        .AddItem "5":         .ItemData(.NewIndex) = 5
        .AddItem "6":         .ItemData(.NewIndex) = 6
        .AddItem "7":         .ItemData(.NewIndex) = 7
        .AddItem "8":         .ItemData(.NewIndex) = 8
        .ListIndex = 4        ' Default to 8 data bits
    End With
```

```
' Stop Bits
With cmbStopBits
    .Clear
    .AddItem "1":       .ItemData(.NewIndex) = 2
    .AddItem "1.5":     .ItemData(.NewIndex) = 3
    .AddItem "2":       .ItemData(.NewIndex) = 4
    .ListIndex = 0      ' Default to 1 stop bit
End With

End Sub

Private Sub btnCancel_Click()
    Hide
End Sub

Private Sub btnOK_Click()
    ' Reset the comm settings
    ResetCommSettings
    Hide
End Sub

Private Sub Form_Load()
    InitializeForm
End Sub
```

NETWORK SETTINGS DIALOG

To create the Network Settings dialog, add a fourth new form to the project and add a CheckBox, a Label, a TextBox, and two CommandButtons (see Figure C-4). Assign control properties as follows:

Object Type	Property	Value
Form	Name	frmNetworkSettings
	Caption	Network Settings
	Border Style	3 – Fixed Dialog
CheckBox	Name	chkEnabled
	Caption	Connection Enabled:
	Value	1 - Checked
Label	Name	lblServerPort
	Caption	Server Port:
TextBox	Name	txtServerPort
	Text	1234
CommandButton	Name	btnOK
	Caption	OK
CommandButton	Name	btnCancel
	Caption	Cancel

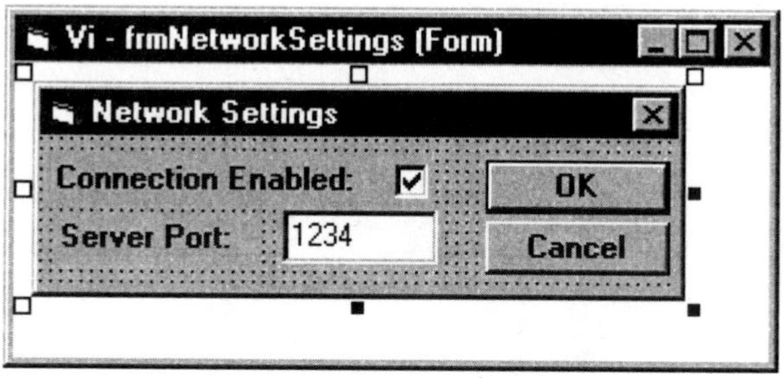

Figure C-4. Virtual Instrument Network Settings Dialog Form design.

Enter the following code into the frmNetworkSettings from Code Window.

```
Option Explicit

Private Sub ResetNetworkSettings()

    ' Reset the flag indicating whether or not the network connection is to be enabled
    If chkEnabled.Value = vbChecked Then
        frmMain.NetworkEnabled = True
    Else
        frmMain.NetworkEnabled = False
    End If

    ' Reset the server port on which to listen
    If IsNumeric(txtServerPort.Text) Then frmMain.ServerPort = CInt(txtServerPort.Text)

    ' Cause changes to take effect
    frmMain.ResetNetworkConnection
End Sub

Private Sub btnCancel_Click()
    Hide
End Sub

Private Sub btnOK_Click()
    ' Reset the network settings
    ResetNetworkSettings
    Hide
End Sub

Private Sub Form_Load()
    ' Upon loading set the interface to reflect the current parameter settings
    If frmMain.NetworkEnabled = True Then
        chkEnabled.Value = vbChecked
    Else
        chkEnabled.Value = vbUnchecked
    End If

    txtServerPort.Text = CStr(frmMain.ServerPort)

End Sub
```

The Virtual Instrument program is complete.

INDEX